Ex Libris

Robert W. Segrell

10-25-04

LATIN
AMERICA
Perspectives on a Region

LATIN AMERICA

Perspectives on a Region

Edited by Jack W. Hopkins

HM

HOLMES & MEIER
New York / London

First published in the United States of America 1987 by
Holmes & Meier Publishers, Inc.
30 Irving Place
New York, N.Y. 10003

Great Britain:
Pindar Road, Hoddesdon
Hertfordshire EN11 0HF England

Book design by Marilyn Marcus

Library of Congress Cataloging-in-Publication Data
Latin America: perspectives on a region.
    Includes bibliographies and index.
    1. Latin America. I. Hopkins, Jack W.
F1408.L3865 1987   980   86-14903
ISBN 0-8419-0917-2
ISBN 0-8419-0999-7 (pbk.)

Manufactured in the United States of America

Contents

15 *Urbanization in Latin American Development* ■ ROBERT V. KEMPER   *900*

16 *The Political Systems of Latin America: Developmental Models and a Typology of Regimes* ■ HOWARD J. WIARDA   *243*

17   *The Military in Latin America* ▪ DAVID SCOTT PALMER   *257*

18   *Latin America in the World* ▪ JACK W. HOPKINS   *273*

PART **IV**   **APPENDIX**
NOTES ON CONTRIBUTORS
INDEX

Preface

An infinitely complex region, Latin America more often than not has been described in stereotypical terms. Such stereotyping may lead to popular misconceptions about Latin America—exactly that has resulted—and, more serious, to erroneous perceptions and conclusions about policymaking issues and international relations. For many people, Latin America remains suspended in time and stage of development. Its richness of culture and wide range of development, among countries and within countries, are obscured by preconceived notions.

Many factors in recent years, however, have brought Latin America to prominence and increasingly to center stage in world affairs. The population of the region has burgeoned to some 364 million; one of the world's highest birthrates, combined with a steadily decreasing mortality rate due to improved health and sanitary conditions, has resulted in dramatic population growth over much of Latin America. Conflicts in Central America, the Caribbean, and the South Atlantic have become internationalized, their effects reaching far beyond the locale of their origin. Revolutionary movements have spread over widely scattered parts of the region. Countries such as Brazil and Mexico legitimately aspire to major power status and play more autonomous, important, and influential roles in the international community every year; Cuba's world influence belies its relatively small size, population, and resource base. Finally, the impact of Latin American culture on the rest of the world, and particularly on the United States, has been dramatic, pervasive, and profound.

The development of Latin America during the past quarter century has been remarkable in many respects. Changes in the region are forcing the United States to reexamine some of its traditional attitudes and policies. The reappraisal, when it has occurred, has sometimes been a painful process. Threats to a nation's hegemony are rarely easy to accept and accommodate, and all too often the United States has acted as if the status quo ante still prevailed. Indeed, in the midst of dizzying change, many characteristics of Latin America persist in their traditional form; the permanence of some features is truly remarkable as they defy the passage of centuries, the throes of economic and social development, and the onslaught of diverse external forces of change. These considerations suggest the central importance of the Latin American region and help explain the need for a better understanding of Latin America's role in the world.

This book is designed to satisfy that need. It is the work of leading experts in the field of Latin American studies, who present the complex mosaic of their subject from a variety of political, economic, esthetic, and cross-cultural perspectives. A primary aim is to convey the region's infinite variations of life and culture while seeking to capture its unity.

The complexity of Latin American culture

and civilization demanded that individual specialists write separate chapters on each subject area. This approach truly makes the book a group effort, and in my judgment the contributors have dealt remarkably well with this challenge of bringing unity from diverse perspectives. My constant concern was that the reader should become aware of the major themes dealt with for each topic. The test is met if every chapter can stand alone and convey such understanding even if it is a person's only reading on the subject. My broader objectives, however, will be achieved if each chapter, and the book as a whole, excites the reader to pursue further the rich literature on this intriguing part of the world: The effort will be infinitely rewarding. In this regard, the bibliographical appendix by Glenn Read takes a somewhat unusual approach. Entitled "Researching Latin America in the Library," it will be invaluable to any reader who wishes to learn more about a particular topic.

Choosing subjects for the individual chapters was not easy. The final selection obviously is not comprehensive; given the great complexity of Latin America, that would be impossible. Rather, the different chapters represent a sampling of viewpoints that should contribute to a fuller understanding of Latin America.

This book is divided into three parts. Part One includes chapters on environmental and social systems, pre-Columbian civilizations, and Latin American societies and people, thus setting the stage for what follows. The foundations of this region's development are discussed in Part Two, with chapters on the Spanish and Portuguese conquests, the colonial era, and the coming of independence and nation building. Part Three focuses on contemporary Latin America, although background material is included when necessary for a better grasp of the subject at hand. These chapters explore a wide range of subjects, from culture to economics and from religion to politics.

Because the book is designed to introduce students to a wide range of approaches to Latin America, it should serve well as the principal text for many courses dealing with the region. Students of art, politics, music and dance, comparative religion, economics, history, anthropology, Latin American literature, and international relations will find the chapters discussing these areas to be solid foundations for further reading and exploration. The book is especially intended for courses treating Latin American culture and civilization.

Latin America: Perspectives on a Region is the product of twenty-two contributors. The authors have devoted many years to research and writing on Latin America. Their individual work reflects their own experience and synthesis of their encounters with Latin American civilization. Inevitably such a collaborative work will contain variations in style, approach, and interpretation. I am convinced that such variations are valuable and that they enrich the overall perspective, much to the benefit of the student.

Jack W. Hopkins

LATIN

AMERICA

Perspectives on a Region

PART

I

BACKGROUND

1

Environmental and Social Systems

EMILIO F. MORAN

The Latin American environmental system involves more than a distinctive continental mass or physiographic unit. Latin America, after all, is a product not only of geography but also of historical and social forces that have altered the physical environment over many centuries of occupation. This chapter examines the surface features, soils and vegetative cover, systems of production, demography and the adjustments made by the population to cope with a variety of environmental conditions present in Latin America. The interaction between the physical environment's constraints and opportunities and the Latin American population is of special interest in this discussion. Social systems are not independent of their physical surroundings, nor is a given society without impact on its own environment.

Latin America has a total land area of about 8 million square miles. Unlike North America it is constituted by twenty nations.* These divisions are not solely a result of geophysical features;

rather they arise largely from the region's political history. Latin America includes the areas that we know as South America and Mesoamerica. Mesoamerica includes Mexico, portions of the southwest United States, Central America, and the Caribbean. Mexico is geologically connected to the North American cordillera region (i.e. the Rockies) that comes to an abrupt end at round 20° North latitude (i.e. the tip of Baja California). Central America forms a geologically distinct region from North America. The Central American-Antillean region (i.e. Cuba, Haiti, Dominican Republic, Puerto Rico, Jamaica, etc.) is composed of folded and faulted rocks with a general east-west trend and is connected to South America by two chains of volcanic ridges and peaks: the Lesser-Antilles and the highlands that run through El Salvador, Nicaragua, Costa Rica, Panama, and Colombia. South America, in turn, is dominated by three major surface divisions: the geologically young Andean chain; the geologically much older Brazilian and Guiana shields (also called *massifs* or *plateaus*); and the lowlands of the great river basins — the Orinoco, the Amazon, and the Paraguay-Paraná-La Plata.[1] How have these features influenced the human groups that have occupied the region?

*Editor's Note: The number of nations depends on the definition used for "Latin America." Twenty countries are clearly dominated by Spanish or Portuguese culture. But the region of South America, Mesoamerica, and the Caribbean includes 32 independent nations.

3

FIGURE 1

Surface Features of Latin America

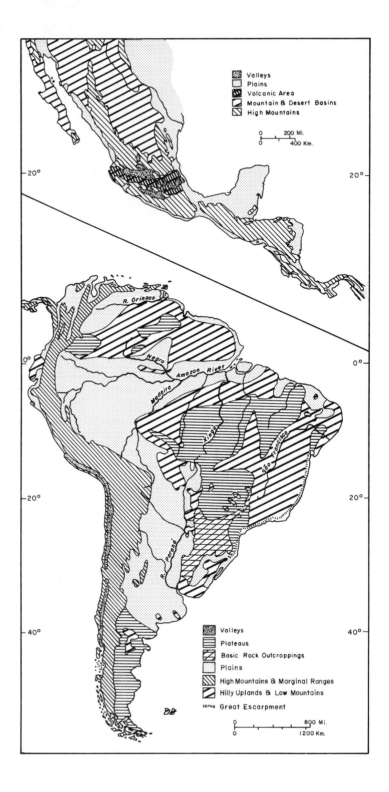

Valleys
Plains
Volcanic Area
Mountain & Desert Basins
High Mountains

0   200 Mi.
0   400 Km.

R. Orinoco
Negro
Amazon River
Madeira
Xingú
São Francisco
R. Paraná

Valleys
Plateaus
Basic Rock Outcroppings
Plains
High Mountains & Marginal Ranges
Hilly Uplands & Low Mountains
Great Escarpment

0   800 Mi.
0   1200 Km.

From Preston James, *Latin America,* 3rd
ed. (New York: Odyssey Press, 1959), pp.
25, 26.

■ Surface Features

Many people tend to think of the physical or surface features of an environment as largely irrelevant to historical or political developments. However, by looking at the northern portions of Mesoamerica from a geological perspective it is possible to understand why they form one unit, and why the area has been a politically disputed one. The Rio Grande boundary, which separates Mexico from the United States, is merely a river that cuts across a region with fundamentally the same physical environment. The area's mineral and petroleum resources are also important to its history. At one time Spanish America, and later Mexico itself, extended over much of this unified geophysical region, although control of it was eventually lost by occupation and military victory on the part of the expanding United States. That earlier Hispanic settlement of the United States Southwest influences to this day the region's ethnic composition and plays a role in the movement of Mexican workers across a border that is a political fact, but does not express geophysical or ethnic realities. This social and environmental situation helps explain the difficulty of negotiations between Mexico and the United States over illegal migration, water rights, and land use.

At about 20° north latitude this unified geophysical area made up of folded mountain ranges separated by either deep troughs or plateaus gives way to an east-west range system of great instability marked by volcanoes. This is an area of considerable strategic significance since it links two large continental masses and two oceans. The Panama Canal is just one of the most obvious strategic pass-throughs; until recently it was a subject of lively controversy between the United States and Latin American nations. The Caribbean and lower Central America have always been of interest to major powers, beginning with the European colonialists who fought for control of various points there — as witness the French, Dutch, British, and Spanish holdings in St. Croix, Curaçao, Barbados, and Hispaniola (today's Haiti and Dominican Republic). Given the activities of the colonial powers on both the Atlantic and the Pacific, a pass-through — whether overland or by canal — was of both military and economic value. Such interests played a role in the political divisions to be found in both Central America and the Caribbean.

The South American continent has the least indented coastline of all continental areas. The Andes form the most impressive physical feature of the landscape, although they do not really form a single mountain chain. Rather, they are a continuous mass of interconnecting mountain systems.[2] There are the permanently snow- and ice-covered uninhabited areas along the Chile–Argentina border; the broad and populated areas of the Bolivian tableland, or *altiplano;* and the densely populated intermontane valleys of Peru, Ecuador, Colombia, and Venezuela. A zone of great aridity sweeps across Peru, Chile, Bolivia, and Argentina, including even the coastal areas of the first two states. Precipitation is profoundly affected by the mountain ranges so that available moisture is very diverse from place to place.

Less dramatic than the Andes but no less significant in shaping the landscape are the Brazilian and Guiana shields. Both shields or plateaus have influenced greatly the occupation of the vast Amazonian lowlands. The plateaus or plains called *llanos* or *campos* are covered in savanna vegetation. The heart of the plateaus is drained by the great Amazon River and its many tributaries. The Brazilian plateau is also drained in a southern direction by the Paraná–Paraguay river system. As the Guiana and Brazilian plateaus drop off into the lowlands, rapids are formed. The presence of these rapids provides the continent with considerable hydroelectric potential that only recently has begun to be tapped. However, in the past and well into the contemporary period, these rapids were obstacles to occupation by European colonists. Settlement of the Amazon Basin by nonaborigines was largely confined to the first 150 kilometers from the main channel of the Amazon. Only in the past two decades have Latin American nations begun to overcome this physical constraint by building highways above the rapids. By doing so, they are opening up the 95 percent of the basin that had remained the preserve of native Amazonians and small settlements that had only seasonal contact with national institutions.

■ **Climates**

Nearly every climate of the world is found in Latin America. Most of Latin America lies in the lower latitudes, the more equatorial zones, where it is broadest in an east-west direction. Where South America's triangular shape narrows, the latitudes are mid to upper and thus characterized by more temperate climates.

The west coasts of Latin America are most influenced by cold ocean streams moving in an equatorial direction — the California Current and the Peru Current. These stabilize the air above them; because they tend to prevent it from rising, they produce very dry conditions. As a result, coastal Peru and the Atacama Desert of northern Chile are among the driest places in Latin America. The desert of coastal Peru, however, is crossed by numerous small rivers coming from the Andes. In pre-Columbian times and into the present, these arid lands have been the object of intensive irrigation agriculture (see chapter 2).

The eastern coasts of South America, by contrast, are bathed by warm currents that bring massive amounts of water vapor into the Amazon Basin and the coastal regions. These areas are characterized by high relative humidities and more moderate temperatures than the dry but hot western coasts. Contrary to common belief, Amazonian temperatures are a relatively even twenty-five to twenty-six degrees centigrade, whereas the hotter areas are found in the Gran Chaco, and in the coastal cities farther south. The high relative humidity, hovering around 85 percent year round, gives the impression of high temperatures noted by visitors to the Amazon.

Three-quarters of Latin America lies within the tropics, but this fact can be deceptive for a number of reasons. Climates are not just a function of latitude. Altitude plays an important role in shaping microclimates, and the Andean chain and the Mesoamerican highlands claim an important proportion of the Latin American habitat. High-altitude environments are characterized by zonation — in other words, by vertical zones that correspond roughly to latitudinal changes. Thus, within a short distance a mountain can have tropical lowlands, temperate grain-and-tuber-growing areas, alpine pastures, and snow-covered peaks. The configuration of the mountain ranges lead to patchy kinds of soils and changing airflows, which cause variations in humidity that offer many opportunities for exploitation. The populations of Latin American highlands in pre-Columbian times, as in the present, have engaged in complex systems of trade across these vertical zones, assuring themselves of a wide range of resources within relative proximity, whereby they reduced the human cost of obtaining a varied diet and other desired resources.

■ **Soils and Vegetative Cover**

Unlike most regions of the world, Latin America still has many significant areas of forested land. Their distribution varies a great deal from country to country. Tropical forests in the Caribbean and Central America have been much reduced, as have those of lowland and coastal Mexico. By contrast, Brazil has the greatest forest reserves in the world, although current rates of deforestation in the Amazon give cause for some alarm. Why be concerned with the fate of Latin American forests? Besides the important place that forests play in protecting the soil below them, there is growing evidence that the humid forests of the tropics recycle vast amounts of water vapor, portions of which affect rainfall in

North America. In addition, one should ask if the uses of such forested land are appropriate or productive. Much of the tropical forest in Latin America has been converted to low-quality pastures. Is that a suitable form of land use, seen from an environmental or social point of view? Later in this chapter we examine this question.

As Figure 2 indicates, the vegetation of Latin America includes vast areas of forests (both tropical and temperate), shrub and steppe, grasslands, and desert and mountain flora. Considerable research in recent years has changed our views about South American tropical forests. Rather than consider them homogeneous masses of evergreen vegetation, investigators now note the great diversity of vegetation and the need to protect the many distinct floras by a complex system of parks. Likewise, the soils are now known to be as variable as in any other area on earth. Thus the tropical rain forest is a multifaceted resource to be used in a complex balance of conservation and development. Severe deforestation took place in the 1970s because of subsidies for the development of cattle-ranching, but a public outcry led to an end to these subsidies and to a reduced rate of deforestation in the 1980s.[3] Much of the tropical moist and rain forest of the Caribbean islands has long been cleared except for steep or mountainous areas that have not been attractive to farmers or plantation owners.

Tropical semideciduous forests are found throughout the West Indies, on the Pacific coast of Central America, and over wide areas of southeastern Brazil and eastern Paraguay (see Figure 2). Many of these have also been eliminated since such areas have been preferred for human occupation and modern urban-industrial development. Tropical thorn forests occur in areas with arid and subhumid climates such as the interior of northeastern Brazil and the northern plateau areas of Mexico. Temperate forests are found in small areas of southern Mexico, southern Brazil, southern Chile, and in mountain areas.

Both tropical and temperate grasslands can be found in Latin America. Dry savannas occur in both the plains of Venezuela (i.e., the *llanos*) and the plains of Brazil (i.e., the *cerrados*) and are characterized by a marked six-month dry season. Wet savannas are richer in grass species and have fewer tree species than dry savannas. Wet savannas occur in the southwest of Brazil and parts of Paraguay. Temperate grasslands are largely confined to the estuary of the La Plata Basin. Here are the well-known *pampas* of Argentina and Uruguay. The pampas are completely treeless except along water courses, unlike the cerrados of Brazil. Grasslands supported native animals that were rapidly eliminated by the colonial population. In their place grew a cattle industry that was so successful that Latin Americans have tried to implant cattle raising almost everywhere they have gone in the region.

The desert areas of Latin America vary considerably in vegetative cover. The semiarid areas of Mexico and northwest Argentina are covered in a scrub forest of stunted dwarf trees. The Atacama Desert is almost completely devoid of vegetation, as is the Pacific coastal margin of Peru and northern Chile. However, even along these extremely dry desert areas, vegetation exists along the west-flowing rivers and streams. These river valleys formed the basis for many complex Andean civilizations of pre-Columbian times. The Sonoran Desert of Mexico is less harsh, and broad-leaved shrubs and succulents may be found. Semidesert conditions prevail in many intermontane Andean plateaus covered in patchy grass and scattered herbaceous growth.

The soils of Latin America are extremely varied, despite their proverbial lack of nutrients, their high acidity, and their potential of turning irreversibly into hardpans. Rich soils may be found along the highlands of Central America and Mexico, the productive agricultural areas of São Paulo and Paraná in Brazil, the coastal zone of northeastern Brazil, and in the pampas of Argentina and Uruguay. These areas are rich for different reasons, the pampas because of their temperate grass cover with deep organic layers

FIGURE 2

Natural Vegetation of Latin America

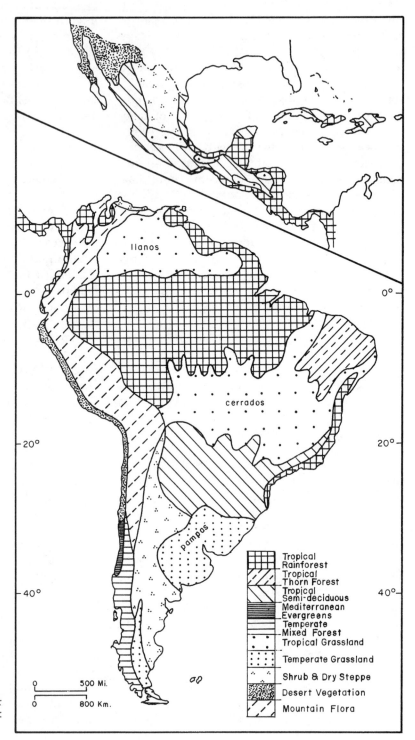

Source: Harry Robinson, *Latin America: A Geographical Survey* (New York: Praeger, 1967), p. 32.

built up over time. The São Paulo-Paraná *terras roxas* (red clay soils), also found in the Amazon in Rondônia and in portions of Altamira, Pará, result from diabase outcroppings and are of high to medium fertility. The *massape* soils of coastal Brazil, black soils rich in clay and organic matter, are derived from decomposition of Cretaceous limestones that supported ancient and now gone forests. The rich soils of the Mexican and Central American highlands originate from volcanic activity and the exposure of basic rocks (i.e., diabase outcroppings, as above) by weathering. Many of Latin America's floodplains are also rich in soil resources that can provide a bountiful agriculture. The Amazon floodplain, although composed of only 2 percent of the total basin, is an area comparable in size to that of many European countries in total land area. Many other river valleys and deltas also support dense populations and still harbor considerable agronomic potential.

■ Human Use of Soil Resources

Most of the best soils of Latin America are already under cultivation, except for some in tropical forest regions only recently incorporated into national economic life. This is not to say that they have always been well managed. The Latin American economy since Columbus has been influenced by a preference for export agriculture over staple food production. This has meant that most of the best soils have been controlled by a few individuals who exploit only small areas of their total estates (about 19 percent in these vast estates or *latifundia*) and then in monocultures that tend to deplete the soil. The rural population has been forced into tiny plots or *minifundia* located on less productive, and sometimes steeper, land wherein forests that previously had been important sources of game and protection for soil resources were cleared.

The use of soil resources of Latin America cannot be judged in isolation from the systems of production imposed by pre-Columbian, colonial, and then national political systems. In most cases, Latin American land use remains dominated by the latifundia/minifundia dichotomy and its associated poverty for the rural masses. The agrarian question in Latin America remains: How might the rural sector be restructured so that national economic goals are achieved and the disenfranchised masses secure greater access to basic resources? Latin American elites have long favored cattle ranches and pasture land as land use systems. Such systems of extensive land use lead to greater deforestation than output of the land justifies, limit access to productive land, and lead even small and mid-size landholders to imitate them, still further compounding the problem. Cattle ranching thus appears to be a strategy not so much appropriate to the Latin American landscape and soil resources as it is a strategy to maintain economic and political control over the all-important rural labor force.

The populations of Latin America have made use of their plant and soil resources in ingenious ways. The main constraint of the lowland soils is now known to be chemical—i.e., nutrients. Native populations cultivated them by clearing forested land, burning the forest, and making use of the substantial amounts of nutrients deposited in the form of ash to grow crops (i.e. swidden agriculture). In areas of volcanic origin, cultivators gave priority to the maize-bean complex with its greater demands upon soil nutrient resources, whereas in the lowlands of the Amazon, often of granitic origin and poorer in exchangeable bases, less demanding root crops dominated, with manioc as the major staple; cowpeas were also grown. Swidden agriculture when population density is low is an effective and economical means to exploit a forested environment. Similar practices could be found in forests along riverbanks in areas surrounded by either savanna or desert conditions.

Pre-Columbian people also adjusted to their own growing population. In areas of Mayan civilization and along the floodplains, recent research has uncovered complex systems of intensive cultivation that involved raised fields, *chinampas* or floating islands created by heaping muck from waterways, and other forms of concentrating organic soil matter in order to increase yield per unit of land.[4] Such techniques were used not only by the lowland classic Maya. Studies have uncovered raised fields in northeastern Bolivia, northwestern Colombia, the Rio Guayas Basin of Ecuador, the Lake Titicaca Basin of Peru and Bolivia, in the Llanos de Mojos of Bolivia, along the Rio Candelaria in western Campeche, Mexico, large areas in the Petén region of Guatemala and in Belize, in Veracruz, and in the upper Mantaro Valley of Peru.

Raised fields appear as the most important form of pre-Columbian hydraulic agriculture, whereby water and soil were carefully managed to make nutrient-poor or poorly drained soils contribute to the feeding of populations. Use of these methods seems associated with high population densities. In the highlands, terracing and gravity irrigation seem far more important because the problem there is not so much poor soils as it is their shallowness and lack of water. Complex systems of hillside terracing near water sources put into production land that otherwise would have been too steep to cultivate. Even to this day many areas that were under intensive production in the highlands and lowlands of Latin America before 1492 have not been returned to cultivation because of the demographic disaster that followed the European arrival and the imposition by Europeans of systems of production oriented toward export crops not necessarily suited to the forms of land intensive agriculture practiced by native populations. A number of countries, among them Mexico, Venezuela, Peru, and others of considerable economic strength appear unable to feed their burgeoning populations—yet they seem to ignore the recent evidence for systems of intensive agriculture capable of cultivating otherwise marginal lands. Instead, countries seem bent on cutting all their forests and maintaining systems of agriculture that are impressive only by their mediocre output when natural conditions are not ideal.

At high altitude, where conditions varied along an altitudinal gradient, native peoples developed systems of terracing and irrigation of considerable sophistication that required enormous labor investment. At high altitude the constraints on cultivation tend to involve soil depth and moisture rather than nutrients. Terracing provided a growing medium of greater depth than that of the natural slope of the land and protected the soil from wind and water erosion. In addition, the terraces were interconnected to water springs so that moisture levels could be maintained that allowed plants to develop properly. At the peak of Andean pre-Columbian civilization, slopes as steep as 60 percent were under cultivation. Many of these were allowed to go into disuse because of the depopulation following European occupation and imported disease. In short, over large areas of Latin America to this day, people rely on ancient systems of land use that reflect conservation-oriented approaches to land management. The erosion problems noted by many scholars have resulted from systems of land use that have overlooked the value of traditional systems or their inappropriateness to levels of population density well above pre-Columbian systems.

These conservation-minded approaches are practiced more often than not by people somewhat isolated from the national economies of Latin America. As noted above, where national priorities govern, the tendency is to favor extensive cattle ranching or export monoculture. Latin American agriculture in most cases has had stagnant productivity. It has kept up with population growth not so much by increasing efficiency but by increasing the amount of land in cultivation. Only in isolated pockets has Latin American agriculture achieved high productivity per unit of land, and then primarily in export crops such as bananas, coffee, soybeans, and oranges.

■ Population

Three major issues dominate studies of the Latin American population: racial mixing or *mestizaje*, slavery, and the explosive rates of growth since

World War II. It is hard to discuss Latin American society without considering the rapid racial mixing that took place in the New World between Iberians and Amerindians, and later with the Africans brought over as slaves. The imposition of a slave-based plantation economy on

Figure **3**

Population of Plateau and Coastal Areas of Central Mexico

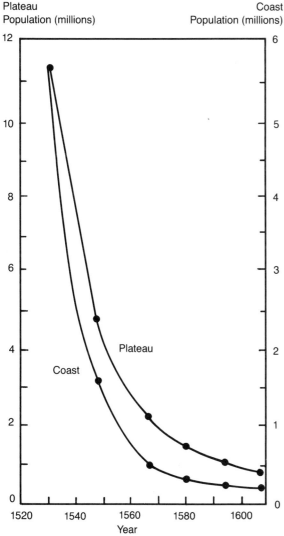

Source: Sánchez-Albornoz, *The Population of Latin America*, trans. W. Richardson (Berkeley: University of California Press, 1974), 49.

most of Latin America has also been understood to have shaped the region and to help explain the rift between classes that persists to this day. A more contemporary issue has been the rapid population growth in the past three decades. This increase results from a drop in the death rate, especially among infants (see Table 1), and from significant improvements in many Latin American economies.

It is impossible to discuss the evolution of Latin American populations without taking note of the demographic disaster that accompanied the Spanish Conquest (see Figure 3 for a glimpse of the scale of the disaster). The arrival of Europeans in the New World brought diseases to which Amerindians had no resistance, and which in large part explain the ease with which a relatively small band of Iberians was able to subdue the complex militaristic kingdoms of the Incas and Aztecs. Historians vary considerably about the size of the pre-Columbian populations. Estimates suggest that mortality in the first century from this biological contact was between 45 and 90 percent. These estimates are in accord with the better-documented mortality rates of native Amazonians in the past decade—populations that had managed to remain relatively isolated from national systems and are now reached by development projects into the Amazon.[5]

Latin America recovered gradually from the demographic calamity of the sixteenth century. In the aggregate at least, the per annum growth rate between the seventeenth century and the third decade of the twentieth century is estimated at between 0.8 percent and 1.3 percent.[6] These figures compare to those of Europe. Indigenous communities appear to have stabilized overall, although decimation due to famine and disease has continued in localized areas. The most significant impact on population since the seventeenth century was from slavery, which brought millions of Africans to the New World. Estimates of the volume of forced migration of Africans vary greatly, partly because of the destruction of importation records in Brazil soon after the abolition of slavery in 1888 and creation

TABLE **1**

Infant Mortality Rate in Nine Countries, 1920–1967 (per thousand live births)

	1920–24	1930–34	1940–44	1950–54	1967
Argentina	100	82	74	65	58
Cuba	135	76	61	—	44[a]
Panama	110	101	81	60	43
Costa Rica	174	160	131	88	62
Guatemala	142	125	127	110	94[b]
Mexico	178	142	105	92	63
Venezuela	153	130	120	88	41
Colombia	159	155	143	125	78
Chile	250	212	170	119	92

[a]1966.   [b]1968.

Source: Sánchez-Albornoz 1974, 200.

of the republic in 1889. The great majority of slaves went to Brazil and Cuba, the last countries to abolish slavery as a system. Between 1761 and 1860, viewed by many as the peak of the slave trade,[7] an estimated 1.7 million slaves were imported into Brazil, Cuba, and Puerto Rico. Total figures for the colonial period and early national period vary around 4 million. In Mexico, Central America, and the Andean nations, the labor in the plantations came from the remnants of the complex societies that inhabited these areas and that were able to survive only by force of their initial numbers. In Cuba, Puerto Rico, and the coast/interior of Brazil, aboriginal societies were less dense and less able to cope with the depopulation. Plantation owners were forced to go to African markets for their labor.

Sharing the ideology of Europeans, Latin American elites in the nineteenth century began to explain the poor condition of their economies by the racial composition of their population. Thus most governments promoted European immigration in order to get "more advanced people" into their countries to stimulate the economy. The greatest number went to Brazil, followed by Argentina, Chile, and Uruguay. However, because of their much smaller populations, the impact of the immigrants was most felt in Argentina, Uruguay, and Chile. "The net in-

flow into Argentine ports between 1881 and 1935 amounted to 3,400,000."[8] Not all who came stayed. In the period just before World War I there was almost as much return migration to Europe as there was migration to Latin America. The millions who went to Argentina and Uruguay were enough to populate both the countryside and the cities. In both Brazil and Argentina the greatest proportion of immigrants came from the Iberian Peninsula and Italy. Brazil is unusual because of the large numbers of Germans and Japanese that it allowed in. A greater proportion of the Japanese appear to have stayed as immigrants than most other nationalities, and their impact is significant in contemporary Brazil.

The massive influx of Europeans and Japanese into Latin America speeded up the growth of countries that received them, changed the geographic dispersion of population, and began the pattern of dynamic population increase that had already begun in southern Europe and Japan. Per annum growth rates in Latin America went from the moderate 0.8 to 1.3 percent of the previous two centuries to the range of 2.0 to 2.3 percent in the 1930–50 period. Uruguay's population increased sixfold in a fifty-year period, due in large part to immigration. During this period only Paraguay experienced a population decline because of the War of the Triple Alliance, which decimated its male population. Brazil increased at a rapid rate, as did Colombia. On the other hand, Venezuela, Ecuador, Peru, Bolivia, and Mexico experienced relatively slow growth (see Table 2).

Following the Great Depression of the 1930s, Latin American population took off. Between 1940 and 1970 the population of Latin America increased from 126 to 277 million. Rates increased in each decade from 1.9 percent in 1940 to 2.3 percent in 1950 to 2.7 percent in 1960 and to 2.8 percent in the 1970s. No area of this size had ever grown at such rates before in recorded history—although Africa has surpassed these rates in the past and current decade. Central America has had the highest rates of growth,

reaching 3.3 percent annually in the 1960s. On the other hand, the rates of increase in Argentina, Chile, and Uruguay have been a more moderate 1.8 percent per annum (see Table 3). In the 1970s, to the surprise of many demographers, Latin American countries as a whole reduced their rate of population growth, except for some countries who were late in developing their economies and in introducing the modernization of public health services responsible for the drop in infant mortality.

The high rates of growth in societies then dominated by a traditional agrarian sector, wherein land was in control of a few, could not be supported without major change. The change in question was not a restructuring of the land distribution system, but massive migra-

TABLE **2**

Birthrate (B) and Death Rate (D) in Ten Latin American Countries

		1900–1904	1910–1914	1920–1924	1930–1934	1940–1944	1950–1954
Uruguay	B	38.9	36.5	30.1	25.8	21.6	21.2
	D	13.7	13.5	12.6	11.5	10.3	8.5
Argentina	B	44.3	40.3	35.0	30.9	26.1	26.1
	D	20.0	15.6	13.8	12.2	10.5	8.8
Cuba	B	44.6	44.7	36.7	31.3	31.9	30.4
	D	23.7	21.4	19.3	13.3	10.9	11.3
Panama	B	40.3	42.0	40.0	37.4	39.5	38.5
	D	21.0	19.0	17.3	15.1	12.7	9.1
Costa Rica	B	46.9	48.9	44.9	44.6	42.8	45.0
	D	28.8	27.2	25.2	21.5	17.4	10.7
Guatemala	B	45.8	46.6	48.3	46.2	45.2	50.9
	D	35.4	33.0	33.7	31.7	28.5	23.4
Mexico	B	46.5	43.2	45.3	44.1	43.8	45.0
	D	33.4	46.6	28.4	26.7	21.8	15.4
Venezuela	B	41.8	44.5	41.2	39.9	41.5	44.2
	D	29.1	28.3	26.0	21.9	18.8	12.3
Colombia	B	43.0	44.1	44.6	43.3	42.2	44.0
	D	26.6	26.0	23.7	22.5	20.3	18.4
Chile	B	44.7	44.4	42.2	40.2	38.3	37.0
	D	31.6	31.5	31.3	24.5	20.1	13.7

Sources: Sánchez-Albornoz 1974, 171, 189.

TABLE **3**

Recent Statistics Concerning Birth-, Death, and Growth Rates
(Annual rates 1965–1970 according to CELADE estimates)

	Births	Deaths	Growth
Argentina	23.0	8.7	15.4
Bolivia	43.8	19.0	23.7
Brazil	37.7	9.5	28.2
Chile	33.2	10.0	23.2
Colombia	44.6	10.6	34.0
Costa Rica	37.3	7.4	22.9
Cuba	27.3	7.5	19.8
Dominican Republic	48.5	14.7	33.8
Ecuador	44.9	11.4	33.5
Guatemala	43.5	15.1	28.4
Haiti	43.5	19.7	24.2
Honduras	49.0	16.9	33.6
Mexico	43.2	8.9	34.3
Nicaragua	46.0	16.7	29.3
Panama	40.5	8.4	32.1
Paraguay	44.6	10.7	33.9
Peru	41.8	11.1	30.7
Puerto Rico	26.7	6.6	15.4
Salvador (El)	46.9	12.9	32.9
Uruguay	21.2	9.0	12.2
Venezuela	40.9	7.8	33.1

Source: Sánchez-Albornoz 1974, p. 189.

tion to the cities, where the concentration of resources promised greater chances of upward mobility and economic well-being than the stagnant agrarian sector, with its low wages and restricted opportunity of access. The movement, too, has taken population from the highlands and coastal areas to the interior and the lowlands in the form of both government-directed and spontaneous colonization. Such movements have not absorbed that much population, but they have bought time for an eventual solution that still remains to be implemented.

Central America and the Caribbean, where some of the highest and most recent high rates of increase have been taking place, have turned to international migration for solutions, given the scarcity of unopened lands in their seabound or latifundia-bound countries. However, worldwide economic slowdowns have led to restrictive immigration laws that have reduced the effectiveness of migration as an escape valve.

Latin American cities and the developed world no longer offer the opportunity that they once did. While the concentration of resources in primate cities like Mexico City and Caracas continue to fuel rural-to-urban migration and to justify the hope of the millions who migrate each year, the level of competition for increasingly scarce jobs has become an explosive problem for urban dwellers. However, there is little evidence that the low quality of life in the rural areas (i.e., lack of schools and teachers, services, and health care) or the concentration of wealth in the hands of a few, motives behind the migration, are being addressed by most countries.

The population of Latin America in the next two decades can be expected to reduce its rates of growth because of drops in fertility, the stabilization in the death rate, and absence of major immigration across national boundaries or into the region as a whole. However, because of the relative youth of the Latin American population resulting from the high rates of annual growth between 1960–80, it can be expected to continue to grow at a rapid rate in absolute terms well into the twenty-first century. More of the population will be living in overcrowded cities. The quality of life in rural areas will depend on what changes take place in the decades ahead in land redistribution and productivity gains. The current evidence is very diverse: major gains in productivity in southern Brazil, side by side with low productivity elsewhere in that country. Mexico and Venezuela have increased productivity in one or two commodities, but their food production is behind population growth. Cuba has improved its sugar productivity after a devastating decline in the 1960s, but this was done by giving up on the original plan to diversify the economy from its traditional dependence on sugar. In short, Latin America's food/population balance depends on what happens in the international markets, in the political systems' response to population needs, and in the adoption of systems of production capable of yielding more per unit of land and per unit of labor. Capital-intensive production, as Venezuela and Mexico well attest, have not proven adequate solutions to the needs for food and fiber of Latin American peoples.

■ Human Adjustment to the Environmental Conditions

What significance might one find in these environmental features of Latin America? While it is risky to attempt to make correlations between environmental features and social features, human occupants of Latin America have had to adjust to the habitat, or they have had to pay a heavy price for ignoring it. Human occupation of the high Andes (above three thousand meters) requires both physiological and cultural adjustments to the stresses posed by high-altitude hypoxia (from oxygen deficiency), cold, and low biological productivity. Over time, native Andean populations developed forms of adjustment that permitted them to exploit those regions, to reproduce successfully, and to build impressive civilizations at high altitudes.[9]

When the Spaniards arrived, they brought their cultural habits and physical adjustments to lower altitudes. Within a few decades, the Spanish moved their capital city from Cuzco to Lima on the lowlands, explicitly because both cattle and women had a high rate of fetal loss due to oxygen deprivation.[10] Thus, the integrity of Andean cultures over the centuries of Spanish occupation can be attributed not only to their value and endurance, but also to their relative isolation because of Spanish preference for denser settlement at lower altitudes.

Among the adjustments made by high-altitude natives one finds developmental, acclimatory, and behavioral-cultural changes. People born or living above three thousand meters during childhood (under age eleven) appear to have a denser capillary bed in the lower extremities and greater lung volume to process more of the low-oxygen air. Other changes result from prolonged residence at high altitude, such as greater red blood cell production to increase the blood's capacity for carrying oxygen to tissues. Behavioral and cultural adjustments address more of the other stresses of high altitude such as cold, aridity, and low productivity. High-altitude populations in the Andes control small plots in various parts of the highlands, giving them access to a variety of plant-growing conditions and crops. This access is guaranteed by intermarriage and trade. Efforts to consolidate landholdings in the Andes and other highland areas of Latin America or to redirect trade to the cities and away from other highland zones is likely to result in the breakdown of many settlements. This would further fuel the rural exodus to the cities. Misinformed urban planners have made, and continue to make, efforts to enhance the marketing of highland goods to the major cities. Once these systems of intramountain trade are disrupted, bound as they are by marriage and regularity of exchange, they may not be easily rebuilt.

Isolation has helped certain Latin American peoples to survive. The survival of many lowland Amazonians is explainable by the difficulty of access created by the rapids of the Brazilian and Guiana plateaus. Many indigenous peoples fled to the areas above the rapids during the sixteenth century to escape enslavement and disease. Portuguese settlements were thus confined below the rapids, and their impact on native people was lessened well into the late nineteenth and early twentieth centuries. The reduced economic value of these inaccessible areas to Portuguese and Brazilian colonists gave native Amazonians several centuries of relief from cultural and biological destruction. Unfortunately, the devastating effort of progress has resumed in the past decade as national economies reach deep into their Amazonian territories for land and mineral resources.

The interplay between environmental and social systems points out the importance of understanding the present in the light of past physical and socioeconomic realities. Current regional developments that often baffle the reader of news from Latin America can be understood in this holistic perspective. It is very hard to explain Latin American preference for coastal settlement without an understanding of the mercantilistic and export-oriented economies that have dominated the region. It is difficult to explain why European settlers who migrated to Latin America during the nineteenth century preferred to go to southern Brazil, Argentina, and Chile unless one understands the oppressive presence of slavery over most of northern and southeast Brazil up to its abolition in 1888 and the poverty of the population of these Latifundia-dominated areas. Concentration of European immigrants in the southern regions provided the human conditions needed to develop systems of production different from the paternalism and large estates dominant in northeastern Brazil and transferred to the center-east. Many Europeans brought to Latin America a preference for urban settlement, for cottage industries, and for intensive production using mixed systems that Brazil and most of Latin America lacked until the late nineteenth century. Despite the presence of these mixed farmers operating successful farms of small to medium size, their example was not followed because elites continued to conform to the earlier pattern of extensive control over land, cattle ranching, and an impoverished rural work force living as subsistence tenants.

Latin America can be treated as a whole, but for clarity its lands must be divided into socioenvironmental systems with varying resources. For example, northeastern Brazil cannot be understood if treated as a whole. Rather, northeastern Brazil must be understood as made up, minimally, of three human ecological systems: the wet coast, the *agreste* (an irrigated area), and the *sertão*, a semiarid interior. The coast is an area of rich soils with abundant rainfall and semideciduous tropical forests. The forests laid down rich soils that supported a thriving sugar plantation economy for well over two

hundred years. The region was so specialized in sugar production that a separate area had to be found to produce staple crops and meat. Such an area was the semiarid interior of the northeast. Thus two distinct and interconnected types of human settlement developed with quite a different environmental impact: the extensive plantation with settlement clustered around the manor house, and the isolated homes of the *sertanejos* (or natives of the semiarid region) who herded cattle through a scrubby, spiny, arid flora (xerophytic) suited to an area where rainfall was unpredictable. The terms of trade were usually unfavorable for the sertanejo, yet the area provided anonymity to many escaped slaves and to others seeking better opportunities than those provided by a slave-owning society.

The *agreste*, an intermediate zone between the coast and the interior, grew into a significant agricultural region only in the nineteenth century with the development of irrigation and the exploitation of river valleys that cut through it. The neglect of these valleys speaks to the single-mindedness of the Portuguese and postindependence Brazilians in viewing the northeast as coastal and sugar-producing—rather than containing the environmental conditions for a productive agriculture geared to annual and staple crops. Even today, national investment in the agreste and in the irrigation of the interior pales in comparison to the investments made in other regions and sectors of the economy.

The northeast has one of the lowest per capita income levels in the world, although Brazil has one of the highest per capita incomes in Latin America and already the tenth-largest GNP in the world. The northeast is hampered by its recurrent droughts, by land concentration in the hands of a few, by limited investment in staple food production, and by unfavorable terms of trade that have in the past drained the profits of its agricultural sector to finance the industrial development of southern Brazil.

Thus the conditions of the northeast are a product of environmental and social processes that reflect the alliance of vested interests in northeastern Brazil with national interests in economic development in areas with the greatest competitive advantage. Land taxes in northeastern Brazil are less than one dollar per square mile per year, and such a low tax provides no incentive to put land into production.[11] Thus the northeast is unlikely to improve its condition until the nation sees fit to overlook the initial economic disadvantages of investment in that region and is willing to restructure access to land resources so that it is used by those willing to work it.

The occupation of Andean South America was profoundly affected by the location of native peoples and the presence of ancient human settlements near important resources. During the early occupation of Latin America the most important resource to be controlled was land—and the labor to exploit it. Thus the early European settlers sought control over native labor in order to extract the natural resources of the New World. In the Andes such a task was easy, since the complex, stratified kingdoms there had already identified many of the resource-rich areas of the region, giving the Spaniards a ready way to locate and to control both land and labor. This structure, as texts on Latin America have often noted, helps to explain why a handful of Spaniards were able to subdue the might of the Incas and the Aztecs. Not only did the native populations believe in a myth of a returning white-skinned god, and not only did confusion arise from epidemic disease, but the Spaniards simply replaced the top of the pyramid of classes, maintaining many of the existing control structures. Thus the many forms of class-based control of labor remained largely unchanged.

In short, the Europeans who colonized Latin America adopted socially stratified systems of control wherever they existed and used them to exploit minerals and other resources. In those areas, like the Amazon lowlands, where political systems were less centralized and control weaker, they sought to concentrate labor into missions and plantations. There they imposed systems of production brought over from southern Spain and Portugal—areas dominated by large properties rather than small, mixed peasant agriculture typical of these countries' northern regions. The initial goal was to extract maximum profit from the new land in the shortest amount of time. Later the aim was to maintain control over the land and the labor force to exploit it, as the settlers made the region their home and abandoned thoughts of returning to the Iberian peninsula.

In recent years Latin American food production as a whole has kept up with population, but there are exceptions to the rule. Mexico and Venezuela, in particular, have had great difficulty because of the abandonment of the countryside by those who are responsible for staple food production. Most capital-intensive food production in Latin America on larger farms is geared to export crops rather than staples. Political figures of every ideological persuasion have given priority to a cheap staple food policy that has depressed production. It simply has not paid to produce staples in most countries because of price controls. At the same time, available credit has been absorbed primarily by the largest operators, leaving very little long-term financing for the small farmer who produces for the domestic consumer. The end result has been less and less food per capita in a number of countries and more urban consumers as the farmers become urban migrants.

Latin American environmental and social systems have changed a great deal since colonial times, yet much remains the same. After World War II Latin America came to have the world's highest rates of population growth. Such growth exacerbated social inequities in most of the countries and brought about considerable ferment and revolutionary stirrings. Many Latin Americans are fully aware of the inequities of their systems. The elites, however, retain a paternalistic outlook resulting from their long-standing control over resources: They hope to maintain the status quo and prevent a loss of power to others.

The masses hold a considerable range of views, depending on relative social status. In countries like El Salvador, where population pressure and land maldistribution prevents significant numbers from eking out even a minimal standard of living, many have little to lose by the overthrow of existing regimes. Larger countries like Brazil have a greater range of opportunities and greater resources to exploit, so there the potential for radical change is considerably reduced. What is most striking about Latin American social and environmental systems is the predictability of the social systems. Time and again their beneficiaries fail to recognize the great diversity of environmental resources possessed by most Latin American countries or to incorporate the vast majority of the population — through education and participation — into a common effort from which all, rather than a tiny elite, benefit. Latin Americans crave such an opportunity, but four centuries of inappropriate systems of land use and labor exploitation, coupled with elites more allied to external capital than to their own people, provide a poor basis for significant restructuring of Latin American social and environmental systems.

■ Notes

1. My description of Latin America is based on H. Robinson, *Latin America* (London: MacDonald and Evans, Ltd., 1961), 2 and James Preston, *Introduction to Latin America* (New York: Odyssey Press, 1964), 23 and 25.
2. Kempton Webb, *Geography of Latin America: A Regional Analysis* (Englewood Cliffs, N.J.: Prentice-Hall, 1972), 33.
3. Emilio F. Moran, ed., *The Dilemma of Amazonian Development* (Boulder, Colo.: Westview Press, 1983).
4. W. Denevan, "Development and the Imminent Demise of the Amazon Rain Forest," *Professional Geographer* 25 no. 2 (1973): 130–35.
5. Ibid.
6. N. Sánchez-Albornoz, *The Population of Latin America*, trans. W. Richardson (Berkeley: University of California Press, 1974), 86.
7. P. Curtin, *The Atlantic Slave Trade: A Census* (Madison: University of Wisconsin Press, 1979).
8. Sánchez-Albornoz, op. cit., 154.
9. P. Baker and M. Little, eds., *Man in the Andes* (Stroudsburg, Pa.: Dowden, Hutchinson and Ross, 1976), Emilio F. Moran, *Human Adaptability* (Boulder, Colo.: Westview Press, 1982).
10. C. Monge, *Acclimatization in the Andes* (Baltimore, Md.: Johns Hopkins University Press, 1948).
11. Webb, op. cit., 97.

■ Suggested Readings

Baker, P., and M. Little, eds. *Man in the Andes.* Stroudsburg, Pa.: Dowden, Hutchinson and Ross, 1976.

Butland, Gilbert. *Latin America: A Regional Geography.* New York: Wiley and Sons, 1960.

Freyre, Gilberto. *The Masters and the Slaves.* New York: Knopf, 1946.

James, Preston. *Introduction to Latin America.* New York: Odyssey Press, 1964.

Moran, Emilio. *Human Adaptability.* Boulder, Colo.: Westview Press, 1982.

———. ed. *The Dilemma of Amazonian Development.* Boulder, Colo.: Westview Press, 1983.

Webb, Kempton. *Geography of Latin America: A Regional Analysis.* Englewood Cliffs, N. J.: Prentice-Hall, 1972.

2 | *Pre-Columbian Cultures*

GEOFFREY W. CONRAD

Brief summaries of Latin American pre-history invariably discuss the two great foci of native New World civilization, Mesoamerica and the central Andes, and ignore the rest of the region. While those two areas did give rise to some spectacularly elaborate cultures, Mesoamerica and the central Andes did not exist in total isolation from the rest of ancient Latin America. Nor were they always at the forefront of cultural development in the region. Therefore, although it emphasizes the two major civilizational traditions, this chapter also covers the rest of Latin America in an attempt to convey some idea of what was happening throughout the region at any given time.

People have occupied Latin America for at least 14,000 years, of which all but the last 500 belong to the pre-Columbian era. Many of the major events and transformations that took place during this vast span of time—along with the reasons *why* they happened—remain elusive. More than anything else, it is what we do not know for certain, and the resulting debates and disagreements, that make Latin American archaeology so captivating to its practitioners.

Latin America may be divided into eight ar-chaeological culture areas: Mesoamerica, the Intermediate Area (lower Central America and the northern Andes), the central Andes, the south Andes, the Caribbean, Amazonia, eastern Brazil, and southern South America (Figures 1 and 2). While there are no precise boundaries, each of these areas was culturally similar and interrelated over a considerable period. All of the areas can be subdivided, and this will be done as necessary in subsequent sections.

■ The First Inhabitants: 12,000(?)–7000 B.C.

The first inhabitants of the Americas, called Paleo-Indians, descended from Asian hunter-gatherers who crossed the Bering land bridge between Siberia and Alaska toward the end of the last Ice Age. We do not know exactly when the Paleo-Indians first reached Latin America, but the most reliable data argue that they began to arrive around 12,000 B.C. The first immigrants dispersed rapidly southward through the mountains of Mexico and Central America to Andean South America, and thence outward to other parts of that continent, reaching the Strait

FIGURE 1

Archaeological culture areas of Latin America (with modern political boundaries added for reference)

FIGURE 2

Archaeological Sites Mentioned in the Text

1. Tula
2. Teotihuacán
3. Tenochtitlán
4. Monte Albán
5. San Lorenzo
6. La Venta
7. Palenque
8. Dzibilchaltún
9. Uxmal
10. Mayapán
11. Chichén Itzá
12. El Mirador
13. Cerros
14. Tikal
15. Kaminaljuyú
16. Chan Chan
17. Moche
18. Guitarrero Cave
19. Chavín
20. Aspero
21. El Paraíso
22. Huari
23. Cuzco
24. Pucara
25. Tiahuanaco

of Magellan by 9000 B.C. There is evidence of human habitation dating from the end of the Paleo-Indian era in most parts of Latin America, with the exception of Amazonia, the Caribbean, and perhaps the tropical lowland zones of Mesoamerica.

Almost certainly, Paleo-Indian social groups were of the type known ethnographically as bands. Such groups are small (usually no more than twenty-five to fifty members), integrated by familial ties of kinship and marriage, and egalitarian in the sense that social distinctions and the division of labor are based solely on age and sex. Each individual band is an autonomous unit, and leadership is informal and ephemeral. Material property tends to be limited, since the band is mobile, and its members carry most of their possessions with them when they move.

Recent investigations portray the Paleo-Indians as eclectic hunter-gatherers. In addition to hunting large Ice Age mammals — mammoths, mastodons, giant ground sloths the size of elephants, and other similarly formidable creatures — they also pursued smaller game and collected a variety of wild plants. Hence, while their subsistence economies were generally predicated upon hunting herd-dwelling and semigregarious animals, the Paleo-Indians exploited a wide range of resources, tailoring their specific diets to the foods available in a particular place and season.

The later Paleo-Indian era (8500–7000 B.C.) witnessed the disappearance of the large Ice Age mammals (probably caused by a combination of overhunting, environmental changes, and diseases) and a concomitant shift to the hunting of a fully modern fauna composed of medium- and small-game species. Reliance on smaller game was associated with decreasing mobility. By 8500 B.C., if not before, most bands seem to have been following a well-defined seasonal round, confining their wanderings to relatively limited territories with which they were highly familiar.

This process of "settling in" also produced an increasingly intensive use, and perhaps manipulation, of some plant species. Indeed, recent evidence suggests that the domestication of certain plants may have begun in later Paleo-Indian times. At Guitarrero Cave in the Peruvian Andes, chili peppers and kidney beans were apparently cultivated in 8500 B.C., and lima beans by 7000 B.C. If the Guitarrero Cave specimens do indeed represent early domesticates, they were not of surpassing importance to the cave's inhabitants. They were simply new plant foods worked into an established seasonal round. Nonetheless, an unimpressive handful of beans and peppers dated to 8500 B.C. may constitute our first glimpse of the agricultural economy upon which all of the great civilizations of Latin America would eventually depend.

■ The Origins of Agriculture and Sedentary Life: 7000–2500 B.C.

The era from about 7000 B.C. to 2500 B.C. is often called the Archaic period. Sites of this age are more numerous and more widely distributed than Paleo-Indian sites, for several parts of Latin America seem to have been first occupied during this time. While there is presently no direct evidence of human occupation in the interior of Amazonia before 2000 B.C., it seems likely that all of Latin America was in fact inhabited by the end of the Archaic period, although population densities were still very low in most areas.

Archaic subsistence economies were characterized by an intensification of the trends apparent in the later Paleo-Indian era: the hunting and gathering of a wide range of resources; adaptations to specific local environments, and thus more pronounced variations in basic economic patterns; and seasonal cycles of changes in residence (a phenomenon known as transhumance). In several areas economic activities involved increasingly frequent experiments with the cultivation of plants and the manipulation of selected animal species. These experiments laid the foundations of native Latin American agriculture.

There are many unresolved controversies surrounding the origins of Latin American agriculture (for example, the genetic history of maize is hotly debated). Nonetheless, in overview we can identify three major indigenous agricultural complexes:

1. A maize-beans-squash complex that developed in the intermontane valleys and basins of the Latin American highlands
2. A high-altitude complex, native to the south-central Andes, based on the cultivation of potatoes and other frost-resistant tubers and the herding of two animal species belonging to the camel family, the llama and alpaca
3. A tropical forest complex that probably originated in the Amazon basin and was based upon the cultivation of manioc, sweet potatoes, and other root crops

As matters stand, most of our direct data on early plant cultivation come from sites in the intermontane valleys of Mexico and Peru. Evidence from a number of locations shows that plant domestication in Mesoamerica and the central Andes developed over several millennia, from late Paleo-Indian or early Archaic times onward, with the maize-beans-squash complex taking shape between 5000 and 4000 B.C. (It is generally agreed that maize cultivation began in Mesoamerica and then diffused southward.) The origins of the south-central Andean high-altitude tuber and herding complex are less well documented, although the available data suggest that it had been established by 2500 B.C.

All in all, the highland picture is one of a slow, steady buildup to a fully agricultural (and in the central and south Andes, pastoral) way of life. The gradual nature of this trend cannot be overemphasized. Despite a great increase in the number of domesticated species, the data argue that at the end of the Archaic period highland cultivators were still obtaining as much as three-quarters of their diet from wild foods. Furthermore, transhumant band organization was still the norm: By 2500 B.C. highland agriculture had not yet produced any permanent, sedentary villages.

Sedentary residence did appear in Meso-

america and the Central Andes during the Archaic period, but in all known instances it was based on concentrated wild foods. The best documented cases come from the central coast of Peru. Here, between 3000 and 2500 B.C., permanent villages were supported by the netting of small schooling fish and the exploitation of other marine resources, including larger fish, mollusks, sea mammals, and birds.

The one subarea where agriculture and sedentary residence did go together was the northern Andes. Along the coasts of Colombia and Ecuador year-round villages were established between 3000 and 2500 B.C. The inhabitants of these villages made the oldest ceramics discovered to date in the New World. The best known of these early pottery-making, village-dwelling cultures is Valdivia of coastal Ecuador. Valdivia sites include both shoreline settlements that exploited marine resources and inland farming villages along riverine floodplain land.

Like the typical Archaic hunting-and-gathering bands, each of the early sedentary villages of coastal Colombia, Ecuador, and Peru was undoubtedly an autonomous unit. However, the permanent villages were probably organized differently from the transhumant bands. The village dwellers should represent what ethnographers call "segmentary societies." That is, a village was probably made up of several social groups, each composed of individuals related to one another by ties of kinship. Positions of leadership were more formally defined than they were in bands, but village social and political organization was still egalitarian. None of a village's kin groups outranked any of the others, and power and authority were divided among a relatively large number of people rather than concentrated in the hands of a few individuals.

■ The First Complex Societies: 2500–500 B.C.

Despite the exceptions noted above, in 2500 B.C. most of Latin America was characterized by Archaic-type hunting-and-gathering societies. In sharp contrast, by 500 B.C. only the Caribbean islands, eastern Brazil, and southern South America were still occupied exclusively by hunter-gatherers. The intervening two millennia, often called the Formative period, had witnessed a major economic and social transformation: the spread of a sedentary, ceramic-making, village-farming way of life across much of Latin America. Many of the region's earliest pottery styles share generally similar features, testifying to widespread, albeit still poorly understood, contacts among Formative cultures.

Many Formative farming cultures were segmentary societies composed of autonomous, egalitarian villages. However, in Mesoamerica and the central Andes the establishment of the first permanent settlements was followed within a few centuries by the rise of a new, more complex form of organization, the chiefdom. In chiefdoms individual villages are no longer independent political units. Instead, a hereditary leader, or chief, has permanent control of a number of communities. Like segmentary societies, chiefdoms are divided into formally recognized kin groups, but in a chiefdom these groups are ranked with respect to one another. People are "chiefly" or "common" from birth, and political authority is vested in the chiefly lineages.

The first chiefdoms arose around 2500 B.C. along the central coast of Peru, where a sedentary way of life had already existed for some 500 years. There was a rapid growth in the coastal population, and towns of several thousand inhabitants appeared among the smaller villages. A number of sites, such as Aspero and El Paraíso contained large, flat-topped pyramidal mounds and other monumental "corporate labor" constructions (architecture built by work gangs drawn from multiple communities). Marked differences in burials, and in particular the elaborate graves of some infants, suggest the beginnings of hereditary social inequality. For the first time in Latin American prehistory, social status came to be determined at birth.

Interestingly, these early coastal chiefdoms arose in a preceramic, preagricultural context.

They were sustained by the same rich marine resources that had supported the first sedentary villages in the area. Maize agriculture appeared as an introduction from the highlands at a later date, around 2000 B.C. Thereafter, between 1800 and 1500 B.C., the seven-thousand-year-long transition to economies based on intensive agriculture was finally completed in the central Andes.

Beginning around 1200 B.C. and persisting over the ensuing millennium, regular contacts among local complex societies produced a remarkable cultural and artistic florescence known as the Early Horizon (or "Chavín" Horizon, after a site in the north Peruvian highlands). The hallmark of the Early Horizon is a series of elaborate art styles emphasizing felines, humanlike beings with feline attributes, birds of prey, and serpents, expressed in a variety of media—stone sculpture, pottery, textiles, goldwork (the first central Andean metallurgy), and so on (Figure 3). The similarities among these styles are thought to reflect the transmittal of religious ideas that were continually reinterpreted as they were incorporated into the various local cultural traditions.

Mesoamerica shows a similar pattern of cultural development, beginning at a later date. Although some earlier examples are known, sedentary villages did not become common in most of the area until 1500 B.C. Subsequently, the centuries between 1200 and 500 B.C. were marked by the rise of chiefdoms and a widespread artistic dissemination comparable to that of the central Andean Early Horizon. The earliest complex society, and the center of artistic diffusion, was the enigmatic Olmec culture of the Gulf coastal lowlands. The major Olmec sites of San Lorenzo and La Venta have impressive corporate labor architecture of an undoubtedly religious nature. The distinctive Olmec art style was expressed in several media, but its most famous products are stone sculptures, including gigantic heads up to three meters tall (Figure 4) and carvings of "were-jaguars" (human beings with feline mouths).

FIGURE **3**

**The "Great Image," one of the
principal stone sculptures in the main
temple at Chavin.**

Gordon R. Willey, *An Introduction to
American Archaeology, Volume 2: South
America* (Englewood Cliffs, N.J.:
Prentice-Hall, 1971), p. 120. Photo: neg.
no. 337603, courtesy Department
Library Services, American Museum of
Natural History, New York, New York.

FIGURE 4
An Olmec monumental stone head.
Photo: courtesy of Government of
Mexico/PAR-NYC.

Olmec artifacts and stylistic influences occur widely throughout Mesoamerica, but their significance is a matter of dispute. One argument treats the Olmec as a "mother culture," the ultimate source of all the other great civilizations of Mesoamerica. A contrasting hypothesis holds that the diffusion of the Olmec style took place at a time when chiefdoms were arising independently in a number of subareas. From this viewpoint the spread of Olmec influence was a consequence, rather than a cause, of increasing social complexity in other places. The debate continues, but recent evidence tends to favor the latter interpretation. In fact, it now seems likely that the Olmec heartland itself was neither culturally nor ethnically homogeneous.

■ The Rise of the State: 500 B.C.–A.D. 250

The period from 500 B.C. to A.D. 250 witnessed increasing social and cultural complexity in many parts of Latin America. Although southern South America and most of eastern Brazil continued to be occupied by hunter-gatherers, village farmers did appear in a few widely scattered sectors of the latter area. In the Caribbean a ceramic-making, village agricultural way of life spread through the Lesser Antilles to Puerto Rico between A.D. and 250; this new adaptation was brought to the islands by immigrants from the Venezuelan mainland.

The dominant trend in the northern Andes was the development of local chiefdoms out of the old Formative village-farming base. Some of the early northern Andean chiefdom-level cultures show extensive evidence of contacts with Mesoamerica and other distant regions. These foreign traits and influences probably reflect the crystallization of formalized trade networks based on earlier, less structured Formative patterns of exchange. Such networks may have been run by socially distinct, hereditary groups of long-distance traders (a phenomenon emphasized in sixteenth-century accounts of Colombia and Ecuador).

The most complex cultures of the period 500 B.C.–A.D. 250 occurred in Mesoamerica and the central Andes, which gave rise to huge settlements that can truly be called cities and to a new form of social and political organization, the state. The origin of the state is one of the most intensively investigated and debated problems in archaeology today, and there are probably as many definitions of the ancient state as there are archaeologists studying the topic. A minimal definition identifies the early, or preindustrial, state as an autonomous political unit with a strong, centralized, hereditary government that controls multiple communities. The governing body has the power to decree and enforce laws, to impose taxes upon the citizenry, and to draft people for corporate labor projects and warfare.

The first definite Latin American state arose in Mesoamerica, in the Valley of Mexico. Its capital was Teotihuacán, one of the most famous archaeological sites in Latin America (Figure 5). Between 150 B.C. and A.D. 250 Teotihuacán grew to cover twenty-one square kilometers; by the end of this time its population was probably about 125,000, although estimates as high as

FIGURE 5
Central Teotihuacán.
Photo: Courtesy of Department of Library Services, American Museum of Natural History, New York, New York.

200,000 have been offered. In fact, it seems likely that in A.D. 150 some 80 percent or 90 percent of the entire population of the Valley of Mexico lived within the city limits of Teotihuacán.

Elsewhere in the Mesoamerican highlands, there is evidence of increasing social and cultural complexity in a number of subareas— for example, in the Valley of Guatemala, where the site of Kaminaljuyú became the center of a prominent chiefdom. Monte Albán (Figure 6), which was founded around 500 B.C., became the predominant site in the Valley of Oaxaca, with a population of perhaps fifteen-thousand people in A.D. 250. A recent, controversial interpretation proposes that Monte Albán began as a "disembedded capital"—a political center founded in neutral territory by a confederation of independent chiefdoms. In any case, by A.D. 250 Monte Albán seems to have been the capital of a unified Oaxacan state.

The Maya lowlands saw the development of a number of local chiefdoms centered on sites such as Tikal in Guatemala and Cerros in Belize. Interactions among these lowland groups and contemporaneous chiefdoms in the highlands of southeastern Mesoamerica (for example, Kaminaljuyú) seem to have laid the foundations for the great florescence of lowland Maya civilization in the next period. However, new data show that El Mirador, one of the largest of all Maya sites, was built largely in the centuries preceding A.D. 250. Current explanations of the

FIGURE **6**
Monte Albán.
Photo courtesy of Richard Blanton, Department of Sociology and Anthropology, Purdue University, West Lafayette, Indiana.

rise of Maya civilization cannot account for the presence of such a huge, precocious site in an environmentally impoverished lowland zone near the Guatemala-Mexico border, and the ongoing investigation of El Mirador will undoubtedly lead to new interpretations of Maya cultural development.

In the central Andes the period from 500 B.C. to A.D. 250 had a number of salient features. Out of the Early Horizon cultural base there arose a series of elaborate local civilizations: Moche, Nasca, Pucara, Tiahuanaco, and others. In the first few centuries A.D. some of these cultures crossed the threshold between chiefdoms and states. The largest and best known of these early state-level societies is represented by the Moche culture of northern coastal Peru, whose capital lay at the site of Moche in the valley of the same name (Figure 7).

Another major theme of central Andean cultural development between 500 B.C. and A.D. 250 is the emergence of the Lake Titicaca Basin as the principal focus of highland civilization. During this time two sites achieved positions of eminence: Pucara in the northern part of the basin and Tiahuanaco in the south. Toward the end of the period Tiahuanaco surpassed Pucara and became the predominant cultural and economic center of the Titicaca Basin.

In the south Andes, the transition from hunting and gathering to a village agricultural way of life was fully completed between 500 B.C.

FIGURE 7
The "Pyramid of the Sun" at Moche.
Photo: Shippee-Johnson, courtesy of Department of Library Services, American Museum of Natural History. New York, New York.

and A.D. 250. During this time the area was characterized by generally similar ceramic styles and other evidence of widespread cultural contacts. This pattern reflects the presence of formally organized trade networks, integrated by llama caravans and directed by pastoral groups from the Titicaca Basin cultures and the highlands of southern Bolivia.

■ The Classic Civilizations: A.D. 250–600

In many parts of Latin America there is little reason to define A.D. 250–600 as a separate period. Some areas did undergo new developments: For example, incipient chiefdoms seem to have arisen along the major riverine floodplains of Amazonia. On the whole, however, the general trends of the preceding epoch, and many of the individual cultures, persisted. Rather than massive, widespread cultural change, the dominant theme of these centuries is the flourishing of the brilliant civilizations of Mesoamerica and the central Andes.

In Mesoamerican archaeology this period is known as the Early Classic, and it has two preeminent characteristics. The first is the unrivaled power and prestige of Teotihuacán. During the Early Classic period Teotihuacán was the single most influential site in all of Mesoamerica, a focus of religious pilgrimages and the center of a vast, state-controlled trade and marketing network. The city's presence was felt everywhere in the Mesoamerican world. Its deities were incorporated into local pantheons; its products were distributed throughout the area and widely copied as well. The precise nature of Teotihuacán's impact is controversial: Some archaeologists interpret it as a largely peaceful phenomenon brought about by merchants and religious pilgrims, while others see Teotihuacán as an aggressive state expanding its political and economic power through military conquests.

The second major theme of Early Classic Mesoamerica is the florescence of lowland Maya civilization. The great cultural elaboration that characterized the centuries following A.D. 300

ranks the Maya among the most renowned civilizations of ancient Latin America. Maya sites such as Tikal (Figure 8) and Palenque are famous for their towering, limestone-faced pyramids topped by small temples and for their carved stone stelae with ornate hieroglyphic inscriptions. The Maya are also noted for their remarkable astronomical knowledge and their complicated calendrical system. The latter included both a 260-day ceremonial calendar and a 365-day solar year, the two of which were integrated in a cycle that repeated itself every fifty-two years.

Major changes in the prevailing view of Maya civilization have taken place over the past two decades. It was once thought that Maya accomplishments rested solely on a long-fallow system of shifting cultivation known as swidden, or "slash-and-burn," agriculture. However, new data show that the Maya employed a variety of more productive farming techniques, including the construction of raised fields in swampy zones and terraces on hillsides. Furthermore, where large Maya sites used to be seen as rather "empty" ceremonial centers, with relatively small resident populations, it is now clear that such settlements had much larger numbers of inhabitants. To be sure, individual households were dispersed, and the overall population density was low, but at Maya cities like Tikal tens of thousands of people lived within a few kilometers of the civic center.

The nature of Maya political organization is still a matter of dispute. The Maya were governed by hereditary aristocracies; traditionally these rulers have been seen as the heads of high chiefdoms or at best independent city-states. However, there are clear differences in the size of Maya centers, and a few — Tikal, for example — are much larger than the rest. In recent years this hierarchical settlement pattern has led a growing number of archaeologists to argue that between A.D. 300 and 800 the Maya lowlands were divided into about a half-dozen states.

In the central Andes the local civilizations

FIGURE 8

Temple I at Tikal.
Photo © copyright by University Museum, University of Pennsylvania. Philadelphia, Pennsylvania.

apparent in the latter part of the preceding period continued to flourish. Probably the most obvious trend during these centuries is the increasing bipolarity of central Andean civilization, with the northern coast and the Titicaca Basin consolidating their positions as the two principal foci of political and economic power. On the northern coast the Moche state expanded until it measured three hundred kilometers from end to end and encompassed nine river valleys. In the Titicaca Basin Tiahuanaco continued to occupy the predominant position, and Tiahuanaco artifacts and influences spread throughout the south Andes. Like Teotihuacán, Tiahuanaco was simultaneously a religious, manufacturing, and political center, and the nature of its influence is unclear. Some archaeologists argue for an increasing Tiahuanaco monopolization of trade networks in the south Andean area, while others speak of military conquests and the rise of a Tiahuanaco Empire.

At this point it might be useful to make some comparisons between the Mesoamerican and central Andean civilizational traditions, since there were some striking differences between them. All major Mesoamerican civilizations had systems of writing, but writing never developed in the central Andes. On the other hand, domesticated animals and metallurgy (eventually including bronzesmithing) played major roles in central Andean civilization but were relatively insignificant in Mesoamerica. The populations of highland Mesoamerican cities tended to be very large and economically diversified, with substantial numbers of agriculturalists to support the resident religious, governmental, and craft specialists. In contrast, central Andean cities were "empty" or "artificial" in the sense that their permanent populations usually consisted almost entirely of official state personnel; the farmers, fishermen, and herders who sustained them lived in outlying villages. The Maya pattern of dispersed agricultural households around a civic center represents a third type of urbanism, distinct from the other two.

Another frequently cited difference — the importance of markets in Mesoamerica and their absence in the central Andes — has probably been overstated. Nonetheless, it is true that (at least in the highland subareas) Mesoamerican states generally had multifaceted economies, supporting themselves through marketing activities, labor drafts, and the exaction of tribute in the form of goods. Central Andean states relied more heavily on systems of labor taxation, in which citizens were required to provide the state with labor services, including work on state-owned agricultural fields, rather than with goods produced at the household or village level.

■ Times of Turmoil: A.D. 600–1000

In stark contrast to the preceding epoch, the four centuries from A.D. 600 to 1000 were a time of widespread cultural transformation. In Mesoamerica and the central Andes the changes reached truly cataclysmic proportions, as great civilizations, some of them a thousand years old, vanished in a process of major cultural realignment. Old centers of economic, political, and religious power fell, to be replaced by new ones — many of which themselves collapsed before the period was over. The major events of this period have yet to be satisfactorily explained, and their causes remain highly controversial.

In Mesoamerica Teotihuacán's power and prestige declined dramatically. Its influence disappeared from distant subareas around A.D. 600, and by A.D. 750 large parts of the city had been abandoned. In the power vacuum left by the collapse of Teotihuacán, new peoples wandered into the Valley of Mexico from the more arid lands to the north and northwest. Most of these immigrants were agricultural groups from the periphery of the old Teotihuacán sphere of influence, but others seem to have been nomadic or seminomadic hunters and gatherers from the northern deserts.

Elsewhere in the Mesoamerican highlands, Monte Albán was almost completely abandoned around A.D. 600, and the Valley of Oaxaca divided into a number of small political units. In the Valley of Guatemala Kaminaljuyú continued to thrive into the later part of the period and then fell, leaving the Guatemalan highlands fragmented into small, warring polities.

One of the most spectacular collapses occurred in the Maya lowlands. Classic Maya civilization reached its peak in the two centuries from A.D. 600 to 800: The lowland population was at an all-time high, and monumental construction proceeded on a massive scale. The ensuing century can truly be described as catastrophic. Between A.D. 800 and 900 nearly all of the major sites in the southern lowlands were deserted, and the total southern population may have dropped by as much as 70 percent. The focus of Maya civilization shifted to the northern lowlands, to sites such as Uxmal and Dzibilchaltún. These centers flourished for about two centuries and then declined rapidly around A.D. 1000.

In the central Andes the centuries from A.D. 600 to 1000 are called the Middle Horizon, and they constitute one of the most poorly understood periods of the area's prehistory. Many of the civilizations of the preceding epoch, such as the Moche state, persisted into the first part of the Middle Horizon, until around A.D. 700, and then collapsed or were radically transformed in ways that are not yet clear.

The outstanding characteristic of the first half of the Middle Horizon was the widespread appearance of art styles related to that of Tiahuanaco. The mechanism underlying this phenomenon is puzzling. Archaeologists once spoke of a Tiahuanaco Empire expanding across the central Andes but eventually dropped the notion in favor of a peaceful religious diffusion. More recently, some scholars have claimed that religious ideas from Tiahuanaco were reworked and then carried outward by a militaristic empire based at the site of Huari in the south-central Peruvian highlands. Other investigators do not believe in the existence of a Huari Empire and argue that the extent of the Middle Horizon

stylistic diffusion is to be explained in terms of intensified interaction among a series of local states or spheres of influence. Whatever its nature, in most of the central Andes the unifying force of the Middle Horizon broke down around A.D. 800. Previously larger cultural units disintegrated into small, competing polities, except in the Titicaca Basin, where Tiahuanaco itself continued to flourish.

The Intermediate Area and the Caribbean witnessed increasing cultural complexity rather than collapse. In the northern Andean sector of the Intermediate Area local chiefdom-level societies consolidated themselves into a series of larger, more powerful chiefdoms. Examples of this trend include the Milagro, Manteño, and Cañari cultures of Ecuador and the Tairona, Quimbaya, and Muisca (Chibcha) cultures of Colombia. Many of the high chiefdoms represented by such cultures persisted until the time of the Spanish Conquest. In the Caribbean there was a marked cultural elaboration that began in Puerto Rico around A.D. 700 and then spread to Hispaniola and Jamaica. These new developments reflect the nascent forms of the chiefdoms that occupied the Greater Antilles during the next period.

The Amazonian pattern remained the same as that of the previous epoch, with chiefdoms along the major floodplains and village agricultural societies elsewhere. In the second half of the first millennium A.D. some of these latter groups — probably speakers of Tupi-Guaraní languages — moved into eastern Brazil and settled in the forested parts of that area. During this period ceramic-making, village farming cultures appeared for the first time in the northern section of southern South America, but the southern two-thirds of that area continued to be occupied solely by hunter-gatherers.

■ **Conflict and Empires: A.D. 1000–1450**

Many of the cultural patterns described in the immediately preceding paragraphs persisted through the last five centuries before European contact. One area in which significant change did occur was the Caribbean. Beginning in eastern Hispaniola and then spreading outward, a further cultural elaboration produced the historically known chiefdoms of the Greater Antilles, the Bahamas, and Trinidad. These peoples—the Taino, Sub-Taino, Igneri, and others—spoke Arawakan languages. They were the first Latin American Indians to be encountered by Europeans, during Columbus's voyage of 1492–1493.

At a still uncertain date after A.D. 1000 Carib-speaking males began to move off the mainland onto the islands. By the end of the fifteenth century they had taken over the Lesser Antilles from the native Arawak populations, and they were raiding throughout the Greater Antilles and the Bahamas. Unlike the Arawaks of the larger islands, the Caribs were organized into autonomous farming villages, not chiefdoms. They were fearsome warriors who ate the bodies of their male Arawak victims in ritual feasts, and they took captured Arawak women as wives, whom they kept in slavelike drudgery. In addition to giving their name to the Caribbean, the bellicose Caribs—via the Hispanicized form *Caribales*—are the source of our word *cannibal*.

Mesoamerican civilization also underwent a series of major cultural transformations between A.D. 1000 and 1450. The overall tenor of the period was one of increasingly fierce military and political competition. In the central Mexican highlands the two centuries after the fall of Teotihuacán had been marked by political fragmentation and the arrival of immigrant groups from the north. Sometime between A.D. 950 and 1000 a new dominant power arose, the Toltec Empire.

Despite both archaeological and ethnohistorical documentation, the Toltecs remain highly enigmatic. When Spanish conquistadors arrived in 1519, the Toltec Empire had long since become a legendary archetype of sophisticated civilization, and Toltec descent was the source of political legitimacy for central Mexican states. However, myths and legends apparently exaggerated the scope and magnificence of the Toltec Empire: It seems to have been basically a loose military alliance among peoples without a Mesoamerican past (northern farmers and nomads) and peoples whose roots reached back to the old Teotihuacán state. Furthermore, while later native histories described the Toltec capital, Tollán, as a paragon of splendor, its archaeological remains—the site of Tula—are those of a sizeable but rather shabby city with decidedly inferior art and architecture. Despite these discrepancies, the Toltecs obviously achieved a position of some power. They are said to have been paid tribute by sites and peoples scattered from the Gulf Coast to western Mexico, and Toltec influence at the lowland Maya center of Chichén Itzá is so strong as to imply military conquest and political domination.

The Toltec state fell apart violently in the second half of the twelfth century, and central Mexico once again fragmented into small city-states, each of which struggled to establish itself as the legitimate heir of the Toltecs. Meanwhile, Toltec-influenced northern groups wandered into the Valley of Mexico and settled among the native inhabitants. These late pre-Columbian valley peoples, natives and immigrants alike, are often lumped together under the label Aztecs, but each group had its own name. Initially, one of the least impressive of the newcomers was a people known as the Mexicas. Simultaneously respected for their ferocity in battle and despised for their lack of sophistication, they served more powerful and prestigious city-states as clients and mercenaries until the mid-1420s. At that time they embarked upon an astounding career of conquests and began to create one of the two largest states ever formed in the native Americas, the Aztec Empire.

In other parts of the Mesoamerican highlands the disunity and conflict apparent by the end of the preceding period continued. The Oaxacan subarea was divided among small, pugnacious Zapotec and Mixtec kingdoms. The Guatemalan highlands were occupied by a variety of petty kingdoms, all of them highly antagonistic toward one another.

The northern Maya lowlands also experienced military conflicts and shifting leadership. Between A.D. 1000 and 1250 the Yucatán Peninsula was dominated by the site of Chichén Itzá. During this interval Chichén Itza's art and architecture so closely imitated Tula's that most archaeologists speak of a central Mexican invasion, with Chichén Itzá serving as the center for Toltec control of Yucatán. Chichén Itzá survived the fall of Tula but was itself overthrown around A.D. 1250, and Mayapán seized control of the northern lowlands. After a stormy rule of about two centuries, Mayapán was destroyed in A.D. 1441, and Yucatán disintegrated into small, quarrelsome polities.

In most of the central Andes the second millennium A.D. opened with a continuation of the turmoil that followed the breakdown of the Middle Horizon states. Small kingdoms and chiefdoms struggled with one another for military and political supremacy. In turn two peoples, one coastal and one highland, arose out of this competition to establish themselves as great imperial powers.

The first of these victors was the Chimú Empire of northern coastal Peru. The Chimú capital, Chan Chan in the Moche Valley, is the largest archaeological site in South America, with ruins that still sprawl across twenty-five square kilometers. Between A.D. 1200 and 1465 the lords of Chan Chan expanded their domain until it encompassed the northernmost one thousand kilometers of the modern Peruvian coast. Throughout the empire a hierarchy of administrative centers enforced the decrees of the Chimú rulers. Local officials mobilized taxpayers to man the Chimú armies and to work on massive construction projects, including multi-valley irrigation systems. In one case the Chimú even succeeded in linking five separate river valleys into a single enormous agricultural complex, the largest ever known in ancient or modern Peru.

In the Titicaca Basin the Tiahuanaco civilization persisted until about A.D. 1200, when its thousand-year domination of the south-central Andes finally came to an end. The resulting power vacuum in the Titicaca Basin gave birth to a series of kingdoms and chiefdoms—the Colla, Lupaqa, Pakaqa, and others—who were the ancestors of the modern Aymará-speaking Indians of the subarea. The late prehistoric Aymará polities were intensely hostile to one another, with each one striving to subjugate its neighbors and assert itself as the rightful heir of Tiahuanaco. The breakdown of Tiahuanaco and the ensuing conflicts also affected the south Andean area, where fortified towns became the prevailing type of settlement in the centuries immediately preceding the Spanish Conquest.

Meanwhile, to the northwest of the Titicaca Basin, in a mountain valley around Cuzco, a new culture developed in the aftermath of the Tiahuanaco collapse. For several centuries this group remained small and unprepossessing. Nevertheless, around A.D. 1440 it started to prevail in the fierce local infighting. Within the next few decades it went on to conquer the entire central Andean area, including the Titicaca Basin and the once-mighty Chimú Empire. These upstarts were the Incas, and they have given their name to the largest empire ever formed in the native New World.

■ The Aztec and Inca Empires: A.D. 1450–1532

As we have seen, the Mexicas wandered into, and the Incas were born out of, the political disarray and constant military conflict of the thirteenth-century Mesoamerican and central Andean worlds. In the last ninety years before European contact these two peoples, hitherto so obscure and unimpressive, emerged out of the competition surrounding them to create the two most famous states of Latin American prehistory, the Aztec and Inca Empires. Both empires rose swiftly, vaulting the Mexicas and the Incas to unrivaled heights of power and affluence, and then collapsed with stunning rapidity before a few hundred Spanish adventurers. The Aztec and Inca cultures both amazed and appalled the sixteenth-century Spaniards who first encountered them, and they have fascinated people ever since.

The Aztec Empire originated as an alliance among the city-states of Tenochtitlán, Texcoco, and Tacuba, but its driving force was the Mexicas of Tenochtitlán. Starting in 1428, the Mexica-led "Triple Alliance" prevailed in the internecine warfare of the Valley of Mexico and took control of that entire subarea. Major conquests outside the valley began around 1450, and soon thereafter the Aztec presence was felt everywhere in Mesoamerica. Through time the Triple Alliance was increasingly dominated by the Mexicas, with Texcoco and Tacuba being relegated to largely symbolic roles. In 1519 the Mexica capital Tenochtitlán was one of the world's premier cities, with splendid palaces and temples and an estimated population of 150,000 to 200,000 residents.

There was an aura of frenzy about the Aztec expansion. Warfare and conquest went on incessantly throughout the history of the empire. At the height of their power the Mexicas nominally controlled almost all of central Mexico and the Gulf Coast, plus large sectors of southern Mexico and the Pacific coast. However, no stable administrative framework was ever imposed over this vast territory: Subjugated peoples were required to pay tribute to Tenochtitlán, but Aztec supervision of the provinces was minimal, and rebellions were frequent. Furthermore, there were large independent enclaves within the boundaries of the Mexica domain. The independent groups, particularly the Tlaxcalans, were a constant threat to the security of the Aztec Empire, and they would eventually help to bring about its downfall.

Tenochtitlán's economy had a threefold base. In the Aztec heartland, around the lake system of the Valley of Mexico, crops were raised on *chinampas*, richly productive artificial islands made by heaping up muck from the lakebeds. Trade was extensive, and professional merchants known as the *pochteca* formed a special group within Aztec society. In addition to their mercantile activities, they often traveled in advance of the Aztec armies, serving as spies. Tribute extracted from conquered peoples formed a third sector of the Aztec economy, and as time went on it became increasingly essential to the support of Tenochtitlán.

A crucial factor in the Mexicas' success—and in their downfall—was a unique state religion that represented a reworking of ancient Mesoamerican beliefs and rituals. In the Mexica vision of the cosmos, the sun was a warrior-god who battled his way across the sky every day, fighting back the forces of darkness. To keep him fit for combat, and thus to stave off the destruction of the universe, the Mexicas had to "feed" the sun with a precious liquid full of vital energy—the blood of warriors captured in battle. Combat provided the necessary captives, who were sacrificed in grisly rituals in which hundreds, or even thousands, of victims perished. Hence, a pattern of conquest without consolidation was actually desirable to the Mexicas, since it led to a perpetual state of war that maintained the supply of sacrificial captives without whom the universe would perish.

However, such an unstable imperial system could not endure forever. In its final years the Aztec Empire was beset by growing economic, military, and political problems. Aztec society became divided against itself, while hatred of the Mexicas smoldered in conquered provinces and the independent enclaves. When Hernán Cortés and his four hundred Spaniards arrived in 1519, they took advantage of this situation to destroy the Aztec Empire within a matter of months. In their final assault on Tenochtitlán, the conquistadors were backed by tens of thousands of vengeful Indian allies.

The Incas called their empire *Tawantinsuyu*, or "Land of the Four Quarters." They began their climb around 1440 by establishing control over the area surrounding their capital district, the Valley of Cuzco in the southern Peruvian highlands. Their first major foreign conquest took place in about 1450, when they seized the northern Titicaca Basin. The resources gained in the Titicaca Basin campaign funded subsequent conquests, and the Incas became the supreme empire-builders of the Andean world. In 1525 their domain stretched from the southern frontier of Colombia to central Chile—a distance of forty-three hundred kilometers spanning thirty-six degrees of latitude.

Tawantinsuyu was politically much more integrated than the Aztec Empire, since the Incas sought not tribute payments and sacrificial captives, but permanent control of land and labor. A hierarchy of administrative centers was established throughout the conquered territories. Each province was supervised by an imperial governor and a set of hereditary officials; native provincial nobles were co-opted into the Inca government whenever possible. In many cases provincial populations were reshuffled and groups of colonists were resettled, either to minimize the risk of rebellion or for economic purposes. The entire empire was linked by a superb network of roads and by relay runners who transmitted messages along them. The Incas had no writing, but detailed records were kept on bunches of knotted strings called *quipus,* which were interpreted by trained specialists.

One of the chief duties of this elaborate administrative structure was to supervise the imperial economy, which was based on the traditional central Andean practice of labor taxation. Citizens of Tawantinsuyu paid their taxes by manning the Inca armies, constructing public works projects, and farming state-owned fields, which were located throughout the provinces. The produce of these fields was gathered into imperial storehouses and then redistributed to support the state's undertakings.

As in the Aztec case, a reworking of traditional religious concepts played a fundamental role in Tawantinsuyu's rampant expansion, which continued even after it had become a major strain on the empire. The Inca kings were held to be divine beings, sons of the sun, and the empire's prosperity was believed to depend on their perpetual well-being. In death they were treated as if they were still alive. A de-

ceased emperor's corpse continued to occupy his palaces, where it received visitors; the royal mummies were brought out to attend all major state ceremonies, and even to greet their friends. Most importantly, the dead rulers continued to own all of the property they had accumulated during their lifetimes, including vast agricultural estates. This fantastic cult of the royal mummies, which was essentially a grandiose version of an ancient central Andean religious tradition of cults of the dead, had a profound impact on Inca society, for it created unrelenting pressures for conquest. Because each emperor ascended the throne without inheriting any of his predecessor's property, he had to strive to amass his own wealth and assure his own eternal welfare by leading the Inca armies to new victories.

For all its size and splendor, the Inca Empire had a number of internal political and economic weaknesses. In its final years it was torn apart in a civil war led by two half-brothers, Huascar and Atahualpa, who were contending for the throne. Atahualpa won and declared himself emperor in 1532, but he did not enjoy his title for long. In the later afternoon of 16 November 1532, at Cajamarca in the northern Peruvian highlands, he was captured by 168 Spaniards under the leadership of an illiterate old campaigner named Francisco Pizarro. Within the next year Atahualpa had been executed and the conquistadors had taken control of Cuzco. They would eventually have to suppress an Inca uprising, but the outcome had already been decided by the Inca civil war and the capture of the emperor. In that sense, the Spanish conquest of Peru was the work of an afternoon.

■ Epilogue

The Spanish and Portuguese conquests put an end to the independent development of native Latin American cultures, but not to the cultural traditions themselves, nor to all of their peoples. After a drastic decline in the early colonial era, Indian populations have rebounded. Nobody knows exactly how many Indians live in Latin America today, but a total of somewhere around 40 million is not unlikely. For countries with large Indian populations, such as Mexico, Guatemala, and the Andean republics, the integration of the indigenous peoples into national life is a major and still unresolved problem. Four and a half centuries after Cortés and Pizarro, the impact of Latin America's pre-Columbian cultures remains strong.

■ Suggested Readings

Adams, Richard E. W. *Prehistoric Mesoamerica*. Boston: Little, Brown, 1977.

Bankes, George. *Peru Before Pizarro*. Oxford: Elsevier, 1977.

Bawden, Garth, and Geoffrey W. Conrad. *The Andean Heritage*. Cambridge: Peabody Museum Press, 1982.

Berdan, Frances F. *The Aztecs of Central Mexico: An Imperial Society*. New York: Holt, Rinehart, and Winston, 1982.

Blanton, Richard E., Stephen A. Kowalewski, Gary Feinman, and Jill Appel. *Ancient Mesoamerica: A Comparison of Change in Three Regions*. Cambridge: Cambridge University Press, 1981.

Conrad, Geoffrey W., and Arthur A. Demarest. *Religion and Empire: The Dynamics of Aztec and Inca Expansionism*. Cambridge: Cambridge University Press, 1984.

Hammond, Norman. *Ancient Maya Civilization*. Cambridge: Cambridge University Press and Rutgers University Press, 1982.

Jennings, Jesse D., ed. *Ancient South Americans*. San Francisco: W. H. Freeman, 1983. Includes coverage of Mesoamerica.

Lumbreras, Luis G. *The Peoples and Cultures of Ancient Peru*. Washington: Smithsonian Institution Press, 1974.

Weaver, Muriel Porter. *The Aztecs, Mayas, and Their Predecessors: Archaeology of Mesoamerica*. 2d ed. New York: Academic Press, 1981.

Willey, Gordon R. *An Introduction to American Archaeology: Volume 2: South America*. Englewood Cliffs, N.J.: Prentice-Hall, 1971.

3 | Latin American Societies: People and Culture

PAUL L. DOUGHTY

Just as Gabriel García Márquez's fictional hero, Colonel Buendía in *One Hundred Years of Solitude,* nostalgically recalled his father showing him ice for the first time, so many contemporary Latin Americans might remember their parents taking them to their first fiesta. Today, thoughts of innocent celebrations shrink before the ominous shadows of civil wars and political corruption, the numbing impact of dictatorships and international power struggles, the life-altering effect of runaway inflation and banal consumerist culture. While the stereotypes of "siesta and fiesta" may still be conjured up by many travel agents, the reality of contemporary Latin American experience dictates another vision. It is well to remember that Colonel Buendía reminisced as he stood before a firing squad.

Finding the "real" Latin America means rejecting the stereotypes that Europeans and North Americans have accepted. Foreign culture, military coercion, colonial dependency, economic exploitation and uncertainty, race and class conflict, and rebellion have molded Latin America's evolution since Hernán Cortés, Francisco Pizarro, and their Portuguese counterparts.

The effects of this history are readily visible. In the small, remote district where I once lived, my Peruvian neighbors were a genealogical surprise. Their English, Scottish, Italian, and Chinese surnames among the Spanish and Quechua ones alone gave pause to any facile generalization about "Latin America": Mery Afon Olivera, Juan Estuart Terry, and Jhony Chauca Machiaveli. These complex forces affecting common people have been ignored.

The first point that must be understood is that the "Latin" classification is little more than a convenient label blanketing a region of thirty two independent countries and seventeen dependent territories of France, Great Britain, the Netherlands, and the United States. Differences in land, climate, and resources in pre-Columbian societies, and in degrees of a cultural influence by European colonial administrations led to major political and economic variations within Latin America. And while there is much commonality deeply rooted in old experience, rapid changes are occurring today as nations participate ever more in world affairs.

Racial and ethnic differences among the nations are clearly evident (Table 1). Only Bolivia and Guatemala report a majority of their citizens

TABLE 1

The Nations, Population, and Social Composition of Latin America, 1983[a]

Nation	Population (000)	Percentage of Total[b]	Race and Ethnic Group (%)				
			Amerind	Mixed	White	Black	Other
Argentina	28,174	7.9		15	85		
Antigua/Barbuda	77	<1			1	99	
Bahamas	215	<1			10	80	10
Barbados	251	<1			4	80	17
Belize	149	<1	19	33	3	11	35
Bolivia	5,600	1.6	55	35	6		4
Brazil	120,507	33.8	2	30	60	8	
Chile	11,292	3.1	7	62	31		
Colombia	26,425	7.4	4	58	20	18	
Costa Rica	2,340	<1	<1	90	6	2	<1
Cuba	9,865	2.7			37	11	52[b]
Dominica	74	<1	<1			99	
Dominican Republic	5,592	1.5		73	16	11	
Ecuador	8,605	2.4	25	55	10	10	
El Salvador	5,087	1.4	4	95	1		
Grenada	110	<1			1	99	
Guatemala	7,477	2.1	55	45			
Guyana	796	<1	4		1	43	52[c]
Haiti	5,104	1.4		1		99	
Honduras	3,818	1.1	2	95	1	1	1
Jamaica	2,194	<1			1	76	23[d]
Mexico	71,215	20.0	29	55	16		
Nicaragua	2,777	<1	5	69	17	9	
Panama	1,877	<1	7	70	8	14	1
Paraguay	3,057	<1	4	95	1		
Peru	17,031	4.7	35	47	15	1	2
Puerto Rico*	3,251	<1		73	2	25	
Saint Lucia	119	<1			1	90	9
Saint Vincent	115	<1	2	1	4	86	6
Suriname	356	<1	3	31	1	11[e]	65[f]
Trinidad/Tobago	1,203	<1		14	1	43	42[g]
Uruguay	2,929	<1		5	90	5	
Venezuela	16,500	4.6	2	67	21	10	
Averages or Totals	364,182	100[i]	10.7	41.4	35.5	6.2	2.4

[a] Estimates based on *World Bank World Development Report, 1983* and Global Studies, *Latin America, 1983.*
[b] Includes mulattos (51%), Chinese (1%).
[c] Includes East Indians (51%), Chinese (1%).
[d] Includes Chinese, East Indians.
[e] Maroons (11%).
[f] East Indians (38%), Indonesians (16%).
[g] East Indians.
[h] Percentage of total Latin American population: < 1 percent is less than one percent of total Latin American population.
[i] total rounded off.
*U.S. associated state.

as native American Indians, while five Caribbean nations claim more than 90 percent black populations and three nations count more than half of their people as white. However, the largest block of Latin Americans is of mixed racial ancestry — American Indian, white, black, Oriental, or East Indian — in varying degrees.

The developmental features of Latin America show similarly broad ranges of variation (Tables 2 and 3). Although the average gross national product per capita places the region as a whole in the World Bank's "upper-middle income" country division, 60 percent of Latin Americans have average incomes far lower, and Haiti, Bolivia, Honduras, and El Salvador rank among the poorest third of the world's nations. In short, although 71 percent of Latin Americans live in countries whose income levels are above those of half the world, the chasms of socioeconomic inequality among and within the countries belie average figures. Furthermore, the overwhelming dominance of the largest city in most nations signals the profound imbalance between these primate cities and their hinterlands.

■ Population, Race, and Ethnicity

Research findings in the past two decades have radically altered traditional views of early American demography. Estimates of the population of pre-Hispanic Latin America have been dramatically increased from 7.5 million (Kroeber) to as high as 112.25 million (Dobyns).

The reason for this discrepancy is that earlier scholars understood neither the great productive and carrying capacity* of pre-Columbian socioeconomic systems nor the extent of population decline caused by disease in combination with the devastating effects of social disruption, cultural demoralization, and the rigors of colonial regimes.[1] There is an ethnocentric dimen-

sion to this miscalculation, compounding the lack of data: How could non-European societies, lacking critical elements of Old World culture and technology (and thus, "civilization"), have developed extensive empires, cities, agriculture, and vast populations? For many years, scholars simply took for granted that the American Indians had not been able to populate or develop this richly endowed hemisphere. They were wrong, as archaeologists and ethnohistorians working today make increasingly clear.

As radical as it might seem, contemporary investigation lends support to high population estimates, although the "final" figures have yet to be determined. The rapid decline of native American populations after contact and conquest by Europeans occurred because New World peoples lacked immunity to the classic epidemic diseases such as smallpox, whooping cough, measles, chicken pox, bubonic plague, typhus, and influenza. This produced dramatic population losses of as much as twenty-five to one over the colonial period in some areas, and losses were particularly heavy in "high culture" regions — the Aztec homeland in central Mexico and the Andean empire of the Incas. Some smaller tribal societies were extinguished altogether in the first century of conquest, and dozens of native languages disappeared in all but name. In Brazil, aboriginal peoples like the coastal Tupi-speaking peoples suffered a similar fate.[2]

By the mid-sixteenth century, the plantation economy focused on sugar production, which had replaced the exploitation of brazilwood and other natural products. The Portuguese soon discovered that the Tupinamba, Potiguar, and other peoples abhorred the coercive routine of plantation labor. The constant need to replenish the enslaved but dying native populations led to the development of a major frontier career: slave raiding of native tribes. *Bandeirantes,* as they were called, explored and exploited the vast Brazilian hinterland for more than a century after 1600. During this long period of violent and chaotic colonization, the labor problem was

---

*Editor's Note: Carrying capacity refers to the potential of the land and resources to sustain a population.

TABLE 2

The Basic Demography of Latin America, 1983[a]

Nation	GNP ($ 1981)	Urban (%)	Primacy Rate[b]	Birth Rate[c]	Death Rate[c]	Life Expectancy	Literacy (%)
Argentina	2,560	83	20	20	9	71	93
Antigua/ Barbuda	1,550	39	nd	30	8	68	89
Bahams	3,620	69	nd	25	5	69	93
Barbados	3,500	04	nd	16	7	71	99
Belize	1,080	54	21			67	
Bolivia	600	45	50	42	16	51	63
Brazil	2,220	68	91	30	8	64	76
Chile	2,560	81	35	25	7	68	90
Colombia	1,380	64	89	29	8	63	81
Costa Rica	1,430	44	28	30	4	73	90
Cuba	nd	66	27	18	6	73	95
Dominica	750	47	nd	21	5	58	
Dominican Republic	1,260	52	29	36	8	62	67
Ecuador	1,180	45	85	40	9	62	81
El Salvador	650	41	21	40	8	63	62
Grenada	850	26	nd	27	6	63	69
Guatemala	1,140	39	10	39	10	59	47
Guyana	720	34	22	29	7	61	85
Haiti	300	28	26	33	13	54	23
Honduras	600	36	83	44	11	59	60
Jamaica	1,180	42	16	29	6	71	90
Mexico	2,250	67	23	36	7	66	83
Nicaragua	860	54	34	44	11	57	90
Panama	1,910	55	19	30	5	71	85
Paraguay	1,630	40	16	32	7	65	84
Peru	1,170	66	15	36	11	58	80
Puerto Rico	4,969	62	20	27	6	71	86
Saint Lucia	970	37	nd	35	7	67	78
Saint Vincent	630	nd	nd	31	10	60	95
Suriname	3,030	40	7	29	7	69	65
Trinidad/ Tobago	5,670	22	18	9	8	72	95
Uruguay	2,820	84	13	20	10	71	94
Venezuela	4,220	84	35	35	6	68	82
Averages	1,790	51	32	30	8	65	79

[a] Estimates based on World Bank *World Development Report 1983* and Global Studies, *Latin America, 1983; Encyclopedia Britannica Book of the Year, 1983.*
[b] Primacy rate (P) compares the largest city (x) with the combined sizes (y) of the next two largest cities. The lower the P figure, the greater the demographic dominance of the primate city.
[c] Birth and death rates per 1,000.

eased by the importation of Africans, who rapidly became the backbone of the plantation system, the frontier of European economy. Along Brazil's long coastal provinces from Bahia to Rio, the Tupi peoples resisted, traded, mated, and fought with the Europeans, but ultimately they died out before the combined onslaught of abuse and disease.

The "great dying" of the native American peoples now stands as a great human tragedy, a biological cataclysm with profound cultural and social consequences. If the high estimates for pre-Columbian population are near the mark, then Latin America did not regain its preconquest population level until about 1940. And even today epidemic disease and cultural extinction remain a threat for native Americans in Amazonian tribal societies.[3]

In the Caribbean region, as the Arawaks met their demise and the fierce Caribs retreated to "safe" havens, they were continuously replaced first by other native peoples brought in from surrounding continental areas, and, after 1518, by a steady stream of Africans from dozens of nations and tribes in west central Africa. While many of these worked the sugar plantations for the European trade, elsewhere (for example, in Peru), the Africans also worked as artisans in the cities. Between 1500 and 1870, when the last arrived, almost 8.5 million slaves made the Atlantic journey to Latin America and the Caribbean region, with 38 percent of these going to Brazil, the last country in the hemisphere to abolish slavery (in 1888).

Today, the black peoples of the New World are widely spread out, forming major segments of the populations of all Caribbean countries and many others. (see Table 1). Nevertheless, they are often underrepresented in censuses in, for example, Peru, Mexico, Panama, Brazil, and Colombia, where people may prefer to identify themselves as persons of mixed ancestry. In this

TABLE **3**

Population Percent and Average Per Capita Gross National Product by Country Group and Region, 1982

Region*		Population	Percentage of Total	Per Capita GNP
I.	Caribbean Area	45,421	12.5	2,103
	A. Group	21,226	5.9	4,122
	B. Group	17,877	4.9	1,267
	C. Group	6,318	1.7	703
II.	Central America	23,376	6.4	1,278
	A. Group	11,694	3.2	1,493
	B. Group	11,682	3.2	703
III.	Southern Cone	45,452	12.5	2,392
IV.	Andean	57,661	15.8	1,082
	A. Group	52,061	14.2	1,243
	B. Group	5,600	1.5	600
V.	Brazil and Mexico	191,722	52.7	2,235

Based on World Bank, *World Development Report, 1983.*

*IA: Venezuela, Trinidad, Suriname, Puerto Rico, Bahamas, Barbados; IB: Antigua, Belize, Cuba, Dominican Republic, Jamaica; IC: Dominica, Grenada, Guyana, Haiti, St. Lucia, St. Vincent; IIA: Guatemala, Panama, Costa Rica; IIB: El Salvador, Nicaragua, Honduras; III: Chile, Paraguay, Argentina, Uruguay; IVA: Colombia, Ecuador, Peru; IVB: Bolivia.

fashion, African ethnicity is often hidden or remains only in cultural fragments, which provide little basis for a sense of ethnic identity.

Strong African cultural patterns do appear where blacks are numerous. This is particularly so in areas where Maroon (from the Spanish for "runaway," *cimarrón*) societies developed and survived. Escaping slaves, from the very first, sought safety in refuge areas in island interiors, as in the Jamaican "cockpit" country or in the tropical forests of the Guianas. Today the Saramaka and Djuka in Suriname remain discrete, numerous, and successful societies. Their cultures, representing an amalgam of African, European, and native American elements, in which the African dominates, reflect a clear sense of their history and identity.[4] Significant numbers of Belizeans, Hondurans, and Nicaraguans represent different cultural expressions of this harsh synthesis, where, long assimilated into Indian groups, they identify themselves not as Africans but as Miskito Indians, "Black Carib," or Garifuna.

White immigrants to Latin America were few in comparison to the Africans during the colonial period, and they largely consisted of men: soldiers of fortune, colonial bureaucrats, clergy, and entrepreneurs. They settled primarily in the viceregal capitals and major ports: Lima, Mexico City, Rio de Janeiro, and Havana. Outside these areas, Spanish and Portuguese officials and adventurers made their ways, often in isolation from compatriots. Iberian women found little to attract them to early colonial life, and even during the later years of colonial stability, they never made up a significant percentage of immigrants.

The combined effects of massive Indian deaths and African and European immigrants forever altered the composition of the New World population. Significantly, Columbus Day is in Latin America called *Día de la Raza* ("Race Day") in recognition of the new mixed population of the Americas. The largest segment of people throughout Latin America today is of "mixed" racial background: identifying themselves as *mestizos* in Mexico and Peru, *ladinos* in

Central America, and *caboclos* in Brazil. The historic progenitors of this group, the whites and Indians, remain discretely identified today as they were four hundred years ago, while those of unmixed African descent are called *negros* in Spanish-speaking countries and *pretos* in Brazil.

The contemporary situation evolved from colonial attempts to maintain a racially based castelike order for purposes of social control and taxation. Throughout the Spanish and Portuguese colonies, elaborate classifications described various types of unions and their offspring. In the case of Mexico, for example, there were sixteen designations.[5]

> Spanish-Indian union produced a *mestizo*
> Mestizo-Spanish union produced a *castizo*
> Spanish-black union produced *mulato*
> Black-Indian union produced a *zambo*
> Spanish-mulatto union produced a *morisco*
> Spanish-morisco union produced an *albino*
> Spanish-albino union produced a *saltra-atras*

Such racial classification at best is a cumbersome and inexact science. In practice, the system was simplified by referring to persons of mixed and "lesser" ancestry as "castes." Those so labeled were relegated to performing menial tasks and to service occupations. In most places they were prohibited by sumptuary laws from doing such trivial but symbolic things as wearing Spanish-style clothing or riding horses.

Many of the caste terms not only survive today but are often used as terms of address or reference in normal discourse. In Brazil, for example, alongside the generic terms *branco* (white), which carries the implication that one is rich and upper class, and *preto* (black), which connotes poverty and lower-class status, there are terms that describe many variations in appearance — in blackness or whiteness.

Similar interpersonal references are common throughout most of Latin America. In Peru, the terms *zambo* and *moreno* are regularly used for persons of black heritage; *Indio*, or *indígena* for Indians; and *cholo* and *mestizo* for those of mixed background. Moreover, if used in the diminutive form (*cholito*, *morenito*) such terms may become somewhat derogatory, and if used with the noun *people* (*gente morena, gente indígena*) they become more polite. The use of such words may carry subtle and negative connotations about a person, and what may pass as an innocent adjective in one country would not in another. Regardless of such differences, it is universally true that whiteness is associated with high status and blackness with low status.

Low status is also accorded to those who appear to have Indian ethnicity. The experience of native Americans under colonial rule and in subsequent periods leaves little doubt that this inferior status is deep-rooted and pervasive.[6] "Looking Indian" is a combination of stature, facial structure, hair, and dress. Behaving like an Indian means performing heavy manual labor, particularly farming; living in rural areas; adhering to highly localized, native customs; and above all, speaking an indigenous language as one's first tongue. "Indianness" is thus defined as much by sociocultural markers as by biological ones although the two are frequently confused. Indians are sometimes regarded as "racially" incompetent because they speak only native languages, as "lazy," or "unteachable." Terms like *brute Indian* and *Indian savage* are heard not infrequently with respect to the rural indigenous population.

From independence onward, various factors — the neocolonial impact of European powers and of the United States, transnational expansion of business interests, massive internal migrations in most countries, and a high volume of international immigration and emigration — have further diversified each country and region. From 1850 to 1950 Argentina received over 4.5 million European immigrants: English, Irish, French, and especially Spaniards and Italians, who accounted for 26 percent and 55 percent of the influx respectively. By 1914 foreigners outnumbered native Argentines by two to one.

Similar influxes elsewhere in the southern cone — in Chile, Uruguay, and parts of southern Brazil — sharply altered the character of these societies, differentiating them from the rest of Latin America. In Chile's southern valleys between Valdivia and Puerto Montt large numbers of German immigrants established ethnic colonies after 1850, challenging the native Mapuche (Araucanian) Indians for their lands. By the end of the century, the Germans formed a virtual nation within a nation, speaking German and maintaining close ties with the fatherland. Germans also populated southern Brazil, coming as refugees after World War II to form very traditionalist ethnic enclaves.

In the second half of the nineteenth century many Chinese were brought to Cuba, Brazil, Central America, and Peru as indentured labor, to help build the railroads and do agricultural work.[7] The ninety thousand who went to Peru and the more than one hundred thousand who were taken to Cuba were welcomed in the declining phases of the slave economies. The descendants have retained ties with China and preserved many ethnic traits and considerable social identity, institutionalized in the form of Chinese clubs. Cities such as Lima and San José, Costa Rica, are notable for their scores of Latin-Chinese restaurants.

Labor needs of the sugar plantations led the British to bring Hindu workers from India into the Caribbean during the nineteenth century. Between 1838 and 1917, over a half-million "East Indians," as they are called in the New World, were distributed throughout the Caribbean where the slave plantations found their labor supply wanting.[8] These immigrants now form the dominant ethnic group of Guyana and constitute almost half of Trinidad and Tobago's population. The international labor migration to Latin America in this century has also been complemented by significant numbers of Japanese immigrants. Often working as businessmen or farmers, they formed strong colonies in Brazil, Bolivia, and Peru.

■ Latin America's Fourth World

The interplay of forces within each nation resulted in both the extensive assimilation of foreigners into the national societies and a variety of accommodations in which cultural pluralism vigorously survives. This process, however, has tended to exclude the preexisting native societies. Throughout Latin America the distinctive native cultural groups, such as the tribal societies of the vast Amazonia, are vulnerably positioned in the national sociopolitical structures. They occupy "regions of refuge," as Aguirre phrased it, or constitute a sort of Fourth World of non-state societies bound within the borders of nations, in them but not of them.[9] In Latin America there are many such societies; their situation differs sharply from one nation to the next, reflecting fundamental differences in national politics and culture.

The Mexicans pioneered new relationships between the state and its native cultures after the 1910–20 revolution developing the strong "Indianist" movement that inspired imitation throughout the hemisphere and led to the organization of the Inter-American Indian Institute and affiliated institutions in most countries. Despite this development, Mexico's strident postrevolution (1920) nationalism is part of an aggressive cultural florescence, *mestizo* in character and pervasive in national life. With its popular *ranchero* music played by ubiquitous *mariachi* bands, its ribald humor, monolithic political style, food, vigorous small towns and burgeoning cities, the national culture of Mexico has recruited members from all Indian groups, blurring but not eradicating ancient internal ethnic boundaries. Indian policy in Mexico remains, four and a half centuries after Cortés, a matter of debate. Indian societies maintain their visibility throughout the country with functioning cultures and large, thriving populations. Almost 30 percent of the Mexican population is identified with one of the forty-five different ethnolinguistic groups such as the Nahúatl (Aztec), Otomi, Maya, Zapotec, and Mixtec. These Mexicans are buffeted by fluctuating national interests: At certain times they are highly valued and exalted ethnographic symbols of Mexican uniqueness and soul, as showcased, for example, in the magnificent national museum. At other times their cultural status is seen

as the "Indian problem," a dilemma of identity, condition, and social value. In the view of some scholars, Mexican Indian groups are vestiges of colonialist society, essentially alienated and exploited by a ruthless system in which they are neither admired nor respected unless they put aside their cultural uniqueness to become part of social class movements at the national level.[10]

The government itself, although formally lauding cultural pluralism, has nevertheless vacillated between outright encouragement of native organization, through such programs as the Indian Patrimony of the Mesquital Valley (Otomi development program) and a deliberate (but quiet) downplaying of such promotion of ethnicity. As a consequence, government decision makers have difficulty even with issues such as whether to permit publication of books written in native languages, because these issues are always viewed as influencing national ideology and policy. Each new government, although symbolically always "pro-Indian," nevertheless consciously reformulates its position.

Despite these uncertainties and fluctuations, Mexico is virtually unique in its approach to native Americans. In neighboring Guatemala, where they represent an even higher percentage of the population, Indians are not only less secure under the law, but at the present time are under active persecution by the conservative ruling forces, which view them as a threat to national unity. The Mayan peoples of Guatemala are divided into more than twenty ethnolinguistic groups and in the highlands and neighboring lowland areas, they are the majority of the population. Although Spanish-speaking *ladino* Guatemalans live among them, each Mayan group dresses, speaks, worships and lives in distinct ways from them. Thus, these are tightly organized communities, whose members generally give allegiance first to their municipal leaders and culture.[11]

In effect they constitute a separate Guatemala. Until recently Guatemalan Indians participated little in the political life of the nation. However, since the late 1970s, with the country undergoing a virtual civil war that has resulted in 70,000 deaths and 500,000 refugees, government forces have attempted to coerce Indians into the national system so as to gain support. Government actions pose a serious threat to Indian cultural autonomy and the survival of the ethnic groups themselves.[12] Not since the Spanish Conquest have events of such scope devastated the Guatemalan Mayas. Entire villages have been dislocated into refugee camps throughout the country, in Mexico, and in the United States. Elsewhere in Central America, other Indian groups such as the Miskito of Nicaragua and Honduras are similarly caught up in events beyond their control.

The largest number of native speakers of Indian languages live in the central Andean countries in the area that was dominated by the Inca Empire on the eve of conquest. The Aymará, located in the southern provinces of Peru around Lake Titicaca and in adjacent areas of the Bolivian altiplano, provide a break in what is an otherwise uninterrupted Quechua population. About 9.8 million Andean Indians speak one of seven Quechua dialects, and 1.4 million speak Aymará. In all, this represents 35 percent of the populations of Peru, Ecuador, and Bolivia, with small numbers in northern Argentina and Chile. Currently, perhaps half of these persons are bilingual: this figure has grown considerably since about 1950.

The Andean Indians, like their Mexican and Guatemalan counterparts, generally work small farms and produce food for local consumption. Many of them reside in the highland valleys and altiplano regions, in settlements that are interspersed with *mestizo* towns and cities. Although there is a remarkable cultural homogeneity throughout the Andean region, clothing styles and other cultural variations distinguish one province from another. Moreover, linguistic differences among the Quechua peoples are such that the dialect spoken in, for example, Otavalo, Ecuador would not be readily intelligible to speakers in Cuzco, Peru, or Salta, Argentina.

In the Andean countries, the governing elites traditionally viewed Indians as an un-solvable problem. Fettered by an archaic manorial system or eking out a bare subsistence on upland slopes, Indian peasants often staged localized revolts against the abuses of *mestizo* landlords, but to little avail. In 1952, however, the Bolivian revolution shattered the status quo, achieving a redistribution of land to Indian communities and other substantive changes. Similar measures in Peru came nearly two decades later. On 24 June 1969, President Velasco announced an agrarian reform in the following revolutionary words: "Peasants, the landlord will no longer eat from your poverty!" In the same speech, President Velasco announced that the word *indio* ("Indian"), because of its derogatory connotations, would henceforth be officially replaced by *campesino* ("peasant").[13]

While Bolivian and Peruvian Indians have been helped by agrarian reform, they continue to face uncertain government policies which have failed to make promised development investments in rural areas and have not followed through on the reforms initiated. Although Quechua is an official language in Peru, it is rarely taught or used by teachers even in areas where children speak no other language. The Aymará in particular suffer from negative stereotyping generally as "sullen" and "troublesome." In recent years, as the Aymará have developed a greater positive consciousness of their own culture and language, a level of Aymará "nationalism" has arisen on both sides of the Peru-Bolivia border.

Further south, Chile's Mapuche Indians have been locked in a battle with external forces since the Incas' invasion in the reign of Topa Inca (1471–1493). The march of the Tawantinsuyu Empire was stopped at the Bío-bío and Maule rivers, which became the boundary between the Mapuche and the Spanish colonial, and later, the Chilean governments. But by 1890, after intermittent, if rather fierce wars, the Mapuche were finally forced onto reservations. Since that time, Chileans have often encroached further on Mapuche lands.

The Mapuche vigorously maintain their independent identity. They have preserved their own language, religion, family and kinship system, and patterns of sociopolitical organization. After centuries of warfare, they are grudgingly respected, if not admired, by other Chileans. In the decade prior to the Pinochet dictatorship, Mapuche fortunes vis-à-vis the Chilean state had slowly risen with educational and agrarian reforms and other changes. These improvements were, however, dramatically rolled back by the military rulers, who in 1979 established a legal process facilitating the breakup and dissolution of reservation lands. Because control of the land is vital to maintaining the social organization of the group, this development poses a major threat to Mapuche existence.[14]

These pressures and the generally poor state of the Chilean economy under the Pinochet dictatorship have led many Mapuche to migrate. At present, the Mapuche constitute an estimated 7 percent of the national population. About 450,000 Mapuche live on reserved lands, for the most part in Cautin and neighboring provinces. Over 350,000 have migrated to Santiago and other urban centers.

Throughout the tropical lowlands of South America, many still autonomous tribes have resisted extinction along the frontiers of "civilization," although increasingly acculturated, pushed into refuge areas, and forced onto reservations. Perhaps the greatest present-day threat to Indian tribes comes in the tropical lowlands of South America as both governments and private concerns become interested in exploiting these areas. (The appropriate number of tribes in tropical South American nations is given in Table 4; the figures are estimates as there have never been uniform censuses of the tribal peoples.) The threat varies in magnitude, stemming from thousands of small-farm colonists as well as huge development schemes such as Brazil's gargantuan Polonoreste project, which covers 410,000 square kilometers occupied by the largest Amazonic tribe, the Campas, and the smaller Amuesha.

Few tribes have been able to defend their legal rights over the lands they have occupied

TABLE 4

Estimated Number of Tribal Societies and Population in Tropical South American Nations[1]

Nation	Tribes	Estimated Population
Argentina	11	54,000
Bolivia	42	187,000
Brazil	116	186,000
Colombia	80	421,000
Ecuador	11	97,000
Guyana	5	27,000
Panama	3	93,000
Paraguay	17	51,000
Peru	56	206,000
Suriname	6	10,200
Venezuela	39	150,000
Totals	386	1,480,800

Sources: Luis M. Uriarte López, "Poblaciones nativas de la Amazonia Peruana," *Amazonia Pervana* 1, no. 1 (1976): 9–58; Enrique Mayer and Elio Masferrer "La Poblacion Indigena de America en 1978," *America Indigena*, 39, no. 2 (1979): 217–335. Luis M. Uriarte López, "Poblaciones nativas de la Amazonia Pervana," *Amazonia Pervana* 1, no. 1 (1976): 9–58.

from time immemorial. Among the South American countries, Peru has the most advanced laws governing the protection of native communities. But, even in Peru, the process of establishing group recognition and territorial ownership is bureaucratically difficult. Thus, of the sixty-seven tribal groups reported, only eleven had legal titles. Because of government failures to execute their programs and promises faithfully even in organized colonization project areas, few tribes have legal recognition.

Throughout the Amazon basin, colonists, oil companies, and lumbering and ranching interests vie for control of "unoccupied" tropical forest, affecting virtually every tribal society, whose members are rarely considered as having citizens' rights. The asocial frontier behavior that has long characterized the area still prevails, and with much greater repercussions.[15] The Brazilian government's attempts to manage the tropical frontier exemplify the problems. Serious problems surround the many government projects and private developments such as the

Amazonic highway, hydroelectric projects, colonization programs, national parks, and tribal reserves. The effectiveness of the government's National Indian Foundation (FUNAI) fluctuated greatly. Also problematic has been the government's role in regulating the gold rush and the struggle over use and ownership of traditional Indian land. A letter about this to Brazil's president from a group of Brazilian tribal leaders expresses their sense of vulnerability before an apparently uncaring state:

> We here present the Indian point of view — the testimony of him who is the only one not invited to testify concerning the emancipation intended to affect him. . . . Perhaps, Mr. President, it is not proper for our people to speak. . . . But no, Mr. President, we are certain that our people would understand that message even in different tongues. . . . Your excellency must agree that our people's blood cannot be held within its veins while we watch how the Whites are usurping the few lands that remain to us out of all that immense Brazilian territory which once was our exclusive domain. . . . What perplexes us most is that . . . we know that several articles of our present law, the Indian statute [of 1973] have not been implemented. . . . (Goias, December 1978)[16]

Some tribal groups have now organized in order to obtain arrangements that will change the structural relationship between themselves and their national governments. But such arrangements are difficult to develop and maintain, as the Mapuche-Chilean experience demonstrates. Elsewhere, native groups are struggling to find ways of gaining formal status in state affairs. Leaders among these are the San Blas Cuna of Panama and the Shuar of Ecuador, whose organizational development and ability to mount efficacious political action represent a major break with past native-state relations in Latin America. In both instances, the change involves the tribal group's ability to take control of its own political and economic organization, direct efforts toward clarifying the group's legal status, and gain cultural self-respect.

The San Blas Cunas' highly developed politi-cal organization includes local and general congresses, which deal with the Panamanian government and run Cuna affairs. Since the construction of the Panama Canal, the Cuna have successfully learned to play national and international interests off against each other for their own benefit. Many Cuna are well educated, and Cuna chiefs maintain representatives in Panama City to keep track of tribal interests. At their home on the Gulf Coast islands, they have been able to fend off unwanted developers and keep the flow of tourists under control.

A different model is that of the Shuar Federation. Once known by the derogatory term *Jivaro*, ("rustic, savage") and internationally famous for their internecine warfare and former practice of shrinking their enemies' heads, the Shuar officially adopted their present name (meaning "people") at the time the federation was founded. The federation has both political and cultural functions.[17] A series of community centers unite the people and permit the development of various services. Seventeen thousand Shuar now pay dues to the federation, which also receives government support and donations from foreign supporters. Although many problems persist, the achievements are numerous. The federation operates a radio station as well as 138 "radio schools." Shuar university students maintain a center in Quito, contract for legal assistance, lobby the government, and in general, help increase Shuar power in their home regions. They have been so successful in fact, that Ecuadoran colonists now complain that the Shuar are too "rich and powerful." The federation has also made considerable headway in tilling native lands through the Ecuadoran government's Agrarian Reform and Colonization Institute (IERAC), and it encourages various economic development projects under Shuar control. But Shuar activisim does not stop at the much-disputed international border between Peru and Ecuador. Jivaroan speakers on the Peruvian side (known as Huambisi and Aguaruna) regularly hear station HCSK broadcasts in the native language. Taken together, such actions are greatly revitalizing this traditional forest society of the Ecuadoran Andes.

■ Ethnicity, Class, and Mobility

It would be wrong to leave the impression that members of Latin American ethnic and racial groups are caught in permanently fixed social conditions. In most Latin American nations there are two interacting systems of socioeconomic order. The first is based on rigid concepts of rural and urban social components and on ascribed social roles and statuses. The second is an urban-based class system characterized by social mobility and, at least to some extent, individuals who have achieved roles and statuses.

The cultural-racial categories in which all Latin Americans place themselves stem directly from colonial practices and function today as personal attributes that imply ascribed roles statuses. Nevertheless it appears that while such classifications remain in use they carry increasingly less significance as indicators of social rank and that old usages are being directly challenged as public consciousness of some discriminatory traditions has risen. The use of "campesino" instead of "Indian" exemplifies this change.

The negative implications of being classified as "black" in Latin America, however, are subtle and often go unobserved by nonblacks. Indeed, governments have paid no heed to the condition of blacks since emancipation in the middle of the last century. The first Congress of Black Culture in the Americas (Cali, Colombia, 1977) challenged this insensitivity, noting that contrary to popular views, blacks in Latin America are the victims of active discrimination.[18] To give just one example, racism abounds in cartoon depictions, in commercial advertising featuring gross stereotypes of blacks, and in endless jokes about the *zambito* who did such and such. Large black populations, for example, in Ecuadoran, Colombian, and Venezuelan coastal regions, are increasingly responding to this growing internal and regional black consciousness.

Monumental social and demographic changes in the past three decades have created unprecedented opportunities for socioeconomic mobility. Even with the high national birth rates (Table 2) most Latin American cities have grown primarily because of phenomenal internal migration rates. Urban populations have surpassed the rural, with many important repercussions. Among these are the "urbanization" of institutional structures and a widespread acceptance of urban cultural behavior by rural populations. Thus, the growth of Latin American primate cities has raised the region to a unique and leading status in world demography and brought about important changes in socioeconomic structures.[19]

Opening paths to political participation has been and remains extremely difficult because most nations hold to policies that not only exclude native peoples from constitutional political action but never really contemplate their participation in national life as cultural groups. The mass of native American peoples such as the Quechua, Aymará, Nahúatl, and Maya have not been part of an organized polity of their own since the conquest. Instead—along with blacks—they have constituted what was, by national practice and tradition if not by definition, the "lower class." Moreover, such persons were traditionally barred from electoral participation by literacy and language laws, or by local elite practices preventing suffrage. As members of unorganized ethnic groups most traditional Indians are culturally defined as a class of lesser citizens. Under these circumstances participation in national society implies the cultural and social assimilation of Indians into a relatively homogeneous national culture. Thus it can be said that the national policies of most countries since independence have been directed at reducing cultural and ethnic differences and not supporting cultural pluralism.

Such policies actually worked in two directions. First, they stimulated the propensity to rid subjects of visible Indian identity. Spanish could be learned, Andean Indian homespuns or

Mexican *calzones blancos* (a white costume) changed for factory-made clothes, and one could insist that he or she was mestizo. Finally, migration to urban centers, and new social and world identities encouraged one to cut one's direct ties to an ethnic past. Abetting this pattern is the nature of urban primacy in Latin America, whereby wealth and access to services and power are disproportionately concentrated in a nation's largest city.

The emergence of strong urban-based social classes has reduced the previous structural importance of the "dual economy" and "caste" structures resting on Indian/mestizo/white/black social divisions. Geographic mobility has enabled rural peoples to assume "working-class" *(obrero)* status, something that peasants view as an advance in social position. Although migrants retain their racial identity, the ethnicity component of "social race" survives the passage from province to city.[20] Even those who return to their home communities do so as bearers of city values and of an internationally oriented, urban metropolitan culture.

Another level in the insatiable quest for modernization and equality is the international migration stream. Throughout the hemisphere, hundreds of thousands seek direct channels of social mobility in numerous "opportunity zones" such as the Brazilian-Paraguayan border area, where vast hydroelectric and irrigation projects on the Paraná River system have created boom conditions. This phenomenon also contributes to a fundamental restructuring of national societies as well as to new international relationships. Major movements within this massive flow of people include those of: Mexicans to the southwestern United States, Cubans to Florida, Puerto Ricans to the northeastern United States, Dominicans to New York, Jamaicans and Trinidadians to Canada and the United States, Haitians to Cuba and Florida, Colombians to Venezuela, and Peruvians to Argentina, Venezuela and the United States.

Civil wars in Central America and political conflict elsewhere are producing major dislocations of individuals and whole communities: for example, tens of thousands of Salvadorans fled to Honduras, Guatemala, Costa Rica, Mexico, and the United States; over 200,000 Guatemalans ran to Mexico and the United States; and thousands of Chileans escaped to other Latin American countries, Western Europe, and North America. This diaspora of Latin Americans of all cultures, races, and socioeconomic classes fundamentally affects both donor and recipient societies.

The processes of acculturation and assimilation that follow the dictates of international metropolitan culture reach into Quechua villages, Amazonian towns, and Caribbean island homes alike through television programs produced in, for example, Brazil, Mexico, Argentina, Spain, Japan, and the United States.

Thus, the issues of cultural pluralism and assimilation have developed dimensions beyond the control of any national policymakers. The rising levels of hostilities between social, cultural, and economic groups in Central America, the Andean countries, Brazil, and elsewhere created by demands for economic mobility, well-being, and social justice are deeply rooted in historical events. The current trends are many and are often contradictory. Knowing from past experience, however, that cultural identities may not only persist but even thrive under the harshest of circumstances, or indeed, because of them, one may confidently predict that there is little danger of sociocultural homogeneity in Latin America.

■ Notes

1. For earlier estimates see Alfred Kroeber, *Cultural and Natural Areas of Native America*, University of California Publications in American Archeology and Ethnology. vol. 38 (Berkeley: University of California Press, 1939); Angel Rosenblatt, *La Poblacíon Indígena y el Mestizaje en América*, 2 vols. (Buenos Aires: Editorial Nova, 1954). Newer accounts are found in William M. Denevan, ed., *The Native Population of the Americas in 1492*

(Madison: University of Wisconsin Press, 1976), 2–4. For works exploring the causes of decline see Noble David Cook, *The People of the Colca Valley: A Population Study,* Dellplain Latin American Studies 9 (Boulder: Westview Press, 1982); Henry F. Dobyns, *Their Number Became Thinned: Native American Population Dynamics in Eastern North America* (Knoxville: Newberry Library and University of Tennessee Press, 1983); Sherburne F. Cook and Woodrow W. Borah, *The Indian Population of Central Mexico, 1531–1610* (Berkeley: University of California Press, 1971–79); and Denevan, op. cit.

2. John Hemming, *Red Gold: The Conquest of the Brazilian Indians, 1500–1760* (Cambridge: Harvard University Press, 1978), 487–501, 139–60.

3. Charles Wagley, "The Effects of Depopulation upon the Social Organization as Illustrated by the Tapirape Indians," *Transactions of the New York Academy of Science,* ser. 2, vol. 3, no. 1; 12–16; and Shelton Davis, et al., *Voices of the Survivors: The Massacre at Finca San Francisco, Guatemala,* Occasional Paper 10 (Cambridge: Cultural Survival and Anthropology Resource Center, 1983).

4. The slave trade and its many ramifications are seen in Philip D. Curtin, *The Atlantic Slave Trade, A Census* (Madison: University of Wisconsin Press, 1969); Frederick P. Bowser, *The African Slave in Colonial Peru, 1524–1650* (Stanford: Stanford University Press, 1974); Franklin Knight, *The Caribbean: Genesis of a Fragmented Nationalism* (New York: Oxford University Press, 1978), 236; Norman Whitten, Jr., *Black Frontiersmen: A South American Case* (New York: Schenkman Publishing Co., 1974); Angelina Pollak-Eltz, *Vestigios Africanos en la Cultura del Pueblo Venezolano* (Caracas: Universidad Católica Andrés Bello, 1972); Richard Price, ed., *Maroon Societies: Rebel Slave Communities in the Americas* (Baltimore: Johns Hopkins University Press, 1979), and *First Time: The Historical Vision of an Afro-American People* (Baltimore: Johns Hopkins University Press, 1983).

5. Social and racial caste configurations are discussed by Magnus Morner, *Race Mixture in the History of Latin America* (Boston: Little, Brown, 1967); Charles C. Cumberland, *Mexico: The Struggle for Modernity* (New York: Oxford University Press, 1968), 54–56; Harry W. Hutchinson, *Village and Plantation Life in Northeastern Brazil* (Seattle: University of Washington Press, 1957).

6. Colonial era impacts are described in John Howland Rowe, "The Incas under Spanish Colonial Institutions," *Hispanic American Historical Review* 37, no. 2 (1957), 155–99; Charles Gibson, *The Aztecs Under Spanish Rule: A History of the Indians of the Valley of Mexico, 1519–1810* (Stanford: Stanford University Press, 1964); and Hemming, op. cit. Contemporary manifestations of these patterns are found in Thomas M. Davis, Jr., *Indian Integration in Peru: A Half Century of Experience, 1900–1948* (Lincoln: University of Nebraska Press, 1974); Gonzalo Aguirre Beltrán, *Regions of Refuge,* Society for Applied Anthropology Monograph 12 (Washington, D.C. 1979); and Richard N. Adams, *Crucifixion by Power: Essays on Guatemala National Social Structure, 1944–1966* (Austin: University of Texas Press, 1970).

7. Aspects of foreign immigration are reviewed by James R. Scobie, *Argentina: A City and a Nation* (New York: Oxford University Press, 1971), 33 ff.; Georg Volveiler, *Colonia "Fritz",* Ph.D. dissertation, University of Florida (Ann Arbor: University Microfilms, 1977); Watt Stewart, *Chinese Bondage in Peru: A History of the Chinese Coolie in Peru, 1849–1874* (Durham: Duke University Press, 1951), 72–76.

8. Knight, op. cit., 143.

9. Aquirre Beltrán. op. cit.; Patricia J. Lyon, ed., *Native South Americans: Ethnology of the Least Known Continent* (Boston: Little, Brown and Co., 1974).

10. The vicissitudes of Mexican Indians and theories about them are seen in Pedro Ramirez Vazquez, et al., *The National Museum of Anthropology, Mexico* (New York: Harry N. Abrams, Inc., 1968); Rodolfo Stavenhagen, "Clases, colonialismo y aculturación: Ensayo sobre un sistema de relaciones interétnicas en Mesoamérica" in M. O. Mendizabal, et al., *Ensayos sobre las Clases Sociales en México* (México, D.F: Editorial Nuestro Tiempo, 1968), 109–69; Pablo González Casanova, "Enjenación y conciencia de clases en México," in M. O. Mendizabal, et al., op. cit., 172–214.

11. Examples of Mayan Indian life are portrayed in G. Alexander Moore, *Life Cycles in Atchalan: The Diverse Careers of Certain Guatemalans* (New York: Teachers College Press, 1973); Robert C. Hinshaw, *Panajachel: A Guatemala Town in Thirty-Year Perspective* (Pittsburgh: University of Pittsburgh Press, 1975); James D. Sexton, ed., *Sons of*

Tecun Uman: A Maya Indian Tells His Life Story (Tucson: University of Arizona Press, 1981).

12. A case study of one of the many tragic situations is retold in Shelton Davis, et al., op. cit.

13. Wilfredo Kapsoli, *Los Movimientos Campesinos en el Perú, 1879–1965.* (Lima: Delva Editores, 1977); William E. Carter, *Aymará Communities and the Agrarian Reform in Bolivia,* Social Science Monograph 24 (Gainesville: University of Florida Press, 1965); Dwight Heath, et al., *Land Reform and Social Revolution in Bolivia* (New York: Frederick A. Praeger, 1969). Henry F. Dobyns and Paul L. Doughty, *Peru: A Cultural History* (New York: Oxford University Press, 1976).

14. The long-running conflicts of the Chilean Mapuche are analyzed in L. C. Faron, *Mapuche Social Structure: Institutional Reintegration in a Patrilineal Society of Central Chile,* Illinois Studies in Anthropology 10 (Urbana: University of Illinois Press, 1961); Inter-Church Committee on Human Rights in Latin America, *Mapuches: People of the Land,* Report of a Fact-Finding Mission to Chile, November 1979, Toronto, 1980, Survival International, *SUISA News,* 2, no. 2.

15. Complex and disruptive events constantly occur. Typical conditions are described by Anthony Stocks, "Notas Sobre los antóctonos tupi del Perú," *Amazonia Peruana* 1, no. 1 (1976), 59–73; Luis M. Uriarte López, "Poblaciones Nativas de la Amazonia Peruana," *Amazonia Peruana* 1, no. 1 (1976), 9–58; Anonymous, *Cultural Survival Newsletter* 5, no. 1 (1981); Hector Martínez, "El saqueo y la destrucción de los ecosistemas selváticos," *Amazonia Peruana* 1, no. 2 (1977), 7–28; Oriol Pi-Sunyer, "The Cultural Costs of Tourism," *Cultural Survival Quarterly* 6, no. 3 (1982), 7–10; Richard C. Smith, "Indian Girls Make the Best Maids," *Cultural Survival Quarterly* 7, no. 4 (1983), 38–39; William T. Vickers, "Ideation as Adaption: Traditional Belief and Modern Intervention in Siona-Secoya Religion," in *Cultural Transformations and Ethnicity in Modern Ecuador,* ed. Norman Whitten (Urbana: University of Illinois Press, 1981), 705–30.

16. David Maybury-Lewis, et. al., *Special Report: Brazil* no. 1 (Cambridge, Mass. Cultural Survival, 1979).

17. G. Alexander Moore, "From Council to Legislature: Democracy, Parliamentarianism, and the San Blas Cuna," *American Anthropologist* 86, no. 1 (1984), 28–42; James Howe, "Kindling Self-Determination Among the Kuna," *Cultural Survival Quarterly,* 6, no. 3 (1982), 15–18; Ernesto Salazar. "The Federación Shuar and the Colonization Frontier" in Whitten, op. cit., 589–613; Michael Harner, *The Jivaro: People of the Sacred Waterfalls* (Garden City: Natural History, 1972).

18. Grace Shubert, "To Be Black Is Offensive: Race Attitudes in San Lorenzo" in Whitten, op. cit., 580–82.

19. Paul L. Doughty. "A Latin American Speciality in the World Context: Urban Primacy and Cultural Colonialism in Peru," *Urban Anthropology* 8, nos. 3–4 (1979), 321–32; Anibal Quijano, "The Urbanization of Latin American Society" in *Urbanization in Latin America,* ed. J. Hardoy (Garden City: Anchor Books, 1975), 109–56; and Bryan R. Roberts, "The Interrelationships of City and Provinces in Peru and Guatemala" in *Latin American Urban Research,* ed. W. A. Cornelius and F. M. Trueblood, vol. 4 (Beverly Hills: Sage Publications, 1974), 207–37.

20. Charles Wagley, *The Latin American Tradition: Essays on the Unity and Diversity of Latin American Culture* (New York: Columbia University Press, 1968), 155–74.

■ Suggested Readings

Adams, Richard N. *Crucifixion by Power: Essays on Guatemalan National Social Structure, 1944–1966.* Austin: University of Texas Press, 1959.

Cumberland, Charles C. *Mexico: The Struggle for Modernity.* New York: Oxford University Press, 1968.

Cultural Survival Quarterly. Cambridge, Mass.

Davis, Thomas M., Jr. *Indian Integration in Peru: A Half Century of Experience, 1900–1948.* Lincoln: University of Nebraska Press, 1974.

Dobyns, Henry F., and Paul L. Doughty. *Peru: A Cultural History.* New York: Oxford University Press, 1976.

Gibson, Charles, *The Aztecs Under Spanish Rule: A History of the Indians of the Valley of Mexico, 1519–1810.* Stanford: Stanford University Press, 1964.

Heath, Dwight, et al. *Land Reform and Social Revolution in Bolivia.* New York: Frederick A. Praeger, 1969.

Hemming, John. *Red Gold: The Conquest of the Brazilian Indians, 1500–1760.* Cambridge, Mass.: Harvard University Press, 1978.

Knight, Franklin. *The Caribbean: Genesis of a Fragmented Nationalism.* New York: Oxford University Press, 1978.

Mellafe, Rolando. *Negro Slavery in Latin America.* Berkeley: University of California Press, 1975.

Lyon, Patricia J., ed. *Native South Americans: Ethnology of the Least Known Continent.* Boston: Little, Brown, 1974.

Price, Richard. *First Time: The Historical Vision of an Afro-American People.* Baltimore: Johns Hopkins University Press, 1983.

Sexton, James D. *Sons of Tecun Uman: A Maya Indian Tells His Life Story.* Tucson: University of Arizona Press, 1981.

Wagley, Charles. *The Latin American Tradition: Essays on The Unity and Diversity of Latin American Cultures.* New York: Columbia University Press, 1969.

Whitten, Norman, Jr., ed. *Cultural Transformations and Ethnicity in Modern Ecuador.* Urbana: University of Illinois Press, 1981.

Wolf, Eric. *Europe and the People Without History.* Berkeley: University of California Press, 1982.

PART

II

FOUNDATIONS OF DEVELOPMENT

4 | *Discovery and Conquest*

JOHN FREDERICK SCHWALLER

The Spanish and Portuguese adventures in discovery and conquest in the late fifteenth and early sixteenth centuries did not emerge dramatically, but rather came as the result of long periods of development. The voyages of exploration and the establishment of colonial empires were logical outgrowths of Iberian history. While the romantic vision of this period favors a view of intrepid, independent, and adventuresome men taking on the whole world, these men enjoyed a depth of cultural and technological support almost unparalleled until recent times. The establishment of Spanish hegemony over much of the Americas and that of the Portuguese in Brazil came through a gradual advance, each step building on past experiences.

■ The Reconquest

At the end of the sixteenth century there were two major factors that would influence Spanish and Portuguese expansion beyond the limits of the European continent. One of these was the reconquest, the *reconquista*. In 711 Muslims invaded the Iberian peninsula and by 718 had conquered as far as the Pyrenees. Only the mountain fastness of the Cantabrian coast re-

mained under Christian control. For nearly eight hundred years the Christians waged occasional war and diplomacy to reconquer this lost territory. In the process, the Christians established institutions and philosophies that would aid them in the integration of the newly won lands and would later prove very important in the Spanish and Portuguese conquest and settlement of the New World.

One of the major factors in the reconquest was the system of incentives offered by the Christian monarchs to recruit followers. At this time the Iberian peninsula was divided into several small kingdoms. Each, on its own, was unable to successfully challenge the Muslims. The necessary strength was gained through alliances and through recruitment. To recruit followers, kings offered various incentives, the most common being the right to govern the newly conquered land. This system was successful for the monarchs in that they gained large numbers of supporters but unsuccessful in that they gave away a great degree of control over the new lands. Thus weakened, the monarchs ultimately came to be mainly arbitrators between factions.

Some territories, after their reconquest, threw off the control of the Christian kings. Portugal, originally granted to a French noble for his participation in the reconquista, became an independent kingdom in the mid-twelfth century. With further successes against the Muslims, the king of Portugal was able to conquer the whole west coast of the peninsula by the middle of the thirteenth century. Unable to expand to the east, or risk war with the Spanish Christians, the Portuguese began to look to Africa and beyond.

By about 1270 the Christian forces of what is now Spain had also driven back the Muslims, confining them to a small mountain kingdom north and east of Cadiz, with its capital at Granada. By this time the rather distinctive institutions of Spanish political culture had become well established. The monarchs were relatively weak and depended on the goodwill of their nobility, the church, and the cities. When the king gave newly-conquered lands to a noble, the legal fiction was that the monarch granted them in trust *encomienda*. The holders of these grants then had jurisdiction over the land and were responsible for settling and integrating it into the Christian sphere.

■ **Portuguese Expansion**

While the Spanish kings were involved in the latter phases of the reconquest, the Portuguese were exploiting their location and becoming a powerful seafaring nation. Venturing into the Atlantic, Portuguese fishermen for centuries had been sailing uncharted waters. In the fifteenth century, the Portuguese royal family became interested in capitalizing on this experience in a very sophisticated attack on the Muslims. Clearly, by this time direct assault on neighboring Muslim territories served only as harassment. In order to break Muslim power, it was necessary to destroy its hold on the vital Middle Eastern trade routes As Europe emerged from the Middle Ages, prosperity brought a growing demand for luxury goods, the provision of which the Muslims controlled. Even the bulk of Europe's gold came from Muslim-controlled lands across the Sahara. The Portuguese

reasoned that if they could outflank the Muslims, it might be possible to capture the zones of production of gold and luxury goods, and thus eliminate the Muslim middlemen; it might also be possible to attack the Muslims from behind and eliminate them entirely.

Notions of geography were still rudimentary. Although the world was known to be spherical, the organization of the continents and oceans was unclear. Some thought all bodies of water to be linked by channels, seen and unseen. Others believed the land surrounded two oceans, while a contrary opinion held that water surrounded the land. For the Portuguese the basic question became the true shape of the African continent. As gold came from across the Sahara, if they could sail to the other side of the Sahara, they might be closer to the site of gold production. From there they might be able to sail on and either link up with eastern Christians who they believed inhabited the area and take the Muslims from the rear, or advance pincer-fashion: while the eastern Christians attacked from the Mediterranean, the Portuguese could move against the foe from their base to the northwest.

To achieve these goals, more technology was needed, particularly in two areas. First, Portuguese ships were unsuitable for this kind of long-distance sailing, in variable winds, carrying either large amounts of provisions or trade goods. Second, cartographers still had not produced the necessary maps. Thus, the prince of Portugal, Dom Enrique (d. 1460), known to English speakers as Prince Henry the Navigator, established a school and base of operations at the southwesternmost point in Europe, Cape Saint Vincent. Here he brought together the leading pilots, cartographers, and shipwrights to develop the technologies needed for this great adventure. The system that emerged was used throughout the fifteenth and early sixteenth centuries by the Portuguese. They would sail farther and farther down the African coast. When each voyage reached the limits to which it could sail, a marker would be placed on the shore, for future voyages. Within Dom Enrique's life the Portuguese were able to reach only Cape Verde, near modern Sierra Leone, but by 1488 Bartolomeu Dias would round the tip of Africa, preparing the way for Vasco da Gama's successful voyage to India in 1499.

■ The Consolidation of Spain

When the Portuguese were thus busy amassing information about cartography, shipbuilding, and long sea voyages, the Spanish kings entered into a period of peace with the Muslims, during which a relatively stable relationship emerged. A frontier developed in Andalucia, from Cadiz north in a semicircle around Granada to reach the Mediterranean. The Christian kings had embarked on a period of consolidation, reducing the number of petty Christian kingdoms through marriage and alliance until by the fifteenth century only three monarchs ruled all of the minor territories. The final unification of the Spanish region became possible in the mid-fifteenth century with the betrothal of the daughter of John II of Castile to the son of John II of Aragon. This was the famous marriage of Ferdinand and Isabella.

Ferdinand and Isabella faced several threats to their power. The Castilian nobility was not ready to accept Isabella, and a civil war (1475–1479) had to be fought between her supporters and those of her half-brother's bastard daughter, Juana la Beltraneja. Ferdinand and Isabella needed a cause that would unify the kingdoms and generate strong popular support to help undermine this formidable internal opposition. The Muslim kingdom of Granada provided just such an opportunity. By engaging in one final crusade of reconquest, the kings hoped to generate unity in the face of a "foreign" threat. Thus in 1482 the campaign on Granada began. Much was won through diplomacy, but finally the Christian forces laid siege to the city in 1490, centering their operations in a newly founded town on the plains outside Granada, Santa Fe. For this campaign Ferdinand and Isabella ap-

pealed to religion, "nationality," and justice to help smooth over divisions in the Christian ranks. The popular outpouring was impressive, and the campaign ultimately succeeded on several counts. It unified the factions and gave the monarchs a groundswell of support that allowed them to begin to limit their rivals' power. For this crusade they won the title "The Catholic Monarchs."

■ Spain Faces the New World

The greatest coincidence occurred in the winter of 1491, when Ferdinand and Isabella were camped at Santa Fe. A Genoese adventurer approached them with a proposal to reach the source of the luxury goods entering Europe, a chance to secure the Orient trade for Spain. The Genoese was Christopher Columbus (or Cristóbal Colón, as he is known in Spanish). He had worked and studied at the Portuguese school for years, served in the Portuguese voyages, and concluded that traditional theories about the size of the world were incorrect. The novelty of his hypothesis was not that the world was round, since most educated people, or people who knew from experience, realized the spherical nature of the globe, but rather that the world was far smaller than generally thought. Columbus, basing his estimate on a host of classical, biblical, and empirical sources, concluded that the circumference of the globe was some 6,000 miles less than commonly believed. It followed that 2,500 to 3,500 miles were all he needed to sail west at his chosen latitude to reach the Orient. That distance was within the realm of current technologies, whereas the ten-thousand-mile voyage dictated by conventional assumptions was not.

Columbus finally convinced Isabella of his case, after failing at the Portuguese court and with other possible patrons. Isabella then offered to serve as a guarantor of the voyage, which meant she did not put up any money but did serve as a backer by granting guarantees and drawing up a contract with Columbus.

Under the contract Columbus was to discover the route to the Indies and begin Spanish hegemony there. In return for this he was to enjoy the title Admiral of the Ocean Sea and serve as viceroy of the newly conquered lands, with other rights and perquisites to fall to himself and his heirs. With this contract Columbus had a relatively easy time raising the funds necessary to carry out his adventure.

■ Columbus's First Voyage

Columbus assembled his small fleet on the south coast of Spain, the Andalucian coast, with ships and crew coming from the small towns on the Tinto River near Huelva, especially Palos de la Frontera. He spent time at the monastery of La Rábida, preparing himself spiritually for the voyage. Columbus refitted his three ships, discarding the Portuguese lateen rigging, good for coasting and sailing into the wind, for the more traditional square rigging, good for the open sea with strong following winds. The three ships set off initially for the Canary Islands. These islands had been pacified several decades earlier by the Spanish and served now as a way station for the African coastal trade. Water and provisions stored, Columbus then set out across the ocean sea.

During the voyage Columbus was keenly aware of his crew's expectations. Many must have realized the potential length of the voyage should Columbus's estimate be wrong. Many modern historians believe that in order to allay those fears, Columbus kept two logs to record the day's sail. In the public log he systematically underestimated the distance sailed. In his own private log he kept a fairly accurate account. Columbus obviously believed that he would hit land after about three thousand miles' sailing. He hoped to arrive before the public log indicated the stipulated distance. Had that mark been passed and no land sighted, he could have faced problems among the crew. The surviving, probably private, log for the voyage has an overestimate of about 9 percent.

As it turned out, Columbus did strike land just about where he predicted it would appear. The land first sighted, where landfall was made on 12 October 1492, was Watlings Island, or as Columbus named it, San Salvador. He began his discoveries in earnest, and in the next two months sailed along the north coast of Cuba and on to the island he named Hispaniola. There on the north coast, on Christmas Eve, the largest of the three ships, the *Santa María*, ran aground and broke up on the rocks. The crew clambered ashore. At this point Columbus had no alternative but to establish a settlement, since the other two ships were too small to carry the entire crew home.

On the return voyage, the *Niña* and the *Pinta* were separated in the mid-Atlantic. Columbus first stopped in the Azores, where the local Portuguese residents nearly threw him in jail, along with his crew, for being interlopers. He then sailed on, hoping to round Cape Saint Vincent for the final leg home. Contrary winds and torn riggings made it necessary to call at Lisbon. There he told of his adventure to an incredulous king of Portugal, who finally sent him on his way. At that point Columbus sailed home as quickly as he could. On 15 March 1493, he and the *Niña* returned to Palos, and later in the day the *Pinta*, under Martín Alonso Pinzón, arrived.

■ Further Voyages of Columbus

The marginal success of the first voyage nevertheless resulted in enthusiastic support for Columbus. Even though he had not found the gold, jewels, and rare goods he hoped for in the Indies, he had found land, more or less where he had predicted. He was now able to mount a much larger expedition, one goal of which was to rescue and relieve the sailors left from the first voyage. Settlers were being taken out to establish a truly permanent community, and Columbus wished to discover the secrets of the Indies. The fleet consisted of about thirteen large ships and a handful of small coasting vessels, a total of about seventeen ships and twelve hundred men, but no women.

Columbus would make a total of four voyages to the Indies. The name *Indies* stuck, since Columbus went to his grave believing that in truth he had reached the Orient. By the end of the second voyage, and assuredly by the third, most experienced pilots and sailors realized that Columbus had found not the Indies, but rather a New World. Nevertheless, it was important that Columbus cling to his illusion. All of his contracts with the monarch were predicated on the understanding that he discover a shorter route to the Orient. No allowance was made for finding an unknown land. Thus to maintain his monopoly and jurisdiction Columbus had to continue to assert that he had landed in the Indies.

By the turn of the century, forces in the Spanish court were seeking the suspension of the Columbian monopoly on voyages to the west. These parties finally convinced the Catholic monarchs, Ferdinand and Isabella, that Columbus had found a New World and therefore his contract was null and void. With this, the epoch of the Columbian voyages ended.

■ Continuing Voyages of Discovery

Just as the reconquest had provided a background for the first impulse to venture beyond the limits of the European world, so the later voyages of discovery built upon the experience of the first Columbian voyages. The period of exploration and discovery in the New World can be divided into four clear phases. The first was the era of the Columbian monopoly, which lasted until 1499. The second phase has been called the Andalusian voyages. These expeditions lasted until about 1508. In that year a rather notable change occurred. Voyages were no longer necessarily mounted in Spain, but locally in the New World. This can be called the period of the Antillean voyages. It lasted until 1519 when Cortés landed in Mexico and began the conquest of the Aztecs. Thus, the fourth and final era was that of conquest.

The eleven Andalusian voyages shared several similar traits. All were organized and launched from Andalusia, as had been Colum-

bus's first three voyages, and all were conducted with express royal licenses and contracts. Their principal zone of discovery was the coast from Panama south along South America to part of modern Brazil. Among these expeditions were Amerigo Vespucci's voyages to South America, and the early expeditions of conquest and settlement to what is now Panama. These latter are important since the first major European settlement on the continent occurred in Panama. The Andalusian voyages provided European explorers and navigators with crucial information about the contours of the landmass of South America, the islands and currents of the Caribbean, and the first contacts with North America from voyages, such as Columbus's fourth, along the coast of Central America.

While these voyages sought to increase knowledge about South America and the Caribbean, the Spaniards had been settling and consolidating their hold on the island of Hispaniola. The structure of government was imported from Spain, while other institutions were used to allocate limited resources among the settlers. Nevertheless, the available resources were quickly depleted by the Spanish settlers. The single most important resource was the Indians, who provided the labor to extract the gold and grow the crops upon which the Spanish depended. Foodstuffs ranked as the single most important factor in the early history of the Americas. The Spanish were loath to eat native American foods. Thus they relied heavily on the importation of European foodstuffs, although transportation costs made these very expensive. In times of need, however, the Spaniards did eat Indian food, and the Indians were required to provide them with it.

One unforeseen event changed forever the course of conquest and colonization in the Americas. The Indians were highly susceptible to European diseases, especially smallpox. The Americas had been largely cut off from the Eurasian landmass for several thousand years, and many Old World diseases were practically unknown in the New World. Each wave of pestilence would kill from one-third to one-half of the native population. Thus by 1508 the island of Hispaniola was facing severe depopulation. Without the Indians the colony stood a chance of starving to death. This situation motivated the third phase of discovery, the Antillean voyages.

While several of these expeditions of 1508 to 1519 still explored the Caribbean region and northern South America, more and more attention was directed northward. Colonists began to eye the neighboring islands either as new frontiers to conquer, or as ready sources of supply of food and Indians.

There were three types of voyages during this phase. Two major expeditions were launched to collect more geographical information. These were voyages of circumnavigation of the islands of Hispaniola and Cuba, for mapping purposes. The second type of voyage was less for this purpose than to acquire slaves. The principal areas of interest were the Lucayo, or Bahama, Islands, and the Guanajo, or Bay, Islands, the latter found off the coast of Honduras. A major result, nevertheless, was the accumulation of important information about the currents and geographical features of the northern Caribbean and Gulf of Mexico. The third type of voyage was the true expedition of discovery and conquest. As resources began to fail on Hispaniola, Juan Ponce de León moved out to settle Puerto Rico. Growing Spanish immigration to Hispaniola further aggravated its difficulties, and slightly later Diego Velázquez undertook the conquest and settlement of Cuba. Cuba had been settled for only a handful of years before pressure grew to look for new areas. This in turn paved the way for the discovery and conquest of Mexico.

The period of the Antillean voyages is of prime importance. The later expeditions into the heartland of the high civilizations of Middle and South America probably would have been impossible without the earlier conquest and settlement. Thus by the time Cortés embarked on his voyage to Mexico the Spanish had already gone through two steps of settlement. The first was the settlement and development of Hispaniola, followed shortly by the pacification and settlement of Panama. From those two points, further expeditions set out to augment the known settled territory. From Hispaniola the surrounding islands were settled. From Panama expeditions struck northward toward Nicaragua. Once these secondary areas were stabilized, then the basis was laid for the later expeditions. Neither Cortés nor Pizarro was totally ignorant of what they sought; both drew heavily on accounts of earlier expeditions.

Following the pattern of exploitation, diminishing resources, and then a new search for resources, in 1517 expeditions began to move out from Cuba, initially to the Bay Islands of Honduras, looking for slaves. One of these, led by Francisco Hernández de Córdoba, caught sight of the Yucatán Peninsula. To capitalize on this discovery, Hernández de Córdoba sought a license from the governor of Cuba to authorize a new expedition. But Hernández de Córdoba did not tell Velázquez the true nature of the voyage. Rather, he merely asked for renewed permission to raid for slaves in the Bay Islands. Nevertheless, Hernández de Córdoba and his pilot, Antón de Alaminos, returned to Yucatán, where they made contact with the Indians. They sailed up the Gulf Coast of Mexico before turning back. Severely wounded in a later encounter with Indians, Hernández de Córdoba reported his discoveries to Velázquez, who immediately organized another expedition to exploit the gains of the first.

The second voyage, led by a close follower of Velázquez, Juan de Grijalva, was clearly prepared for conquest and perhaps settlement. Alaminos served as head pilot. But again, rather than make permanent landfall, Grijalva sailed the Gulf Coast of Mexico and returned to Cuba. The crew was angered by being deprived of what it thought would be a sure opportunity for wealth. Velázquez then organized a third expedition, under Hernán Cortés. Cortés took the commission, but privately indicated that he was not willing to fulfill the specifics imposed by Velázquez. The governor tried to stop Cortés from setting sail, but the latter got away, leading a ten-ship flotilla manned by over five hundred men.

■ Cortés and the Conquest of Mexico

The conquest of Mexico required nearly two and a half years. It was achieved not in a single dramatic thrust, but rather in several distinct phases. After Cortés reconnoitered the coast, engaged several Indian groups in battle, and won some captives, he decided on a landfall near modern-day Veracruz. Since the site was chosen on Easter 1519, Cortés named his camp La Villa Rica de la Vera Cruz (the rich town of the true cross). By this point in his adventure, he realized that to maximize his gains, he should throw off Velázquez's supervision and strike out on his own. Lamentably, the royal contract for the expedition was in Velázquez's name. Thus, if he ignored his superior, Cortés would engage in an illegal expedition and possibly court a charge of treason.

In a stroke of genius, Cortés decided on a method of declaring his campaign independent of Velázquez. Harking back to the experience of the reconquest, Cortés and his followers set about founding a town, of which they were the sole inhabitants. A town council was elected, Cortés was chosen governor, and the streets and lots of the place laid out. All this done, representatives were chosen to request a charter from the king, thus incorporating the adventure as a legal entity with clearly recognized rights. In this fashion, operating as a Spanish town, the expedition could claim authority throughout the land until its jurisdiction met that of another Spanish town.

Cortés, now endowed with new authority, sent representatives to the king to seek official approval. To sweeten the deal, he also sent along the king's share of all of the booty that had been collected up to that point. Under contractual arrangements with the conquerors and explorers, and in keeping with Hispanic tradition, the king received one-fifth of all booty,

treasure, and salvage. This done, Cortés could set out to explore and conquer without fear of being restricted by Velázquez.

After securing his position in Veracruz, Cortés and his band began to advance inland. He had met with emissaries of the Aztec emperor, who had urged him not to advance and not to make the arduous journey up into the highlands. Their presents to him and their urging only piqued Cortés's curiosity and stimulated his desire to find the Aztec leader.

The first major confrontation of this campaign came when the expedition entered the lands of Tlaxcala. Tlaxcala was an independent polity within the Aztec Empire. Governed by a council of four nobles, the territory had maintained its independence through stiff resistance to Aztec expansion and because it served a practical purpose for the Aztec alliance. One of the major purposes of Aztec warfare by this time was the acquisition of captives for use in sacrifice. By allowing Tlaxcala to remain unconquered, the Aztecs always had a ready opponent against whom they could make war and capture warriors for sacrifice. This feature of Aztec warfare was shared by many of the groups of the Mexican highlands, including the Tlaxcalans. Thus when Cortés engaged them in battles, at least from a strategic point of view, the Indians had a disadvantage, since they sought to take captives, not kill the enemy.

After a fierce battle the Spanish defeated the Tlaxcalans and entered into a peace parley. In the ensuing encounters, the Tlaxcalans decided that they, perhaps, had more in common with the strangers than they had thought. They could, after all, make common cause with the Spaniards against the mutual foe, the Aztecs. In allying with the Spaniards, the Tlaxcalan nobles also accepted Christianity. Their baptism became an important moment in the spiritual conquest of Mexico, since it signified the first conversion of important Mexican rulers.

From Tlaxcala Cortés and his followers, their ranks now swelled with Tlaxcalan warriors, set out for the holy city of Cholula, en route to the

Aztec capital of Tenochtitlan. In Cholula Cortés met with the local nobility, who turned out to greet him warmly and peacefully. Again ambassadors of the Aztec emperor urged the Spanish to go no farther, but Cortés was now adamant in his desire to seek out the emperor. During the night, while the Spanish rested, the Cholulans prepared an ambush. Notice of this treachery reached Cortés's interpreter, Doña Marina, who warned him. Thus when the Indians attacked, the Spanish were already on the offensive. The battle was bloody, but the Spanish escaped.

The role of Cortés's interpreter was crucial to the overall success of the campaign. Doña Marina, or La Malinche, had earlier, before the landfall at Veracruz, been given to Cortés as a prize of war. According to legend, she was the daughter of an Aztec noble, who had been sold into slavery among the Maya-speaking people of the Gulf Coast. As a result she was fluent in both the Aztec language, Nahúatl, and Maya. Near the beginning of his exploits in Mexico, Cortés had rescued a survivor of an earlier expedition, Gerónimo de Aguilar. Aguilar had lived among the Maya, taken a Mayan wife, and learned the Maya language. Thus, with these two Cortés could communicate with most groups in central Mexico. In speaking with the Aztecs, Cortés had Aguilar translate from Spanish to Maya, and Doña Marina translated from Maya to Nahúatl. As time went on, Doña became Cortés's concubine and thus learned Spanish herself, eliminating the need for Aguilar.

After the battle at Cholula, Cortés crossed through the mountains that ring the Valley of Mexico, through the pass that today bears his name. It is spectacular, winding between the snow-capped peaks of Iztaccihuatl, the White Woman, and the volcano Popocatepetl, Smoking Mountain. The vision that greeted the Spaniards was literally like something in a dream. Bernal Díaz del Castillo, a member of the expedition and chronicler of the conquest, reported that the sight was like something out of fiction, it was so beautiful and exotic. Tenochtitlan, the Aztec capital, lay on two islands in the middle of lake Texcoco. The valley, called Cem Anahuac (the center of everything) by the Aztecs, was filled with smaller villages, and at that time must have supported one of the densest populations on the globe. The multicolored city shone like a jewel in the blue-green lake. The valley was historically known for its crystalline air, being called "the most transparent region of the air."

The party advanced to the capital, making camp that night in the valley. The next day, they prepared to enter the city. Just as they had begun to pass over the broad causeway that linked the city to the southern shore, they were met by the imperial party, which had come out to greet them. Motecuhzoma Ilhuicamina, known to us as Montezuma, stepped down from his litter onto a pavement of fresh flowers, carpets, and feathers, and warmly greeted Cortés. He escorted the Spanish into the heart of the city and housed them in one of the several palaces near the religious precinct.

This warm and open reception caused much confusion, both among the early Spaniards and later scholars. The most popular explanation is that the Aztecs, Montezuma in particular, believed the Spanish to be either gods or the gods' emissaries. Cortés was supposedly linked with Quetzalcoatl (the Plumed Serpent), an Aztec culture hero who had sworn to return to Mexico one day and drive out the usurpers of his power. Whatever the cause, the Spanish took advantage of their luck and slowly gained control over Montezuma, until they finally placed him under house arrest. The situation is difficult to imagine: a small band of Spaniards taking control of the ruler of an empire of some 25 million subjects, and the foreigners met little or no resistance.

Cortés's days of prosperity in Tenochtitlan, the modern Mexico City, did not last very long. While he was residing there news came up from the coast that an army of Spaniards under Panfilo de Narváez had been sent out by Velázquez to capture Cortés and take him back to Cuba in chains. Cortés took half of his army out of Tenochtitlan to go meet Narváez in battle. He left the remainder under the control of Pedro de Alvarado, known to the Indians as Tonatiuh (the sun), since he was well over six feet tall, with reddish-blond hair. Cortés engaged Narváez and defeated him. The Spaniards who came out with Narváez were given the option of returning to Cuba themselves or joining Cortés. The vast majority joined. His ranks filled, Cortés returned to the capital.

During Cortés's absence the Aztec nobility had requested permission from Alvarado to celebrate one of their religious feasts by holding a ceremony of dancing in one of the palaces. Alvarado consented, and on the appointed day the flower of the Aztec nobility and warrior class assembled to participate in the religious dance. At the same time, Alvarado posted armed guards on the rooftops surrounding the patio where the celebration was to occur, fearful that the assembly of nobles might be a pretext for attacking the Spanish. For reasons that are still not clear, Alvarado gave orders to fire on the Aztecs. In the ensuing massacre scores of nobles died. The event caused a fury of hatred to run through the Aztec capital. When Cortés returned he attempted to pacify the city, but to no avail.

The Spanish presented Montezuma to the populace, hoping that he could calm their rage. During his address to the multitude the emperor was struck by a stone hurled from the mob. A few days later Montezuma died. With this the Spaniards' protection evaporated. The city became an armed camp. Rather than being lords of the place, the Spanish found themselves imprisoned.

On the night of 30 June, they attempted to escape the city. As they approached the causeway leading to the western shore of the lake, the cry went up. All of the causeways to the shore had breaks in them, to allow canoe traffic to pass unimpeded on the lake. These openings were covered by wooden bridges to allow foot traffic on the causeway. All of the bridges had been removed, thus isolating the city but also

keeping the Spanish captive. In their flight the Spanish had to cross numerous such gaps. Many drowned, unable to swim or weighted down by gold and treasure they sought to carry off. Many more died at the hands of the Aztecs that night, while others met their death in ritual sacrifice atop an Aztec temple. Finally Cortés and the main body of Spaniards reached the shore, regrouped, struggled around the lake, and took refuge atop a small peak. With this the *Noche Triste* (Sad Night) ended. The Aztecs did not pursue their advantage and, other than harassing the stragglers, did not interfere with the retreat.

The Spanish slowly marched back to Tlaxcala, where they cured their wounds and planned. The ultimate order of battle was decided upon here by Cortés. Rather than launch an immediate assault on the city, he sent out expeditions to conquer or seek alliances with all the communities that surrounded the Valley of Mexico. With that territory secure, he could then reenter the valley and do battle with each valley town. The plan of attack went well. When Cortés had gained control of the surrounding valleys, and much of the Valley of Mexico, he made camp in Texcoco, the capital of the eastern part of the valley. From there he oversaw the invasion of Tenochtitlan. By cutting off all the causeways, Cortés could lay siege to the city.

Nevertheless, the causeways accounted for only a fraction of the commerce entering the city. The bulk came by boat, and Cortés could not totally cut off boat traffic on the lake without a navy himself. So he ordered the construction of twelve so-called brigantines, in reality more like floating gun platforms. He had metal fittings and gear brought up from the ships that had been left in Veracruz, ordering those ships burned, thus cutting off possible retreat should his own troops mutiny. Timber was cut in the surrounding mountains, and the ships were built in Texcoco. Twelve captains were commissioned, and the little fleet set out to accomplish a two-fold purpose: to interdict the canoe traffic to the city, thus drawing the siege even tighter, and to serve as mobile attack fleet to engage the Aztecs on the water and on land.

The campaign began. The brigantines' guns would blast away at the houses and buildings of the city, clearing out areas that the Spanish troops could then secure. The Spanish worked from the south end of the islands to the north, with the Aztec defenders finally taking refuge atop the main pyramid of Tlatelolco, the market district of the city. Finally, on 13 August 1521 the city fell to the Spanish, and the last emperor, Cuauhtemoc, was captured. To commemorate the victory the patron of the city became Saint Hippolyte, on whose feast day the city had fallen.

Many have questioned how such a small band of Spaniards defeated the Aztec Empire. The Spanish army probably never amounted to much more than a thousand men. They were, however, aided by tens of thousands of Indian allies, principally Tlaxcalans. Likewise, the differences in styles of warfare gave the Spanish an advantage, since they fought to kill. But this advantage was brief, for ultimately the Indians countered with the same. Certainly the Spanish war technology was superior. They had horses, war dogs, cannon, harquebuses, crossbows, and steel swords, all of which were unknown to the Indians. In fact initially the Indians had thought the horse and rider to be one being. But again, familiarity with these weapons could have given the Indians the opportunity to counter them better. Likewise, a mass attack of several thousand Indians could have rendered even these technological advantages useless.

In studying the Spaniards' advantages over the Aztecs, two things stand out. First, the Indians seem to have lacked the will to press on to victory, as in the Noche Triste. They could have annihilated the Spaniards but chose not to. Basically the Aztecs probably underestimated the Spaniards' designs. The Aztecs wished to rid themselves of the problem, not necessarily massacre the foe. Second, the Spanish had pestilence on their side. Between the Noche Triste and the final assault on the city, smallpox had entered the Valley of Mexico. After Montezuma's death, Cuitlahuac had come to the throne. He ruled for only eighty days before succumbing to smallpox. Thus while the Spanish were laying siege to the city, its inhabitants were dying by the thousands from the disease. This weakened the already debilitated city, allowing for a quicker conquest. Finally, the Spanish were able to seize power following the fall of Tenochtitlan rather easily because they merely replaced the Aztecs in ruling the empire. The subject peoples now paid tribute to the Spanish, rather than to the Aztecs. They were now forced to venerate the Spanish god rather than the Aztec pantheon. At the basic level, immediately following the conquest, very little had changed.

■ **The Empire Expands**

Following the fall of Tenochtitlan, the Spanish proceeded to launch expeditions of discovery and conquest from this new base. Cortés led an army down into what is now Honduras. Pedro de Alvarado became the captain of the conquest of Guatemala, and established himself as leader there. In the west, a somewhat later expedition was organized by Nuño de Gúzman, who conquered the kingdom of Michoacán and established the Spanish Kingdom of New Galicia, stretching into the modern southwestern United States. Later columns opened up even more territory in the north, such as Francisco Vázquez de Coronado's expedition to what is now Kansas, and the various explorers and conquerors of the Gulf Coast and Florida, including Narváez, Hernán de Soto, Tristán de Luna y Arrellano, and others.

Significantly, most of Cortés's followers had had some prior experience in the New World. These were not men fresh from Spain seeking their fortune in the new land, but rather, men who had come out and found themselves just a little too late for earlier conquests. Many had first settled on Hispaniola, gone to Panama, then on to Cuba, each time just missing the main exploits of conquest. Not having fought in these adventures, these men did not participate in the ensuing division of the spoils. Indeed, this probably served as an added incentive to persist till the end in Mexico.

■ The Conquest of Peru

The case of the conquest of Peru is somewhat different. The leader, Francisco Pizarro, had had extensive experience with the New World before his conquest of Peru. In fact, it was while serving in Panama that he acquired the information that led him to believe that there was an Indian civilization ready for conquest in the Andean highlands. Under the authority of the governor of Panama, Pedrarias Dávila, Pizarro undertook a voyage of exploration down the west coast of South America. In 1526, his pilot had sailed far enough down the coast to gain certain evidence of the Indian civilization. A year later, dissension in Pizarro's ranks caused word to get back to the new governor of Panama, who declared that any men under Pizarro who wished to return could do so without fear of retribution. This brought about the famous decision on Gallo Island, where thirteen men remained loyal to Pizarro. During this whole time, more and more information was being collected about the coast, the coastal Indian communities, and indications of civilization further inland. By 1528 Pizarro felt that he had sufficient information to justify organizing a full expedition. Well aware of the troubles Cortés had had serving as an agent of Velázquez, Pizarro decided to return to Spain to seek direct royal approval for his plan, and to recruit additional men, especially men from his home town of Trujillo, whom he could trust completely.

By 1531 Pizarro returned with his men and his royal license, and the actual conquest of Peru was under way. As in the previous voyages of exploration, Pizarro began his expedition by sailing down the west coast, making stops and collecting information. As they painfully made their way down the coast, additional troops joined up with the main body of the army. Allies and partners of Pizarro had been sent to various parts of the New World, such as Nicaragua, to seek additional men. Finally, in 1532, the main group made a more or less permanent landfall and began to march inland. Following a pattern already set by Cortés and earlier conquerors, Pizarro founded a city near the Indian city of Tumbez. This Spanish city, San Miguel, became a permanent base of operations and gave Pizarro additional legal justification for his actions. The older and ailing members of the party were left in San Miguel.

Scouts and information gained from the Indians now indicated that the Inca emperor, Atahualpa, was currently at one of his capitals, Cajamarca, in the relatively nearby highlands. Knowing this, the Spanish set out to meet him. Their climb to the highlands was basically uneventful. Needless to say, they were wary of an Indian attack, although none was forthcoming. They sighted movements of Indians but no outward hostilities. Finally they reached Cajamarca, only to find that Atahualpa was not in the city itself, but encamped a short distance away. Pizarro sent Hernán de Soto, later to gain glory on the Mississippi, to parley with the Inca. Arrangements were made for the emperor to meet with Pizarro in Cajamarca the following day.

On the new day, 16 November 1532, the preparations for the entry of Atahualpa occupied the entire city. The Spanish too began their preparations. They had decided to capture the emperor and use him as a tool to gain the entire empire, an action not unlike Cortés's capture of Montezuma. It took nearly the whole day for the thousands of followers of the Inca to fill the city and prepare the way. Finally, with great ceremony, music, and activity, Atahualpa himself arrived.

The Spanish plan was to frighten the Indians with artillery and horses, and in the confusion capture the emperor. Upon Pizarro's signal, cannon and muskets were fired. The cavalry detachment came thundering into the main square of the city, where Pizarro was standing with the emperor. Save for a few misfired rounds, the plan worked; Atahualpa was taken prisoner. The Indian troops guarding him and filling the square were routed; perhaps thousands were killed without one Spanish life lost. The conquest of Peru was largely over.

Pizarro and the Spanish now held Atahualpa for ransom. Specifically, they wished to have a room in the palace filled with gold and silver. Most likely the possibility of releasing the Inca was never seriously considered, since the Spanish plan of conquest was based upon taking over the authority of the emperor. Slowly the treasure began to come to Cajamarca and fill the chamber. The total booty of the escapade turned out to be just over one-and-one-half million pesos, literally a king's ransom. Nevertheless, in May 1533 when the ransom was paid, Atahualpa was executed. The treasure was divided among the 160 men who were present at Cajamarca when Atahualpa was taken, except for the king's fifth, which went to Spain. Some lucky ones were allowed to return to Spain to accompany the royal share. The bulk of the men stayed on in Peru to complete the conquest.

The military phase of the conquest took about one more year. Traditionally, the end of the conquest is dated from March 1534, when a Spanish city was created in Cuzco, the capital of the Inca Empire, Tawantinsuyu. From this base in the central highlands, additional expeditions then went off for the conquest of Quito and Chile. There were subsequent Indian uprisings in Peru, notably in 1536–1537, but the region was generally pacified. The major cloud on the horizon was the internal disputes between the conquerors, which would end in a series of bloody civil wars.

As in Mexico, one wonders how such a relatively small band of Spaniards could conquer such a tremendously large and populous empire. In many ways the reasons are similar. Perhaps the single most important factor, again, was pestilence. Before the arrival of the main expedition in 1531, the people of the Andean highlands had been scourged by epidemic disease caught from the Spanish. In the epidemic

the Inca emperor, Huayna Capac, had died, leaving his office to be contested between Atahualpa and Huascar. Huascar was aided by the priests and establishment of Cuzco, while Atahualpa received support from the northern region of modern Ecuador. The ensuing internecine fighting served to debilitate the empire even further. Thus when the Spanish arrived, the Incas had just gone through a very trying period of epidemic disease and civil war. Another important factor in the Spanish conquest was the tremendous degree of cohesion and strength within the empire. In spite of the struggle between the two pretenders to the throne, the political structure of the empire was very strong and highly centralized. Once the Spanish did away with Atahualpa, they were able to place themselves at the pinnacle of this efficient administrative machinery.

The conquerors of Peru differed slightly from the victors in Mexico. As noted earlier, many of these men came directly from Spain, mostly from the region of Extremadura, and more specifically Trujillo, having come over with Pizarro. Nevertheless, Pizarro himself and several of his captains had long careers in the Indies before Peru. While only one veteran of the conquest of Mexico also participated in the conquest of Peru, it seems certain that Pizarro did know quite a lot about that earlier adventure. Several men went on to follow equally impressive careers after Peru, notably Hernán de Soto, Pedro de Valdivia, conqueror of Chile, and Sebastián Benalcázar. As with the conquest of Mexico, the conquest of Peru brought a very wealthy and populous region under Spanish dominance, a region that could be, and was, used as a base of operations for further expansion.

■ The Portuguese in Brazil

The Portuguese experience in Brazil was far different from the Spanish conquest of the main Indian civilizations. The Portuguese tended to follow patterns they had developed in the explorations of the African coast. Rather than make permanent settlements populated by large numbers of colonists, as the Spanish had first done on Hispaniola and then repeated throughout the Americas, the Portuguese merely established trading entrepôts (trading stations) on the coast. The Portuguese discovery of Brazil was more of an accident than a conscious attempt at exploration. Although the Portuguese had signed the Treaty of Tordesillas with the Spanish, drawing an imaginary line through the globe 370 leagues west of the Cape Verde islands, they had never expected that lands to the west of Africa might be included. Rather, they placed the line so far to the west merely to assure their own shipping routes in the Atlantic. Nevertheless, in 1500, Pedro Alvares Cabral, commanding a fleet of twelve large ships en route to India, caught sight of land to the west, and made landfall on 22 April. This course had been advised by Vasco da Gama, the man who had first sailed to India, as a means of avoiding the contrary winds off the west central African coast. Although Cabral made a formal declaration of discovery for Portugal, he and his contemporaries in Lisbon imagined the land to not be worth the effort to conquer it.

Brazil offered little or no immediate gain to the Portuguese. The only product of immediate benefit was a dyewood called brazilwood, which lent its name to the place. Between 1501 and 1503 more expeditions were sent out to explore the coast. Finally, a Lisbon merchant, Fernão de Noronha, was given a license to pursue the dyewood trade. This meant the establishment of permanent trading posts, called factories, along the coast. Soon others became involved in the trade, and Brazil had its first spurt of prosperity. The area of this operation stretched from Pernambuco in the north to São Vicente in the south.

In spite of the treaties, other European powers coveted these new possessions, notably the French, who routinely defied both the Spanish and Portuguese claims. In the face of threats to the budding trade with Brazil, the Portuguese set about securing the land more firmly. The first major attempt at settlement was made in 1532 when Martim Afonso de Souza founded a permanent colony near the modern port of Santos, in São Vicente. At the same time, the Portuguese monarch was settling the entire coast.

The plan to colonize Brazil was based upon quasifeudal arrangements with private entrepreneurs. Each leader was donated a large parcel of land along the coast line. For this purpose the coast was divided into fifteen territories. Each recipient, or *donatario,* was given extensive powers to exploit and settle the land. Twelve men received these donations and began the settlement. Nevertheless, only two of them ever had any reasonable success. The donatory could give land grants, exercise administrative and judicial authority, and collect taxes in his territory. He was ultimately responsible to the monarch in a feudal relationship. Nevertheless, he also oversaw the development and exploitation of the region, and thus had certain capitalistic goals. All in all the attempt was a failure, but it indicated Portuguese resolve to hold the territory.

Thus the conquest and settlement of Brazil differed markedly from the Spanish experience in the Americas. Rather than undertaking a step-wise expansion of permanent colonies, the Portuguese moved from purely exploitative entrepôts to more permanent settlements only in the face of outside competition. Additionally, the very nature of the Indian population of Brazil differed markedly even from the large islands of the Antilles. The Portuguese did not find a large civilized and tractable Indian population, but rather a somewhat fierce, seminomadic hunting-and-gathering people, in the Portuguese' minds, not at all suitable to settlement. As far as they were concerned, slavery was the only means of exploiting the labor of these Indians.

■ The Development of the Empire

The discovery and conquest of the Americas by the Spanish and Portuguese fit into a much larger continuum, which began with the Muslim invasion of the Iberian peninsula. Even before Columbus set sail for the New World, there were two major precedents that would influence the adventure. One of these was the experience of the reconquest, and with it the institutions developed by the Spanish and Portuguese for the incorporation of newly conquered lands and people into the realm. The second was the Portuguese experience of discovery along the African coast. The technological and scientific knowledge developed in this adventure was essential to European expansion across the oceans.

Once Columbus made his crucial first voyage, the rest of the conquest and settlement of the New World came as an orderly series of improvements on earlier discoveries with the settlement of Hispaniola and voyages out to Panama and into the Caribbean. As the Indian population of Hispaniola began to fail, causing famine and severe labor shortage, adventurers went out to find sources of Indian labor and new lands, initially Cuba and Puerto Rico, and ultimately leading to the discovery and conquest of Mexico. Both the adventures of Cortés and Pizarro had their own developments, building upon the sucesses of the past, acquiring knowledge about the land and its peoples, until victory was won. Finally the Portuguese followed a similar pattern of development in Brazil beginning with trading posts and moving ultimately to full colonies.

Thus, although the period of European expansion is filled with tales of derring-do, the overall pattern was one of systematic development, each leader building on the knowledge recently gained, slowly but surely pressing forward until the Americas had been conquered.

■ **Suggested Readings**

Boxer, Charles. *The Portuguese Seaborne Empire.* New York: Knopf, 1970.

Díaz del Castillo, Bernal. *The True History of the Conquest of New Spain.* New York: Farrar, Straus, and Giroux, 1966.

Elliot, John H. *Imperial Spain, 1469–1716.* New York: St. Martin's Press, 1963.

Hanke, Lewis. *The First Social Experiments in America.* Cambridge: Harvard University Press, 1935.

Heming, John. *The Conquest of the Incas.* New York: Harcourt Brace Jovanovich, 1970.

Lockhart, James. *The Men of Cajamarca.* Austin: University of Texas Press, 1972.

Morison, Samuel Eliot. *Admiral of the Ocean Sea: A Life of Christopher Columbus.* 2 vols. Boston: Little, Brown, 1942.

———. *The European Discovery of America: The Northern and Southern Voyages.* Oxford: Oxford University Press, 1971–74.

Parry, John H. *The Age of Reconnaissance, Discovery, and Settlement, 1460–1650.* New York: Praeger, 1963.

———. *The Spanish Seaborne Empire.* New York: Knopf, 1963.

5 | *Colonial Latin America*

JOHN V. LOMBARDI

■ The Colonial Past in Hispanic America

The discovery of America initiated a long-term program of exploration, conquest, and colonization in the new land. Spanish conquerors and colonists went out to the New World authorized by the crown but financed by private investors interested in speculative enterprises. The Spanish crown, with neither resources nor manpower of its own for the domination of America, relied on independent entrepreneurs who carried out the conquest of America in stages.

In the Caribbean islands, beginning in Santo Domingo and expanding later to Cuba, the first wave of conquerors created a facsimile Spanish society, culture, and economy. The success of this operation led directly to the second stage, the conquest of Mexico, and from then on the conquest and settlement of America depended primarily on support, financing, and equipment provided from American bases.

The Spanish conquest, designed to capture and control urban centers, moved from Indian town to Indian town, leaving the pacification of the rural areas for another time. Through this process, a small imperial force conquered large areas in a short time by dominating strategic urban centers and thereby acquired nominal control over the surrounding countryside.

Throughout the campaigns, the Spanish conquerors projected Iberian urban forms and functions onto the Amerindian structure. Everywhere they founded towns with church, plaza, and council. Without this careful attention to municipal organization and the linkages provided by the bureaucratic town structure, Spanish America would never have come into existence so quickly.

■ Land and Labor: The First Generation

From the conquest until about 1550, America had only one strategic resource required for a share of its wealth: Indian labor. Without that labor there could be no gold, no silver, no crops, no food, no security, nothing at all. Therefore, the first economic competition in America involved the control of this strategic resource. In the conflict, three loosely defined interest groups appeared: the colonists and conquerors; the clergy or the church; and the crown or, better put, the central government in Spain. Each came with a proposal for the Indians and each with a claim that made its proposal an important alternative.

The Spanish empire in America rested on the work of colonists and conquerors. They discovered Mexico and Peru; they controlled and pacified the Indians, coercing them to produce gold, silver, and other wealth; and they had to be rewarded. None of these conquerors wanted to suffer and fight in America only for the glory of God and crown. It was largely the opportunity to get rich that had moved them to leave Spain for America. So the colonists and conquerors expected that they would receive rights to the essential Indian labor, rights they could pass on to their children as part of the family inheritance.

This arrangement would ensure that some colonists would get rich, the Indians would be kept working, and that more colonists would come to America to expand the settled region in hopes of finding more Indians and establishing a family fortune based on hereditary rights to Indian labor.

Both the church and crown regarded this proposal with considerable suspicion. Such a solution would have delivered control of Spanish America's main strategic resource to individuals, weakening the state's control over America. Given hereditary rights to Indian labor, the colonists might have controlled the development of Spanish America. With the Indians under the colonists' jurisdiction, the church's Christianizing mission would surely have been difficult.

Given these objections, the clergy put forward a proposal. Their claim to a respectful hearing came from the terms of the papal donation that constituted Spain's title to the Americas. In recognition of Spain's mission to Christianize the American Indians, the pope had awarded Spain an exclusive title to most of the New World. Without such a strong title to the Americas, the Spanish monopoly in the New World might have been even more difficult to maintain against the claims of such rivals as England, France, or the Netherlands.

The church had to be helped with its mission, so the clerics proposed that they be as-signed the natives for Christianization. Indians in the hands of the church would be protected against exploitation by the colonists, their labor would be parceled out by the church to needy colonists, and the Indians would gradually become good productive Christian Spanish citizens.

If the church gained control of the Indians, America's main strategic resource, the church could have become the most powerful force in America. Moreover, the church might protect the Indians so well that the colonists would not have sufficient Indian labor to make America pay. If America did not pay, the colonists would go home, no wealth would be produced, and the crown would lose its empire in the New World.

The king, of course, had the final say. Without the crown, colonists and clergy could not settle disputes or establish fortunes in America. Everyone recognized the importance of the crown's role as guarantor of success achieved in America. The ability of the government to legitimize success and guarantee its perpetuation gave the crown its dominant position in the discussion. To retain this position, it had to remain the ultimate controller of strategic resources, in this case the labor of the American Indian. The crown had to prevent either the colonists or the clergy from acquiring excessive, independent power in America, power that might later challenge state control. Therefore, the crown sought a solution that would channel all strategic resources through the king's agents. At the same time, the solution had to provide enough incentive for colonists and clergy to remain in America, working for the greater profit of monarchy and country.

In the end, the crown declared Indian tribute labor the property of the king. Then the royal government distributed temporary rights to this labor to the colonists according to their needs and merits. The king also assigned the responsibility for Christianization to the clerics, but without any effective control over Indian labor.

As a result of this solution, anyone who

wanted to share in America's riches had to get it from the state. Anyone who succeeded did so thanks to the king's permission and largess. No perpetual control of a strategic resource remained in the hands of individuals who might later think themselves more important than a distant monarch, but all of America's Indian resources became available to help the colonists produce wealth.

Much of the evolution of Spanish policy toward the Indians during the first generation focused on the development of two principal institutions: the *encomienda* and the *repartimiento*. With the encomienda, the crown conferred a set of rights and responsibilities on deserving conquerors and colonists *(encomenderos)*, including the right to a portion of the labor of a number of Indians in a specified geographic area. This institution provided a focal point for much controversy in early Spanish America; conquerors argued long and vehemently that not only should they receive the labor tribute of the Indians in encomienda but the rights to this labor should become part of a conqueror's patrimony, to be inherited generation after generation.

The regular clergy fought this argument with its counterproposal to control and Christianize the native Americans and by emphasizing the ruthless cruelty of Spanish conquerors. This opposition to the encomienda proved most important in forming the crown's rationale for retaining control of Indian labor tribute. The clerics' arguments, powerful, polemical, and exaggerated, provided the material used by Spain's enemies, especially in England, to enhance an unrealistic interpretation of Spanish exploitation and cruelty towards native Americans during the first generation of conquest and settlement known as the Black Legend.

The crown's partial solution to the controversy between church and encomenderos denied the colonists perpetual hereditary rights to Indian labor, but invented a successor institution to the encomienda. The repartimiento in Mexico and the *mita*, its Peruvian analog, orga-

nized the distribution of Indian labor through a government bureau that allocated it on the basis of applications by colonists but involved no right to any specified amount of labor or any guarantee of perpetual control over that labor.

Epidemic disease and malnutrition probably had a greater impact on Indian policy in Spanish America than any direct mistreatment or exploitation. The catastrophic decline of Indian populations under Spanish rule constituted one of the most dramatic consequences of the European intrusion into America and provided an important incentive for the crown, convinced that harsh treatment by the colonists caused the decline, to take control of Indian labor.

Spain's colonial rivals often used this population decline as evidence of Spanish brutality in the conquest and colonization, but other European colonists in America demonstrated similar behavior. Much of the population decline may well have been the inevitable consequence of the disruption of Indian societies and economies and the introduction of new diseases, an unavoidable part of the conquest and colonization process.

The significance of the struggle over control of Indian labor lay in the precedent established for continued and active royal control of American affairs throughout the colonial period.

■ Spanish-American Government

The Spanish system of government for the Americas before 1700 had two major bureaucracies, one in Spain and one in America. The king ruled, and all other officials governed in his name and by his authority. Nevertheless, he governed not as an absolute monarch, but in consultation with a number of councils. The Council of the Indies, located in Spain, provided advice on American affairs.

Founded in 1524, the Council of the Indies had responsibility for American affairs except for the Royal Exchequer and the Holy Inquisition, which had separate administrations. With the king's approval, the council appointed all important officials, civil and ecclesiastic, and approved all legislation for America. It functioned as the last court of appeal for cases involving America, collected information on all aspects of American affairs, and supervised American officials. Few important activities took place without council involvement. Although all its members were born in Spain, a few had American experience.

Perhaps the best way to see the complexity of Spanish-American government in the New World is to imagine it as a layered structure composed of interlocking levels of government based on territorial divisions. At the top level appeared the most powerful administrative offices and the largest territorial units, the viceroys and their viceroyalties, with subsequent layers extending down to the lowest and territorially smallest units, the town councils.

The viceroy served as the king's surrogate in America with responsibility for the organization and control of the area included in his viceroyalty, although the degree of his authority varied from place to place. Always Spanish born, he received a high salary and usually came from the upper nobility, frequently the second son of an important family. Most of these viceroys turned out to be reasonably competent. Usually their appointments came as the result of court influence or as a reward for success in other royal activities, especially wars. Viceroys had short terms of office, about five years on the average, and formed few attachments to local elites. Viceroys reported mostly to the Council of the Indies, and on special occasions or in times of crisis directly to the king. They were expected to maintain the majesty of royal law and custom in America and to work in close concert with the *Audiencias* in their jurisdiction.

Audiencias were both royal courts and the name for the jurisdictions of those royal courts. Three varieties of audiencia operated in America. Viceregal audiencias in Mexico City and Lima had the greatest prestige and power. Although presided over by the viceroy, the royal court was not directly subordinate to him and could act against his wishes. The audiencia served as the tribunal for a variety of civil and criminal cases, some on appeal, others in the first instance. The court also issued legislation that took effect immediately, although such laws required subsequent approval by the Council of the Indies.

Superior audiencias, usually headed by a nonlawyer (a man of *capa y espada*, or "cape and sword," in the picturesque Spanish phrase), were the most prestigious of non-viceregal courts. Usually located in remote areas or in the center of large jurisdictions, the heads of these audiencias might be captains-general with military as well as civil authority in their districts. The viceroy usually exercised only minimal supervision over these courts, which reported directly to the Council of the Indies. Otherwise, their functions were similar to those of viceregal audiencias.

Inferior audiencias governed smaller areas, generally accessible to a viceregal capital. The inferior court had a president appointed by the king with the advice of the council. The president usually had a law degree and frequently came with experience as a judge in some other court. More closely supervised by the viceroy, the inferior audiencias usually reported to him rather than to the Council of the Indies.

Three main jurisdictions composed the provincial or sub-audiencia level. *Gobiernos*, generally large and remote, reported to a governor who usually had quasimilitary powers. Appointed by the king with the advice of the Council of the Indies, governors had high status and pay and reported to the royal court of his jurisdiction. The governor enjoyed considerable freedom of action, exercising judicial and administrative functions within his district.

Corregimientos de españoles, based on sizable Spanish towns, reported to a *corregidor*, an official with middle-level prestige and salary. Appointed by the king with the advice of council and subordinate to the local audiencia, he exercised judicial and administrative powers within the area.

Designed to serve predominantly Indian areas, *corregimientos de indios* were based in large Indian towns with few Spanish residents. The *corregidor de indios,* appointed by the viceroy from among that worthy's retainers, had both low prestige and a low salary, but the position offered outstanding opportunities for graft and corruption. The corregidor de indios reported to the closest audiencia.

Whatever the significance of other jurisdictions, Spanish legal theory placed popular sovereignty in town councils. In the early years of the conquest of America, town councils had extensive powers as the sole representatives of royal government in America. They handed out Indian labor and legitimized conquests. With the establishment of viceroyalties, audiencias, and corregimientos, the role of the *cabildo,* or council, declined.

Municipal government regulated urban life by managing local markets and administering urban properties. The town council often represented certain colonial points of view before audiencia, viceroy, Council of the Indies, and on occasion, before the king. Members of a cabildo were almost always Creoles; that is, born in America. In the seventeenth century, they frequently purchased their offices, using the town council as a mechanism for defining local elites and preserving individual privileges. In the early nineteenth century, town councils articulated local elite interests in the independence movements.

Even with this elaborate chain of territorial divisions and authorities, Spanish citizens, whether in Spain or America, reserved the right to take their problems and complaints to practically any level of the bureaucracy. Although there was a specified procedure for handling complaints, especially judicial matters, dissatisfied Spanish Americans could always appeal directly to the king or council. The right to petition the king was much more effective in the early years of colonial rule than in the later ones. But even during the independence period, Spanish-American colonials believed it possible to attract the attention of the monarch, attention that might eventually lead to the resolution of injustice.

Information and Control

Believing that the key to imperial control lay with accurate information, the Spanish empire systematically collected data that can be classified as routine, survey, or extraordinary in nature. Routine information came through letters, reports, comments, and the like from officials in the normal chain of command; it involved primarily day-to-day imperial operations such as law enforcement, economic development, and bureaucratic management. Officials frequently double-reported to ensure accuracy and guarantee that self-serving bureaucrats did not distort the data. The multiple channels of communication and authority guaranteed that no official could control the information flow to the crown.

Surveys provided occasional in-depth reports on the Spanish American empire. One of the most famous sets of these reports, called *relaciones geográficas* (geographical reports), described the total physical and human environment. Especially important in the sixteenth century and then again in the eighteenth, these relaciones geográficas provide some of the best information available about life in Spanish America.

A second category of special survey included the censuses and other population-related materials collected throughout the Spanish empire, an incredibly detailed set of materials maintained more or less consistently throughout the Spanish colonial period.

As a result, the royal bureaucracy received an enormous amount of information, most of it excellent in quality, but in a volume surpassing what the receiving officials could handle. Even so, the passion for information-gathering continued until the very end of Spanish rule in America.

When the normal information-gathering

proved inadequate or insufficient to resolve conflicts, the Council of the Indies or the king sent out officials called *visitadores* (inspectors) with wide powers to investigate and resolve problems within a particular jurisdiction.

Another institution, the *residencia* (Review of Administration), provided a confidential inquiry into the activities of a viceroy by his successor, the incoming viceroy. It offered those opposed to the previous viceroy an opportunity to describe injustices. The report of the residencia went to the council, and the council punished or rewarded as it saw fit.

Finally, according to Spanish law and practice any citizen had access directly to the king and the council, and throughout the colonial period citizen complaints uncovered many illegalities or improprieties in the behavior of government officials. This sort of special complaint provided an independent source of information outside the bureaucracy, turning even greed and jealousy into a useful reporting device.

Although this elaborate information system served the king and council well during the first generations of empire, it could not be sustained in the long run. Effective for a small empire with few officials, it failed to adjust to the increasingly complex empire of the seventeenth and eighteenth centuries. The council ultimately came to rely on secretaries to read and summarize mountains of data, giving these functionaries excessive control over the flow of information. The collapse of the information system neatly illustrates the decline of the Spanish-American bureaucracy by the middle half of the eighteenth century.

■ The Spanish-American Economic System

For Spanish America, we can identify three major periods in colonial economic history: conquest and settlement, 1492–1550; the controlled colonial economy, 1550–1700; and the liberalized colonial economy, 1700–1800.

During the period of conquest and settle-ment, the conquerors modified the American environment to fit their requirements by planting food crops suited to Spanish preferences, crops such as wheat, rice, grapes, and sugar. They introduced domestic animals such as horses, mules, cattle, sheep, and pigs, and they increased the productivity of the land through a combination of new crops and better agricultural techniques. The conquerors also gained control of the American Indian population for use as laborers and and established effective territorial control through the foundation of administrative cities throughout the empire.

Although accompanied by controversy, especially over the question of Indian labor, by 1550 the crown had imposed its system on America, and because the basic conflict of interest had been institutionalized, the economic development of America proceeded apace in the three major areas of agriculture, commerce, and mining.

Agriculture provided food for Spanish-American colonists and their labor force. This meant especially the cultivation of cereals and domestic food animals plus the continuance of native production of maize, turkeys, and potatoes. As a result of its importance, the production of food became a major source of prosperity for many Spanish colonists.

Commerce involved primarily the importation of Spanish and European goods, the sale of cattle and grain, the transportation of gold and silver, financial operations (principally loans to finance crops and trade), speculative financing of explorations, and the private collection of public revenues, or tax farming.

Based on the assumption that the more gold and silver a country had the better off it would be (the bullionist theory of wealth), the Spanish government often pursued precious metals with single-minded intensity. Necessary to support Spanish international policy, especially foreign wars, precious metals offered the quickest way to maximize the crown's American profit. The Inca and Aztec treasure, the result of many years of accumulation, encouraged the Spaniards to use the best European techniques to discover many new mines, begin deep shaft mining, and introduce advanced metallurgical techniques for extracting the metal from ore.

The Spanish colonial economic system in the second period, from 1550 to 1700, depended on the success of four policies: control, order, regularity, and conformity.

Control came from the management of import and export trade to America, through regulating economic relationships between Spain and America, and by creating complex local regulations for economic activity and an elaborate tax structure. The prime economic goal involved the maximization of metal production (mostly silver) and imperial economic policy subordinating local economic development in manufacturing, trade, and finance to the maintenance and expansion of bullion flow to Spain.

Traffic to and from America had to be on Spanish ships. Commerce, essentially finished goods to America, went through Spain and Spanish ports. Bullion shipments, whether private or state-owned, also went through Spain, specifically Seville. To keep the system working correctly, Americans were not supposed to develop local manufactures that would compete with Spanish industry.

Such a complex system proved difficult to sustain. As an essentially agricultural nation, Spain could not supply America's non-agricultural requirements, and Americans began supplying themselves through domestic manufactures. To keep up with American demand, Spain imported goods for reexport to the colonies, becoming a conduit rather than a producer of goods for the American market. The passage of so much money and goods through Spain led to inflation and severe economic difficulties without much corresponding industrial development, difficulties exaggerated by Spain's expensive military adventures in Europe.

The Spanish system relied on regularly scheduled and closely monitored fleets to America for much of its control and organization, but by the middle of the seventeenth century the expense of maintaining the fleet system became more than many merchants wanted to pay. Fleets from Spain to America came irregularly and infrequently, and where the Spanish merchants could not trade, foreigners were more than eager to substitute, especially in relatively out-of-the-way places such as Buenos Aires, the coast of Venezuela, and parts of the Mexican Gulf Coast. The absence of a regular supply of manufactures encouraged illegal local production and increased prohibited intercolonial trade.

Spain's international wars and dynastic quarrels required more and more revenue from the treasury. The treasury responded with confiscations and forced loans which in turn fostered more fraud and evasion, all of which reduced the Spanish commercial system's efficiency.

Inevitably, more and more of the wealth produced in America failed to pass through Spain. Figures on bullion imports and production make clear that much of it never went through the hands of Spanish middlemen in the peninsula but went directly to the North Atlantic nations to pay for contraband imports.

By the beginning of the eighteenth century, any rational observer could have seen that the Spanish imperial economic system did not work. America had developed an economic life independent of Spanish control, and Americans had come to depend on supplies and trade that came from outside Spain. During the period of the Bourbon reforms (1750–1800) one last effort was made to patch up the system, but it came too late and proved to be too little.

The gradual disintegration of the Spanish imperial system represented the transition of economic control and American dependency from the Spanish government to the merchants of the North Atlantic. Once this process was well under way, the subsequent independence movement provided the political readjustment needed to complement the economic realities of an American commerce tuned to the needs of northern Europe, not peninsular Spain.

■ Colonial Brazil

Until now we have focused mainly on the conquest and settlement of Spanish America, but for a complete understanding of colonial Latin America we must turn now to Brazil, the Portuguese outpost in the Americas. Indeed, because the Portuguese were the pioneers of early European imperialism, we need to know why they were not more ambitious there.

Except for occasional visits to the coast of Brazil, the Portuguese showed little interest in America. This was largely due to the large rewards reaped by the Portuguese from trade in Asia. Most of the profit in the Portuguese empire was based on quick exploitation and trade, not long-term colonization and control, and in Brazil about the only product of interest was brazilwood, an exotic tropical tree used to make dye.

During those early years brazilwood was harvested under contract from the Portuguese crown. The traders set up a barter system along the coast of Brazil: Ships from Lisbon would stop at a series of trading posts there to pick up cotton, wild pepper, animal skins, parrots, Indian slaves, and, of course, brazilwood. The growth of trade in these products produced a string of such posts from Pernambuco south to São Vicente, but few were really permanent settlements. If the Portuguese were relatively uninterested in Brazil, that was not the case with the French, who established a competing trading system there, especially along the southern coast. So successful were they that by 1530 they had almost driven the Portuguese off the coast, and this threat finally moved Portugal to make a more strenuous effort in Brazil.

At the end of 1530 Martim Afonso de Souza set out for Brazil with extensive powers from the Portuguese monarchy to establish a permanent colony. Because of the success of this initial venture, the Portuguese crown decided to expand its commitment in Brazil by introducing the captaincy system, designed to settle and control the coast through a series of fifteen large land grants stretching from Maranhão to Santa Catarina. Each of these captaincies included a generous strip of coastline and all the hinterland behind it to the Tordesillas Line that separated Portuguese from Spanish territory in the Americas. The captain or *donatario* who received this grant accepted an obligation to find colonists, bring them to the New World, and establish a colony. Most grantees underestimated the difficulty of this enterprise and failed to establish viable settlements. While the captaincy system can be judged a political failure, it did prevent the French from taking over the colony and laid the basis for the subsequent urban development and plantation economy of Brazil.

Disappointment in the captaincies and increased conflict between Portuguese, Indians, and French led the crown to establish a central government in Brazil; in 1549 it sent a governor-general, thereby changing the direction of colonial Brazilian development.

The progress of Portuguese expansion in Brazil was greatly hindered by the continuing French and Indian raids and by the lack of adequate labor for plantation agriculture. To resolve these problems the royal government introduced institutions not previously very important: the Jesuits, an irregular military force, and black slavery. Thus emerged, almost by accident, three of the most powerful and enduring influences on Brazilian history.

The Portuguese plan used the Jesuits, a new and zealous religious order, as the crown's agents for Indian affairs. Their task was to pacify, Christianize, and concentrate the Indians in towns, where their labor could be most readily exploited. The second element of the plan called for an irregular militia made up of Portuguese settlers and their retainers. These irregulars supplemented the efforts of royal troops against the French and any rebellious Indians. The large landowners, as a result, organized impressive private armies to protect themselves, and on occasion, to assist in the common defense. The third element in the plan helped eliminate the critical shortage of plantation labor. Slave traders brought black slaves into Brazil in large numbers to provide workers for the sugar plantations.

During the period before 1600, Brazil experienced a number of important demographic changes. More Portuguese entered the colony, the number of civilized Indians declined dramatically, black slaves from Africa entered in significant numbers (by 1600, slaves equaled perhaps a quarter of the population), and a category of mixed races, combinations of European, American Indian, and African, appeared in substantial numbers.

At the beginning of the seventeenth century, Brazil was settled only along the coast, and only a small portion of its territory had been thoroughly explored, although the pattern of plantation society and Portuguese-dominated culture and government institutions had been firmly established.

Most of the early expansion into and exploration of Brazil's vast *sertão*, or interior regions, took place through sporadic entries, sometimes by Jesuits in search of Indians to convert, more often by colonists in search of Indians to enslave. Although sporadic, this expansion permitted Brazil and Portugal to claim much more of South America than would have been allowed by the Tordesillas Line, and its success can be explained by a combination of dynastic, international, and local circumstances.

From 1580 to 1640 the crowns of Portugal and Spain were united. Although the two countries did not integrate either economically or politically, the Spanish felt little concern about Portuguese expansion in America beyond the Tordesillas Line because the Spanish monarchs never expected to lose Portugal. This period of cooperation came at the same time the French threat to Portuguese control of Brazil ended, and so Brazilians turned their attention to the interior. The Dutch made a major effort in the mid–1660s to capture part of the Brazilian northeast, an effort that was partially successful for a time and that pushed some of the Portuguese sugar and cattle interests inland from the coast.

If these international events permitted a temporary reorientation of interest from the coast to the interior, it was the potential profit in the Indian slave trade that provided much of the motive for expansion during the first half of the seventeenth century, especially in the south from São Paulo, directed against the Jesuit missions in Spanish Paraguay. In the north, there was considerable movement into the upper São Francisco River Valley. Originally, in the early 1600s, these expeditions were undertaken to acquire slaves for the labor-hungry planters along the coast, but after 1650, when the African slave trade began to supply the needs of the coastal planters, the expeditions turned to the search for gold, silver, and precious stones.

There were four major centers of Brazilian expansion into the interior, each with its characteristic type of exploration activity. The Amazon valley as a separate administrative region of Brazil was created in 1626. It was surveyed and more or less conquered by expeditions sent out from Belem at the mouth of the Amazon. These expeditions, unlike others in the expansionist drive, were officially sponsored.

The southernmost part of Brazil to the Rio de la Plata, the regions of Santa Catarina and Rio Grande do Sul, were explored by military enterprises sponsored by the governor-general in Bahia and the crown in Lisbon.

In the northeastern backlands, the sertão behind Pernambuco and Bahia, it was a heterogeneous group of mixed bloods and renegades who occupied and pacified the region. Most of these individuals had fled the closely regulated coast; they were cowhands for the most part, and the crown made little effort to supervise or control this area until long after the initial expansion.

These first three centers, while important for the establishment of Brazil's boundaries, did not constitute the primary expansionist force in the colony. That distinction belonged to the *bandeira*, quasimilitary expeditions sent out from São Paulo that roamed the backcountry areas of Brazil in the first half of the seventeenth century. The life-style and social organization of these *paulistas* gave them the reputation as semibarbarians, but a crisis in the more cultured parts of the colony often found the paulistas called upon to defend the country.

The major bandeira cycle occurred from 1600 to 1750, clearly a profit-oriented, private-enterprise venture. Most of those before 1600 and after 1650 prospected for gold, silver, and gems. The slave-raiding bandeiras were concentrated between the 1550s and the 1650s, beginning as part of the effort to subdue and pacify rebellious Indians, but they rapidly became slave raids. The major slave-raiding cycle ran from 1600 to 1650 and developed in response to the Jesuit success in concentrating Indians in missions in Paraguay and the Rio de la Plata region. These raids, frequently aided by Spanish officials in the Rio de la Plata area, succeeded; and the Jesuits soon began to arm their Indians, thereby increasing the cost of attacking the missions.

After 1640 dissolution of the Spanish-Portuguese union closed off the Spanish territories to Portuguese raiders, and the expansion of the African slave trade reduced the demand for Indian slaves in the sugar regions. This in turn brought about a decline in the number of bandeiras organized for slave raiding. Thus, after 1650 the bandeira became more and more a prospecting venture. The *bandeirantes* turned their attention from the southern Jesuit missions to the north and west of Brazil where, it was hoped, a new Peru or Mexico could be found. Indeed, by 1700, the paulista expansion into the interior discovered the long-sought-for gold, thereby initiating the mining boom of eighteenth-century Brazil.

From 1650 on, the future of Brazil was closely tied to Portugal's course as a colonial power. During the period known in Portuguese history as the Spanish Captivity (1580–1640), Portugal lost its best possessions in the Orient; and in Brazil the Dutch established a beachhead in Pernambuco. When Portugal achieved its independence from Spain in 1640, it found the empire in sorry condition. Spain did not give up its claim to Portugal for another twenty-five years, and given the opportunity, seemed prepared to invade it. Moreover, weakened by its loss of Oriental trade, the Portuguese crown did not have the resources to defend its colonial territory. In a period of increasing imperial expansion by other European powers, Portugal feared it could not survive as a neutral. The question, then, was what alliance would provide the Portuguese empire the most protection at the least cost.

The first effort involved overtures to the Dutch; negotiations that failed because Dutch internal political problems prevented the pursuit of a consistent foreign policy. The Dutch also felt sure of their own seapower and believed that eventually all Brazil would fall into their hands. So the Portuguese turned instead to the English, who agreed in a series of treaties (1642, 1654, and 1661) to an alliance with Portugal that would last for at least two centuries and shape the destinies of both Portugal and Brazil. In spite of the advantages gained by England in these arrangements, it is important to note that without English support Portugal would never have been able to keep any part of its colonial empire intact. While Portugal may have given up considerable sovereignty and become semidependent on England, the treaties made possible Portuguese participation in the eighteenth-century Brazilian economic boom.

British merchants obtained a special position within the Portuguese empire with broad extraterritorial jurisdiction, freedom of trade with the Portuguese colonies (principally Brazil), control over customs duties on British merchandise imported into Portugal and the colonies, and a host of other privileges. The English became extremely powerful agents in Portugal with great influence over the government.

Unfortunately for the Portuguese, the prosperity of the Brazilian sugar economy declined from the middle of the seventeenth century. The government looked for other solutions for the prosperity of Portugal's major colony and began to emphasize the search for precious metals. Although the paulista explorers knew the interior of Brazil well, they had never found the desired gold or silver—in part, it turned out, because they did not know what to look for. By the end of the seventeenth century, Portugal had provided the technical knowledge required to recognize gold-bearing sands, and by the beginning of the eighteenth century, a gold boom had begun in the interior of Brazil.

Before the mining cycle, Brazil had been tied into an economic system based on a few large sugar mills. Emigration from Portugal held little promise for men of small means, for only individuals with enough money to finance some large scale enterprise could prosper in Brazil's plantation economy. The mining boom started a new cycle of migration dominated by men of limited wealth.

The gold in Brazil was placer gold, alluvial metal taken from streambeds, requiring no complex organization or sophisticated equipment. The low investment required to start mining in Brazil and the high potential returns meant that the gold rush in the Minas Gerais region attracted many new immigrants. The number of Portuguese who decided to migrate to Brazil is impossible to determine with any degree of precision, but many came, so many that the Portuguese authorities worried about a possible depopulation of Portugal and imposed restrictions on migration to Brazil. A tenfold increase in the European population of Brazil during the eighteenth century would probably be a close estimate.

Although the mining economy in the interior of Brazil used slave labor, it functioned differently from the black slave-based plantation economy of the coastal sugar region. Black slaves never formed a majority of the population in the mining regions, and slavery there became less restrictive than in the areas growing sugar.

Slaves in mining had greater freedom of movement, opportunities to work on their own initiative, and ultimately, a better chance to earn their own freedom.

The same expansion of opportunity in the mining economy affected free men as well. In the sugar regions, a free man not of the planter class had few opportunities to improve his status; only those with substantial resources had any chance of succeeding in the sugar economy. As the sugar sector itself declined during the seventeenth century, more and more marginal men appeared along the coast, individuals unable to withstand the hard economic times. The Minas Gerais gold rush attracted these people, for it gave them a chance to succeed.

The special character of placer mining in Minas Gerais had other consequences for the local economy. Placer miners in Brazil had a limited attachment to the land, which was valuable only as long as it produced gold. The placer deposits were quickly exploited, and once the good sand had been washed out, a miner had to move on to new, richer claims. Most prospectors showed little interest in improving the land, building permanent structures, or doing anything that would prevent a rapid shift to new and better claims.

This impermanence and rapid movement were reinforced in a number of ways. For example, mining was a highly specialized and very profitable activity. A miner could, at the beginning of the boom, make more money devoting all his resources to mining rather than diverting any labor to food production. As the mining community grew larger and larger, food supplies became less and less adequate. The resulting scarcity and high prices of food led to a distribution of the economic gains from mining to other parts of Brazil. Mining in the interior of Brazil fostered a wide range of complementary economic activities outside the mining region. For example, it brought about an important modification of Brazil's transportation network. Mining took place far from the established agricultural areas of Brazil, and its specialized nature made the entire population of the gold region dependent on food supplies packed into Minas. The great inland distances and poor roads meant that the transport system was dependent on mules. Their breeding became one of the more profitable activities of the Brazilian economy, for without them, no supplies could get in to Minas and little gold could come out.

Gold exports grew throughout the first half of the eighteenth century, reaching their peak about 1760. By 1775, however, they were already declining, and by 1780 the exports ran at about half the peak volume. The greatest period of prosperity for the mining economy spanned the 1750s, but even at the peak of the boom, gold economy never produced as much, in per capita terms, as the sugar economy at the same time.

In summary, then, it is clear that during the eighteenth century mining acted as a seed industry for a stagnating Brazilian economy. It stimulated immigration, encouraged social and economic mobility, opened new areas of Brazil to settlement, encouraged industries such as cattle and mule raising, and served as an economic link between various regions.

The last quarter of the eighteenth century was a period of considerable economic difficulty for Brazil. Exports dropped from 5 to 3 million pounds sterling. Sugar faced increased international competition and gold exports declined steadily. Viewed in the larger perspective, Brazil can be seen as a series of economic systems. Some were interrelated through either the gold economy of Minas Gerais or the sugar economy of the northeastern coast, and others were isolated. The sugar economy was linked to the gold region through the cattle-breeding hinterland of the São Francisco River Valley, and the gold economy was linked to southern Brazil through the cattle and mule trade through São Paulo. In the north, two relatively autonomous centers in Maranhão and Pará functioned with little attention from the rest of Brazil. Pará lived exclusively on a forest extractive economy organized by the Jesuits and based on the

exploitation of Indian labor. Although the Jesuits probably made a good profit from this activity, the region remained isolated.

While the sugar and mining regions suffered economic decline and hardship, the productive center in Maranhão prospered. It had the initial advantage of careful attention from a Portuguese government that saw the colonists of Maranhão as a bulwark against the growing prosperity of the Jesuits in Pará. As the Portuguese crown was engaged in a struggle with the Jesuits in the second part of the eighteenth century, careful attention to Maranhão seemed good politics.

The royal government helped settlers establish a highly capitalized trading company responsible for the financial development of the region. Equally important was the change in the world market for tropical products caused by the American Revolution and the English industrial revolution. The Maranhão Company's directors saw cotton as the tropical product with the fastest growing demand. They saw rice as another good export not restricted in European trade. The company therefore concentrated on cotton and rice production, and when the rice production of the future United States was excluded from the world market by the American Revolution, Maranhão found itself in a favorable economic position. In addition, the growing demand for cotton for the textile mills of England kept Maranhão's cotton growers prosperous.

Yet with the exception of Maranhão, the Brazilian colonial economy suffered a period of serious depression in the last decades of the eighteenth century. The gold region's decline was especially serious and would last for at least half a century. Of course the decline of the gold region brought hardship to the southern cattle-and-mule raising regions as well.

When Napoleon invaded the Iberian peninsula in 1808, the Portuguese royal house moved to Brazil, transferring the seat of imperial government to America. This set the stage for the peaceful separation of Brazil from Portugal in 1820 after the emperor returned to Lisbon and reestablished it as the capital of what remained of the Portuguese empire.

■ The Independence of Spanish America

A series of events from at least 1750 made independence possible in Spanish America even though the region appeared much the same in 1810 as it had a decade earlier.

The disintegration of the Spanish imperial economic system and the emergence of new regions of importance within the old imperial structure created and strengthened new elites less attached to the Spanish commercial and bureaucratic networks. Further weakening authority in America were the governmental and economic measures of the Bourbon regime, which brought new officials, jurisdictions, and restrictions along with more freedom of trade and an improvement in commerce. The better efficiency of government hurt those American colonials profiting from the traditional graft, corruption, and incompetence, and the new opportunities for trade excited the ambition of merchants who found even the liberalized regulations too restrictive. The reforms implicit in Bourbon social policy threatened white elite status while raising the expectations of the non-white masses beyond society's ability to satisfy them. Finally, increased contact between Spanish America and the North Atlantic nations expanded trade with them making visible their industrial accomplishments, so that Spanish-American colonials began to hope they could participate in the same kind of prosperity.

In spite of the importance of these phenomena, it is easy to exaggerate the weakness of the Spanish empire in America. Most of the elite, whether born in America or Spain, feared change. Most viewed the French Revolution and its consequences in the New World, such as the Haitian revolution, with horror. Still, self-interest, a small but capable radical element among the elite, and the proper international conditions would make a revolution for independence possible.

During the decades preceding 1810 a number of revolts against Spanish rule failed, not only because they found little local support but also because they lacked international support. Success in 1810 can be explained only by the change in external conditions, not by dramatic changes in the lives and outlook of Spanish Americans.

The precipitating cause of independence came in 1808 with Napoleon's invasion of Spain and capture of the Spanish monarch Charles IV and his heir, Ferdinand. Charles abdicated in favor of Ferdinand, who then became Ferdinand VII, and both were forced to agree to the installation of Joseph Bonaparte, Napoleon's brother, on the Spanish throne.

Spanish loyalists opposed to Napoleonic rule established a committee, or *junta*, in Seville to rule Spain and all its possessions in the name of Ferdinand VII until he could be restored to the throne and the usurper and his French supporters could be expelled from Spanish soil. This series of events left Spanish Americans unsure how to respond. If they accepted the French rule of Spain, and then Ferdinand VII were restored, those who supported the French would be punished as traitors. If they allied themselves with the junta of Seville, then the French, if they won, might punish them as traitors and rebels. Most chose a form of lukewarm support for the rights of Ferdinand VII without following the junta's lead.

In Spanish legal theory, the king was sovereign only because the people gave him that right. With the king out of Spain and unable to rule, sovereignty reverted to the people who could then exercise it through elected town councils. By citing this legal argument, the American elites justified the creation of local juntas that would hold the colonies in trust for Ferdinand VII until the disposition of the Spanish throne could be resolved. These juntas also gained Americans time to discover which side was likely to win and under what conditions Spanish America might accept a return to Spanish government control.

This procedure, by its nature transitory and unstable, eventually led the radical members of some local elites to force a declaration of independence, first in Venezuela and then in Argentina, primarily in response to the continuing French control of Spain. Some of the impetus for independence may have come from the people, but not much. Independence was essentially the work of Spanish-American Creole elites.

Independence was easier to declare than achieve. Even in Argentina and Venezuela, where the sentiment for independence was strongest, it took a civil war to establish freedom from Spain. None of the Spanish-American areas had the institutions, national organization, or experience to create viable governments. All had strong royalist parties to contend with.

Spanish-American patriots believed that all of America had to become independent. It would do no good to have Venezuela independent but not Peru or Colombia, because independent American republics were too weak to prevail against any of their neighbors who remained under Spanish control. Many Spanish Americans had long-established interests that linked them to Spain. Many competent royal officials, and in some places the royal army, resisted a break with Spain. Under these circumstances, wars of liberation broke out. In some areas a short, perfunctory war sufficed; elsewhere the wars lasted over a decade, causing great destruction and loss of life.

The political systems that emerged in Spanish America after independence tended to be highly unstable, based on temporary alliances between powerful local leaders, with shifts in the alliances resulting in changes in government. These newly independent nations found themselves unable to establish an independent economy, in part because of the costs of their political instability. This situation encouraged the local elites to fight among themselves for the privilege of administering the dependent local economy for the benefit of the North Atlantic community.

Independence contributed to the instability within Spanish-American countries throughout the nineteenth century by destroying traditional authority patterns and traditional means of resolving disputes while failing to significantly modify traditional interest groups, social categories, or patterns of resource distribution. The demands of competing groups continually impeded whatever progress might have been made during the short periods of peace and prosperity.

Three major groups defined the conflict: the owners of agricultural wealth and land, the military chieftains who provided political control and authority, and the North Atlantic financiers and merchants whose loans and trade were essential to economic life. The latter group required that Spanish-Americans produce primary agricultural products, sell them at a reasonable price, and guarantee foreign businessmen the legal protection necessary to invest and collect their money and carry on their trade.

Although the chronic instability and endemic warfare of much of Spanish America represented an inconvenience to most foreign businessmen, they apparently regarded these conflicts as of no major importance. While they supported factions favorable to their interests, most of the costs of this internal strife were borne by the Spanish-Americans themselves. The conflicts of the early nineteenth century can be seen primarily as contests within the local elite for the opportunity to manage the state in the interests of North Atlantic commerce. Those who won this prize, even if only for a short time, could be assured of considerable wealth from commissions, taxes, tariffs, and graft stemming from the profitable trade with England, France, Germany, and the United States.

■ **Conclusion**

Although we have traced the evolution of Spanish and Portuguese America from the first days of conquest and settlement through imperial organization and economic life to the emergence of politically independent nations, the history of

Latin America's dependence did not come to an abrupt halt in 1810 or 1820. Instead, the economic, political, social, and cultural dependency of the area shifted during the late eighteenth and early nineteenth centuries from a system of Iberian control and domination to a more complex arrangement of North Atlantic control.

Yet within the dramatic changes that have subsequently occurred in the Americas, especially the rapidly accelerating pace of change in the twentieth century, many patterns of colonial society, colonial economy, and colonial politics remain virtually untouched. Beneath the veneer of modern forms and the protocols and styles of modern fashion, contemporary Latin America bears a striking resemblance to the Latin America of the 1700s.

■ Suggested Readings

Boxer, Charles. *Portuguese Seaborne Empire*. London: Hutchison, 1969.

———. *The Church Militant and Iberian Expansion*. Baltimore: Johns Hopkins University Press, 1978.

Castro, Américo. *The Structure of Spanish History*. Princeton: Princeton University Press, 1946.

Cortés, Hernan. *Hernan Cortés: Letters from Mexico*. New York, 1971.

Díaz del Castillo, Bernal. *The Discovery and Conquest of Mexico*. New York, 1956.

Elliot, John H. *Imperial Spain, 1469–1716*. New York: St. Martin's Press, 1963.

———. *The Old World and the New*. Cambridge: Cambridge University Press, 1970.

Foster, George M. *Culture and Conquest: America's Spanish Heritage*. New York: Viking Fund, 1960.

Hemming, John. *The Conquest of the Incas*. New York: Harcourt Brace Jovanovich, 1970.

———. *Red Gold: The Conquest of the Brazilian Indians, 1500–1760*. Cambridge: Harvard University Press, 1978.

Iglesia, Ramon. *Columbus, Cortés, and Other Essays*. Berkeley: University of California Press, 1969.

Kirkpatrick, F. A. *The Spanish Conquestadores*. London: A. & C. Black, Ltd., 1934.

Portilla, Miguel Leon. *Broken Spears: The Aztec Account of the Conquest of Mexico*. Boston: Beacon Press, 1962.

Lockhart, James. *The Men of Cajamarca*. Austin: University of Texas Press, 1972.

López de Gomara, Francisco. *Cortés: The Life of the Conqueror by His Secretary*. Berkeley: University of California Press, 1964.

Merriman, Roger B. *The Rise of the Spanish Empire in the Old World and the New*. 4 vols. New York: Cooper Square Publishers, 1918–1934.

Morison, Samuel Eliot. *Admiral of the Ocean Sea*. 2 vols. Boston: Little, Brown, 1942.

———. *The European Discovery of America*. 2 vols. New York: Oxford University Press, 1971–1974.

O'Gorman, Edmundo. *The Invention of America*. Bloomington: Indiana University Press, 1961.

Parry, John H. *The Establishment of the European Hegemony*. New York: Harper & Row, 1961.

———. *The Age of Reconnaisance*. New York: New American Library, 1963.

———. *The Spanish Seaborne Empire*. New York: Knopf, 1966.

Prescott, James H. *The History of the Conquest of Mexico and the History of the Conquest of Peru*. New York: The Modern Library, 1843–1848.

Sauer, Carol O. *The Early Spanish Main*. Berkeley: University of California Press, 1969.

Vigueras, Andre. *The Discovery of South American and the Andalucian Voyages*. Chicago: University of Chicago Press, 1976.

Vives, Jaime Vicens. *Approaches to the History of Spain*. Berkeley: University of California Press, 1967.

6

Independence and Nation Building in Latin America

LAWRENCE S. GRAHAM

A crucial point to be established about independence and nation-building in Latin America is that these are essentially nineteenth-century phenomena. The transformations of that era ruptured the fabric of colonial society and fostered the cleavages that followed. What makes the experience of the Latin American states so different from that of other Third World countries is the timing and sequence of these social, political, and economic changes and the way in which they led to the formation of the present state system. On the eve of World War I the Latin American state system had already taken definitive form. Elsewhere—in Asia, the Middle East, and Africa—the nation-state concept, national revolution, and the assertion of non-European cultural traditions as the basis for organizing autonomous governments are developments following from and stimulated by the two great wars of this century.

This chapter surveys the nation- and state-building process within Latin America in such a way as to call attention to the importance of the immediate postindependence experience for the evolution of these states.* The focus is on those aspects that are most relevant to understanding the present. This chapter does not offer a historical narrative of the major events leading to the dissolution of the Spanish and Portuguese empires in the Americas. Nor does it chronicle the aftermath of independence, with its succession of *caudillos* (military rulers) and civilian dictators. Instead it seeks to identify and explore five themes: (1) the transition from colonies to independent states; (2) centralization versus decentralization; (3) the contrast between state institutions and informal political realities; (4) ten-

*Editor's Note: By "state building" and "nation building" the author refers to two of the major problems in political development. State building means the integrated "differentiation of new roles, structures, and subsystems which penetrate the countryside." Nation building is the task of building loyalty and commitment to a state or larger political system. See Gabriel A. Almond and G. Bingham Powell, Jr., *Comparative Politics: A Developmental Approach* (Boston: Little, Brown and Co., 1966), 36 and passim.

sion between elites and masses; and (5) the myth of state supremacy in economic development. These themes are integral to the development of Latin America in the nineteenth century and are still essential for understanding Latin America in the twentieth.

■ Transition to Independence: Continuities and Disjunctures

The first theme is that of continuities and disjunctures in the transition from colonial dependencies to independent states. The easiest way to conceptualize this transition is to think in terms of the competition between "conservative" and "liberal" forces in society, albeit these labels have a very different meaning in Latin America from that present in the United States. Latin American conservative thought is largely "corporatist" in character.* Those supporting this view of society emphasize the importance of fidelity to traditional Iberian values — hierarchy, order, authority, religious orthodoxy, and collective obligations as opposed to individual rights and liberties. Nineteenth century Latin American liberal thought rejected these values. Seeing in them the source of the region's backwardness, those favoring change turned to the political thought engendered by the French and the United States revolutions and the economic successes of Great Britain as more appropriate models for their newly independent countries.

Once fidelity to monarchs in Spain and Portugal was broken, local elites entered into intense competition with each other to give shape to the new political order. In those instances where independence did not lead to ruptures in the social order, it is more appropriate to emphasize the conservative character of the independence movement and the transfer of power from more cosmopolitan bureaucratic elites to more provincial local elites. Elsewhere, political

change coincided with a conscious decision on the part of local elites to build new states patterned after European and North American models which would decisively break with the Iberian past.

For example, Dr. José Gaspar Rodríguez Francia (1811–1840) in Paraguay and Gabriel García Moreno (1860–1875) in Ecuador strongly embraced traditional values. Both structured new states that were essentially authoritarian and theocratic. Dr. Francia insured the continued ascendency of conservative social forces in the new republic, maintained close identification between church and state, and identified the independent Paraguayan regime with his own personality and monopoly of power. García Moreno's regime built on reaction against the liberal, anticlerical, pro-Enlightenment values of those who had held power in Ecuador from 1845 to 1860. Economic chaos, combined with abject poverty, a non-Spanish-speaking Indian mass in the highlands, and strong popular backing for a theocratic government, produced the support essential to the consolidation of García Moreno's dictatorship, culminating in his dedication of the republic to the Sacred Heart of Jesus.

Equally important to the process of nation building, however, were the values that Latin American conservatives rejected — political liberalism (with its emphasis on individual rights), anticlericalism, and other articles in the Enlightenment credo. The oscillation between the two orientations, which colored Ecuador's post-independence experience, influenced the rest of Spanish America as well. Against the Dr. Francias and the García Morenos were arrayed those for whom Simón Bolívar represented the best of a new world, the hope of a free society, and the illusion of Hispanic America unified by closely cooperating independent republics. The 1855–1876 era in Mexico and the reform movement led by Benito Juárez posed liberal against conservative political values even more dramatically. The irreconcilable differences represented by these two opposing views of state and society underlay much of the conflict cutting across

---

*Editor's Note: See Chapter 16 "The Political System of Latin America" for further discussion of corporatism.

nineteenth-century Latin America. Where neither set of values dominated throughout the immediate postindependence period, nation building was delayed and, in most cases, consensus over the nature of the state failed to emerge until well into the twentieth century.

The tension between change and continuity was also reflected in the conflict between "liberals" and "conservatives" over the role of the church in the new states. This conflict was at the heart of the intensely personal competition among those who sought to control the new governments. Whereas the liberal faction wished to sever church and state in order to create a firm foundation for modern, European-style secular states, conservatives pressed for a central role for the church in postindependence society and politics. Conservatives, recognizing that monarchy no longer had popular support, saw in the institutional church of the Counter-Reformation a crucial mechanism for reestablishing and maintaining order and continuity. Thus they argued that Roman Catholicism ought to enjoy the status of an official religion and that the *patronato real* (royal patronage) of colonial times should be transferred intact to the newly independent governments. They wanted to make the church one of the pillars of society closely integrated with the state. Conservatives believed that granting the new governments church patronage (the right to select the church leadership within their own domains) would sustain barriers against heretical ideas and alien religious concepts and reinforce hierarchical order in society. Above all, they were frightened by the civil disruptions and anarchy that had followed the collapse of Spanish power. Such was the case especially in the Andean republics of Ecuador, Peru, and Bolivia.

Nineteenth-century Latin American "liberals" believed as strongly that the time had come to secularize civil society. Although most of them were practicing Catholics, they argued for a clear separation between politics and religion. Consequently, whenever they gained control, they pressed for confiscation of church property and its redistribution by public sale to private individuals. These liberal ideas originated in postrevolutionary French hostility to the political and socioeconomic power of the Catholic Church, an attitude known as anticlericalism. Continental European anticlericals and their Latin American counterparts believed that one of the primary obstacles to economic progress was the church's anticapitalist precepts. They considered the church's extensive worldly possessions to be a dead weight on the economy. They maintained that nationalizing church property would release nonproductive holdings to more productive members of society. Equally important, according to the more radical wing of the liberal faction, was the secularization of education. But generally speaking, until the Mexican Revolution that issue did not become as salient in the Latin American context as it did in Continental Europe.*

Out of this debate emerged the first political parties in Spanish America. Composed largely of factions within the region's elites, they called themselves Liberals and Conservatives. Over time, the significant differences between these two groups disappeared; as most of the republics entered the twentieth century these parties had come to reflect the more conservative interests in society. They eventually either merged into a single party (for example, the National party in Chile) or they became identifiable as a single set of interests (the conservative parties in Argentina). However, in one case—that of Colombia—this initial lineup became the foundation of a twentieth-century two-party system based on more extensive political participation. For this reason Colombia's political history is characterized by extended elite rule, a gradual expansion of the electorate to include mass elements, major shifts in internal party alignments as the two parties accommodated themselves to changes in society, and con-

---

*Editor's Note: For a fuller discussion of the liberal-conservative conflict, see Chapter 7, "Religion in Latin America."

siderable regime continuity. That continuity was marked by a long tradition of civilian government, little military interference in politics, and general respect for election results.

These three aspects of Latin American political history — the liberal-conservative split over nation building, the debate on the church's role, and initial party alignments — highlight the importance of the era between independence and World War I as one that gave definitive structure to these new states. State- and nation-building ideas took root early on, well before issues of participation and redistribution became paramount. This is especially true of the South American states — except for Venezuela. Because they were relatively isolated from great power politics and the constant external intervention in domestic affairs characteristic of the Caribbean Basin, these states were able to develop their own political systems with a degree of autonomy absent among the states bordering on the Caribbean.

Generally speaking, however, throughout Latin America concepts of nationality emerged well before the creation of viable states and stable governments. Within Spanish America this formation of national consciousness among local elites both preceded independence and varied greatly in its impact on relations with the mother country. It ran the gamut from early moves for independence in Argentina (1810), to independence forced upon a reluctant local elite by the outcome of war (Peru in 1821), to the accommodation of both modernizing pressures and elite national consciousness in Cuba within the confines of empire until the Spanish-American War of 1898.[1] Regardless of regional variations, independence coincided with the collapse of bureaucratic organizations and an institutional order identified with Spanish rule, and left a power vacuum that local elites sought to fill in a variety of ways. The first elites to organize a coherent independent state apparatus were in Chile. Others soon appeared in Colombia and Argentina. Yet whatever the local response to the formation of independent governments, the experience was broadly similar: Most local elites formed new states that sought to break definitively with Hispanic institutions.

Brazil alone stands apart from this experience. Herein lies a basic distinction that must always be drawn in approaching Latin America for the first time: the difference between Portuguese and Spanish America. Only in the case of Portuguese Brazil was there significant continuity in the elite political culture during the move to independence so that a single political unit was able to emerge, instead of a plurality of independent states. In Spanish America, by contrast, independence coincided with political fragmentation. Coalescing around former imperial administrative centers, local elites sought to create their own independent governments. While Brazilians coalesced around the creation of a constitutional monarchy, which maintained national unity in the midst of considerable diversity, Spanish-Americans faced a legitimacy crisis from the outset. In order to meet this crisis, local elites turned to a variety of countries for institutional models: to France (the concept of a republic supported by an elaborate central administrative apparatus); to England (the concepts of constitutionalism and limited government); and to the United States (federalism and the separation of powers). Only much later, once unity had been established, did Brazilian elites begin to experiment in the 1890s with such concepts as presidentialism, federalism, and the separation of powers.

■ Centralization Versus Decentralization

The second theme cutting across state- and nation-building in Latin America since independence is the tension between centralization and decentralization. The centralist tradition in Latin American political experience is better understood and more fully documented than are the pressures for decentralization.[2] The governing elites perennially feared that the loss of control from the center would lead to disintegration of their fragile polities. Such fears were the natural consequence of the diversity of lands and peoples once embraced by the Portuguese and Spanish empires. Internal colonial forces had continually posed a threat to rule from Lisbon and Madrid. Cultural cohesiveness among the upper strata of society and their hold on the regulatory apparatus of government served to maintain order and stability. Against that social and political background the complaint registered at independence — "From the Spanish lion hath emerged a thousand pups" *(Del león español han salido mil cachorros)* — takes on special meaning. Once the Spanish Empire in Latin America was dismantled, it proved extraordinarily difficult to hold together the former colonial peoples in larger political units.

No sooner had Spanish hegemony disappeared than it was replaced by a wide range of aristocratic republics. Local elites now sought to re-create central authorities from the competing geopolitical centers of earlier administrations. Thus former viceregal capitals and the seats of captaincies became the core of new states. These new centers' control over their peripheries — over rural areas and subordinate cities and towns — varied widely. Not surprisingly, those capital cities that first established strong control over their peripheries became the first to reproduce European concepts of the nation-state within the Americas. Santiago de Chile, Buenos Aires, Montevideo, and Asunción led the way, followed by Bogotá, Guatemala City, Mexico City, and Lima. There was never a viable alternative to the initial four administrative centers, which were also seats of judicial, religious, and commercial power. But challenges to the central authority claimed by the second group were frequent, producing bitter conflict in the formative period after independence.

Center-periphery tensions varied greatly in their impact on state formation. Competing power centers appeared in Central America quite early, giving rise to a plurality of small states and ending the hegemony of, first, Mexico City and, later, Guatemala City, in that region. In contrast, in Gran Colombia (northern

South America), dispersion of economic resources, combined with elite cohesiveness among urban residents in well-developed urban centers, produced consensus on the desirability of having Bogotá continue its role as a governmental center in exchange for acceptance of considerable local autonomy for such cities as Medellín, Cali, Popayán, Cartagena, and Barranquilla. But that did not occur before an independent Venezuela centered on Caracas had emerged to the east.

The reestablishment of central authority and control was particularly difficult in Mexico. Rapid change and violent conflict characterized Mexico's formative period (1821–1876), until Porfirio Díaz took command. A succession of dictators, presidents, monarchs, and *caciques* (local political bosses) sought to establish their own personal rule, but none of them could offer an effective alternative to the dominance of Mexico City's increasingly important urban agglomeration. In the Yucatán and along portions of the Caribbean coast south of Veracruz, local elites experienced greater or lesser autonomy during the nineteenth century. But independence never really became a viable alternative for them.

As a consequence, both during the *porfiriato* (1876–1910) and under the hegemony of the PRI (1940–present) — the two eras of governmental stability — the effectiveness of central authorities depended on their ability to concentrate political power and control of economic resources in Mexico City.

In similar fashion Lima, despite the absence of a sense of nationhood among the Indian majority in highland Peru, remained the natural center of government for provincial elites in towns scattered along the coast and across the sierra. Without question they continued to look to the City of the Kings — as Lima was known in popular parlance. This did not preclude significant regional autonomy and the separation of the country into competing power centers dominated by local political bosses. Regionalism thus reigned supreme in Peru throughout the nineteenth century and into the first two decades of the twentieth; Lima was an isolated city facing the sea without effective control over its hinterland. Elsewhere, throughout continental Latin America, centralizing dictatorships arose during the latter part of the nineteenth century and established the supremacy of the central government once and for all. In Peru, by contrast, a combination of calamity, factionalism, and war prevented that from occurring until the Leguía dictatorship of 1919–1929.

In Portuguese America — where a single polity (Brazil) took form — the question of national union hung in balance from time to time, but wider consciousness of cultural unity and shared national experience overcame the movement toward independent Portuguese-speaking states grouped around regional administrative centers. Brazil, in contrast to the Spanish-American countries, owed its formation as a state and nation to the continuity of its central government institutions and to a federalism that allowed expression of its diversity in political culture without fracturing the still-fragile nation-state.

Whether as a unitary state (under constitutional monarchy, 1822–1889) or as a federal republic (with executive supremacy, 1889–present), Brazil has almost always respected two distinct spheres of government authority. Offsetting the national government, housed for most of its history in Rio de Janeiro and only more recently in Brasília, have been the state governors, with their officials and supporters drawn from cities and towns in the surrounding countryside. As a consequence, one can identify distinct cycles of centralization and decentralization. Since the conversion from monarchy to republic, there have been two eras of centralized government (1937–1945 and 1967–1985). But, even in those periods, the federal government could implement policy only by brokerage with local elites and the grant of de facto autonomy to state governments for day-to-day administration.

This "functional federalism" permeates Brazilian political experience since independence and constitutes a pattern of power markedly different from that encountered in Spanish America. Early on, it prevented the imposition of a centralizing monarchy on provincial elites, isolated as they were in self-contained urban centers scattered like an archipelago along the coast.[3] Military rulers in the 1970s were no more able than their civilian counterparts in the 1870s to impose their will from the center without the support or acquiescence of regionally based political and economic elites.

Underlying the centralist tradition in Spanish-American governance is the day-to-day reality of countless localities, the *patrias chicas* (literally, "little countries") that exist in all the Spanish-American states. Nevertheless, the absence of functional federalism does not mean that central rule is absolute or that there the center-periphery dynamic is unimportant. What is different about the tension between centralization and decentralization in these countries is the experience that relaxation of central authority from the capital city has coincided far too often with the disintegration of a viable national government and has become identified with separatist movements. For this reason it is important to understand that concepts of nationality within individual Latin American states are frequently complex mixtures of national and regional symbols of identity. Even in Mexico's case, where the revolution of 1910 gave the concept of nationality new and vibrant meaning, nationality is not so much a single concept as it is a common set of revolutionary symbols linking Hispanic and Indian pasts. Likewise, at the opposite end of the hemisphere where there is far greater ethnic homogeneity, enormous contrasts exist between Buenos Aires — that immense port city into which the vast majority of Argentina's Italian immigration poured — and the provincial interior. Independent Argentina began not as a centralized republic but as the federal United Provinces of the Río de la Plata. Juan Manuel de Rosas was later to impose his authority over these fourteen disparate, semiautonomous provinces, yet the nation first took form in a fertile, rural hinterland for which the port provided access to world markets. Or, to cite Peru's case, for a thousand isolated Indian communities in the Highlands, Lima and the coast were — and are — little more than hostile, alien forces to be contended with and accepted by necessity. Revolutionary military officials of the Velasco Alvarado government (1968–1975) and the declaration of Quechua as an official second language could do little to change this.

The successful wars of independence against Spain thus produced a political vacuum in its former colonies, one which had to be filled by new governments. Local elites could not reconstruct colonial society and still claim legitimacy. Instead they had to search out new political symbols. This was as true for conservatives as for liberals. The organizing ideas for both came from Europe and North America. As applied to newly developing national societies, these ideas were associated with contrary political forms of organization. From the outset, much of the debate was between unitarists and federalists. Federalist views were strongly advocated well into the present century. Federalist theory eventually received constitutional recognition in Argentina, Venezuela, and Mexico, but Spanish-American practice ultimately favored the unitary state (the idea that all power and authority should be concentrated in the hands of central government authorities).

However, power relations among local elites needed redefinition before these abstract political issues could be resolved. In this connection it is important to emphasize the personal relations among a relatively small group of men in each of the republics to understand how individuals vied for power. The political expression of personal ascendancy within an elite became *caudillismo*, and the important historical landmarks in the evolution of each of the Spanish-American states are those left by the dictators who centralized power in those self-contained regions that were to become new states.

An example of the appeal of the unitary state in Spanish-speaking America, as a way to transcend the dispersal of power into smaller and smaller political units, is to be found in the case of Chile. Among the Spanish-American republics, it was the first to establish a coherent and stable government transcending any one individual and pulling together disparate localities in the region immediately surrounding its core urban center (Santiago). While the political history of this region was as chaotic as that of any other in Spanish-America at the outset, Chile was the first Spanish-American nation to experience centralizing dictatorship. It was also the first to develop a more stable form of rule, sharing power more widely among a small group of men rather than vesting it in a single individual.

Three points need to be understood regarding this observation. First, the personality of the leader who first amassed sufficient power to transcend local differences in the region that was to become an independent state had a decisive impact on the initial structuring of power relationships. Where that leader used his personal appeal to build loyalty to a wider sense of political community — a new nation — an adequate foundation was laid early on for building a viable independent state. Where that leader used personal loyalties solely to aggrandize his own personal power, little was accomplished in the way of nation- and state-building until much later. In those instances the state remained largely an artificial creation until well into the twentieth century. The contrast between Chile and Venezuela is instructive in this regard. In the former the man who first centralized power successfully, Diego Portales, never once held power as president. A solid foundation was thus established for the Chilean state between 1829 and 1837: Nationhood was not identified with a single leader. By contrast, not until well into the twentieth century did Venezuelans prevail over a succession of caudillos and dictators, each of whom gave his own particular definition to the state and linked government to his own personal authority. The anecdote frequently repeated about José António Paez, the man responsible for Venezuelan independence, illustrates this point especially well. His partisans — Venezuelan plainsmen *(llaneros)* who fought with him for independence from Bogotá — are reputed to have greeted him on the occasion of their independence with the words, "General, you are the country."[4]

The second observation pertains to the reliance on the unitary structure of government in the Spanish-American states. Again, Chile's experience can best be used to clarify this point. The constitution of what Chileans call the aristocratic republic (1829–1861) merged the separation of powers doctrine from United States experience with Napoleonic concepts of the unitary state. The goal was to create a strong central government without permitting the abuse of power. The presidency's extensive powers thus were checked by vesting control of the budget in congress. On the other hand, the unitary structure of government insured the center's dominance over the periphery.

Third and lastly, the new institutional structures created in Latin America after independence broke decisively with the institutions of Spanish colonial government. Again, Chile provides a clear example. Chilean reformers were very much influenced by postrevolutionary French political thought and administrative practice. They also favored a strong presidency along lines laid down by the United States Constitution. Consequently, the division of powers between central and state governments was never a prominent feature in Chilean government. What they sought to create was a new state apparatus sufficient to deal with local conditions, as they knew them, to permit the building of an autonomous nation-state. This experience was replicated subsequently throughout the rest of Spanish America: the state model utilized was an amalgamation of nineteenth-century European and North American political thought.

■ The Contrast of Forms and Political Realities

The contrast between official and informal political realities has always existed in Latin America. The difference between juridical intent and actual practice increased in direct proportion to the distance from capital city to hinterland in each of the new republics.

Because of its longevity, the Argentine Constitution of 1853 perhaps best symbolizes this discrepancy between form and reality. The modernizing elite that took power after the Rosas dictatorship was overthrown in 1852 sought consciously to build consensus around common national institutions. One of these institutions was representative democracy, although suffrage was limited to a minority. (During the nineteenth century most "liberals" believed that voting rights should be restricted to the more responsible, propertied, male citizens.) Another institution trusted to unify the nation was mass education. It would be the primary tool for civilizing the population and for building a modern state. Given such institutions, the elite believed, masses of immigrants could be channeled into making a fertile and largely unpopulated land productive.

Against those aspirations stood the realities of rural life. The book that best captures this aspect of nineteenth-century Latin American reality is Domingo Faustino Sarmiento's *Facundo: Civilization and Barbarism in the Argentine Republic* (1845). The harsh life of the countryside, centered on the symbolic figure of the *gaucho* (the mounted herdsman) and the unbroken continuity of the *pampas* (plains) was far removed from urbane Buenos Aires. There are many different literary manifestations of this contrast between South America's coastal cultures, thoroughly imbued with Western European values and styles, and life in the interior, as exemplified by Euclides da Cunha's *Os Sertões (The Backlands)*, a tale of popular rejection of republicanism and mass rebellion in the backlands of northeastern Brazil.

These are familiar themes which frequently appear in accounts by Latin American intellectuals of how their national experience differs so greatly from that found in Europe and North America. Of particular relevance here are discussions of the artificiality of the European state model when applied in the New World context. Behind this lies a much larger cultural reality. Intellectual histories of Latin America dealing with the arts, the humanities, and philosophy often call attention to the slavish imitation of European models in the formative period of Latin American culture. Such histories trace the gradual evolution and development of ideas and artistic forms that express a cultural milieu very different from that of Europe and North America. Sympathy for the distinctive qualities of Latin American culture is especially strong among scholars and artists whose perceptions have been shaped by contact with indigenous peoples—in what the Peruvian *Apristas* (members of a mass-based, social democratic, nationalistic party) call Indian America: the Andean countries, Mexico, and Guatemala. There the contrasts between Iberian-styled cities, built in uniform architectural format, and the surrounding countryside have always been striking. The geography of Latin America — and the peoples inhabiting its tropical jungles, Andean highlands, or fertile pampas — have always belonged to a world fundamentally different from and alien to the artificiality of its capital cities, with their European orientation.

The modern nation-state idea all the same has very real application to Latin America. It is artificial only in that official forms, as sanctioned by constitutional writ and executive decree, frequently stand in marked contrast to political behavior, especially the farther one is removed from the influence of the capital city. This is as true today as it was in the past, which is why there is such a contrast between the political-economic views shaped by national authorities at the center and the views of those who work at the grass roots level, such as government officials, anthropologists, or volunteers.

As a consequence, throughout Spanish America one must continually weigh the concentration of politics and administration in the capital city against the countryside's tendency to counterbalance action by the central government. This enormous contrast between center and periphery points up the wisdom of discussing the internal heterogeneity of the more advanced states and dealing cautiously with generalizations about them.[5]

While many scholars reject the concept of dualism in economics, politics, and society as simplistic, it provides a useful means for an initial grasp of Latin American reality. Government (the apparatus of the modern state) and politics (the informal patterns of behavior centered on power relationships) are affected by and reflect this dualism between traditional and modern sectors.

Seen in terms of policy, the contrast between policy formation and policy implementation takes on special meaning in the Latin American context. The unitary state model implies that bureaucratic decision making is concentrated at the top in the presidency of the republic and a myriad of central ministries and independent public organizations. From above, the state looks like a network of complex organizations in which coordination and control have become enormously difficult. Compounding this is the diffusion of responsibility among government bureaucrats, extensive delays in processing routine paperwork, and complex government regulations designed at the top to impose accountability.

Yet bureaucratic complexity at the center does not necessarily imply extensive and well-developed administration farther afield. Most state employees are found at the center; financial and human resources decline rapidly as one moves to the periphery. Central organizations may well boast elaborate mechanisms, scattered throughout the country, for carrying out policy. But form and good intent do not translate readily into practical operation. Middle-level bureaucrats — those responsible for managing the day-to-day operations of government — are, above all, middle-class urbanites for whom the concept of extended service in the interior is frequently anathema. At best they are found in small numbers in provincial capitals; rarely, if ever, in smaller towns and rural areas. The administrative network is thus essentially urban in character, most fully developed at the center, adequate in provincial centers, and deficient if not absent at the periphery. Only reorganization from the bottom up, as it were, can provide the needed corrective to government's tendency to behold its own work and find it well done.[6]

■ Tension between Elites and Masses

Recognition of the need to examine public administration performance from a grass roots perspective leads directly to consideration of the fourth theme crucial to understanding Latin American nation building: the tension between the elites and the masses. Even more in Latin America than in Europe, this division was of fundamental importance in the emergence of independent nation-states. The European state model applied to Latin American experience produced a number of aristocratic republics in Spanish America; in Brazil it led to constitutional monarchy before that country also adopted republican institutions to promote economic growth.

Political stability and economic progress during the late nineteenth and early twentieth centuries came mostly to those countries in which governing elites established agreement among themselves on the rules that would govern politics and the development of economic resources. The vast majority of the population was effectively excluded from civic life. As local economies prospered and import-export trade boomed, the separation between elites and masses increased. What had begun as isolated economic enclaves, concentrating on export agriculture, mining, or substitution of local manufacturing for imports, became centralized economies focused on capital cities and ports

tied to external markets.[7] At the forefront of these developments stood Chile, Argentina, Uruguay, and Brazil. But in none of the three larger states was the developing market economy congruent with state boundaries. In Chile it revolved around the central valley, the port of Valparaíso, and Antofagasta; in Argentina around the great port and province of Buenos Aires; and in Brazil around the center-south — Rio de Janeiro, São Paulo, and Minas Gerais. Uruguay was an exception: but it alone was a city-state. Montevideo, focused on its port and an urban sprawl extending along the coast, dominated a small hinterland, where prosperity came from sheep *estancias* (ranches) and the wool trade.

Late nineteenth- and early twentieth-century Chile, Argentina, Uruguay, and Brazil stood out as the Latin American countries with the greatest success in adopting the model of European nation-states. After World War I they were first to experience the entry of new groups into politics and to experiment with adjustments aimed at incorporating the masses into national life. Despite a stormy political history, Chile had the greatest success in accommodating expanded political participation, at least until the debacle of 1973 (when the military overthrew the elected government of Salvador Allende). Abandoning political participation by a greatly restricted group (the aristocratic republic of 1829–1861), Chile extended suffrage to virtually the entire upper sector of society (the liberal republic, 1861–1891) and eventually to all significant social forces within the country (the parliamentary republic, 1891–1971). All four countries experienced the entry of large numbers of people into politics and the consumer market. In Uruguay, for example, this took place through the peaceful development of a modern welfare state, from the 1920s through the 1960s, before military rule intervened. In Argentina social conflict dominated the scene. After Juan Perón imposed his authoritarian populism in the 1940s politically, urban labor became a given in Argentina political life.

Only with the dictatorship of Porfirio Díaz did independent Mexico overcome elite dissension over the direction it should take and how it should deal with the masses. Centralized, continuous one-man rule from 1876 to 1910 permitted the establishment and consolidation of a state apparatus that filled, for the first time since independence, the political vacuum left by Spain's withdrawal. Economic progress followed, since with government stability came guarantees for foreign investment. Mining and petroleum extraction expanded rapidly, and a rail system developed that gave access to foreign markets for these commodities and the import of manufactures desired by the more affluent members of society.

But Díaz's regime gained stability at a tremendous cost. Out of the *porfiriato* (the dictatorship of Porfirio Diaz) erupted the Mexican Revolution, accompanied by the forceful entry of the masses into national life. After three decades of chaos and gradual reestablishment of central government authority, a new regime finally emerged, congruent with national reality and far different from that of other Latin American states. Political crisis and institutional breakdown characterized the latter as they confronted the issue of mass participation after World War II. Mexico arrived at its own way to reconcile this through the PRI (*Partido Revolucionario Institucional,* or Institutionalized Revolutionary Party). This dominant party — despite authoritarian practices, institutionalized corruption, and limited economic benefits for the poor majority — has retained mass appeal by its effective use of revolutionary symbols. Its governmental apparatus is able to intercede in the name of patriotism between the nation and foreign interests.[8]

The Mexican state has become by far the most stable and predictable of any in the region. Its capacity to rule without internal challenge and to sustain its autonomy vis-à-vis foreign powers has no parallel. That experience, however, belongs to the twentieth century, and the post-1940 Mexican regime bears little resemblance to the weak governments that ruled during most of the nineteenth century.

■ The Myth of State Supremacy

Consideration of Mexico's unique response to elite-mass tensions raises the fifth and final issue under discussion: the myth of state supremacy versus the state's limited capacity to assure sustained economic growth. Economic historians have frequently called attention to the state's heavy involvement in the economy, both in Iberia and Latin America. They have pointed out how the strict regulatory practices of bureaucratic empires formed under the monarchy inhibited the development of capitalism and the industrial revolution, just when northwestern Europe was undergoing the fundamental socioeconomic change that led to its world ascendancy. Imperial constraints on trade and commerce kept the Latin American region especially isolated.

Independence immediately opened up these emergent nations to free trade and to direct influence from the then-dominant economic power: Great Britain. Those formulating economic policy, however, did not intend to continue state control of the economy. Instead, as good nineteenth-century liberals, they wished to dismantle the remnants of the Hispanic regulatory state and create a new set of conditions that would encourage trade, investment, and development.

As elsewhere, the state helped create conditions attractive to foreign investment, including development of transportation, finance, energy resources, and the like. This did not involve a reversion to traditional policies. It was a response to the need for foreign capital and domestic private entrepreneurship. The resulting "mixed economies" were tied to those of the more developed countries. In time, successful economic development produced centralized economic systems. Yet no more continuity from colonial times existed in the economy than in the governmental bureaucracy. Rather, one finds the Latin American world imitating and adapting successful models from Europe. Economic practices observed in the United States were later adopted as well.[9]

Accounts of economic modernization in nineteenth-century Brazil, Argentina, and Chile demonstrate little historical continuity in their economies. Eighteenth-century mercantilism tried to maximize exports through various forms of state regulation, ownership, and subsidy. Nineteenth-century free trade, by contrast, was designed to attract foreign trade and investment. Finally, the twentieth century has found a special role for the state in triggering internal economic development. Economic nationalism arose largely from the recognition that domestic investment of foreign capital could not or would not create the conditions for self-sustained internal development.

This development belongs to the era immediately preceding World War II, and especially to that which followed it. Within the most successful centers of economic modernization (Argentina, Chile, and Brazil), a new generation of political leaders argued for stronger national governments able to impose regulations and controls in defense of national interests. They believed government action was necessary to offset foreign domination of the domestic economy, which was vulnerable to external market conditions: The aristocratic republics had failed to protect the national economic interest in this respect.

Thus, seen in historical context, the activist state — the state that initiates domestic economic development and regulates external economic forces — represented a reaction to the weak governments of the nineteenth century.

The appeal of activist-state solutions is now drawing to a close. Not only have the major Latin American states reached the limits of growth under activist-state auspices, but their leaders are increasingly aware that they need new approaches. Among these are experiments with reduced state economic direction, attempts to make public enterprise more efficient and

effective, the introduction of market concepts into the public sector, and, in the more innovative economies, greater enthusiasm for private initiative.

The Latin American states are not alone in the search for new answers. State intervention in and regulation of the economy and the proliferation of public enterprises has characterized virtually the entire post-World War II world. Although advocates of privatization in the United States are mostly conservatives preoccupied with the milieu at home, the debate abroad is much broader. In developed as well as developing countries, in capitalist as well as socialist economies, the problems are similar. Disappointment with the inefficiencies and delays that seem inherent in public bureaucracy, the tremendous costs incurred by bloated state apparatuses, and the increasing intractability and incoherence of the modern state transcend national and regional boundaries.

None of this denies the saliency of the state in the Latin American economies. On the contrary, the accelerated growth of public enterprise was characteristic of post-World War II Latin America, but it was not restricted to that region. It was a worldwide trend whose most visible manifestation was the proliferation of state-owned enterprises (SOEs). An international comparative perspective shows that one is dealing with a structural problem in Latin America — the institutional consequences of rational economic-policy choices designed to accelerate self-sustaining economic growth — not a cultural phenomenon.[10]

However, since the mid-1970s the increased role of the state in Latin America — an understandable manifestation of the desire to control and stimulate the national economy — has become counterproductive. State expenditures today consume an increasing share of the nation's economic resources. In Brazil, for example, "some 600 SOEs account for 70% of total government investment, employ 1.4 million people, and are responsible for half the nation's $90 billion foreign debt. All of the ten largest Brazilian companies are SOEs."[11] Similar situations have arisen in Argentina, Chile, Mexico, Venezuela—the most developed countries in Latin America today.

The limited states of the late nineteenth and early twentieth centuries served as vehicles for the first phase of economic modernization in Latin America's independent national economies. So too the expanded states of the mid-twentieth century have served to to promote import substitution and export diversification as means for economic development.* The current international debt crisis—which is worst in Latin America—has shown that this model of political direction to economic development is now obsolete. Certainly the size of the state apparatus, its diversity, and its complexity preclude finding easy solutions to today's economic difficulties. It is equally certain that these developments in economics and politics since World War I have few ties with nineteenth-century Latin America and that the growth of the state in twentieth-century Latin America happened for reasons which affected most other regions as well. We now stand in the midst of another transition in this hemisphere as significant as any since independence and nation building began. Today's changes and challenges are likewise a response to the underdevelopment first perceived a century ago and represent a further stage in the evolution experienced by these states over the last century.

■ **Notes**

1. Jorge I. Domínguez, *Insurrection or Loyalty: The Breakdown of the Spanish American Empire* (Cambridge: Harvard University Press, 1980).

2. The most articulate expression of this perspective is in Claudio Véliz's *The Centralist Tradition of Latin America* (Princeton: Princeton University Press, 1980).

3. "Functional federalism" further elaborates an idea developed by Djacir de Menezes. It is more fully explained in a comparative context in my essay "Yugoslav and Brazilian Experience with Federalism," *Technical Paper Series* no. 43 (Austin: Institute of Latin American Studies, University of Texas, 1984).

4. John A. Crow, *The Epic of Latin America* (Garden City: Doubleday, 1946), 609.

5. Guillermo O'Donnell, *Modernization and Bureaucratic-Authoritarianism: Studies in South American Politics* (Berkeley: University of California, Institute of International Studies, 1973).

6. Richard F. Elmore, "Backward Mapping: Implementation Research and Policy Decisions," in Walter Williams et al., *Studying Implementation: Methodological and Administrative Issues* (Chatham, N.J.: Chatham House Publishers, 1982), 18–35.

7. For further elaboration of these points, see the discussion of Latin American industrialization contained in Véliz, op. cit., 250 ff., and the overview of nineteenth-century export economies in Spanish America provided by Roberto Cortés Conde in *The First Stages of Modernization in Spanish America* (New York: Harper & Row, 1974).

8. For a discussion of the formative period in Mexican nation building, consult Richard N. Sinkin, *The Mexican Reform, 1855–1876: A Study in Liberal Nation-Building* (Austin: Institute of Latin American Studies, University of Texas, 1979). The best overview of the origins and development of the modern Mexican state is probably Roger D. Hansen, *The Politics of Mexican Development* (Baltimore: Johns Hopkins Press, 1971). Two sources that definitively establish the collapse of central government institutions at independence are Doris M. Ladd, *The Mexican Nobility at Independence, 1780–1826* (Austin: Institute of Latin American Studies, University of Texas, 1976) and Linda Jo Arnold, "Bureaucracy and Bureaucrats in Mexico City: 1741–1835," unpublished doctoral dissertation (Austin: University of Texas, 1982).

9. A useful summary of these developments is to be found in William P. Glade, *The Latin American Economies: A Study of Their Institutional Evolution* (New York: American Book Co., 1969).

10. Two essays provide excellent insight into this wider problem: John F. Coburn and Lawrence H. Wortzel, "The Problem of Public Enterprise: Is Privatization the Solution?" and Horacio Boneo, "Some Preliminary Thoughts on Privatization,"

*Editor's Note: See Chapter 14, "The Economics of Latin America."

William P. Glade and Horacio Boneo, eds. *State Shrinking: A Comparative Inquiry into Privatization* (Austin: Institute of Latin American Studies, University of Texas, 1986).

11. Coburn and Wortzel, op. cit., 1.

■ **Suggested Readings**

Bruneau, Thomas C. and Philippe Faucher, eds. *Authoritarian Capitalism: Brazil's Contemporary Economic and Political Development.* Boulder, Colo.: Westview Press, 1981.

Burr, Robert N., *By Reason or Force: Chile and the Balancing of Power in South America, 1830–1905.* Berkeley: University of California Press, 1967.

Cortés Conde, Roberto, *The First Stages of Modernization in Spanish America.* New York: Harper & Row, 1974.

Crow, John A., *The Epic of Latin America.* Garden City, N.Y.: Doubleday, 1946.

Domínguez, Jorge I., *Insurrection or Loyalty: The Breakdown of the Spanish American Empire.* Cambridge: Harvard University Press, 1980.

Glade, William P., *The Latin American Economies: A Study of Their Institutional Evolution.* New York: American Book Co., 1969.

Glade, William P., and Horacio Boneo, eds. *State Shrinking: A Comparative Inquiry into Privatization.* Austin: Institute of Latin American Studies, University of Texas, 1986.

Hansen, Roger D. *The Politics of Mexican Development.* Baltimore: Johns Hopkins University Press, 1971.

O'Donnell, Guillermo. *Modernization and Bureaucratic-Authoritarianism: Studies in South American Politics.* Berkeley: University of California Institute of International Studies, 1972.

Sinkin, Richard N. *The Mexican Reform, 1855–1876: A Study in Liberal Nation-Building.* Austin: Institute of Latin American Studies, University of Texas, 1979.

Véliz, Claudio. *The Centralist Tradition of Latin America.* Princeton: Princeton University Press, 1980.

PART

III

CONTEMPORARY DIMENSIONS

7 | *Religion in Latin America*

THOMAS G. SANDERS

Although a religious outlook directs the individual consciousness toward concerns — such as God and salvation — that lie beyond nature and history, in all cultures and historical periods religion has also strongly influenced human activities and the forms of society. Attitudes toward the ultimate, the beliefs, doctrines, symbols, and forms of worship that are associated with it, and their social or political applications — all of these aspects are interrelated and represent the total framework of a religion.

In Latin America the unity of religion's transcendent and historical dimensions is important. In all epochs the faithful have interpreted their beliefs in ways that have an explicit or implicit impact on society. Among the preconquest populations, religious beliefs and practices were integrative — that is, religion provided a rationale to explain culture and the social system — and commitment to religion gave people a sense of loyalty and participation in both the natural and social world around them. The intervention of the Europeans disrupted the indigenous systems, but the newcomers, in turn, established a new religious synthesis that provided an explanation of ultimate human concerns and a justification for the new society they established.

■ The Religious Panorama

Today Latin America contains a number of religious groups, each somewhat different in the way it affects people's attitudes toward society. Nevertheless, all of the religious expressions of Latin America combine the transcendent dimension dealing with consciousness, beliefs, and worship with the historical dimension dealing with culture and society. This combination can take a variety of forms, even within a single religion. Some accept the existing culture and society totally, seeking to integrate people and defend prevailing values. Other religious views reject the existing culture and society, either on the basis of transcendent or ultimate values and goals or on the basis of other historical and political alternatives.

Although Latin America has the highest percentage of the population baptized as Roman Catholic in the world — some 90 percent — the people themselves hold a wide variety of beliefs and express them in quite different ways. There are several explanations for this diversity or "pluralism."

One explanation is that religious variety is a consequence of Latin America's racial and ethnic diversity. In some areas descendants of the region's original inhabitants maintain beliefs and practices that reveal strong continuity with those of their preconquest ancestors. Although a small minority, they may be found where indigenous communities, as in parts of the Amazon Basin, have preserved their cultural integrity relatively unaffected by outside influences. The Spanish and Portuguese, in turn, brought Roman Catholicism with them, and the influx of immigrants from Iberia, along with the conversion of the native inhabitants, laid the basis for Catholicism's majority status in Latin America today. The Africans imported as slaves brought their own religious concepts and ceremonies with them. Although over the centuries most of their descendants became Catholic, small groups remain faithful to African patterns. Finally, the more recent immigrants to Latin America also brought their religions with them: various forms of Protestantism, Judaism, Islam, Buddhism. Contemporary Latin America is open to the world, via immigration or missionary endeavor, and its citizens include believers in all of the world's well-known religions as well as more obscure movements and sects.

A second explanation for Latin America's religious pluralism stems from the tendency of religions to develop internal variety. While this phenomenon is best known with respect to Protestantism, where it has produced a number of separate denominations, it is true of Catholicism and other religions as well. In addition to Catholicism, one finds in Latin America the classic Protestant churches of the Reformation — Lutheran, Anglican, Presbyterian — usually established by immigrants from Germany, England, and Scotland. Invariably the most common and rapidly growing Protestant groups are the "evangelicals" such as Baptists, especially the Pentecostals. Both the Protestants and the Catholics are divided, sometimes on theological

grounds (traditionalists versus modernists), but more often (and in complex fashion) in their attitudes toward society and politics. Such divisions also exist within the other religious communities. In Buenos Aires, for example, the ultraorthodox Hasidim compose a part of the Jewish population along with university-educated, often secularized Jews. Buddhists in the large Japanese-Brazilian ethnic group of São Paulo have been influenced by the rise of new Buddhist movements and sects in Japan.

It is obvious from this diversity within major religions that religions undergo change. What causes them to do so? In some instances new interpretations spring from reading authoritative books like the Bible, but more often changes result from social factors — the impact of new environments or confrontation with fresh problems. The early divisions among Protestants in Latin America were based on national backgrounds, but over the centuries new groups have emerged — especially among the lower classes. "Traditional" Catholics or Hasidim hold firmly to past values, which they recognize as having greater authority than current versions of their faiths or the prevailing secular values.

One of the most interesting forms of change, knowledge of which is indispensable for understanding Latin American religion, is "syncretism." This term refers to the fusion or mixture of two or more distinct religions. Although a pure indigenous or African religious outlook is rare in Latin America today, mixtures of Catholicism with indigenous (preconquest) and African religions are common. The origins of the practice lie in the encounter of the conquering religion with the original inhabitants and Africans who were expected to adopt Catholicism even though they did not understand it and could not or would not abandon their previous beliefs. Over a period of time an adaptation was reached in which elements of the two religions coexisted, so that believers perceived no contradiction between them. Thus, in the Andean region of South America peasant communities maintain an essentially indigenous religion along with a number of Catholic beliefs and symbols, including devotion to saints as well as to the traditional forces of nature. In Brazil and certain Caribbean countries Afro-Catholic syncretisms are common and expanding rapidly. Umbanda in Brazil is essentially an African religion, but it has added many elements from Catholicism and from the indigenous component of Brazilian culture.[1] There is a broad spectrum of syncretisms. At one end of the spectrum, the dominant outlook is essentially that of Catholicism with certain indigenous or African "survivals," while at the opposite end it is essentially indigenous or African but incorporates certain Catholic features.

The fundamental contradiction between Catholicism and native religion at the time of conquest was between historical and nature religions. Catholic faith was based on the ultimate significance of certain historical events: the Creation, the birth and death of Jesus, the founding of the church, and the response of the church to new events. Native religions, on the other hand, were centered on natural forces that were powerful but could be understood or influenced by human actions. The capacity for conversion to Catholicism or syncretism was facilitated by two factors: (1) the array of Catholic saints, who were also powerful and could be identified with or replace the natural forces; (2) the fact that Spanish and Portuguese Catholicism as practiced by the masses was itself still close to nature, for it retained beliefs and ceremonies inherited from the nature religions that preceded it.

Although the chief aspect of native culture that the conquerors found intolerable and tried to wipe out was its religion, these two factors helped both sides to come to terms with each other through what is usually called "popular" Catholicism. As anthropologist George Foster has lucidly shown in his *Culture and Conquest*,[2] the Spanish and Portuguese radically transformed the native religious outlook, replacing it by a sixteenth-century Iberian Catholicism, replete with practices drawn from diverse geographical and cultural settings. Dramatic presentations, special ceremonies, and symbols from pre-Christian European culture had already mixed with more clearly Catholic manifestations in the religious system that found its way to America. Many practices that outsiders assume are vestiges of indigenous beliefs when they observe a Latin American fiesta today really came from popular Catholicism in Europe. Indigenous elements were also incorporated, to be sure, but the basic structure of religion, especially in the small cities, towns, and countryside of Latin America, stems from late medieval Iberian village Catholicism.

Millions of contemporary Latin American Catholics continue to practice a popular Catholicism centered on fiestas, pilgrimages, and devotion at the family altar.[3] Fiestas are usually held during the week before Easter or in honor of the patron saint of a town, but they are accompanied by special meals, drinking, dancing, and other customs. They function as a means of uniting friends and relatives, and especially of giving coherence to the community. Pilgrimages, in turn, are visits to shrines dedicated to the Virgin Mary or to saints, who are believed able to help petitioners or to perform miracles. Individuals go on a pilgrimage to seek divine intercession or to thank a saint who has previously responded to their prayers. Every Latin American country has numerous places of pilgrimage; one usually has a special national significance such as the shrines of the Virgin Mary at Guadalupe (Mexico), Aparecida (Brazil), Luján (Argentina), or Maipú (Chile). However, the most important and intimate locus of popular Catholicism is the home, which usually has an altar decorated with flowers, candles, pictures of saints, and other holy objects. Most Latin Americans pray frequently, usually at the family altar in response to problems like health, money, or family conflicts. Studies indicate that participants in popular religion have a minimal understanding of basic church doctrines like that of the Trinity or salvation and that they do not participate frequently in the official ceremonies of the church such as mass or the sacraments. This is partly because of their low levels of education, but also because popular religion is their real faith, the one that makes sense to them and meets their needs. Nevertheless, the consciousness of being Catholic is strong.

From the sixteenth through the nineteenth century popular Catholicism channeled the religious life of Latin America, where at least 90 percent of the population lived in small towns or rural areas. The local priest was often the most important leader in the community, and he shared in and gave legitimation to the practices of popular religion. Virtually all identified themselves as Catholics, even if certain elements from indigenous religions or local customs had a part in fiestas or determined the location of shrines. Devotion to the local saints, and the "brotherhoods" that took care of them, provided communal unity and organization, and the culture's values were expressed in Catholic terms. The prevalence in Latin America today of saints' names for persons, streets, and towns is a striking reminder of this tradition.

This insulated and secure world was already challenged in the nineteenth century by intellectual and political movements that viewed the colonial system of religious and social integration as a source of backwardness. In the twentieth century additional social forces and perspectives have further diversified the range of alternatives. Migration from the countryside to the cities undermined the social framework in which popular Catholicism had thrived, and Protestantism, secularism, and several political movements, including Marxism, offered a wide gamut of options. Within the church itself, popular Catholicism confronted a variety of interpretations as Catholic leaders attempted to relate the faith more clearly to new intellectual and political alternatives.

■ The Church and the Empires

Upon the discovery of America, the papacy granted an unprecedented concession to Span-

ish and Portuguese monarchs. Although the church had long been in conflict with various rulers to maintain autonomy in its internal decision making and control over territory, Pope Julius II in 1508 allowed the Spanish and Portuguese kings to exercise the right of "patronage" over the church in America. This meant that they could appoint church officials, establish dioceses and parishes, and collect the tithes ("tenths"—a major source of church wealth in Europe). Furthermore, no decision by the pope could be published or carried out in America without the kings' agreement. In return for these privileges the kings assumed responsibility for organizing and maintaining the institutional structure of the church, paying its personnel, and encouraging the conversion and pastoral care of the native inhabitants of the New World. Under this arrangement the American church became an administrative agency of the Spanish and Portuguese governments, more directly controlled by the monarchs than by the pope in Rome.[4]

Church personnel came to have an influential role in politics, society, and culture. Bishops and priests, as the most educated elite, held important governmental posts. The church itself conducted all schools, hospitals, orphanages, and hospices for the elderly. As a result of donations from the pious, it eventually came to own much of the land and other material assets in the colonies. Catholic values and interests completely dominated the culture. Education, even in the universities, was based totally on theology until the mid-eighteenth century, when the ideas of the Enlightenment began to have an impact in Latin America. The Holy Inquisition was a church institution operating with the backing of government to guarantee strict religious conformity.

The movements for independence that broke out in the early nineteenth century reflected hostility by the Americans (*criollos*, or "colony-born") against the political, economic, religious, and cultural control of Spain and Portugal. In the Spanish colonies, the church, nearly all of whose bishops were Spaniards, represented an arm of the state, part of the enemy against which the colonists fought. The leaders of the rebellion were not anti-Catholic; in fact, the new republics established Catholicism as their official religion. Though the higher clergy remained loyal to Spain, most of the lower clergy, who were not Spanish- but American-born, sympathized with independence. Because priests represented a select and educated group of leaders, many of them played prominent roles in the rebellions, including Miguel Hidalgo and José María Morelos in Mexico and Camilo Henríquez in Chile.

During the wars for independence popes took the traditional view, bolstered by the attitude of the post-Napoleonic European monarchies, that order and established authority represented the divine will and all revolution was bad. The popes demanded that Americans submit themselves again to the king of Spain. Only after a number of years did the papacy gradually accept independence as irreversible; and in the 1830s it began to cooperate in reorganizing and appointing new personnel to the church.[5]

■ The Church after Independence: From Conflict to Resolution

In many parts of Latin America an intellectual and political movement had emerged by the 1820s that called for a radical transformation of the traditional role of religion in society. The movement was inspired by Enlightenment ideas, especially as mediated through France and the American and French revolutions. The liberals, as they called themselves, favored a republican political system; in economics they advocated laissez-faire capitalism and free trade. They associated the Catholic church with authoritarianism, and the popes proved them right by reacting to the French Revolution and early nineteenth-century turbulence in Europe and Latin America by defending order, authority, and the monarchical system. Since the church owned much property, the liberals

wanted to expropriate the church's land and put it to more productive use by selling it to private individuals. In some cases it was clear that the liberals wanted to buy the church's land themselves. Another major concern of the liberals was the *fueros*, or special privileges, of the clergy, which allowed them to be tried in their own ecclesiastical tribunals rather than in secular courts.

Liberals were divided on several issues. Some favored a church-state separation on the United States pattern; others wanted a state-established Catholicism that would be under the control of national governments. Still others were totally opposed to Catholicism, which they hoped eventually to eliminate, while some were willing to reach an accommodation with the church and even considered Catholic unity and values important for social unity and well-being. In education the former wanted to abolish religious schools and replace them with secular institutions; the latter were willing to accept parallel public and Catholic schools, often with religious instruction even in the public ones.

The conflict between defenders and opponents of the church led to the formation of Conservative and Liberal parties, the former representing the interests of the church and the latter an anticlerical movement. After the 1860s a second anticlerical party, the Radicals (who were more middle-class than the Liberals) appeared in some countries. Conservatives and Liberals often represented other interests as well; for example, the Conservatives represented landowners and the Liberals represented urban professionals and merchants. Or the Conservatives supported a strong central government with somewhat authoritarian powers, while the Liberals favored more decentralized and democratic forms. Fundamentally, though, the church question was the chief issue dividing the two groups; and the struggle between them was the major political conflict in nineteenth-century Latin America.

Pope Leo XIII (1878–1903) was the originator of modern Catholic social teaching. He distinguished between political forms animated by hostility to Catholicism and those that aimed at the common good in politically and religiously pluralistic societies. Leo also set out a distinct church position that rejected socialist doctrines favoring the abolition of private property, but was also critical of laissez-faire capitalism, which did not utilize property in ways that were beneficial to workers and society as a whole. He called on the rulers of nations to intervene in favor of the victims of economic exploitation, and he advocated a variety of workers' rights, including a just wage and the opportunity to establish unions.

The social teachings of Pope Leo XIII represented an important milestone for Latin American Catholicism. Though the pope did not alter traditional doctrine, he displayed a more open and progressive attitude, which was especially reflected in the church's perspective on modern society. Henceforth, Catholics did not have to be "reactionary" defenders of the past, but could lend their efforts to constructive solutions for a range of modern problems. This papal shift stimulated an interest in social problems among Catholics throughout Latin America.

By the 1920s the issue of the relationship between government and church had been settled, with the liberals usually having won and defined the terms. Sociologist Ivan Vallier distinguishes four different patterns of church-state relations in twentieth-century Latin America.[6]

1. The church holds a privileged position as the official religion of the country, with the church having almost full autonomy in its internal affairs.
2. The government establishes Catholicism and exercises certain rights of patronage, which in practice entail control.
3. Church and state are separated with the church maintaining full freedom in its internal affairs, control of its own educational institutions, and the right to exercise influence on society.
4. Church and state are separate, but the legal terms of separation restrict certain church activities. The Constitution of 1917 in Mexico, which continues to govern church-state relations, is the best example of this type.

■ Change and Reaction

In the 1950s the Catholic church found itself in an ambiguous situation in Latin America. On the surface, it seemed to have considerable strength. All of the countries were predominantly Catholic, and in most of them, no matter what the system of church-state relations, the hierarchies (bishops) held positions of respect. The church sponsored networks of institutions, especially schools, that provided education to a substantial portion of the young people. In some countries most secondary schools were Catholic.

Under the surface, however, the church was in crisis. In most of Latin America attendance at official ceremonies was low, and most of the population had only a rudimentary understanding of Catholic beliefs. Few young people were entering full-time religious careers, with the result that many Catholics rarely had contact with a priest. Bishops had to depend on clergy from other countries, especially in Europe, to supply essential parish and educational functions. Catholic schools were concentrated in middle- and upper-class residential areas, and the lower class was drifting away from the church, especially in the rapidly growing cities. Faced with urban expansion, bishops lacked the financial resources or personnel to bring the church to the mushrooming squatter settlements and proletarian residential areas. The Neo-Thomist revival, which had such an impact in the 1930s, was of little appeal to the new educated generation, which often was more attracted by Marxism or simply by a secular, materialistic outlook. Among the lower classes sectarian Protestantism, especially the Pentecostal congregations that were based on small communities and intense personal religious experience, was growing rapidly, as were Afro-Catholic syncretistic religions in Brazil and in the Caribbean region.

Although the early 1960s were especially important for change through the Second Vatican Council, the groundwork for this transition was already being laid by church thinkers and institutions in Latin America and elsewhere. Many Catholics harbored a deep dissatisfaction with the church as it was and wanted to make it more relevant to contemporary issues, though they had little support from the highest church authorities to do so. In the 1950s a number of religious innovators were active in Latin America, experimenting with new modes of Catholic thought and fresh forms of social outreach. They often had difficulty because their innovations clashed with accepted patterns. But Pope John XXIII also believed that the church needed drastic renovation. He stunned the Catholic world by announcing his intention to hold a general council, the first in ninety years. To the surprise of many people, the council instituted many long-pending reforms. Latin American bishops played an important role at the council, not only because their numbers gave them special weight but because they came from a region that was losing the allegiance of many Catholics, which made the bishops open to new strategies for recovering the faithful.

One of the most important changes was in the church's self-conception. Previously the church had defined itself in terms of its structure and system of authority, but at the Vatican Council it was described as "the People of God." For the first time, the lower levels — ordinary priests, laity, and women — had the opportunity to share in decisions. Parish and diocesan councils were established that included a broad range of participants. A variety of approaches to theology, heretofore unknown in Catholicism, appeared and did not even pretend to meet the approval of official leaders. Catholics for the first time engaged in "ecumenism," cooperation with people from other religious traditions. Bishops and priests cast off the symbols of status and

formality, adopting ordinary clothing and manners.

Latin American church leaders were especially concerned with improving their pastoral relations with the people. A major innovation was to decentralize the parish by promoting smaller meetings of Christians. Previously Catholics had attended large impersonal services in a church that served a geographical area. Now the church emphasized small groups called ecclesial base communities, CEBs, where the participants were in close contact with each other. CEB leaders often came from the laity; the program included Bible reading and discussion, prayer, songs, and attempts to apply Christianity to the problems that people faced in their daily lives.[7] Many priests and nuns doubted the need to spend so much of the church's limited resources on middle- and upper-class schools, so they turned them over to lay administrators and teachers, themselves shifting to pastoral work, especially in lower-class areas. This decision was in conformity with the Vatican Council, which also favored giving priority to the poor.

On social and political matters the council expressed its preference for church-state separation, because this arrangement left the church free of political interference. Laity were urged to participate in politics, directing their activities toward greater justice and the well-being of society, but bishops, priests, and other full-time religious personnel were expected to focus on specifically religious and pastoral functions. The institutional church on the regional, national, and diocesan levels accepted responsibility for defining the principal social problems in their geographical areas and for providing guidelines to Christian response.

The changes approved or inspired by the Vatican Council provoked reactions in two directions. Many Catholics, especially laity, opposed the innovations and preferred to maintain traditional beliefs and practices. They often combined religious traditionalism with a very conservative political stance. Upset by the reformist spirit taking hold within the church, they felt more comfortable with things as they were or as they had been. In many Latin American countries the "Society for the Defense of Tradition, Family, and Property" has grown significantly in recent years. Its title conveys its concerns: defense of traditional religious and cultural values against changes in church and society; family integrity against the secular acceptance of divorce; and the right of property against government programs of agrarian reform or other redistribution of wealth and social benefits.

In an opposite direction, a number of Catholics have taken advantage of the church's new atmosphere of freedom to propose views that Popes Paul VI and John Paul II, as well as most of the Latin American bishops, felt compelled to resist. At issue was the relationship between unity and diversity within the church. As a result of the Vatican Council, the church opened itself to new ways of interpreting Christianity, but Roman Catholicism is distinctive among Christian churches in its insistence on a teaching authority located in popes and bishops. The proliferation of views among Catholics and the nature of some of them led church leaders since 1970 to question their legitimacy and to define more clearly what they considered to be correct Catholic teaching.

■ Liberation Theology

Part of the controversy in Latin America has centered on what is called Liberation Theology.[8] This viewpoint first appeared in the mid-1960s among an outstanding group of Catholic (and Protestant) thinkers who wanted to make Christianity more relevant to contemporary intellectual and social concerns. To many people, being a Catholic had traditionally meant submission to a set of theological propositions and moral rules. In contrast, these thinkers highlighted an important biblical theme, that being a Christian meant liberation — from sin, death, and the expectations of the world. They also emphasized socially liberating motifs in the Bible like the escape of Israel from Egypt, the prophets' de-

nunciation of injustice, and the vision of a future time when the oppressed will inherit the Kingdom of God. Liberation Theology envisions history as a process in which God is acting to free humanity from the bonds of oppression. Although Liberation Theology reformulates Catholic doctrines using biblical themes, it also represents an analysis of society and advocates political action in a way that contrasts with previous approaches. To understand the controversy it aroused, it is important to describe other Catholic responses to questions of development and social change.

■ The Church Responds

During the late 1950s and early 1960s the church in a number of Latin American countries underwent a wrenching shift in its way of dealing with social and economic issues. In the period immediately after World War II, church leaders were principally concerned with maintaining Catholic values and influence in public life, while resisting new religious and political points of view. During the 1950s a vanguard reached the conclusion that the church needed to understand and participate constructively in the major transformations then under way. Individual bishops and, later, national bishops' conferences took positions supporting economic development and a series of reforms in land tenure, public administration, taxation, and distribution of social benefits. Building on the longtime church support for labor unions, they favored organizing groups, especially among the poor, to press for a better share in public services. A number of activist priests dedicated themselves to establishing credit unions, setting up cooperatives, or developing housing programs. But it was among the laity that important political movements emerged. The church opposed direct political involvement by its own personnel, but it encouraged the laity to become active. The Conservative parties had arisen to serve church interests, but after World War II that issue was no longer a live one.

■ Christian Democracy

The principal modern political movement led by Catholic laity was Christian Democracy.[9] Movements similar to Christian Democracy go back to the early twentieth century in Latin America, but they never had a major impact on political life. In the 1930s the foundations of modern Christian Democracy were laid, owing much to the influence of Neo-Thomism. (Neo-Thomism was the attempt among contemporary Catholic thinkers to make the views of St. Thomas Aquinas — a thirteenth-century theologian — relevant to modern issues. The Neo-Thomists developed an important critique of authoritarianism, asserting the autonomy of the individual and the natural rights that accompanied that autonomy, which the state was morally prohibited from violating. Neo-Thomism became a vital intellectual weapon in defense of democratic tendencies in Latin America.) The Chilean example is helpful for understanding this process. A group of young Catholics were inspired by the social teachings of Popes Leo XIII and Pius XI to become involved in politics. At that time the Conservative party was the natural choice for politically active Catholics in Chile, so they founded within it a group called the Young Conservatives. They eventually reached the conclusion that the Conservative party was not faithful to the orientations of social Catholicism; in 1938 they left to form a new party, the *Falange Nacional* (National Phalanx). For nearly twenty years the Falange Nacional remained small; but in 1963, after playing an important role in the discussion of national development and changing its name to the Christian Democratic party, it became Chile's largest political movement, winning the presidency with Eduardo Frei at its candidate in 1964.

Christian Democratic parties became major contenders in a few countries like Chile, Venezuela, El Salvador, and Peru in the early 1960s; but in most other countries they remained small, and activist Catholics chose to involve themselves in other parties. Whether through Christian Democracy or other options, during this time a Catholic outlook appeared that favored a broad development program based on a mixed economy, plus peaceful and gradual reforms in agrarian structures (such as land distribution), taxation, and banking. Christian Democrats have also encouraged many kinds of cooperatives and other organizations (such as labor unions) as part of a philosophy of a "third way" between capitalism and socialism.

■ Leftist Approaches

Alongside the moderate reformism of Christian Democracy an alternative political approach appeared, usually called the left. It favored a more radical course and stressed the identity of interests between Latin America and the rest of the Third World. Many of its leaders were influenced by Marxism, from which they adopted concepts like class struggle and the need for a revolutionary socioeconomic transformation. The left emphasizes cooperation with other political movements, including those which are Marxist, that also want radical changes.[10] The left has played its most prominent role as part of the governing coalition of President Salvador Allende in Chile (1970–1973), as participants in the Nicaraguan revolutionary government that took power in 1979, and as an important component of the revolutionary forces in El Salvador.

The appearance of a leftist revolutionary movement within Catholicism was a source of concern among most church leaders. Liberation Theology was largely a product, in its origins, of thinkers on the left. Some interpretations of Liberation Theology incorporated Marxist concepts and insisted that the only truly Christian option was to participate in the revolutionary process of liberating the oppressed. In response, church leaders at the Puebla Conference of CELAM formulated an interpretation of Liberation Theology that consciously avoided Marxist concepts and was explicitly presented as official church teaching.[11]

■ The Church Faces the Future

Latin American Catholicism, by the early 1980s, had worked out a serious reformulation of its social and political attitudes. To understand the current view of church leaders, it is helpful to distinguish between the church's institutional role and the role of the Catholic laity. Although the church itself supports development through moderate peaceful change, as shown by papal declarations and the resolutions of national bishops' conferences, ordinary Catholics in practice follow a variety of political positions, ranging from the left to the right. Church teaching encourages the laity to be active in politics, but it does not want to specify any political position and merely urges individuals to make decisions according to Christian values and with the aim of a just society. Official teaching includes two caveats: Individuals should not support a political movement that is clearly incompatible with Christianity, and they should not claim that their own political views represent the only valid Christian choice.

The institution, in turn, defines its own role as communicating the Christian faith and dealing with the personal and religious problems of individuals. Pope John Paul II has insisted that church personnel not be active in politics because doing so causes confusion about their pastoral role and might alienate people with differing political views. The church as institution believes, however, that it can play a constructive role in achieving a better society. One way is to serve as a mediator in conflicts. Society benefits from an institution that is not identified with partisan political positions but has the confidence of all and can promote internal peace by emphasizing values that all citizens share. In addition the church defends human rights. In countries like Chile, Brazil, and El Salvador, where authoritarian governments have killed and tortured citizens, the church has been the principal defender of the victims by providing legal counsel for them and assistance for their families.

The church in all Latin American countries issues periodic analyses of national problems. It tries to avoid partisanship, defining this function as a moral rather than a political one. Its documents discuss problems like poverty, economic injustice, or forms of discrimination, indicating in general terms the way in which society should deal with them. The bishops usually insist that they lack the technical or political expertise to suggest concrete policies, which instead are the responsibility of political parties, interest groups, and the government.

The role of the church seems more politically direct in authoritarian regimes, often involving a defense of human rights and a call for the restoration of democratic procedures, than in more open contexts, in which the church defines problems and exhorts the country's political forces to take effective measures for dealing with them. In cases of violent conflict like that prevailing in El Salvador, the church tries to promote dialogue among the contenders and presents itself as a mediator for a negotiated solution. The church favors an open society with a mixed economy. It also encourages people to organize because it believes that they can defend their interests more effectively when they are united. The church, furthermore, is now committed to the interests of the poor, both in its pastoral work and in its moral support of their cause. The extent to which the institutional church follows through on this outlook varies greatly depending on the country, the interests of the bishop or priest, and the social groups with which it is working.

In any analysis of the public role of the Catholic church, one must recognize that even though it has political influence, that influence takes a special form that is not the same as that of a political party. Since the principal interests and activities of the church are religious and pastoral, it is a distinctive institution among the interest groups in a given nation. In practice, the time of Catholic personnel and active laity is centered around religious services, counseling, and church institutions, including parish organizations, schools, and other projects of various kinds.

Currently there is great interest within the church in the CEBs and other small groups. Church leaders hope that the new pastoral strategies will provide more depth to the awareness and understanding of ordinary Catholics. The CEBs in many places have also encouraged participants to apply their religious convictions to problems of their community or class. The CEBs have become controversial especially in Brazil because of the strong partisan political views reflected in some of the literature they use. Pope John Paul II admonished the CEBs themselves not to be agents for political action, but rather church organizations where people become concerned and then decide to act through community institutions, unions, or political parties. Church leaders would like for participants to be active politically, but they are concerned lest the CEBs be associated with any particular party.

■ **Protestantism**

Protestantism is much weaker in Latin America than Catholicism, but (especially since World War II) it is growing more rapidly. Guatemala has perhaps the highest proportion of Protestants, nearly 20 percent; Brazil and Chile, about 6 to 8 percent.

Protestantism was introduced to Latin America by foreign missionaries, but for a long time its churches have been led by native-born personnel. In the late nineteenth and early twentieth centuries Protestants were especially active in establishing high quality secondary schools, which attracted many children of prominent families. During this period the principal churches were those that originated in the sixteenth and seventeenth centuries — the Lutherans, Anglicans, Baptists, and Presbyterians — plus the Methodists. The Protestant churches transmitted an ethic of hard work and aspiration that led to considerable social mobility among their members.

In recent decades the largest and most vig-

orous Protestant groups have been the newer churches. Pentecostals represent a majority of the Protestants in most Latin American countries. Other very active groups are Seventh-Day Adventists and Mormons. The Pentecostals attract people for several reasons. Their services are informal, with popular music styles, and participants play a very active role in the services. Ministers are not sent from outside, but are drawn from the congregation based on proven spiritual qualities and leadership talent. Pentecostals emphasize "gifts of the Spirit," spontaneous utterances believed to be communicated by the Holy Spirit. Their congregations are found largely in the lower classes, but as with earlier Protestant groups, many of their members have risen economically because of the austerity and hard work they derive from their religious outlook. The principal social effect of Protestantism in Latin America has probably been to produce socially mobile people.

Protestant groups have also taken social and political stands based on their religious outlook. Through much of the twentieth century Protestants voted for parties, like the Liberals and Radicals, that were critical of Catholicism. In the period since World War II, however, some Protestants, like the Catholics, became concerned with economic development and social change. After the 1960s, with the emergence of the ecumenical movement, many of them cooperated with Catholics. In Chile, for example, the initial human rights organization, the Committee for Peace, which was founded in 1973, was an ecumenical enterprise including Catholics, members of several Protestant churches, Jews, and Eastern Orthodox Christians. Some Protestants have also joined Catholics in reformist or radical publications and activities.

To understand Protestant social positions, it is important to distinguish the older Protestant denominations from the newer ones. Many Lutherans, Presbyterians, and Methodists have become directly concerned with social and political issues or run for public office as an application of their religious and ethical views. As in

Catholicism, this has created a division of opinion among conservatives, reformists, and leftists. The Lutheran Church of Chile, for example, split into two groups over the military government that seized power in 1973.

The newer groups, including the Pentecostals, have tended until recently to place little or no emphasis on political issues. The reason is that their theology views politics as unimportant, focusing instead on the resolution of problems in the afterlife. Members of the church spend their spare time in evangelization and often completely reject activities they describe as "worldly." However, because they were hostile to Catholicism, these groups often voted for anticlerical parties in the past. More recently they have sometimes taken anti-Marxist positions. In 1973, for example, Chile's extremely fragmented Pentecostal groups managed to unite in support of the military government, which they said saved the country from Marxism. A few members of the sects would like for them to have a broader social vision. In practice, Catholics and Protestants, including Pentecostal churches, often collaborate with other groups to improve conditions in local residential areas and to make representative organizations more effective.[12]

The Protestant concern for evangelization sometimes causes a reaction against its activities. Evangelists are often charged with undermining indigenous or local cultures through their attempts at conversion. In 1984, for example, the Mexican government took advantage of the anticlerical features of its constitution to expel over fifty foreign missionaries for illegally preaching in Indian villages in the state of Chihuahua. Protestant spokesmen charge that the government did this at the instigation of the Catholic church. The Summer Institute of Linguistics, an organization of evangelicals who study indigenous languages, has been accused of working for the U.S. Central Intelligence Agency. The special concern of Protestants to persuade people to change their faith thus brings them into conflict with society in a way

that Catholics, who are the predominant religious group, do not experience.

■ Judaism

Jews represent only a small percentage of the population in Latin America, though Brazil, Mexico, and (especially) Argentina have relatively large communities concentrated in the major cities. As in the United States, many Jews are secularized and do not participate in organized religious activities, or if they do, only on special occasions like Rosh Hashanah and Yom Kippur.

Jews entered Latin America in several waves. Some came to Brazil during the colonial period because they were tolerated in the New World. Others were part of the massive eastern European outmigration of 1880 to 1920, while still others came to Latin America, fleeing persecution, before and after World War II.

Jews represent a disproportionate segment of university students and have played a prominent role in highly skilled professions, above all in Argentina. Many have been radical political activists, partly due to the influence of socialism in the Europe they left and partly because many belong to the Latin American intelligentsia.

Jacobo Timerman, a prominent Argentine publisher and Jew, was imprisoned and tortured by the post-1976 Argentina military regime. When allowed to emigrate, he charged the regime with anti-Semitism, claiming that Jews experienced exceptional repression under it. Although many Argentines agree with Timerman, some leaders of the Jewish community denied his charges. Latin America has been relatively free of anti-Jewish attitudes, except during the 1930s when many Latin Americans were influenced by nazism and fascism.

■ Religion and Society

Probably the major difficulty in interpreting Latin American religion today is the preeminent interest that observers have in its social and political importance. Much of the best research on contemporary Catholicism in the region has been done by political scientists who naturally ask political questions, and this essay itself has concentrated on those issues because of their complexity and the interest of readers in the influence of religion on Latin America.

The religious groups themselves, even when they emphasize a political role for individuals and the institution, consider the religious experience per se of prime significance. All of them regard evangelization and pastoral care as their basic function. The analysis of religions differs from that of political organizations because it must take seriously the self-definition of the churches. That self-definition involves a vision of reality quite different from conventional historical or social-scientific world views.

The enormous stress on social change (or lack of it) and politics in the interpretation of Latin America also leads to neglect of what is probably the most important social contribution of the churches. Religion has helped forge and continues to strengthen a range of attitudes and values that link people together, providing coherence to society and making peaceful change and development possible. These include family ties (which all religious groups stress), friendship, neighborliness, civic responsibility, and concern for the welfare of others. Religious values seem, then, to have at least three referents: toward God, interpersonal relations, and political activity. In Latin America the principal political actors are political parties, the military, and economic groups. Religion plays a role, but a secondary one. It provides a set of values and concerns that people internalize and seek to apply in various ways. From an authentic religious point of view, the chief contribution of religion is to bring people into relationship with God; socially religion has had its principal impact by strengthening the bonds that unite people and enable society to function. This is true of popular Catholicism, mainstream Catholicism, the various forms of Protestantism, and other religious expressions of Latin America.

■ Notes

1. The best way to encounter Andean religion is through the film *Magic and Catholicism,* which is available from the University Field Staff International, Box 150, Hanover, N.H. See also the essay that accompanies the film; on Brazilian Umbanda, see Seth and Ruth Leacock, *Spirits of the Deep* (Garden City, N.Y.: Doubleday, 1972); and on Caribbean spiritism, see Migene Gonzalez-Wippler, *Santeria* (New York: Julian Press, 1973).
2. George Foster, *Culture and Conquest: America's Spanish Heritage* (New York: Wenner-Gren Foundation for Anthropological Research, 1961).
3. On popular religion, see *ibid.*
4. J. Lloyd Mecham, *Church and State in Latin America: A History of Politico-Ecclesiastical Relations* (Chapel Hill: University of North Carolina Press, 1966), 3–37.
5. *Ibid.,* 61–87.
6. Ivan Vallier, *Catholicism, Social Control, and Modernization in Latin America* (Englewood Cliffs, N.J.: Prentice-Hall, 1970), 34–36.
7. On CEBs, see Thomas C. Bruneau, "Basic Christian Communities in Latin America: Their Nature and Significance (Especially in Brazil)," *Churches and Politics in Latin America,* ed. Daniel H. Levine (Beverly Hills: Sage, 1979), 225–37.
8. Selections from a number of Liberation Theologians are in Rosino Gibellini, *Frontiers of Theology in Latin America* (Maryknoll, N.Y.: Orbis, 1979).
9. On Christian Democracy in Latin America, see Edward J. Williams, *Latin American Christian Democratic Parties* (Knoxville: University of Tennessee Press, 1967).
10. Michael Dodson, "The Christian Left in Latin American Politics," In Levine, op. cit., 111–34.
11. Thomas G. Sanders, "The Puebla Conference," *Field Staff Reports,* South America Series, 1979.
12. On Protestant social views, see Tommie Sue Montgomery, "Latin American Evangelicals: Oaxtepec and Beyond," in Levine, op. cit., 87–107.

■ Suggested Readings

Bruneau, Thomas C. *The Political Transformation of the Brazilian Catholic Church.* London: Cambridge University Press, 1974.

————. *The Church in Brazil: The Politics of Religion.* Austin: University of Texas Press, 1982.

Foster, George. *Culture and Conquest: America's Spanish Heritage.* New York: Wenner-Gren Foundation for Anthropological Research, 1961.

Gibellini, Rosino. *Frontiers of Theology in Latin America.* Maryknoll, N.Y.: Orbis, 1979.

Landsberger, Henry, ed. *The Church and Social Change in Latin America.* Notre Dame, Ind.: University of Notre Dame Press, 1970.

Levine, Daniel H., ed. *Churches and Politics in Latin America.* Beverly Hills: Sage, 1979.

Levine, Daniel H. *Religion and Politics in Latin America: The Catholic Church in Venezuela and Colombia.* Princeton: Princeton University Press, 1982.

Mecham, J. Lloyd. *Church and State in Latin America: A History of Politico-Ecclesiastical Relations.* Chapel Hill: University of North Carolina Press, 1966.

Pike, Frederick B., ed. *The Conflict Between Church and State in Latin America.* New York: Knopf, 1964.

Ricard, Robert. *The Spiritual Conquest of Mexico.* Berkeley: University of California Press, 1966.

Sanders, Thomas G. *Catholic Innovation in a Changing Latin America.* Cuernavaca; CIDOC, 1969.

Schmitt, Karl M., ed. *The Roman Catholic Church in Modern Latin America.* New York: Knopf, 1972.

Smith, Brian H. *The Church and Politics in Chile: Challenges to Modern Catholicism.* Princeton: Princeton University Press, 1982.

Thought (Spring, 1984). Special edition on Latin American Catholicism.

Vallier, Ivan. *Catholicism, Social Control, and Modernization in Latin America.* Englewood Cliffs, N.J.: Prentice-Hall, 1970.

8 | *Latin American Education*

ROBERT F. ARNOVE
MICHAEL CHIAPPETTA
SYLVIA STALKER

Education from its inception in the Spanish and Portuguese conquests of the New World was integrally tied to the extension and consolidation of elite power. The first educational institutions in Latin America were universities. Founded in 1538 in Santo Domingo and subsequently in 1551 in Mexico City and Lima, they tended to be both royal and pontifical. Their principal functions were the preparation of clergymen to propagate the Catholic faith, the training of civil servants to administer a colonial empire, and the education of the sons of the rich and powerful families. Education, from these early beginnings, was long restricted to the male offspring of Spanish-born settlers and their descendants, who came to be known as *"criollos."* Gender and race were for centuries bars to education, as was lower-class status.

Primary education has its origins in the nationalist period following the Wars of Independence (1810–1825). Many of the new republics began to offer rudimentary education on a limited basis to the children of the poor. Frequently, however, the church was responsible for the provision and supervision of education well into the twentieth century. In a number of countries, Liberal-Conservative battles of the latter half of the nineteenth century were fought over whether education would be a state function or would be left in private hands. The first nations to provide extensive basic education were the southern cone countries of Argentina, Chile, and Uruguay. Education was closely related to the integration of large numbers of European immigrants and to state-building. Following the Mexican Revolution of 1910, education was disseminated as part of the reforms designed to create a new and more just social order. Generally, however, universal primary education, the extension of secondary education to a substantial number of youths, and the development of institutions responsible for planning, coordinating, delivering, and assessing education are all phenomena of the post–World War II period.

This chapter focuses on the growth of schooling in the post–World War II period as well as on the persisting inequalities in educational opportunities and outcomes. Education in Latin America continues to discriminate against children of the lower classes, rural areas, and indigenous populations. It also fails to provide the same range of opportunities for females, particularly at the university level, as it does for males. By and large, education in Latin America continues to fulfill the central social purpose that dominant groups assign to it; that is, maintenance of the status quo.

In the final sections of the chapter, we will discuss the potential and limitations of a variety of educational reforms now sweeping Latin America. We also will examine educational change in two societies (Cuba and Nicaragua) that have undergone revolutionary shifts in political power and economic arrangements. In these cases, transformations in social structures preceded school reforms designed to achieve greater equity in educational provision and attainment.

■ **Post–World War II Expansion**

Since World War II, there has been a remarkable expansion of education in Latin America. In 1950 there were 16 million students enrolled at the primary, secondary, and higher levels of education in all of Latin America; thirty years later there were 85.9 million. While primary education enrollment more than quadrupled from 14.2 million to 64.5 million between 1950 and 1980, secondary education increased more than ten times from 1.5 million to 16.5 million, and higher education registered the most dramatic growth, increasing nearly twentyfold from 265,818 to 4,893,000.[1]

As Table 1 indicates, the percentage of students enrolled in different levels of the educational systems in Latin America exceeds that of other developing areas. Not only are more students going to school, but a greater percentage of students are attending higher levels of education. In 1950, secondary students represented 9.6 percent of all enrollment, and higher education 1.6 percent; in 1980, the corresponding figures were 19.2 percent and 5.7 percent.[2]

These figures, however, mask great variations within and across countries in access to

TABLE **1**

Percentage of Appropriate Age Group Enrolled in Different Levels of Education, for All Developing Areas and Latin America, 1960 and 1980

	1st Level	2d Level	3d Level
All Developing Areas			
1960	60.8	12.6	2.1
1980	85.5	31.8	7.2
Latin America			
1960	73.4	14.2	3.0
1980	102.3ª	45.1	14.9

ªThis figure is largely explained by high repetition rates and the substantial number of overage youths who were absorbed into the school system when opportunity was extended to previously excluded populations.

Source: UNESCO, *1981 Statistical Yearbook*, 11–35 and 36.

education—variations based on social class, residence (urban/rural), ethnicity, and gender. Moreover, student attendance rates do not indicate dropout and repeater rates, which again vary greatly by demographic factors.

■ **Different Access and Outcomes in Primary Education**

In most countries, a majority of students who enter the first grade do not complete the period of "compulsory" schooling, which is usually a six-year period (see Table 2). Indeed, as of 1976, Rama and Tedesco report that

even in the countries of higher educational development, the percentages of students enrolled who are not able to complete the cycle of compulsory schooling continue to be very high. "Data on dropouts during the 1970s show, for instance, that" out of [100] students enrolled in first grade only the following reached the 6th grade of primary education: 14 in Brazil, 19 in Nicaragua, 21 in the Dominican Republic, Honduras and Guatemala, 30 in Paraguay, 32 in Colombia, 38 in Peru, 42 in Ecuador, 53 in Argentina, 54 in Venezuela, 60 in Panama, 61 in Bolivia, 64 in Uruguay and 76 in Costa Rica.[3]

As a case in point, Chile historically has had one of the most developed educational systems in Latin America. Yet data reveal a similar pattern of attrition as well as inequalities in who succeeds in schooling. During the period 1967–74, only about 43 percent of a group of students entering grade 1 completed an 8-year primary education. Moreover, social class background heavily influenced which students continued with their studies.[4]

Data marshalled by Solari on school completion rates indicate that, in addition to social class factors, there are significant urban-rural differences in equality of educational opportunities and outcomes. In Argentina, for example, 74 percent of the students who started 1st grade in greater Buenos Aires in 1969, were in 6th grade in 1975. The percentage of students reaching 6th grade in other cities such as Córdoba and Mendoza varied from 53 to 60 percent; and in most rural and impoverished areas of the country, only between 31 and 38 percent attained this grade. In Costa Rica, a country noted for its educational efforts, urban students were twice as likely as their rural counterparts to complete primary schooling during the 1960s.[5]

By contrast with the urban elites, the masses in rural locations are politically weak and disorganized. Historically, their interests have been poorly served by educational systems. Rural areas have the highest illiteracy rates, often two to three times greater than that of cities; they have fewer primary schools, inadequate schools resources, and often no form of secondary or higher education at all.

To take the case of Colombia, out of an edu-

TABLE **2**

Compulsory Education, Entrance Ages, and Duration of Schooling at First and Second Levels—Latin American Countries and the United States

	Compulsory Education		Preprimary Entrance Age	First Level		Second Level	
	Age Limits	Duration (Years)		Entrance Age	Duration (Years)	Entrance Age	Duration (Years)[a]
Argentina	6–14	7	3	6	7	13	3 + 3
Bolivia	6–14	8	4	6	8	14	4
Brazil	7–14	8	4	7	8	15	3
Chile	6–13	8	4	6	8	14	4
Colombia	7–12	5	5	6	5	11	4 + 2
Costa Rica	6–15	9	5	6	6	12	3 + 3
Cuba	6–11	6	5	6	6	12	4 + 3
Dominican Republic	7–14	6	3	7	6	13	2 + 4
Ecuador	6–14	6	4	6	6	12	3 + 3
El Salvador	7–15	9	4	7	9	16	3
Guatemala	7–14	6	4	7	6	13	3 + 3
Haiti	6–14	6	2	6	7	12	3 + 4
Honduras	7–13	6	4	6	6	12	3 + 3
Mexico	6–11	6	4	6	6	12	3 + 3
Nicaragua	7–12	6	3	7	6	13	3 + 3
Panama	6–15	9	4	6	6	9	3
Paraguay	7–14	6	5	7	6	13	3 + 3
Peru	6–11	6	3	6	6	12	3 + 2
Uruguay	6–15	9	3	6	6	12	3 + 3
Venezuela	7–14	6	4	7	6	13	3 + 3
United States	6–16	11	3	5	6	12	6

[a] UNESCO, 1985 Yearbook. Tables 3.1 and 3.1A

cation budget of nearly $125 million in 1970–71, the rural areas received less than $12 million, although the rural population constitutes approximately one-half the total national population. At that time, rural education served approximately 43 percent of the 3,118,300 children (ages seven to eleven) attending primary schools, but received less than 10 percent of the education budget.[6]

The results are evident in the deplorable conditions in most rural schools: dilapidated buildings, overcrowding, and lack of educational materials. A study done by a team of sociologists in 1970–71 at the Pedagogical and Technical University in Tunja examined rural schools in Boyacá, one of the least urbanized areas of Colombia. The team found that more than three-fourths of the schools had only one classroom. With few exceptions, schools were without electricity, running water, or sanitary services (a situation common throughout rural Latin America). A typical school consisted of one room, a dirt floor, and forty-five to fifty students in three grades studying at the same time. Teachers attempted for the most part simply to maintain a semblance of order while getting students to go through several routine assignments. Little learning took place; instead, teachers frequently communicated misinformation.[7]

Rural teachers throughout the Southern Hemisphere are as a rule the least qualified, the most overburdened in terms of student-teacher ratios, and the most poorly paid. They tend to be not only dissatisfied, but psychologically and socially distant from their students and estranged from the communities where they work. The rural teacher often comes from the rural bourgeoisie or middle class and uses the teaching profession as a springboard for social mobility and movement out of the countryside. When poor salaries and inadequate living conditions are also taken into account,[8] it is not surprising that turnover is extremely high in the countryside — frequently approaching half the teaching force in any single year.[9]

The textbooks (when in sufficient supply) and the curriculum contain little to engage the interest of children in rural areas. This problem is particularly acute in countries that have substantial indigenous populations, such as Bolivia, Peru, Ecuador, and Guatemala. Recent curriculum trends in Latin America tend to blur the differences between rural and urban areas. As Arnove has noted elsewhere, the rationale for a uniform curriculum is to provide a core of instrumental knowledge that equips the student to participate in national life and share common values and perspectives.[10] The problem with this approach is: Whose values will form the core curriculum? As an earlier (1968) United Nations study on education, human resources, and development in Latin America observed: "For the most part, the rural school has been an exotic and sickly import from the cities, deriving from national policy rather than local demands."

With some exceptions, Latin American countries have a national curriculum with a centralized system of supervision and evaluation. Under this system, students are given the same national examinations whether they attend poorly endowed schools with unqualified teachers or resource-rich schools with highly qualified teachers.[11] Invariably, many students fail to pass these examinations and either drop out (as noted earlier) or repeat the same grade. This pattern is evident from the beginning of primary school. It is not uncommon for one-fourth to one-fifth of the students to repeat first and second grades.

Despite these obstacles an increasing number of rural as well as urban lower class students throughout Latin America are completing primary education, often at great sacrifice.[12] Yet those who do complete primary schooling are unlikely to obtain an attractive job or to change their social position. A primary school certificate leads nowhere, except possibly to higher levels of education and to a quest for a more prestigious degree.

■ Advancing through the System: Characteristics of Secondary Education

To advance through the educational system in Latin America, an academically talented or socially ambitious youth will have to go to the cities, for that is where most secondary schools are located. In a number of countries, well over 90 percent of all educational facilities are located in urban areas and a handful of cities contain the bulk of secondary schools.[13]

In recent decades, the great demand for secondary education has led to an impressive numerical expansion at this level of schooling. In 1950, approximately 10 percent of fourteen-to-nineteen-year-olds attended secondary education; by 1980, 45 percent attended. But as the United Nations Project on Development and Education in Latin America and the Caribbean notes, the quantitative change generally has not been matched by a qualitative change in the aims, content, and pedagogy of secondary education. Secondary education, developed long after university and primary school education, has traditionally served as merely a junior appendage to university education providing elite youth with the prerequisite educational background.[14] In time, a second branch of secondary education developed, consisting of technical, commercial, and normal (teacher training) schools. This vocationally oriented sector of secondary education has primarily served children of the lower-middle class and the upwardly mobile working class. Until recently, it was of a terminal nature, that is, it did not lead to higher education. Thus it contributed to the dual-track character of schooling.

With the increasing demand for further education, the first cycle of secondary education—in most countries grades seven through nine (see Table 2)—has become an integral part of an introductory or "compulsory" cycle of eight to nine years of schooling. Latin American countries are increasingly moving away from channeling post-primary students by means of tests.

In fact, the trend is toward "homogenization" of the different branches of secondary education with regard to content and function up to grade 9.[15] General, university-preparatory studies have become standard. Such studies represented over 70 percent of secondary school enrollment in 1950 and over 80 percent by 1975.[16] This pattern has unfortunate consequences for the substantial number of students who drop out or who are otherwise unable to go on to higher education. That is, these students are ill prepared to enter the work force.

Technical education, however, has not been an attractive option for upwardly mobile students, primarily because it has not led to the expected payoff in jobs in the modern industrial sector. In many countries, employers may have a bias against technical school or vocational program graduates, feeling that they are inferior to students in the academic track and yet will demand greater salaries and benefits than students with less education.[17] Employers frequently prefer to hire students with lesser qualifications and give them on-the-job training.[18] In a number of countries—e.g., Brazil, Colombia, Venezuela—graduates of occupational training organizations (SENAI, SENA, and INCE, respectively) may be preferred to technical school dropouts or even graduates.[19] These organizations promote apprenticeship training as well as education for upgrading of existing skills or the acquiring of new skills. The training programs of these organizations have the advantage of being linked to and supported by industrial and commercial firms.

From the government's point of view as well, expansion of technical education may not be appealing. It is costly, and its graduates often do not find appropriate employment. To take the case of Argentina, which has an established tradition of technical education, less than one-fifth of the work force with technical degrees actually finds jobs as technicians.[20] Moreover, those graduates who do find employment often work only until they can save up enough money to go back to school for a college degree.[21] A related source of problems is that students in technical schools—given their middle-class background or aspirations—push to have their academic programs resemble those of the university-preparatory high schools. This contributes to the homogenization mentioned above.

Homogenization does not, however, imply overall modernization of content. According to the United Nations Projects on Education and Development, scientific and technical studies tend to be found predominantly in the upper cycle of secondary education (grades nine through eleven or twelve). Modern curricula in the sciences, mathematics, and technology are added in an unplanned way to the existing liberal arts curriculum. The result is a conglomeration of often unrelated subjects—poorly articulated with either primary or higher education, as well as irrelevant to the marketplace and the transformations occurring in Latin American society. Students have to take as many as twelve or more subjects per year, following a prescribed curriculum that allows little, if any choice. The United Nations project notes that pedagogically most courses involve student memorization of teacher lectures and seldom emphasize inquiry-oriented or group-learning activities. Moreover, teaching-learning methods tend to isolate individuals—setting them against one another in their desire to advance through the system.[22]

While technically it may be true that Latin American educational systems do not set up barriers between primary and postprimary education, or between the different cycles of secondary education, the system does rigorously screen out students at both the primary and secondary levels. The dropout rate for the latter is usually within the range of 40 percent to 50 percent. Characteristically, the children from working-class and rural backgrounds fare poorly. The rigorous screening is partially attributed to the gatekeeping function of teachers, who view themselves as passing on only the most qualified to higher levels of the education

system. Whether or not there is overt bias by teachers against students from lower-class backgrounds, the curricula, pedagogy, and examinations of most Latin American education systems favor the knowledge, language, and learning styles of the middle and upper classes.

In addition, children from elite backgrounds generally go to private schools, where examination pass rates and promotion rates tend to be higher. Although private schools are not always better endowed and their teachers are not necessarily more qualified, the student-teacher ratios are generally favorable to more individualized attention and instruction is organized to ensure student success on examinations. Given the dependence of these schools on student tuition, instructional staff may be more reluctant to fail students; and, in many cases, the common class background of staff and students facilitates communication and the possibility of assisting students who are having academic problems.

In a number of countries, most secondary schools are privately owned and run, albeit subject to varying degrees of government regulation and supervision. Many students are unable to afford the fees charged by these schools and find the competition for admission to the public schools exceedingly stiff. In such situations of restricted access, it would be more appropriate to speak of "lockouts" rather than dropouts.

In the competition to succeed academically, students who attend private schools have a higher probability not only of completing secondary education but also of passing university entrance examinations. The reasons include those described above, as well as the greater resources and support for learning provided by the upper-class families of students attending private schools.

■ At the Top: Characteristics of Higher Education

We now discover an ironic pattern: until recently, students who attended private high schools frequently continued to a public university, where tuition fees were nominal because of generous public financing. In effect, the children of the middle and upper classes were subsidized by the government to attend public universities and thereby to confirm their higher social status.

This pattern has begun to change as increasing numbers of students attend private institutions of higher learning. While higher education has grown faster than primary or second education, and its growth rate in Latin America is the highest for any region of the world (approximately 12 percent annually between 1965 and 1980), it is the private sector that has registered the most dramatic gains. In the 1970s, approximately 5 percent of higher education students were enrolled in private institutions; in the 1980s over 30 percent attend private universities and colleges.

Overall, the growth rate of higher education in Latin America in the post–World War II period has been remarkable — in absolute terms and with regard to the corresponding age group.[23] In 1950, there were approximately 1.5 million students in higher education; in 1980, approximately 5 million. By 1950, there were 105 universities in Latin America. By 1975, there were over 290 universities and altogether more than 1,000 institutions of higher learning, including teacher colleges, technical institutes, and junior colleges.[24]

Latin America is unique among developing regions. Although many Latin American countries still do not offer a basic education to many of their citizens, enrollment ratios at the higher education levels are comparable to that of many developed or industrialized countries.[25] High illiteracy rates (25 percent in the 1960s, and 15 percent-plus in the 1970s) coexist with a university-going population proportionally larger in some cases than that of European countries. For example, in 1975 Ecuador and Venezuela respectively had 22.4 percent and 19 percent of their relevant age group enrolled in some form of

higher education as compared with 19 percent in England, 17.5 percent in Greece, 12.2 percent in Czechoslovakia, and 11.7 percent in Hungary.

Among the factors behind the growth of higher education, especially in the private sector, are overall population growth and the increasing numbers of students at the lower levels. More students, with their parents' encouragement, are demanding access to higher education, which is widely viewed as the gateway to the modern sector of the economy, to more prestigious and higher-paying jobs. Coupled with this social demand for education are government perceptions that economic development will require human resource development, especially of high-level professionals and skilled technicians. Today, although 80 to 90 percent of university students still come from the middle and upper classes, increasing numbers of "popular sector" or lower-middle and working-class youths are gaining access to higher education institutions — notably the public universities.[26]

Many believe that the rapid expansion of higher education has led to a deterioration of quality and a devaluation of educational credentials. Such fears, together with ongoing upheaval and student political activism in public institutions, have led to a movement of elites to private institutions. Thus, there has emerged a stratified system in which students from non-elite backgrounds attend two- or four-year public institutions and colleges and a variety of nontraditional "open universities" or "universities without walls" (which use radio and television transmissions and correspondence materials), while those from elite backgrounds attend more prestigious institutions that are often private or, if public, organized along the lines of private universities (e.g., Simón Bolívar in Venezuela).

There are, of course, differences in public-private higher-education patterns from country to country. Brazil, for example, has seen a rapid expansion of private higher education institutions that are generally of lower quality than their public counterparts.[27] These institutions absorb students who have failed to pass rather rigorous public university entrance examinations, and/or do not have the time to study on a demanding, full-time basis.

Public-private differences also emerge with regard to field of study. Most medical students are enrolled in public institutions because the cost of facilities adequate to prepare physicians is very high and usually must be borne by the state. On the other hand, fields requiring minimal expenditure, such as the social sciences, are disproportionately represented in private institutions. Increasingly the study of economics, business, and administration takes place in the private sector. Engineering tends to be equally divided, more or less, between public and private universities.

The above discussion is pertinent to changing enrollment patterns, by discipline, over the past two decades. Around 1960 the most commonly studied fields were, in order of importance: (1) medicine, (2) law, (3) social sciences, and (4) engineering. Around 1975 the order had changed to (1) social sciences, (2) medicine, (3) education, and (4) humanities.[28] (It is noteworthy that although the largest number of students were enrolled in social sciences, the dropout rate here was also higher than in the more selective field of medicine. Thus, in terms of number of students graduating, medicine still ranked first.)

The enrollment patterns by field of study bear little relation to the so-called human resource needs of Latin American countries. Despite the agricultural basis of many Latin American economies, often fewer than 5 percent of students are enrolled in courses in agricultural sciences. Cuba, with university admissions quotas geared to national economic plans, is a possible exception, but even there, enrollments in agriculture, forestry, and fishery studies in 1982 comprised less than 10 percent of total enrollments (15,189 out of 173,403 students).[29]

One consequence of these enrollment patterns is that graduates in overpopulated fields such as the social sciences and law have great difficulty finding employment. On the other hand, graduates in highly specialized scientific fields may also be unemployed because the national economies — whether because of their dependent or distorted nature — are not geared to employing professionals in newer fields.[30] Only graduates from the most prestigious institutions and fields — and in many cases with the traditional advantage of family connections — may be able to find employment to suit their expectations. One familiar outcome of these frustrated expectations is the "brain drain" of high-level talent to the metropolitan centers of North America and Europe. Between 1961 and 1966, for example, over 19,000 professional, technical, and kindred workers entered the United States from Latin America with immigrant visas.[31]

In our discussion of higher education expansion, fields of study, and social change, it is critical to note the gains made by women over the past two to three decades — as well as the way discrimination against them persists. One factor accounting for the increased level of enrollment in higher education is the greater number of women now attending postsecondary institutions. Women constituted about 40 percent of the increased enrollments in higher education during the period 1960–1980. Prior to 1960, women had made up around 20 percent of the total university enrollment. By 1980 women constituted 40 percent or more of the higher education enrollment in Brazil, Costa Rica, the Dominican Republic, Chile, Paraguay, Uruguay, and Venezuela—and over 50 percent in Argentina and Panama.[32]

These statistics, however, may present an overly optimistic picture. Women are channeled toward careers that conform to the social image of their roles in society. Typically, women tend to be concentrated in education, the humanities, fine and applied arts, social and behavioral sciences, and medical and health-related fields.[33] By contrast, women represent 14 percent or less of the enrollment in engineering. (While women are underrepresented in such fields, these figures resemble those for female participation rates in more industrialized countries.) Moreover, a greater percentage of women are found in nondegree programs and institutions.

To understand Latin American higher education fully, it is essential to note the role of university students as political actors. Latin America has an old and continuous tradition of student political activism, going back at least to 1918 in Córdoba, Argentina. In that year and place, students initiated a major protest movement that was to stimulate student activism throughout Latin America. Students have championed not only academic reform but also social change. The university reforms they have advocated and on occasion won include the following: student participation (along with faculty and alumni) in the governance of universities; a student voice in the selection and evaluation of faculty; academic freedom; university autonomy (i.e., self-regulation and freedom from government interference); tuition-free higher education; elimination of entrance examinations and attendance requirements; greater facilities for workers to attend college; and a curriculum more relevant to national issues. In the political realm, students have consistently opposed dictatorships and fought for national independence, economic development, and social justice. In effect, universities, for most of the twentieth century, have been one of the testing grounds for political leaders and ideologies.[34]

■ Change and Reform

Educational systems in Latin America continue to share many features in common with the systems established in the past century to complement new national political and economic programs.[35] They remain linked to the worldview, the values, and the ideals of elites of that century. The objectives of the educational systems have not changed substantially, although there have been newer influences on them (coming mostly from the United States). Previously, the colonial nations of Spain, England, and France had great influence on education in the region.

Despite the tremendous ferment of the nationalist period in the past century and the continuous upheavals plaguing the region then and now, the position of Latin America in the world economy and the basic geographical, class, and race cleavages of these societies have not changed fundamentally. Therefore it should not be surprising that the educational system still does not serve more egalitarian goals. After all, neither the economic nor political structures of the region have manifested significant democratization.

In Latin America, as in other regions of the world where some democratization of social structures has occurred, educational systems seem to be the most reluctant to reform themselves. Instead they have expanded their enrollment and suffered a deterioration of their traditional standards—thereby causing new kinds of stresses between the educational and other sectors of society.

A uniquely Latin American phenomenon is that in education change is wont to be called "reform." As described earlier, one of the first major reforms in Latin America in this century was the Córdoba Declaration of 1918. Besides the politicization of higher education stemming from this student protest movement, there were two other significant changes in higher education, both occurring in the post–World War II period.

The first change was a broadening of the higher education framework to include a host of new institutions. Technical and agricultural, engineering, and teacher-training institutes have come to be accorded the status and support usually reserved for universities. Moreover, the United States idea of junior colleges, community colleges, and regional campuses of existing universities has been adopted. Recently added to these new institutional forms of higher education have been "universities without walls," based on the British Open University. This model uses a combination of correspondence materials, radio and television broadcasts, and intensive tutorial sessions at selected sites to extend higher education programs to isolated areas.

A second major reform involves the establishment of centralized campuses for university activities—a clear move away from the European concept of university life toward the United States version. Traditionally, the Latin American university was a confederation of separate faculties or schools dispersed throughout a capital city. Each "faculty" offered a full range of both preprofessional general studies and professional courses; courses were one year in duration; and students' grades were largely determined by final examinations. These changes, which are financed to a great extent by technical assistance agencies external to the region, include these features: full-time student bodies and full-time faculty; university cities with a central campus and main library; general studies courses offered across departments; integration of teaching and research activities within the same departments and institutes; a more flexible curriculum with semesters, credits, electives, and periodic evaluations of achievement; and the upgrading of faculty through graduate studies, either at home or abroad.

While these changes might appear to be progressive, the more militant Latin American students and faculty have resisted some of them, which they claim represent the imposition of foreign models. They further claim that many of the reforms (such as full-time study and more frequent evaluation) are designed to curb student political activity.

Curriculum changes have also occurred at the secondary education level—again along lines similar to North American schools and paralleling some of the efforts to introduce general studies into institutions of higher education. As discussed earlier, these changes can best be described as moving toward comprehensive educational reforms. In the new comprehensive high schools students take a core curriculum as well as pursue specific interests

related either to higher studies or entry into the work force.

The case of Brazil illustrates such reforms and their limitations. The 1972 Brazilian educational reform known as Law 5692/72 stipulates that the secondary education (grades nine through eleven or twelve) curriculum must be complemented with work-oriented training. This law attempts to harmonize the previously irreconcilable goals of preparing students both for further schooling and entry into the labor market. The reform envisions that students willing and able to do so will, as before, continue on to universities and that the masses of students for whom secondary school will terminate formal education will be ready to seek employment. However, the work-oriented training has been unpopular with much of its clientele; it is also considered inconvenient, expensive, and—at least initially—beyond the reach of most schools. In order to meet legal requirements, many schools have changed the names of classes they offer, making it seem as though they are "professionalizing"; but they have not modified content at all. For example, chemistry classes became "fundamentals of laboratory techniques" and mathematics became "applied calculus," but students in these classes continue to do what they always have: prepare for university entrance examinations, even when they know that their chances of passing them are very slim because of the large number of students applying and the few available places in entering classes.[36]

Another tendency of change over the past thirty years consists of efforts to decentralize school administration. Most Latin American countries cling tenaciously to highly centralized educational systems dominated by government ministries. Outside influences, mostly from the United States, accompanied by the promise of training for administrators and supervisors and funds for development by agencies such as USAID have pushed some countries into greater local administration—but the United States pattern of local financing and accountability has not been adopted. Case studies indicate that attempts to decentralize decision making within general guidelines and standards set by national authorities frequently fall prey to local and regional politics that override educational considerations.[37] In those countries where political parties alternate in power, changes in government frequently lead to dismantling of previous efforts at reform. Overall, decentralization confronts an overwhelming legacy of concentration of authority and resources in metropolitan centers, particularly capital cities.

The major educational trends in Latin America include development of alternative delivery systems. One of these involves industry-based pre-service and in-service training. Innovative arrangements have emerged for financing such programs. They usually involve a 1 to 2 percent payroll tax on all firms over a certain size and capitalization. Funds are returned in accordance with the number of employees or apprentices involved. Firms that undertake extensive and innovative programs receive government bonuses. Among the well-known organizations that have been looked to as models for other developing countries are SENAI in Brazil, INCE in Venezuela, and SENA in Colombia.[38] The educational programs of these organizations tend to complement rather than undercut existing technical education programs offered by the formal school system, as they may provide apprenticeship programs for school dropouts or extend and upgrade the knowledge and skills of school graduates.

Instructional technologies constitute another system of delivery. For the past three decades, Latin America has been in the forefront of experimentation with correspondence, radio, and television schemes to extend education to rural regions as well as to urban slums, where more conventional education programs are unlikely to succeed. In a number of countries (for example, Colombia, Peru, Brazil, Bolivia, Ecuador, and Mexico) there have been significant attempts to substitute television and radio courses for formal education at the primary level and in a few

instances (Colombia and Peru) for earning secondary-level certificates. In El Salvador, educational television during the late 1960s and early 1970s was an integral part of an overall reform of grades seven to nine, and eventually the entire education system. The television component of the reform, by the late 1970s, was downgraded because of teacher opposition and lack of economic support. But the more liberal content and pedagogy of the reform, in combination with the heightened political activity of teachers, is considered by some observers to have contributed to raising the political consciousness of a substantial number of students.[39] The arena of greatest creativity in the use of instructional technologies seems to be that of adult literacy. Throughout the region far-reaching programs utilizing television, radio, cassettes, and even daily and weekly newspapers are reaching "marginal" populations in inaccessible rural areas.

The repeated failure of traditional literacy campaigns has given credence to the radical pedagogy advocated by Brazilian educator Paulo Freire, who describes the adult literacy process as cultural action for freedom.[40] At the center of Freire's pedagogy are *círculos de cultura*. These círculos are predicated upon dialogue between teachers (as facilitators) and illiterate adults. The interchange builds on the broad experience and rich variety of expression characteristic of adult learners to develop teaching materials appropriate for each community, focusing on its most pressing social problems. The pedagogy seeks to awaken *(concientizar)* learners' awareness and understanding of their historical situation while providing them with the tools to participate in the creation of culture and the transformation of their social conditions. Literacy is acquired in the process of "naming the world" and participating in efforts to change it. To date, Freire's pedagogy has been tried out on a national scale in only two Latin American countries — Chile during the Popular Unity Front of Salvador Allende (1970–73), and Nicaragua following the 1979 Sandinista triumph. The 1961 Cuban literacy campaign also shared many similarities with the philosophy and pedagogy of Freire.

In addition to campaigns for literacy and adult basic education, community-based education programs address specific learning needs of youths and adults outside the framework of formal schooling. Such programs, encompassed by the rubric "nonformal education," are voluntary and usually of short duration; they involve a variety of instructional personnel and may or may not confer a certificate.[41] Such activities are common in the private sector, operating under the auspices of church groups, peasant and trade union organizations, youth associations, and cooperative movements.[42] More recently there have been efforts by national governments and their educational agencies to assume a greater role in the planning, coordination, and regulation of nonformal education and to bring it in line with the formal education system.

Many nonformal education programs develop new levels of awareness among adult learners and lead them to demand a greater share of national goods and services, but such programs have serious limitations as agents of social change. Most are highly localized. The acquisition of new knowledge or changes in behavior will result in few improvements in people's lives without support from outside institutions and services. For example, it is well known that knowledge of new crop techniques is of little value without access to adequate land and water, the credit to buy seeds and fertilizers, or the opportunity to sell goods at fair prices. The attainment of literacy or a general education will not lead to jobs with adequate pay and benefits if government policies do not favor job creation for a large number of those concerned.

For these reasons some of the most impressive gains — particularly in extending literacy and basic education — have been made by countries that have experienced political and social revolution. Cuba and Nicaragua are two significant instances.

Since 1959 Cuba has been experimenting with its schools and with a variety of nonformal educational institutions. Cuban authorities view education as a critical agency for the development of a new socialist conscience and the creation of a political culture based on principles of "equality and development, dignity of work, and mutual respect."[43] Other key roles for education are the teaching of basic skills and the development of high-level human resources to strengthen and diversify the economy.

Among the new formulations developed by the revolutionary government are "schools in the countryside." These junior high schools (grades seven to nine) are among the most innovative educational institutions to emerge in Latin America or any developing area. Students receive a well-rounded education that not only combines academic study with some two-and-one-half hours of fieldwork per day, but includes a full range of cultural, recreational, and extracurricular activities as well. In a poor country whose economy is based on agricultural exports, the government is attempting to extend quality secondary education to virtually all rural inhabitants. The income derived from the agricultural plots of the "schools in the countryside" is in many cases more than sufficient to cover their annual operating costs.[44]

The establishment of a network of elite polytechnic high schools thoughout the island, based on the Lenin Institute in Havana, is also noteworthy, for three reasons in particular: (1) they attract the most academically talented students; (2) they emphasize the value of skilled manual labor (students engage in some form of productive work on a daily basis); and (3) in some of the institutions, a majority of the rigorously screened entering students are females. At the university level the emphasis is on the study of education and on scientific, engineering, and agricultural fields. The results of this emphasis are reflected in the following comment by a recent visitor: "Cuba's leap into twentieth-century science and engineering in only one generation has hurtled this island in most fields far beyond its Latin American neighbours."[45]

Nicaragua, while still in the initial stages of revolutionary development, is notable for its "crusade" against illiteracy—modeled in part on the 1961 Cuban campaign that reduced illiteracy from 23.6 percent to 3.9 percent. But the Nicaraguan case is perhaps even more dramatic. Mounted in the first year of the revolutionary Sandinista regime—with the country still devastated by the civil war and its economy in ruins—the campaign succeeded in reducing the illiteracy rate from 50.3 percent of the population ten years of age and older to approximately 15 percent in just nine months. Given its scope and rapidity, and the conditions under which it was carried out, this campaign is perhaps the most impressive undertaking in the history of such efforts.[45]

The massive literacy campaigns in both Cuba and Nicaragua formed part of an overall effort by these regimes to extend citizenship benefits to the previously excluded rural populations and urban poor, to integrate countryside and city, to win the youth to their revolutions, and to overcome past educational inequities based on class, race, and gender. The Cuban and Nicaraguan successes in promoting literacy raise a critical issue for all developing countries: Can they expand education without first making fundamental changes in their socioeconomic and political structures in order to incorporate the newly educated into the nation-state?

With regard to countries like Cuba or Nicaragua it remains to be seen whether their emphasis on high-level professional and technical training and the creation of advanced schools will not introduce a new elitism to their societies. For example, many of the youths at Lenin Institute are children of professionals, party members, government functionaries, and members of the intelligentsia.

It is also questionable whether Cuba and Nicaragua will be as innovative in their formal school programs. Beyond the quantitative need

for more teachers, there is a qualitative need for teachers whose outlook, values, and classroom behavior measure up to a dramatically changing world. Educational systems, in revolutionary societies as elsewhere, are hampered by the persistence of didacticism, heavy emphasis on memorization, excessive competition for good grades, lack of opportunity for student inquiry or critical analysis of course material and, more fundamentally, by failure to study the basic premises and directions of their revolutions.[47]

■ Conclusion

The story of education in Latin America over the past four hundred years has been one of continuity amidst change. Among the persisting patterns that derive from the colonial period are these: an orientation toward foreign educational and cultural models; the centralization of educational decision making; the influence of the private sector at the higher levels of education; and the primary role of the urban centers in determining the organizational form and content of education. In general, education has helped to maintain a rigid status quo. Since colonial times, school systems have prepared and certified individuals, allocating them to different social roles based on their origins, thereby perpetuating class-based structures in Latin America.

Although much of the history of Latin American education conforms to the maxim that the more things change, the more they remain the same, there are also indications of robust experimentation and occasional success stories that countries in other developing areas of the world have attempted to emulate. Good examples are innovative adult literacy programs (based on the pedagogy of Paulo Freire and industry-based training programs such as SENAI).

Overall, the main line of educational development in the region supports the thesis that significant social change causes educational change and not vice versa. There seems to be no reason to expect that new investments in and expansion of education will by themselves make a meaningful contribution to social, economic, or political improvement. It is possible that educational change may *indirectly* contribute to societal change.

The roots of fundamental change seem to reside in the very contradictions of Latin American societies—contradictions that characterize their school systems. That is, aspirations aroused by school systems through their promise of social mobility and the frustration of these aspirations may cause enough discontent to inspire action leading to more just societies. But, in general, although struggles in the field of education may go hand in hand with struggles in the political domain, it is not likely that the education hand will do the leading. Rather, educational systems have constituted a drag on social change since they have functioned to legitimize the successful and unsuccessful in their "proper" places.

■ Notes

1. 1950 data from UNESCO/CEPAL/PNUD, *Desarrollo y Educación en América Latina: Síntesis General*, informe final 4 (Buenos Aires: Proyecto Desarrollo en América Latin y el Caribe, 1981), Table VIII-1; 1980 data from UNESCO, *1982 Statistical Yearbook* (Paris: UNESCO, 1982), Table 2–2.
2. Ibid.
3. German W. Rama and J. C. Tedesco, *Education and Development in Latin America* (Buenos Aires: United Nations/Economic Commission for Latin America, 1980), 3. The figure on the retention rate for the Bolivian school systems seems to be unusually high.
4. Ernesto Schiefelbein and Joseph C. Farrell, "Selectivity and Survival in the Schools of Chile," *Comparative Education Review* 22 (June 1978): 336–37.
5. Aldo Solari, "La Desigualdad Educacional en América Latina," *Revista Latino Americana de Estudios Educativos*, vol. 10, no. 1 (1980), pp. 14–19.
6. Robert F. Arnove, "Educational Policies of the National Front," in *Politics of Compromise: Coalition Government in Colombia*, ed. R. Elbert Berry, Ronald G. Hellman, and Mauricio Solaún (New Brunswick, N.J.: Transaction Books, 1980), 381–411.
7. Gonzalo Cataño and Elvia Caro, La Educación Rural en Boyacá: Inventario de Problemas (Tunja, Colombia: Instituto Tecnológico y Pedagógico de Colombia, 1971); cited in Arnove, "National Front," 387.
8. Robert F. Arnove, "Education and Political Participation in Rural Areas of Latin America," *Comparative Education Review* 17 (June 1973): 203.
9. On turnover, see Cataño and Caro, op. cit.
10. Arnove, "Education in Rural Areas," 204.
11. Rama and Tedesco, op. cit., 5; also see Abner Prada, *Educación para el Desarrollo Rural en América Latina* (Buenos Aires: CEPAL, c. 1978); and Jose P. Núñez, *La Escuela en Areas Rurales Modernas* (Buenos Aires: CEPAL, 1978).
12. See, for example, Norman Gall, *Peru's Schools: Words and Letters*, AUFS Report, South America, 1978, 21–38.
13. In the case of Colombia, 80 percent of all secondary schools are located in three urban areas—Bogotá, Medellín, and Cali. See Ministerio de Educación, *Educación ante el Congreso* (Bogotá: same, 1978), 335.
14. This was the case, for example, in Uruguay up to 1935; see UNESCO/CEPAL/PNUD, *Síntesis General*, VII-1.
15. Ibid., VII-2.
16. Rama and Tedesco, 20; and Francisco O. Ramírez and John Boli-Bennett, "Global Patterns of Educational Institutionalization," in *Comparative Education*, ed. Philip G. Altbach, Robert F. Arnove, and Gail P. Kelly (New York: Macmillan, 1982), 26.
17. Thomas La Belle and Robert Verhine, "Non-formal Education and Stratification," *Harvard Educational Review* 45 (May 1975): 28–42.
18. UNESCO/CEPAL/PNUD, *Síntesis General*, VII-5.
19. See, for example, Jeffrey M. Puryear, "Vocational Training and Earnings in Colombia: Does a SENA Effect Exist?" *Comparative Education Review* 23 (June 1979): 238–92; and Robert E. Verhine and Rainer H. Lehmann, "Nonformal Education and Occupational Obtainment: A Study of Job Seekers in Northeastern Brazil," *Comparative Education Review* 26 (October 1982): 374–90.
20. UNESCO/CEPAL/PNUD, *Síntesis General*, VII-26.
21. Ibid.; and Jeffrey M. Puryear, "A Cost-Benefit Analysis of the SENA Industrial Apprenticeship

Program," paper read to the Annual Meeting of the Comparative and International Education Society, 27 March 1975, San Francisco, 28; and his "Comparative Systems of Occupational Training in Colombia: The National Apprenticeship Service" (unpublished Ph.D. dissertation, University of Chicago, 1973).

22. UNESCO/CEPAL/PNUD, *Síntesis General*, VII-17, VII-15–20; and Rama and Tedesco, op. cit., 7–8.
23. On higher education trends in Latin America, see Daniel C. Levy, *Higher Education and the State in Latin America* (Chicago: University of Chicago Press, 1986).
24. Robert F. Arnove, "Latin American Universities," in *Academic American Encyclopedia*, vol. 12 (Danbury, Conn.: Arête 1980), 232.
25. Rama and Tedesco, op. cit., p. 3; and Ralph K. Irizarry, "Overeducation and Unemployment in the Third World: The Paradoxes of Dependent Industrialization," *Comparative Education Review* 24 (October 1980), p. 349.
26. UNESCO/CEPAL/PNUD. *Síntesis General*, Tables VIII-8, 9, and 10.
27. Levy, op. cit.
28. UNESCO/CEPAL/PNUD, *Síntesis General*, Tables VIII-12 and 16.
29. UNESCO, *1985 Statistical Yearbook* (Paris: UNESCO), Table III-292.
30. For further discussion, see Irizarry, "Paradoxes of Dependent Industrialization."
31. Carlos Cortés, ed., *The Latin American Brain Drain to the United States* (New York: Arno Press, 1980), p. 7.
32. UNESCO/CEPAL/PNUD, *Síntesis General*, VIII-20. In Argentina, however, the number of women in higher education declined to 43 percent in 1982; see UNESCO *1985 Statistical Yearbook*, p. 111–296.
33. UNESCO, *1982 Statistical Yearbook*, 111–12.
34. Arnove, "Latin American Universities"; and his "Students in Politics," in *Venezuela: The Democratic Experience*, ed. John D. Martz and David J. Myers (New York: Praeger, 1977), 197–214. One prominent example of university faculty and student opposition to a government has been that of El Salvador, which was closed by the military for a five-year period beginning in 1980.
35. Emilio F. Mignone, *Relación entre el Sistema Político y El Sistema Educativo en la Argentina (1853–1945),* (Buenos Aires: Facultad Latinoamericana de Ciencias Sociales, 1978), 9.

36. We are indebted to Beatriz D'Ambrosio for comments concerning the reform of secondary educaion in Brazil.
37. For example, see E. Mark Hanson, "Administrative Develoment in the Colombian Ministry of Education: A Case Analysis of the 1970s," *Comparative Education Review* 27 (February 1983): 89–107.
38. See, for example, Thomas J. La Belle, *Nonformal Education and Social Change in Latin America* (Los Angeles: UCLA Latin America Center Publication, 1976), 87–88.
39. We are indebted to Joaquin Samayoa for comments on the political impact of the Salvadoran educational reform; also see Henry Ingle, "Reconsidering the Use of Television for Educational Reform," in *Educational Television: A Policy Critique and Guide for Developing Countries*, ed. Robert F. Arnove (New York: Praeger, 1976), 114–39.
40. Paulo Freire, "The Adult Literacy Process and Cultural Action for Freedom," *Harvard Educational Review* 40 (May 1970): 205–23; and his *Pedagogy of the Oppressed*, rev. ed. (New York: Herder and Herder, 1972).
41. Thomas La Belle, "Goals and Strategies of Nonformal Education in Latin America," *Comparative Education Review* 20 (October 1976): 328-45; and Philip Coombs, *Attacking Rural Poverty* (Baltimore: Johns Hopkins University Press, 1974).
42. Sanders, op. cit., 15–17, for descriptions of private sector programs in Argentina, Chile, Paraguay, and Uruguay.
43. See Samuel Bowles, "Cuban Education and the Revolutionary Ideology," *Harvard Educational Review* 14 (November 1971): 472–500; and Richard Fagen, *The Transformation of Political Culture in Cuba* (Stanford: Stanford University Press, 1969).
44. For a cost-benefit analysis of "Schools in the Countryside," see Arthur Gillette, *Cuba's Educational Revolution* (London: Fabian Society, 1972), 31–33.
45. Robert Ubell, "Cuba's Great Leap," *Nature* (April 1983): 745.
46. Robert F. Arnove, "The Nicaraguan National Literacy Crusade of 1980," *Comparative Education Review* 24 (June 1981): 244–45; and Fernando Cardenal and Valerie Miller, "Nicaragua 1980: The Battle of the ABCs," *Harvard Educational Review* 51 (February 1981): 1–26.
47. For example, see Gillette, op. cit., 21–25.

■ **Suggested Readings**

Arnove, Robert F. *Education and Revolution in Nicaragua* (New York: Praeger, 1986).

Fagen, Richard. *The Transformation of Political Culture in Cuba*. Stanford: Stanford University Press, 1969.

Freire, Paulo. *Pedagogy of the Oppressed*. New York: Herder and Herder, 1972.

Gillette, Arthur. *Cuba's Educational Revolution*. London: Fabian Society, 1972.

Hirshom, Sheryl, and Judy Butler. *And Also Teach Them to Read*. Westport, Conn.: Lawrence Hill and Co., 1983.

Thomas J. La Belle, *Nonformal Education and the Poor in Latin America and the Caribbean: Stability, Reform or Revolution?* New York: Praeger, 1986.

————. *Nonformal Education and Social Change in Latin America*. Los Angeles: UCLA Latin American Center, 1976.

Leiner, Marvin. *Children Are the Revolution*. New York: Viking Press, 1974.

Levy, Daniel C. *University and Government in Mexico's Autonomy in an Authoritarian System*. New York: Praeger Special Studies, 1980.

Negron de Montilla, Aida. *Americanization in Puerto Rico and the Public School System, 1900–1930*. Rio Piedras, P.R.: Editorial Universitaria, 1975.

Silvert, Kalman H., and Leonard Reissman. *Education Class and Nation: The Experiences of Chile and Venezuela*. New York: Elsevier, 1976.

9 | Women in Latin America: The Impact of Socioeconomic Change

HELEN I. SAFA

The past decade has seen growing interest in the status of women in Latin America. This is shown not only by increasing research and publication on the topic, but by the growth of an articulate and vocal women's movement in several Latin American countries. The mass media now discuss women's issues, and strong, stable feminist organizations have emerged in Brazil, Chile, Colombia, Cuba, the Dominican Republic, Mexico, Peru, Uruguay, Venezuela, and elsewhere. A feminist magazine, *FEM,* is now published in Mexico and circulates throughout Latin America. The international climate has favored consideration of women's issues, starting with the UN conference on women in Mexico City in 1975, which launched the Decade on Women. Research and seminars have been supported by private and government foundations such as the UN specialized agencies, the Ford Foundation, the Inter-American Foundation, AID, and the Social Science Research Council. The Latin American Studies Association now regularly includes several panels addressed to women at its meetings, as do other professional associations in the social sciences and humanities. But what is perhaps most impressive is the number of international conferences on women held in Latin America and organized by Latin American women during the past decade, including those in Mexico in 1977, Rio de Janeiro in 1979, Costa Rica in 1981,Barbados in 1982, and Cuba in 1984. During the 1980s special *Encuentros Feministas* (Feminist Meetings) have brought together hundreds of Latin American women not only in research, but as activists involved with centers for battered women, feminist magazines, peasant organizations, and political parties.[1]

Feminism had to struggle to gain legitimacy in Latin America, where it was accused of being another form of cultural imperialism imported from the United States, and inappropriate to the region's historical and cultural context. In order to combat this charge, the first priority was to make women visible by documenting and assessing their economic, social, and political roles. Most initial studies were descriptive and focused on fertility or on labor force participation (still the most popular and fundable issues). By the end of the 1970s, however, research findings on women began to raise fundamental questions that posed a challenge to traditional social science concepts and methods. For example, studies of female labor force participation documented the failure of official statistics to reflect women's productive role accurately. This has led to greater attempts to measure women's non-wage labor as housewives and as unpaid family workers in home production and on peasant farms.

The growing concern with linking theory and practice led feminist scholars to work with other social scientists who seriously questioned the objectives of traditional research and, more particularly, the relationship between the researcher and the object of study. This concern has been taken seriously in the women's centers that arose in Latin America in the mid- and late 1970s. Feminist activities are diverse, taking in research, social action, service provision, and training. Many of these activities crosscut the class distinctions that seemed insurmountable during the early years of the women's movement. Feminists now have a much stronger commitment to the priority of women's issues, although the question of autonomy versus incorporation within political parties or larger social movements remains a topic of heated debate.[2]

This chapter takes stock of the past decade of research and action on women in Latin America in order to assess the significance of these accomplishments within a broader theoretical framework. What has been learned about Latin American women? How does it portray their changing role in Latin American society? In what way has the women's movement itself begun to change this role? These are some of the questions this chapter will address.

The focus here is on four main areas: 1) the invisibility of women's labor both in production and reproduction; 2) the impact on women of recent economic development and the growing debt crisis, including female migration, the feminization of farming, and the increased participation of women in the labor force; 3) the effect of these changes on family structure, including the increase in female-headed households; and 4) female employment in export-oriented industrialization. Clearly these issues reflect some of the broader changes occurring in Latin America during the past decade, such as the shift from a rural agrarian to an urban industrial economy, the increase in urban poverty and growth of an informal economy, and the increasing integration of Latin America into a global economy. Thus, the focus on women is a way of looking at these other issues from a new perspective.

■ The Invisibility of Women's Labor

For many researchers the key to understanding women's subordination lies in analyzing women's role in production. As long as women's work is undervalued, they can never be considered equal partners with men, who are presumed, in a modern industrial society, to be the principal breadwinners.

The struggle for recognition of women's role in production requires a redefinition of the term *work*. At its simplest level, it is often thought to apply only to wage labor. Since men constitute the great bulk of wage earners in any modern industrial society, the common definition leads to the conclusion that men have a greater role than women in production. However, equating work with wage labor reflects the bias of advanced industrial societies such as the United States, where census techniques and models have been developed. *Work* is defined in terms of production for the market, yet nonmarket production is still very prevalent in Third World countries, including Latin America. Growing food for home consumption, or making clothes or pottery for the family are examples of nonmarket activities often carried out by women.

If work is defined in terms of market production, it would have to include self-employed peasants and artisans, who still constitute a large percentage of Latin America's economically active population. Among peasants and artisans, production is centered in the home, where unpaid family members, including women and children, do the work. Yet in many Latin American countries, these unpaid family members are not counted as economically active members of the labor force. This, then, is one large area in which women's role in production is seriously underestimated.

Women also predominate in subsistence agriculture, or production for home consumption. Subsistence agriculture has until recently been totally neglected in census figures, resulting in a gross underestimation of women's economic contribution. Deere's survey in the Andean region found that the proportion of women participating in agricultural work was 21 percent instead of the 3 percent officially reported.[3] Such research findings have led critics to question the assumption that economic development is necessarily beneficial to all segments of the population, particularly women. Studies in Latin America demonstrate the need for a fundamental reevaluation of women's role in agriculture and the importance of women in subsistence production.[4]

Census surveys reveal a clear male bias: they automatically designate any adult male in a family as the "household head." In reality, the household head is often determined by a complex of factors, such as who contributes the most to expenses and who owns the house or land. Nevertheless, women will often maintain that a man is head of the household, even when he is not the principal breadwinner, because of ideological assumptions regarding male dominance to which they also subscribe. Even women who make major economic contributions to the family see themselves dependent on men as economic providers and spokesmen to the outside world.[5]

Women seldom regard domestic labor as "work," nor is it so regarded in census surveys,

agains because of the emphasis on market production and paid labor. However, the increasing attention given to the household economy in Latin America reveals that women's domestic labor makes a critical contribution to the reproduction and maintenance of the labor force. Women not only raise future members of the labor force, but by cooking, cleaning, doing the laundry, and other kinds of housework lessen the costs of maintaining current workers, who would otherwise have to pay for these services. By lowering labor costs, housework also makes it possible to produce more cheaply, and should, in the opinion of some feminist economists, be counted in estimating national productivity.[6] This is particularly true in Latin America and other Third World countries, where household production is more important and more intense than in industrialized, wage-labor economies. Housework is harder and takes many more hours of a woman's time because of the lack of canned or frozen products, household appliances, and even basic amenities like running water or electricity. Women try to stretch and supplement insufficient wages through home production and networks of exchange to substitute for purchased goods and services. Thus the neglect of domestic labor in defining "work" is again a bias of industrialized societies, where housework generally is less critical to the family's survival than in most low-income Latin American households.

■ The Impact of Development on Women in the Labor Force

It is often assumed that economic development automatically leads to increased female participation in the labor force. A growing number of studies question this assumption, both because women's prior role in the production process has been undervalued, as seen above, and because women have actually been forced out of work by changes such as the shift to capital-intensive industrialization and commercialization of agriculture.

Since the 1940's Latin American countries have experienced an unprecedented period of capitalist expansion in commercial agriculture. This has added, along with population growth, soil erosion, and land fragmentation, to pressure on the land. Unable to earn a living from the land, men have left to seek supplementary income elsewhere, particularly in the cities. However, because of the low wages and high unemployment in the cities, the family is often left behind, with the women caring for subsistence plots, contributing to what has been called the feminization of farming. At the same time, the commercialization of agriculture has reduced the need for cheap female wage labor by mechanizing harvesting, weeding, sorting, and other menial tasks. Both men and women have lost jobs in agricultural wage labor, but women have been expelled at a faster rate. Except for some of the new areas of agribusiness, where women are employed in processing plants, it is increasingly difficult for them to find wage labor in the rural area.

Lack of rural employment and scarcity of land has led to increasing female migration to urban areas. The rate of such migration in Latin America is higher than in any other Third World area. It is estimated that some 3.8 million rural women migrated to Latin American cities between 1960 and 1970.[7] While some women migrate to join their families in the city, increasing numbers migrate on their own to find jobs there. These women are often female heads of households seeking to support their families, or daughters sent by their families to earn supplementary income.

Most of the young migrant women find work as domestic servants. Approximately one fifth of the female labor force in Latin America is employed in this way, even in the more industrialized countries such as Chile and Mexico. While some researchers have regarded domestic service as an avenue of upward mobility for Latin American women, others have argued that domestic servants generally end up in the informal economy as petty vendors or even prostitutes. Once they have one or two children they can no longer be employed as live-in servants and are forced to seek other sources of income.[8]

Some writers maintain that women prefer work in the informal sector which includes the self-employed and other jobs that do not provide a steady wage. Informal work does allow for more flexibility, so that petty vendors, for example, can keep their children with them as they set up their wares on the street or in a market stall. Day-care facilities are almost nonexistent, and many migrant women lack the family support network they could have turned to in the rural area.

A more important factor, however, is that migrant women seldom find jobs in formal wage labor, particularly if they have only recently come to the city, are married, and/or have dependent children. Preference in factory employment is given to young single women who are either urban-born or -bred and have completed at least a primary education.[9] Thus most migrant women and the less educated urban women are relegated to the informal sector. Ironically, married women are often put at a disadvantage by the rather liberal maternity benefits to which permanently employed women in some Latin American countries are entitled, and with which employers would rather not be encumbered, even when they are paid by the state (as in the case of Brazil). Moreover, employers perceive married women as more prone to absenteeism. And, indeed, if a child is ill or has to go to the doctor, it is almost invariably the mother who is expected to assume the responsibility.

The use of capital-intensive technology, which reduces the need for labor, also accounts for the relatively low number of women in industrial employment. Both men and women are displaced, but women are more affected because of their concentration in such traditional labor-intensive industries as textiles and food processing, both of which have undergone rapid technical change. In the textile industry, for example, there has been a switch from female to male production workers, who appear more suited to working with the complex machinery associated with mechanized plants, particularly in synthetics. The switch to capital-intensive industrialization took place all the more rapidly in Latin America because much of the industry was foreign owned and able to import the more advanced technology already developed abroad. Labor-intensive industries such as textiles also declined because of competition with foreign imports such as synthetics.

As a result of the causes just described, until the 1970s the percentage of all women employed in industrial jobs generally declined, or at best remained stable. For example, Brazil experienced a very rapid growth of industry during the 1960s, but the proportion of all women employed in this sector remained at 10 percent in 1970, no higher than 1950, whereas the percentage of all men employed in industry during the same period doubled, from 10 percent to 20 percent. In Argentina the percentage of women in industrial jobs declined from 31.9 percent in 1950 to 21 percent in 1970, while in the service sector it increased from 55.8 percent to 74.8 percent during that same period.[10]

In the 1960s, the growth of female labor force participation was concentrated among young, single women, primarily in white-collar jobs. Yet who are the white-collar workers employed as secretaries, saleswomen, teachers, or social workers? Are they women who have moved up from domestic service or factory jobs? Apparently not. Most of them appear to be middle- and upper-class women who moved into the labor force for the first time as jobs commensurate with their status opened up. Most of these jobs require a secondary or higher education, access to which is still largely limited to non–working-class women despite considerable educational expansion after World War II. [Editor's note: See chapter 8, "Latin American Education."] The relationship between jobs and educational attainment is illustrated by Brazil, where in 1970 female domestic and industrial workers generally had an average of less than

four years of education, whereas workers in intermediary white-collar occupations had an average of four to eight years of schooling.[11]

In the 1970's adequate employment became more difficult than ever to secure because of the acute economic crisis now plaguing most Latin American countries. The crisis was brought on by rising oil prices, unfavorable terms of trade, and a growing foreign debt and public-sector deficit. It is characterized by high rates of inflation, which increased consumer prices by 50 percent to 60 percent or higher, and by a decline in real wages and employment, resulting in general economic stagnation. For example, between 1973 and 1981 wages in the industrial sector in Argentina fell by around 21 percent, while in Chile they contracted by over 41 percent.[12]

Economic crisis hit working-class families especially hard. Faced with rising prices and falling wages, more women joined the labor force to provide much needed additional income for their families. In Brazil, for example, the economically active female population almost doubled from 1970 to 1980, a much faster rise than that for men. Female participation in industry grew even more rapidly, by 181 percent between 1970 and 1980, thus reversing the declining trend of the previous decades. According to the 1980 census, the percentage of all economically active women employed in Brazilian industry rose to 18.6 percent. The reasons for this dramatic increase appear to be due both to the increased supply of female labor (for the reasons noted above) and to increased demand in new industrial sectors such as electrical machinery and metalworking.[13]

The economic crisis has also forced more women into the informal sector, often in a new form of subcontracted piecework at home now known as industrial homework. In Colombia, for example, half of the women employed in labor-intensive industries such as food processing, textiles, and shoes work at home and are paid by piecework; most of them are housewives who also carry heavy family responsibilities. In Mexico City, there are large numbers of unregulated sweatshops and home production of electronics, toys, and clothes subcontracted by multinational corporations.[14] Although industrial homework may provide needed employment for these older, married women, it is also an effective way for employers to cut wages and dilute labor solidarity, particularly in a time of economic crisis. A similar restructuring and deskilling of the labor process is taking place in the United States and other advanced industrial countries, where women also constitute a cheaper source of labor for this unskilled work than men.

In most of Latin America, however, the greatest increase in female employment has been in the tertiary sector, commerce and services. In Latin America as a whole, 67 percent of women workers are in the service sector, but the majority of these are still in domestic service.[15] As in manufacturing, the informal sector has grown to include the sale of nontraditional products such as perfume, digital watches, and single cigarettes; in Brazil it is now estimated to account for 30 percent of the gross domestic product. The growth of this informal sector is attested by the increasing number of self-employed and unpaid family workers, even in relatively advanced countries like Argentina, Chile, and Uruguay. From 1975 to 1978 the percentage of self-employed workers in these countries grew at a higher rate than wage workers, and in Chile accounted for one-fifth of the female labor force.[16]

The growing importance of the informal sector in these countries is in part the result of stabilization models imposed by the International Monetary Fund, which emphasized privatization of the economy and reduction of public expenditures in areas such as health and education. These cutbacks hit working-class families particularly hard, especially since most have no recourse to unemployment insurance or other welfare schemes. Similar stabilization models have now been imposed in Mexico, Brazil, and other Latin American countries.

In short, the increasing number of women in the labor force cannot in itself be seen as a sign of progress. As mentioned earlier, women often have to seek paid employment because of the growing difficulty faced by men who seek stable work. They also have to compensate for rising prices, lower wages, and cutbacks in social services. Women take the lowest paid, most unstable jobs in the informal sector or in industrial homework, because of the decline in formal wage work and because they provide a cheaper, more docile labor force. The way this economic crisis affects family structure is discussed in the next section.

■ Female Employment and Family Structure

It is a curious paradox that in Latin America, as earlier in the United States and Western Europe, the ideology that equates higher-class status with housewives has begun to influence working-class women at the same time that its influence has begun to wane among middle-class women. Middle-class women and men previously feared that a working wife would be taken as a sign that the man was unable to provide adequately for his family and needed his wife's contribution. Although some men still feel threatened by their wives' employment, this is no longer the norm as more and more middle-class women enter the formal labor market. Attitudes have also changed because of the increased demand for consumer goods in most middle-class households. In order to afford a car (or two), color television, stereo, and various household appliances, many women have to work to keep up the installment payments. The critical difference is that these middle-class women work to support a certain life-style, whereas working-class women work for their family's survival.[17]

The two class groups also differ in their degree of household responsibility. Middle- and upper-class women generally have at least one domestic servant to help take care of the children and do the household chores. (Men still refuse to assume such responsibilities in most Latin American homes.) Thus, elite women do not face a "double day" in the same way as do working-class women, who can rely only on relatives and neighbors for assistance. In a 1977 study conducted in Colombia, 69 percent of low-income women workers continued to have domestic responsibilities compared to 47 percent of upper-income working women. One-fourth of the lower-income working women in the Colombian study had no help at all, compared to much lower percentages in the higher-income groups. This helps to explain why working-class women often regard retirement from the labor force as a sign of upward mobility and prefer staying home to keeping a menial, low-paying job. Because of the work most of them do, a job does not mean self-development or even added autonomy: Their wages go largely to support their families, not to their own self-advancement or personal needs.[18]

The struggle to survive is particularly difficult for female-headed households. These are increasing rapidly in Latin America because of many of the socioeconomic changes noted above, like migration, urbanization, and the growing economic crisis. Census data for thirteen Latin American countries reveal that the proportion of female-headed households is 60 percent higher in urban than in rural areas.[19] As mentioned earlier, some female-headed households may migrate to the cities in search of employment; others may form subsequently through separation, divorce, or abandonment. Working-class women in the city often cannot bring community or family pressures to bear on men to remain with or support their families. Women may also prefer to be rid of a man who does not support them and/or is abusive.

Many studies have tried to determine the socioeconomic reasons behind the formation of female-headed households, particularly in the Caribbean, where this has been the predominant form of family structure since slavery and the colonial period. Historical and cultural explanations have now been largely abandoned in favor of socioeconomic factors such as migration, poverty, and unemployment. Studies in the Caribbean have shown a negative correlation between per capita income and the proportion

of households headed by women. High levels of unemployment make it impossible for many men to act as economic providers, so they often abandon their families and leave women with this burden.[20] The decline in male employment and increased percentage of women working as a result of the economic crisis is likely to aggravate this problem.

Female heads of households are at a great disadvantage in the labor market. They have low educational levels and heavy family responsibilities, which often restrict them to jobs in the informal economy. One study in Belo Horizonte, Brazil, found that 53 percent of the female heads of households had jobs in the informal sector compared to 12 percent of the male heads.[21] As a result, women heads of families generally fall into the lowest income categories, even though they have higher labor force participation rates than women in general. They also rely heavily on their children for economic support once the latter are old enough to work. Female-headed households, like poor families generally, survive through multiple wage-earning strategies in which all adult members of the household seek income in the formal or informal economy.

The increasing percentage of female-headed households clearly shows that development has not been beneficial to all women in Latin America. On the contrary, poverty and inequality appear to be greater than before, despite rapid growth of the middle class. White-collar workers in this middle class seem to be the only ones to have really benefited from the vast socioeconomic changes of the postwar period, and even they suffer because of increasing inflation and unemployment. The economic crisis of the past decade has led to a search for new development models appropriate to Latin America. These models concern women in a very real way.

■ Women and Export-oriented Industrialization

Those who criticize Latin American development, particularly from a dependency perspective, argue that most of the socioeconomic problems of women, especially of poor women, stem ultimately from development policies that have made Latin America dependent on trade with the United States and other advanced industrial countries. Despite efforts to foster domestic industries that can diminish reliance on foreign goods ("import substitution"), continued subservience to imported capital and technology has resulted in a new form of dependent capitalism, one mediated through multinational corporations.

Some Latin American countries have now entered a new stage in the industrialization process. They are becoming producers of manufactured goods, not only for their own domestic markets, but for export as well. In order to compete in an international market, the primary criterion is to keep production costs as low as possible. In the case of these labor-intensive industries, low costs translate into utilization of largely female labor. Women are estimated to number 80 to 90 percent of the workers in export-processing, as this kind of manufacture is called. This is partly due to the predominance of the garment and electronics industries, which have traditionally employed mainly women. Management often explains its preference for female labor by reverting to sex stereotypes that depict women as having more nimble fingers and visual acuity — and greater patience for tedious jobs than men. A more adequate explanation, however, appears to lie in the higher profits that can be extracted from female labor because of lower wages. In 1978 minimum wages in industry ran as low as 23 cents per hour in Haiti, 45 cents in Jamaica, 50 cents in the Dominican Republic, and 71 cents in Mexico, which is by far the largest single source of imports to the United States. Under special tariff items certain assembled goods enter the United States almost duty-free.

Export-oriented industrialization has become the new development model for several Latin American and Caribbean countries and is promoted by international agencies such as UNIDO (United Nations Industrial Development Organization). In addition, the trade provisions of the Caribbean Basin Initiative set forth by President Reagan would turn virtually the entire Caribbean into a free-trade zone, eliminating tariff barriers for many manufactured and agricultural products over a twelve-year period. In Haiti alone export processing has grown in value from $3 million in 1970 to $8 million in 1980; it represented 16.7 percent of the gross domestic product in the latter year. Nevertheless, annual per capita income in Haiti in 1981 was still only $297, the lowest in Latin America.

In order to examine the advantages and disadvantages of export-oriented industrialization for women in Latin America and other Third World areas, it is necessary to look at who is employed, what kinds of jobs are created, and where they are created. Most of the women workers are young and have not worked very long. These industries are often located in areas of high unemployment, for both men and women. For example, the Border Industrialization Program in Mexico was instituted to replace the employment formerly provided by the *bracero* program, through which male agricultural workers had been employed on temporary contracts in the United States. Yet, whereas the *bracero* program had almost exclusively employed men, the Border Industrialization Program employs primarily women. The unemployed men, meanwhile, continue to migrate to the United States, often as undocumented workers.[22]

As we have seen, however, employment per se does not necessarily increase women's status and authority; the kind of work they have and what they earn are what count. Jobs in export-processing industries are very often low paying and have relatively low status. Moreover, since the firms do not have a heavy investment in capital plants, they are able to relocate quite easily so that jobs are often not secure. Puerto Rico, for instance, has lost much of its garment industry because of wage increases and the lure of cheaper wages elsewhere. In addition, firms may offer women only temporary contracts, so that they have no claim to fringe benefits, such as severance pay and maternity benefits, that permanent employees receive.

Many factors limit worker solidarity in these industries—low wages, high turnover, the recency and youth of this new industrial labor force, and state control.

The preceding discussion suggests that employment in export processing is not leading to a marked improvement in women's status. True, the job provides a working-class woman with a certain amount of income and economic autonomy, but the possibilities for upward mobility are quite limited given the high turnover, low wages, and unskilled nature of factory employment. Women are a source of cheap labor for the expanding global economy.

■ Conclusion

In assessing the impact of socioeconomic change on women in Latin America, it is important to differentiate between their objective and subjective condition. In many objective respects, women seem to be worse off than they were a decade or so ago. Many have lost access to land as a result of the exodus of the peasantry, and those who remain in rural areas often have to cope for themselves and their children on small subsistence plots while their menfolk work in the city. The percentage of domestics has not declined as a consequence of economic development, largely because the growth of jobs in the formal labor market for women has not kept up with heavy rural-urban migration. As a result of migration, deepening poverty, and unemployment, the percentage of female-headed households in Latin America has increased substantially, particularly in urban areas. Despite a significant rise in female employment, many of these women work in the informal sector, which has grown rapidly because of the persistent economic crisis; white-collar jobs have gone mostly to educated middle- and upper-class women.

There is an increasing number of female industrial workers as a result of the move toward export processing in several Latin American and Caribbean countries, but these jobs also are poorly paid and highly unstable.

Though the socioeconomic level of most Latin American women may have declined in the past decade, their awareness of these problems and their willingness and ability to confront them appears to have increased substantially. This is largely a result of the women's movement and of the expanded research on women in Latin America carried out during the past few years. Women's centers, conferences, training and action programs, and publications have greatly increased the visibility of women's issues and have begun to bridge the gap between elite and working-class women, which is larger in Latin America than in the United States. Feminist organizations have begun to form their own political power base and to penetrate mainstream institutions like the universities and political parties. However, women's organizations feel a need for greater coordination among themselves to achieve common goals.[23]

Authoritarian political regimes and the recessive economic policies demanded by the IMF have worsened the plight of women, who have been adversely affected by the reduction of state investment in social services, increasing unemployment, lower real wages, and inflation. In response to the economic crisis and other problems, women have banded together to obtain such necessities as schools, drinking water, housing, and medical care. Among the best-known women's movements is one in São Paulo, where neighborhood women organized collectively to protest the high cost of living and formed consumer cooperatives. In many ways, women's collective action, particularly among the poor, holds the key to improving their status. It is clear that the state, political parties, unions, or international agencies will not act on their behalf unless women constitute a political force exerting pressure on them to meet specific demands. Women should be conscious of their own needs and abilities and not have these defined for them by outside agencies. This is true in socialist countries like Cuba or Nicaragua, where women's organizations such as the Federation of Cuban Women, are still largely an instrument of government policy.

Women are beginning to challenge the status quo in Latin America. They are organizing collectively, articulating their demands, and designing their own action programs. They are rejecting subordination while maintaining great pride in their roles as wives and mothers. Their primary identification as wives and mothers is one reason women can be mobilized in defense of family and neighborhood interest such as urban services, the cost of living, or even against state repression. A dramatic example of such female political action is to be seen in the Argentine Mothers of the Plaza de Mayo, who for years protested the "disappearance" of their loved ones at the instigation of the ruling military junta. Women may start with immediate, local issues, but as they grow more confident in their capacity to articulate and pursue their demands, they could represent a real threat to the existing system of class and gender inequality in Latin America.

■ Notes

1. Marysa Navarro, "First Feminist Meeting of Latin America and the Caribbean," *Signs: Journal of Women in Culture and Society* 8,1 (1982): 154–57.

2. Marianne Schmink and Carmen Barroso, "Women's Programs for the Andean Region and the Southern Cone: Assessment and Recommendations." Report submitted to the Ford Foundation, 1984. For example, some of the more well-known research institutions on women in Latin America include: Asociación Colombiana de Estudios y Población (ACEP), Colombia; Asociación Mexicana de Estudios de Mujer y Sociedad (AMEMS), México; Centro de Investigaciones para Acción Femenina (CIPAF), Dominican Republic; Centro Flora Tristán, Perú; Federación de Mujeres Cubanas (FMC), Cuba; Fundação Carlos Chagas, Brazil; Círculo de la Mujer, Chile; Grupo

de Estudios sobre la Condición de la Mujer en el Uruguay, Uruguay.

3. Carmen Diana Deere, "Changing Social Relations of Production and Peruvian Peasant Women's Work," *Latin American Perspectives* nos. 12, 13 (1977): 48–69.

4. For example, Magdalena Leon de Leal, C. D. Deere, et al., *Mujer y Capitalismo Agrario* (Bogotá: Asociación Colombiana para el Estudio de la Población, 1980); Magdalena Leon, ed., *Debate sobre la Mujer en América Latina y el Caribe*, vols. 1, 2, and 3 (Bogotá: Asociación Colombiana para el Estudio de la Población, 1982); and Catalina H. Wainerman and Zulma Recchini de Lattes *El Trabajo Femenino en el Banquillo de los Acusados* (Mexico: The Population Council and Editorial Terra Nova, S.A., 1981).

5. Helen I. Safa, "Class Consciousness among Working Class Women in Latin America: Puerto Rico," in *Sex and Class in Latin America*, ed. June Nash and Helen Safa (New York: Praeger, 1976).

6. Lourdes Beneria, "Accounting for Women's Work" in *Women and Development: the Sexual Division of Labor in Rural Societies*, ed. L. Beneria (New York: Praeger, 1982), 119–48.

7. Lourdes Arizpe, "Women and Development in Latin America and the Caribbean: Lessons from the Seventies and Hopes for the Future," in *Another Development with Women*, Development Dialogue 1–2 (Uppsala, Sweden: Dag Hammarskjold Foundation, 1982), 79.

8. For a description of domestic servants and other informal sector workers see Gloria Gonzales Salazar, "Participation of Women in the Mexican Labor Force," in Nash and Safa, op. cit., 187. Ximena Bunster and Elsa Chaney, *Sellers and Servants: Working Women in Lima, Peru.* (New York: Praeger, 1985). CEPAL. *Cinco Estudios sobre la mujer en América Latina.* (Santiago, Chile, 1982).

9. Helen I. Safa, "Women, Production and Reproduction in Industrial Capitalism: A Comparison of Brazilian and U.S. Factory Workers," in *Women, Men and the International Division of Labor*, ed. June Nash and M. P. Fernandez-Kelly (Albany: State University of New York Press, 1983).

10. For discussions of changes in manufacturing and its effect on women see: Eva Alterman Blay, *Trabalho Domesticado: A Mulher Na Industria Paulista* (São Paulo: Editora Atica, 1978), 144–46; David Chaplin, *The Peruvian Industrial Labor Force* (Princeton: Princeton University Press, 1967);

Glaura Vasques de Miranda, "Women's Labor Force Participation in a Developing Society: The Case of Brazil," *Signs: Journal of Women in Culture and Society* 3,1 (1977): 261–74; Arizpe, op.cit., 79.

11. For data on women white collar workers and their relationship to education, see: Economic Commission on Latin America (ECLA), "Participation of Women in Development in Latin America," UN, World Conference of the International Women's Year. E. Conference 66/BP/8 Add.1 (1975); Helen I. Safa, "The Changing Class Composition of the Female Labor Force in Latin America," *Latin American Perspectives* 9, 4 (1977): 126–31; Miranda, op. cit, 19.

12. Victor E. Tokman, "Wages and Employment in International Recessions: Recent Latin American Experience," Working Paper no. 11 (The Kellogg Institute for International Studies, University of Notre Dame, 1984), 16.

13. John Humphrey, "Trabalho Feminino na Grande Industria Paulista." *Cadernos CEDEC* no. 3. São Paulo.

14. For an analysis of industrial homework, see Nohra Rey de Marulanda, "La Unidad Producción-Reproducción en Mujeres del Sector Urbano en Colombia," in *La Realidad Colombiana. Debate sobre la mujer en América Latina*, vol. 1. ed. Magdalena Leon de Leal (Bogotá: Asociación Colombiana para el Estudio de la Población, 1982). See also Lourdes Beneria and Martha Roldan. *The Crossroads of Class and Gender: Industrial Homework, Subcontracting and Household Dynamics in Mexico City.* (Chicago: University of Chicago Press, 1986).

15. Lourdes Arizpe, op. cit., 79.

16. Suzana Prates, *Women's Labour and Family Survival Strategies under the "Stabilization Models" in Latin America.* (Vienna: Centre for Social Development and Humanitarian Affairs, 1981).

17. Marianne Schmink. "Women in the Urban Economy in Latin America," in June Nash and Helen Safa, eds. *Women and Change in Latin America* (South Hadley, Mass.: Bergin and Garvey Publishers, 1986).

18. Rey de Marulanda, op. cit., 65; Helen I. Safa, "Female Employment in the Puerto Rican Working Class," in Nash and Safa, eds., op. cit.

19. International Center for Research on Women (ICRW), *Women Headed Households: The Ignored Factor in Development Planning,* Report submitted to AID/WIS by M. Buvinic, N. Youssef with B. Voh Elm. (Washington, D.C.: 1978), 80.

20. For a discussion of the reasons behind the formation of female-headed households see: Joycelin Massiah, *Women as Heads of Households in the Caribbean: Family Structure and Feminine Status,* (Paris: UNESCO, 1983); ICRW, op. cit. 81; Safa, *The Urban Poor of Puerto Rico: A Study in Development and Inequality* (New York: Holt, Rinehart and Winston, 1974).

21. Thomas W. Merrick and Marianne Schmink, "Households Headed by Women and Urban Poverty in Brazil," in *Women and Poverty in the Third World,* ed. M. Buvinic, M. A. Lycette, and W. P. McGreevey (Baltimore: The Johns Hopkins University Press, 1983).

22. For a discussion of the impact of export-oriented industrialization on women, see: Helen I. Safa, "Runaway Shops and Female Employment: The Search for Cheap Labor," *Signs: Journal of Women in Society and Culture.* 7,2 (1981): 418–33; Maria Patricia Fernandez-Kelly, *For We Are Sold, I and My People: Women and Industry in Mexico's Frontier* (Albany: State University of New York Press, 1983), 55; A. Lynn Bolles, "Kitchens Hit by Priorities: Employed Working Class Jamaican Women Confront the IMF," in Nash and Fernandez-Kelly, op. cit.

23. See for example Schmink and Barroso, op. cit.

■ Suggested Readings

Beneria, Lourdes, ed. *Women and Development: The Sexual Division of Labor in Rural Societies.* New York: Praeger, 1982.

Bunster, Ximena, and Elsa Chaney. *Sellers and Servants: Working Women in Lima, Peru.* New York: Praeger, 1965.

Fernández-Kelly, Maria Patricia. *For We Are Sold, I and My People: Women and Industry in Mexico's Frontier.* Albany: State University of New York Press, 1983.

Knaster, Meri. *Women in Spanish America: An Annotated Bibliography from Pre-Conquest to Contemporary Times.* Boston: G. K. Hall, 1977.

Nash, June, and M. P. Fernández-Kelly, eds. *Women, Men and the International Division of Labor.* Albany: State University of New York Press, 1983.

Nash, June, and Helen Safa, eds. *Sex and Class in Latin America.* New York: Praeger, 1976.

Nash, June, and Helen Safa, eds. *Women and Change in Latin America.* South Hadley, Mass.: Bergin and Garvey Publishers, 1986.

10 | *Political Ideology*

JOHN D. MARTZ

At the core of Latin American political thought rest preoccupations with the individual, his place in society, and the role of the state in supervising the conduct of public affairs. This has emerged through the evolution of three basic schools of thought: monism, liberal pluralism, and Marxism. The last of these reached the Americas within the past century, while the two earlier traditions date back to colonial times.[1] The oldest intellectual tradition, the monist, was a unique synthesis of notions derived from natural law and feudalism. The governing of man was viewed in terms of centralization working in harmony with an organic community to realize the full potential of society.* Monist thought became powerful in sixteenth-century Spain, especially as developed by Francisco de Vitoria and Francisco Suárez.

Monism stressed the community—and that the community's institutions of governance required discipline, order, and authority. Citizens should defer to the power of the ultimate authority, in effect, their *patron* or "protector." The universe was hierarchically ordered and marked by natural inequalities. Governance was therefore necessary to preserve social harmony and order. Such was the intellectual impulse that was transplanted from Iberia to the colonies over a period of three centuries. Yet this was complemented by Enlightenment ideas as well.

Natural law was given a new twist in the seventeenth-century social contract theory of John Locke which provided a rationale for subsequent liberal constitutionalism. Emphasizing that private property had existed as a matter of natural right preceding the establishment of government, Locke believed that governments should serve as instruments for the preservation of individual rights. Because they had been established for that purpose, they might legitimately be overthrown when they failed to accomplish it. Locke's ideas were invaluable to those committed to reform in the name of liberty and individual rights.

Spain was not wholly immune to new ideas. By the 1700s there was an evident impact from French, German, and English Enlightenment thought. Universities modernized their curricula accordingly, and the flow of ideas to the New World also began to reflect the Enlightenment as

*The notion of "organic community" sees society as one in which all the parts interact with one another. Each is to function as a perfectly integrated portion of the whole. Thus the community is closely knit in all of its actions and activities.

144

well as the monist tradition. From France, the writings of Charles de Montesquieu, Voltaire, and Jean Jacques Rousseau were familiar to educated Latin Americans. Montesquieu, for example, influenced them with his admiration of British parliamentary forms, and his contention that government should balance the legitimate needs of society with respect for individual rights. By the close of the century there was also growing knowledge about the revolutionary struggles of France and the United States. Tom Paine, Thomas Jefferson, and Benjamin Franklin were among those whose works were discussed. Pervasive in all the new political philosophies was a concern for individual liberties over against the state — the origin of the word "liberalism" itself.

By the beginning of the 1800s, then, Latin America was familiar with both monist and liberal ideas. The richness of Latin American political thought and ideology was indebted to the vitality of these ideas and of the debate and exchange among them. This was evident during and after the revolutionary wars of the nineteenth century. The rebellion against colonial authority defined freedom more in political than in socioeconomic terms. The individual was to be protected against abuses of power. It was assumed that the attainment of individual freedoms would permit a resolution of other national problems. Once the royalists had been defeated, however, controversy over individual rights and the role of the government grew more heated.

The heritage of the Enlightenment was reflected in two distinct schools of thought. One placed individual rights at the core of its political philosophy and gave the highest possible priority to liberty and self-expression. Its advocates stressed the capacity of the people to rule themselves. Liberty and equality before the law were to be strengthened by broad civic participation.

Others — the institutionalists — trusted laws more and liberties less. They sought to define the role of the state and how it should govern. Somewhat guarded about the ability of the people to shape their own society wisely, these *pensadores* ("thinkers") placed their faith in laws and constitutions. Typically, there was concern that governmental structures rest upon the protection of the judiciary; democracy and individual rights would depend for their protection upon the constitutional mechanisms that were devised. Moreover, it was important to recognize human inequality as a given, rather than uphold what they considered the pious myth of total and unqualified equality.

Though Enlightenment thought was popular, the nineteenth century was also intellectually indebted to monism. This was true of Simón Bolívar himself. The Liberator, an advocate of pluralistic Enlightenment ideas in his youth, came increasingly to question them. As early as 1813 he asked if his fellow citizens were yet equipped with the virtues necessary for republican government. In time his disillusionment over the capacity of the masses deepened, and his Angostura Discourse warned of the need to guard against the disorder threatened by unfettered liberty. He declared that "all our moral powers will not suffice to save our infant republic from this chaos unless we fuse the mass of the people, the government, the legislation, and the national spirit into a single united body."[2]

Others followed who also agonized over the conflict between freedom and order. For them the revolutionary ideal of individual freedom was counterbalanced by fear of the uneducated masses — unless they could be subjected to the paternalistic authority of a small elite. During the latter years of the nineteenth century this attitude was mirrored in positivist thought, which the Latin Americans adapted from the Frenchman Auguste Comte as well as the British thinker Herbert Spencer. Positivism was innately antidemocratic in spirit, calling for government by those most capable of ruling. Thus the positivists by no means viewed the popular franchise as the appropriate means to select political leadership. A kind of priesthood of experts would conduct the affairs of the masses as a service to humanity. Popular participation would thus be curbed by a gradual, orderly evolution shaped from above in accordance with scientific principles.

Positivism registered its most direct political impact in Mexico and in Brazil. The dictatorship of Porfirio Díaz in the last third of the century was supported and guided intellectually by such Mexican *científicos* ("scientific ones") as José Yves Limantour. They held that freedom and liberty could too easily turn into social disorder; hence a highly centralized state authority was justified. In Brazil positivism became virtually the official ideology of the republic following the overthrow of the emperor in 1889. Although the zenith of Brazilian positivism passed swiftly, to this very day its motto, *Ordem e Progresso* ("Order and Progress"), is at the center of the Brazilian flag.

At the start of the twentieth century, then, the traditions of monism and of liberal pluralism were strong, but conflicted with each other in many ways. There was also cause for disillusionment, since the exercise of political liberty had become episodic. Alternating cycles of representative government and of authoritarian centralism appeared equally incapable of creating a just society and economic well-being for all. This helps to explain in part the seductiveness of Socialist thought when it in turn reached Latin America after earlier expressions in the Old World.

Questions about the role of the state and its relationship to the individual began to receive more precise analysis. The state came to be viewed as directly responsible for the welfare of society, the instrument whereby society might be transformed. This signified a turning away from more individualistic notions of society. Thus contemporary ideology further developed both monist and pluralist thought, while Socialist ideas also flowered.

The growing collectivism of political ideology could be traced back to antecedents in the late 1800s, when intellectuals had been intrigued by early, or "utopian" Socialist thought.

Yet Latin America was little concerned with class struggle on behalf of social justice, either in the wake of Europe's 1848 revolutionary upheaval or later in the century. Not until the 1900s did Marxist thought gain a significant number of converts. After the Russian Revolution of 1917, however, greater attention was directed toward both Marxist and Leninist concepts. More broadly, the collectivist thrust was reflected in other ideological schools, including what became known as social democracy.

■ Social Democracy

The pervasive blending of intellectual traditions gave birth to several powerful political movements led by prominent activists. Well before midcentury the social democratic movement became a force to be reckoned with; among its notable leaders were Víctor Raúl Haya de la Torre of Peru, and Venezuela's Rómulo Betancourt. The first was perhaps the most philosophically creative of all the social democrats (although in the 1980s his heirs in Peru rejected the label). For five decades—until his death in 1979—Haya was the unrivaled *caudillo* (chief) of Peru's APRA, or American Popular Revolutionary Alliance. Having spent his early years immersed in Socialist writings, he engaged in a flirtation with Marxist political organizations during the 1920s. *Aprista** doctrine subsequently recognized the importance of Marx and his interpreters, accepting the division of society into classes and the struggle of those classes as an inevitable historical process.

In 1933 Haya called the APRA a Marxist party. At the same time he argued that there was a disparity in the historical evolutions of Europe and of Indo-America, as he termed his own region. Problems were different; they demanded different solutions. Communism was a European movement inappropriate for Indo-

---

*Editor's Note: *Aprista* is used both as an adjective meaning "of or belonging to APRA" and as a noun meaning "a member of APRA."

America. The APRA would therefore be a multi-class party, for the proletariat of European capitalist countries was not like that of countries with only incipient industrialism. This reasoning led to Haya's reinterpretation of Marxism, at the core of which was an unorthodox treatment of imperialism, at least as Lenin had defined it.

> In Europe imperialism is "the last stage of capitalism" — meaning the culmination of a succession of capitalist stages — which is characterized by the emigration or exploitation of capital and the conquest of markets and of productive zones of primary products toward countries with incipient economies. But in Indo-America what in Europe is "the last stage of capitalism" becomes the first. For our peoples, immigrating and imported capital establishes the initial stage of its modern capitalist age. The economic and social history of Europe is not repeated in Indo-America.[3]

Thus, imperialism became not the final but instead the first stage of capitalism for developing areas. This was almost diametrically the opposite of the Marxist concept of historical stages that was derived from the experience of industrialized Western Europe.

Only the advent of imperialism would foster the conditions from which a proletariat grown knowledgeable about capitalism and imperialism itself might move toward Socialist revolution. Haya's reformulation of stages and revolutionary preconditions proved more apt for the Peru of his early adulthood than was orthodox Marxism. At the same time, it contradicted his own anti-imperialism. It was unclear how Haya proposed to cooperate with imperialism as a means of developing the capitalism that created the preconditions for Socialist revolution, itself a response to imperialism.

Haya's writings also insisted upon a renewal of democratic institutions, with the moral and material well-being of the individual dependent upon the erection of a large and active state machinery. The APRA's five-point "maximum" program called for the nationalization of land and industry as well as extensive state ownership in other economically significant sec-

tors. Haya's anti-imperialist state was to limit private initiative while controlling the production and circulation of wealth. The state would direct the national economy, and might have to deny individual or collective economic rights in order to combat imperialism. For Peru he envisaged a democratic, anti-imperialist state founded on the three oppressed classes — peasantry, proletariat, and urban middle class.

The prolific Haya as well as later aprista thinkers paid greater attention to the role of the state than to individual rights. Discussions of the latter generally revolved about the Indian population, identifying its problems more as economic than racial or social in character. The movement's commitment to social justice for all seemed to demand special treatment for the indigenes. Fundamentally, Haya de la Torre enunciated a social democratic vision that relied upon a strong centralized state to protect individual rights. Yet he did not fully elaborate upon the problems and possible solutions involved in the state–individual relationship. This was reserved for Rómulo Betancourt, whose statist orientation consciously incorporated a profound commitment to democratic institutions and individual liberties.

In his early years the Venezuelan leader, much like Haya, had viewed Marxist teachings as a convenient framework within which to analyze national problems and the means to their resolution. In time, political experience both clandestinely and in exile led to an alteration of these views. Well before the official founding of his *Acción Democrática* (AD) party in September 1941, Betancourt rejected the concept of class conflict. Multiclass parties of a comprehensive national revolutionary character were necessary, rather than narrowly based workers' organizations, and the AD considered itself broader than simply a party of the proletariat.

Betancourt's belief in centralized state action was evident from the first moment of the AD's 1945 assumption of government authority. He saw no way for Venezuela to leapfrog the capitalist stage of economic development. The problem initially was not that of socializing economic wealth, but rather of producing it. Movement from colonial to modern structures was the responsibility of government planning and regulation, with those holding power also accountable to the social conscience and aspirations of all citizens. In the final analysis, a democratization of the national economic system would permit the free play of social forces, abolishing subservient relationships and protecting those least able to defend their own interests.

Betancourt had a deep faith in the citizenry, in civic virtues, and in the innate capacity of the masses for self-rule. He rejected the thesis that the people of Latin America were ill suited to perform the great civilizing functions and believed that it was inaccurate to view the political destiny of Latin America as wavering between the extremes of dictatorship and anarchy. He saw Venezuela and its sister nations as fully capable of creating economic and sociopolitical order. "We are a people disposed to being governed legally and democratically. We are determined to find our own way, to make our own history; we no longer wish to maintain a contemplative gaze backwards, burning incense before the portraits of our liberators and behaving like their unworthy grandchildren."[4]

For the AD leader, a responsive state capitalism could enhance individual freedoms. Sovereignty resided in the people, who exercise it through the organs of public power. Civil liberties were to be fully guaranteed; the party pledged absolute respect for all beliefs and creeds. Political involvement enabled the citizen to see in practice the nature and relative importance of national problems, as well as the difficulty of readily resolving them. In conjunction with participation, political education took on a major role in assuring the viability of democracy. As the prefatory passages of Venezuela's National Organic Law — an AD-formulated document — put it:

> Education is an essential function of the State . . . [having] as object the achieving of the harmonious development of the personality, forming citizens preparing for the exercise of democracy,

fortifying the sentiments of nationality, nourishing the spirit of human solidarity and promoting national culture. . . .[5]

Betancourt, like Haya de la Torre in Peru and José Figueres of Costa Rica, was a ranking social democratic figure for two generations, generating much of his country's political momentum. The Venezuelan served twice as president of the republic, and Figueres was chief of state on three occasions. For a time toward the close of the 1960s, it seemed that the vitality of social democracy might be waning. However, today the movement is lively and thriving. Successors of the Betancourt and Figueres parties hold power in their respective countries, while Haya's heirs won power in Peru in 1985. Elsewhere the movement is flourishing, most notably in the Dominican Republic and Ecuador.

■ Christian Democracy

If the thought and ideology of social democracy have contributed to its tradition of effective political action, much the same can be said of Christian democracy. It resembles social democracy in its debt to two distinctive intellectual currents. Rather than building on Enlightenment and Socialist thought, however, it combines liberal and monist theories. The influence of the latter can be traced back to nineteenth-century traditionalist thought, which contributed to the early conservative impulses of Christian democracy. Whereas the early years of social democratic thought adopted Marxist elements, Christian democratic theory began with strong roots in organicist* and authoritarian worldviews.

---

*Editor's note: *Organicist* refers to a body of political beliefs that conceives society as analogous to a biological organism. Societies are born, grow to maturity, and die. Individual members of a society or political community are subordinate to that community and must sacrifice their own wishes to the good of the whole. The good of the community is determined by the leadership, just as the head determines what is best for a biological organism. And just as the parts of an organism follow the direction of the head, so individual members of a community must follow the direction of the leadership or the community will decline and die.

In time, however, progressive elements began to appear. Neo-Thomist thought in Latin America† proved receptive to the French school of "New Catholicism," and to such philosophers as Jacques Maritain, Yves Simon, and Etienne Gilson. Growing papal concern over social issues also exerted a powerful impact on intellectuals, especially as expressed in Pius XI's *Quadragesimo anno* (1931) and in John XXIII's *Pacem in terris* (1960). The Brazilian Alceu Amoroso Lima was a notable early voice of Christian social action: he said that respect for labor was fundamental to a just balance of social forces. Otherwise society would never achieve the common good, falling instead either into atomized individualism or authoritarian, dehumanizing collectivism.

Christian democracy became a potent force through the formation and evolution of political movements espousing its traditions and perspectives. This was particularly true in Chile and Venezuela, where the movement's leaders included distinguished thinkers who later became presidents. In Chile, Eduardo Frei was inspired by the values and principles of Christian philosophy. He saw Christian democracy as "an interpretation of man and his fate and, as a reflection of it, a concept of the human personality that cannot be based on money, class, or race."[6] Frei described Christian democracy as a fundamental moral force, dedicated to the rights and freedoms necessary for collective fulfillment. Approaching social problems with "an inflexible democratic will," Christian democracy advocates a humanizing process whereby people generate power, create wealth, and share in the distribution of both. Society is a social organization in which the common good must come from integrating individual rights and duties. To harmonize justice with liberty requires social pluralism, which assumes the legitimacy of many and diverse units in society — the most fundamental of which is the family. The state exists as an instrument for the benefit of its members, understood not primarily as individuals, but as participants in an increasingly complex network of associations that ascends from the family upward.

The emergence of state-regulated capitalism brought with it the danger of authoritarian tendencies, against which democratic counterbalances had to be built. To do so required the participation of citizens in democratic political parties. Two days after Frei's 1964 election he told an interviewer that political participation was necessary to create an organic basis for democracy. For the full realization of individual rights, a constant interplay between the state and pressure groups was mandatory. The state would promote the consolidation of such groups so that they would be protected against direct state intervention when they voiced their interests. At the same time, the higher organisms of the state should reflect the wishes of basic popular organizations. Through the guidance of a responsive state, Christian democracy could affirm its democratic will in adhering to liberty and freedom. "We are ready to fight for freedom of speech, for freedom of conscience, because that is the only way to live with dignity; and we will never fall into the trap of those who talk of order to protect privilege. . . ."[7]

Venezuela's Rafael Caldera, the single most influential spokesman of Latin American Christian democracy for the past decade, has been similarly dedicated to the achievement of social justice while stressing the fundamental importance of the family unit. Extending the notion of social justice to the international sphere, Caldera further argued that the nation itself should strive for global progress. The obligations of international social justice obligate the economically developed countries to aid the less advanced. This notion represents a corollary of democratic theory itself.

---

†Neo-thomist thought derived from the revival in the late nineteenth century of the ideas of Saint Thomas Aquinas. Aquinas had written in the thirteenth century of an all-embracing harmonious society, one in which there was a universal synthesis in which the whole of human knowledge constituted a single piece. Pope Leo XIII's encyclical *Rerum novarum* provided powerful impetus for the revival of Thomistic thought. Among its more significant aspects was the conception of labor as being a natural community with the right to organize. For a discussion of Neo-thomism, see Chapter 7, "Religion in Latin America."

Democracy to Caldera means government by the citizenry, which constitutes an organic unity of component parts. Human dignity is fundamental to democracy, so constant dialogue between rulers and ruled is a necessity. Although the two parties stand in an organic rather than atomistic relationship to each other, democracy must recognize competing social interests and organizations. Political parties are necessary to guide the evolution of society: Such organizations are inherently nonconfessional, democratic, popular, and national. They require internal democracy and all-inclusive, not class-based participation.

Profound social change becomes an overriding necessity whose realization depends on nonviolent social revolution. "Revolution must be understood as the acceleration of history . . . [and] the rupture with that part of the past which retards the accomplishment of social aims, and the adoption of those measures and systems which can bring about the realization of the Christian concept of man.[11] Either there will be a peaceful and constructive Christian revolution, or the people will be swept up in violence, materialism, and destruction: This is the choice Caldera has emphasized, whether in or out of power, for more than a generation. The reformist, democratizing thrust of Christian democracy has similarities to social democracy, but in many important areas, a distinction between the two is clear.

In recent elections in Latin America, Christian democrats have been overwhelmed by their principal rivals, the social democrats. The only recent bright spot for the movement in this hemisphere was the return to office of José Napoleón Duarte as the result of his election victory on 6 May 1984. The founder of El Salvador's Christian democratic movement, he assumed power amid civil strife that was complicated by the involvement and intervention of foreign powers. Yet Duarte campaigned and attempted to rule as a quasipopulist reformer and healer of national divisions, rather than as a Christian democratic ideologue. Moreover, he himself had never been philosophically oriented. Unlike Caldera and Frei, or even the luckless Herrera, Duarte was frank in admitting his ideological weakness. As revealed to his biographer, Duarte "devoted his time and talent almost exclusively to the mechanical aspects of party organization, leaving theory to the lawyers and humanists. Whenever he did speak on ideology or program, [others] would carefully coach him in advance."[9]

■ Marxism and the Collectivist Impulse

Socialist thought first reached Latin American shores before the turn of the century. Marx, Engels, Lenin, Kautsky, and other European theorists had not, however, found much to interest them in Latin America. Thus would-be disciples were hard pressed to cite doctrinal sources and were left to construct an original Marxist interpretation of Latin American reality. Few have demonstrated such creativity, but a striking exception was the Peruvian José Carlos Mariátegui, sometime colleague and later rival of Haya de la Torre before Mariátegui's premature death in 1930.

Mariátegui set himself the task of adapting European doctrine to American reality. Preoccupied with economic problems and the demands of social justice, he saw the efficient collectivism of the Incas as having been destroyed by the *conquistadores*, producing a feudal economy. By the twentieth century feudalism existed side by side with the communal Indian economy in the isolation of the Andes, and there was in addition a coastal bourgeois economy dominated by international capitalism. European thought was inadequate for theoretical explanation, or as a basis for action. Only a reshaping of Peru's class structure would permit the fulfillment of the individual. Notwithstanding his admiration for the Russian Revolution, Mariátegui thought it held few lessons directly applicable to the Americas. "In Latin America we are not interested in a copy of socialism. Our socialism must be an heroic creation. We must give life, with our own reality, in our own language, to Indo American socialism."[10] The renewal of preconquest economic development required a liberation of the Indian, whose enslaved plight was central to Mariátegui's analysis. He saw the socialist future for Latin America as dependent upon the peasantry—an assertion that provoked condemnation from Stalinist Communists as ideological heresy.

Mariátegui agreed with Haya that Peruvian socialism could not follow European historical experience. Because the industrial proletariat was too small to sustain true revolutionary activity, he emphasized the Indian masses. Only they could bring about the desired recasting of society and an uplifting of the human spirit. The awakening of the Indians to socialism depended, however, upon renewed urban activism. Mature capitalism, accompanied by modern means of production, would help to radicalize the urban proletariat. This in turn would lead to the Socialist revolution in which the Indian rural proletariat would become a major actor.

His impassioned defense of the Indian has somewhat obscured Mariátegui's broader views concerning the role of individuals and their relationship to the state. For urban dwellers as well as the peasantry, he held that the absence of collective organization and commitment was a serious hindrance to self-fulfillment. Individual liberty set people against each other in the struggle for material well-being, while in a Socialist society the individual would be protected through collectivist institutions. Furthermore, the revolutionary quest was an ethical matter. The revolutionary struggle would give meaning to the workers' lives. Their class consciousness in turn required a theory of revolutionary action.

From 1923 to 1926 Mariátegui was in exile in Italy, where he observed the fall of Italian socialism. This alerted him to the danger of fascism and explains his belief that nationalistic sentiment was a peril to democracy, which required a mobilized, enlightened intelligentsia.

His first book, *La escena contemporánea* (The Contemporary Scene), asserted that workers could not attain their revolutionary destiny without class consciousness. Social democratic efforts to work through the existing institutions of bourgeois democracy were doomed. For Peru itself, the existing system had to be destroyed, after which the democratic myth would give way to Socialist reality.

If Mariátegui's Socialist creed embraced both a caring sense of humanity and an unswerving belief in the need for revolution, these attitudes also characterized the thought of Ernesto "Che" Guevara more than a generation later. Perhaps best known as a guerrilla fighter, Guevara also developed a doctrine of Socialist revolution in Latin America. His writings, if less than rigorous, were suffused with three recurring themes: the degradation of life for Latin Americans; tactics and strategy for revolution; and the lessons of the Cuban experience for the hemisphere and for the Third World. For Guevara, the poverty and misery of generations, oppression of the individual, and socioeconomic bondage created the unrest and social violence that ruptured ties between the ruling oligarchy and the parasitic middle classes.

Revolution itself could be undertaken even if its classic "objective" conditions did not exist. Rather, "subjective" awareness that victory was possible could encourage upheaval. The masses could be sparked to revolt if effective revolutionary leadership were available. Contradicting classic European Marxism, Guevara underlined the politicizing function of guerrilla insurgents in arousing the peasantry. He depicted the peasantry as an instrument of liberation, whereas the urban proletariat was relevant but never decisive. Given the successes of the Cuban movement, Guevara insisted that it was the vanguard of Latin America's anticolonialist, anti-imperialist struggle.

Latin American Socialists have debated these issues for over two decades. Marxist orthodoxy, long the dominant Soviet ideology, insisted upon the leadership of urban industrial workers rather than a rural-based insurgency and denied the universal relevance of the Cuban experience. Guevara himself conceded that Cuba had special characteristics: the charisma of Fidel Castro, the disarray of North American imperialism, and the prerevolutionary condition of Cuba's rural proletariat. Nonetheless he wrote in 1960 that fundamental conditions in Latin America were sufficiently similar to justify imitation of the Cuban model. He foresaw "an army of peasants, working out of the countryside and seeking the noble objectives for which the rural population is fighting, [destined to] provide the great liberating army of the future, as it has already done in Cuba."[11]

While his emphasis on revolutionary techniques was politically interesting, it led more importantly to his denial that a peaceful transition to socialism was possible in Latin America. Guevara also denied that the struggle to build socialism required a subordination of the individual to the state. The masses were not to follow their leaders slavishly; neither was the state to be seen as infallible. Should leaders err, "a decline in collective enthusiasm is reflected by a resulting quantitative decrease of the contribution of each individual, each of the elements forming the whole of the masses." With the gradual institutionalization of revolution, the masses would make history "as a conscious aggregate of individuals fighting for the same cause."[12]

Guevara thought the creation of a new society through socialism required an active egalitarianism. The individual would be encouraged to develop a selfless spirit, to accept voluntary work for economic progress, and most particularly to develop the human conscience. The individual's everyday labor would create new riches for societal distribution while improving the laborer as well. Socialism entailed compassion and love. It had to be built upon a bedrock of spiritual as well as economic resources. A spiritual rebirth in the individual's thinking about daily social tasks is necessary before transition to communism itself becomes possible.

For Guevara socialism meant creation of a new kind of individual — the twenty-first century man.

To contrast Guevara with another figure of historic importance for Latin American socialism, we may look to Salvador Allende. As cofounder of Chile's Socialist party in 1933, he worked for its self-definition as revolutionary, anticapitalist, and class-oriented. He also emphasized, as in his 1964 and 1970 presidential campaigns, the belief that the word "revolutionary" signified a radical change in the social order through democratization. Vital structural and constitutional reforms, mandated by the will of the majority, would make socialism possible. Allende insisted on charting a nonviolent course to socialism. "We have said that we are going to create a democratic, national, revolutionary and popular Government which will open the road to socialism because socialism cannot be imposed by decree. All the measures . . . lead to the revolution."[13]

Allende's support of diverse Marxist methods and techniques throughout the hemisphere did not impair his belief that in his own country the ballot box offered a realistic opportunity. When he gained a narrow victory in 1970 elections, Allende described it as simply one more step along the path to socialism. He accurately observed that there were no meaningful precedents to follow, so Chile would be experimenting with new forms of political and socioeconomic organization. Of necessity he concentrated more on the tactics for consolidating the regime during its transitional period than on theoretical definitions of its ultimate objective. Nonetheless, he stressed the importance of political freedom as a requisite for social freedom. Unity of the masses was crucial. It would emerge with the resolution of class struggle, after which revolutionary transformations could break the bonds of national dependency. The working class would have gained control of the state by peaceful, institutional means. The welfare of the masses would be accompanied by full realization of individual potential: "The building of the new social regime is based on the people, who are its protagonist and its judge. It is up to the State to guide, organize and direct but never to replace the will of the workers. In the economic as well as in the political field, the workers must retain the right to decide. To attain this means the triumph of the Revolution."[14]

The Nicaraguan Revolution, whose history is of course still being written, contrasts with Allende's emphasis on institutional reform. In ideological terms, however, it has not produced striking or original ideas. The *Frente Sandinista de Liberación Nacional* (FSLN) frequently refers back to Augusto César Sandino, a revolutionary leader of the 1920s and 1930s whose ideas were only vaguely and partially formulated. FSLN ideology has been more precise and coherent, advocating Marxism as modified by Lenin with regard to national revolution. Carlos Fonseca Amador, the most important FSLN founder, articulated programmatic goals, as did others who now direct the revolutionary government.[15] FSLN theory broadened its scope and diluted its Marxism-Leninism only when the revolutionary regime attempted to incorporate ideologically disparate groupings.

From its victory in 1979 through 1981 the emphasis was on nationalism and on reformist measures. Following its seizure of power, the Sandinista ideology "expanded and evolved to encompass a broad program of reforms to redistribute income, wealth, power, and status and to alter foreign policy and the roles of external actors. It has also, with certain necessary tensions with its populist origin and framework, pursued the somewhat contradictory goals of moderating popular redistributive demands while expanding support for the FSLN and for the revolution."[16] As pressures grew — both inside the country and from the United States—the less ideologically committed elements were driven out of the party. By the time Daniel Ortega Saavedra became the FSLN presidential candidate in 1984, the Marxist orientation was much stronger than in the 1960s, when the movement began. Pronounced differences among the ranking leaders of the movement remained. All the same, ideology was subordinated to pragmatic political questions. Whether the Nicaraguan Revolution evolves a well-articulated political theory remains uncertain. Its example as a movement to oust an entrenched tyranny is presently of far greater importance than its contributions to revolutionary ideology.

Just as Sandinista thought does not constitute a neatly ordered or internally consistent ideological statement, so too socialist interpretations of contemporary Latin American run at considerable variance with one another. Socialist leaders agree in their condemnation of (capitalist) Latin American society, but they vary in their assessment of objective and subjective conditions in their own countries. The collectivist impulse toward dominant state authority is often accompanied by humanistic concern that seeks to blend socioeconomic progress with elevation of the human spirit. In practical terms, "the Nicaraguan and Cuban revolutions and what occurs . . . in El Salvador lead Latin America's Marxist intellectuals to conclude that they can interpret the world but that only the people have the power of numbers to change it."[17]

■ Individual, Society, and State

The intellectual heritage for contemporary Latin American political thought and ideology has several distinctive sources. Monism was embedded in Iberian soil by the sixteenth century, and its concepts were later exported westward to the New World. Derived from medieval corporatist institutions and an organic conception of society, monism was in the natural law tradition. Individual fulfillment could take place only within a disciplined community.

A different theoretical dimension came from the Enlightenment. The ruler was seen as a representative of the people with an explicitly limited sphere of power, while individuals shared basic and inalienable rights and obligations with their fellow citizens. Social contract theory sought to define sovereign authority while protecting the constituent members of society. It was argued that a stable government supportive of social change over time required constitutions and laws. There was a basic commitment to rationality, which, by harmonizing the relationship between ruler and ruled, would make liberty, equality, and individual fulfillment possible.

By the close of the colonial era, other perspectives had been transported to the Western Hemisphere. During the revolutionary wars of independence and through the remainder of the nineteenth century, pensadores and political activists developed innumerable variations on the basic monist and liberal themes. By the dawn of the next century a gradual rise of popular participation encouraged receptivity to new social and political theory. Soon a third generalized view of the individual, society, and the state took hold in Latin America. This was a radical tradition, focusing as it did upon problems of social inequality. Consequently, the early 1900s saw three intellectual foci, each inspiring multiple adaptations and themes for coming to grips with the relationship between individual, society, and state.

"Modern" intellectual perspectives on Latin American politics and society reflect the increasingly complex social and economic conditions, conditions that have encouraged a commitment to enlarge state responsibilities. Still, the liberties and rights of the individual have also required protection: Pluralists, monists, and champions of collectivism have all paid obeisance to individual freedoms, although their worldviews are far apart. Thus social democracy and Christian democracy, stemming initially from distinctive intellectual traditions, have moved toward one another in their perceptions. Although the former had Marxist roots and the latter was based on Thomistic doctrines consistent with monist conceptions of the state, both shifted toward the political and ideological center. This convergence owed more to electoral than ideological factors, as political parties moved toward the political center in the quest for votes.

Recent liberal thought, whatever precise label, has generally advocated some form of state-regulated capitalism as fundamental to the full realization of individual freedom. Popular sovereignty has been postulated as the framework within which to introduce reforms. Power should be shared by all citizens, with individual participation encouraged. For many, party-political organization has become the essential element in assuring social justice. The belief is widespread that opposition is a healthy democratic corrective to the power of the state.

The monist tradition, in contrast to the pluralist, has projected the Platonic vision of an ideal state, of a unity of political power with wisdom and reason. Thus the preferred form of government might be rule by an enlightened philosopher-king. Notions of this sort have been associated with such advocates of one-man rule as Venezuela's Juan Vicente Gómez, and more recently with Juan Perón of Argentina. In one form or another, this kind of elitism suggests quasi-Fascist government forms: It is feared that liberal democracy, plagued by the political ignorance of the masses, simply encourages mob rule. The truly just society recognizes human inequality; individual fulfillment comes through the policies of a wise, all-knowing leader of a highly centralized state.

Exponents of socialism have maintained, of course, that both monist and pluralist thought lead to elitist and narrow rather than broad-based popular rule. Socialism holds that individual liberation comes not from a reconciliation of conflicting class interests, but rather through the destruction of capitalism. For the Marxist, the injustices of capitalism provide the stimulus needed to mobilize the masses. Hence Marxists devote much attention to questions of revolutionary strategy and tactics. Socialist theories, like other currents of Latin American political thought, need to adapt ideas originating in Europe to social reality in the New World.

Marxist interpretations range widely, from the *guevarista* emphasis on the peasantry as the agent of revolution inaugurating a Communist society to Allende's belief in a peaceful road to socialism within a liberal democratic framework. Orthodox pro-Moscow Marxists, of course, have insisted upon classic European formulations and have suffered from their failure to adequately evaluate unique Latin American conditions. Whatever their approach to the seizure of power, Socialists have been preoccupied with the ultimate relationship of the individual to the state. While the problem is elusive, it remains integral to Marxist treatments of developing societies. By the 1980s growing numbers of intellectuals, aware of the flaws and inconsistencies of earlier theories, eclectically sought new approaches. Influenced perceptibly by Lukács and even more by Antonio Gramsci, they have come to attribute a more important role to individual consciousness in the revolutionary process and the construction of socialism.

The traditions of monism, pluralism, and socialism each constitute an integral part of the philosophical and intellectual heritage of Latin America. To understand politics is to recognize the presence of disparate perspectives. If better and more insightful theories of change are to be formulated, the new generation must build upon existing traditions. Ideally, the result will be a synthesis consistent with prevailing needs as the twenty-first century approaches.

■ Notes

1. The argument is presented in detail by John D. Martz and David J. Myers, "Understanding Latin American Politics: Analytic Models and Intellectual Traditions," *Polity* 16, no. 2 (Winter 1983): 214–42.
2. Vicente Lecuna and Harold A. Bierck, Jr., eds. and comps., *Selected Writings of Bolívar,* vol. 1 (New York: Colonial Press for the Banco de Venezuela, 1951), 191.
3. Víctor Raúl Haya de la Torre, *El antiimperialismo y el Apra* (Santiago: Ediciones Ercilla, 1936), 51.
4. Rómulo Betancourt, *Trayectoria democrática de una revolución* (Caracas: Imprenta Nacional, 1948), 245–46.
5. República de Venezuela, *Ley orgánica de la educación nacional,* Chapter I, Articles 1 and 2 (Caracas: Imprenta Nacional, 1948).
6. Eduardo Frei Montalva, "Paternalism, Pluralism, and Christian Democratic Reform Movements in Latin America," in *Religion, Revolution, and Reform: New Forces for Change in Latin America,* eds. William V. D'Antonio and Fredrick B. Pike (New York: Praeger, 1964), 37.
7. Frei, *Una tercera posición* (Lima: Ed. Universitaria, 1960), 101.
8. Rafael Caldera, "Crucial Test for Christian Civilization," in *The Alliance for Progress: A Critical Appraisal,* William Manger (Washington: Public Affairs Press, 1963), 23.
9. Stephen Webre, *José Napoleón Duarte and the Christian Democratic Party in Salvadoran Politics, 1960–1972* (Baton Rouge: Louisiana State University Press, 1979), 53.
10. José Carlos Mariátegui, *Siete ensayos de interpretación de la realidad peruana* (Santiago: Ed. Universitaria, 1955), 196.
11. Ernesto Guevara, "Cuba, excepción histórica vanguardia en la lucha anti-colonialista," *Verde Olivo,* 9 April 1961, 28.
12. Ernesto Guevara, "Notes on Man and Socialism in Cuba," 1965 letter reprinted in *Che Guevara Speaks: Selected Speeches and Writings,* ed. George Lavan (New York: Grove Press, 1967), 123, 129.
13. Allende quoted in Regis Debray, *The Chilean Revolution: Conversations with Allende* (New York: Vintage Books, 1971), 117.
14. Ibid., 201.
15. Carlos Fonseca Amador, ed., *Ideario político de Augusto César Sandino* (Managua: Secretaría Nacional de Propaganda, FSLN, 1980).
16. John A. Booth, *The End and the Beginning: The Nicaraguan Revolution* (Boulder, Colo.: Westview Press, 1982), 216.
17. Sheldon B. Liss, *Marxist Thought in Latin America* (Berkeley: University of California Press, 1984), 290.

■ Suggested Readings

Arciniegas, Germán. *Latin America: A Cultural History.* New York: Knopf, 1967.

Crawford, William Rex. *A Century of Latin American Thought*. Cambridge: Harvard University Press, 1961.

Davis, Harold Eugene. *Latin-American Social Thought: The History of Its Development Since Independence, with Selected Readings*. Washington: University Press of Washington, D.C., 1963.

Dealy, Glen Caudill. *The Public Man; An Interpretation of Latin American and Other Catholic Countries*. Amherst: University of Massachusetts Press, 1977.

Franco, Jean. *The Modern Culture of Latin America: Society and the Artist*. New York: Praeger, 1967.

Jorrín, Miguel, and John D. Martz. *Latin-American Political Thought and Ideology*. Chapel Hill: University of North Carolina Press, 1970.

Liss, Sheldon B. *Marxist Thought in Latin-America*. Berkeley: University of California Press, 1984.

Silvert, Kalman H. *Essays in Understanding Latin America*. Philadelphia: ISHI, 1977).

Véliz, Claudio. *The Centralist Tradition of Latin America*. Princeton: Princeton University Press, 1980.

Zea, Leopoldo. *The Latin-American Mind*. Translated by James H. Abbott and Lowell Dunham. Norman: University of Oklahoma Press, 1963.

11 | *Arduous Harmonies: The Literature of Latin America*

JOHN P. DYSON

Latin American literature in Spanish and Portuguese engages a critic or literary historian initially in much the same way that the New World itself affected the discoverers. Its novelty, abundance, and variety dazzle and stun, but a less dumbfounded response is eventually required in order to come to terms with it. This discussion attempts to do that by assuming an identifiable and expressable community for the literature as a whole. Writing in Latin America is discernible in some special way from other Western literatures despite all it owes to and shares with them. Its unity is not particularly that of common languages or of universal religious, social, or political organizations. Rather, it is a set of constants in the imaginative faculty, an increasingly lucid vision of what it means *to be* in a New World, first as intruder, then as resident, and finally as native, but at the same time to be paradoxically bound and beholden to the Old World for the words to express that new reality. The clear sense of an over-here-now versus a back-there-then creates a tension that is the chief characteristic of Latin American writing, a kind of luminous and tortured baroque quality, vibrant in the literature from 1492 until today. More than any other writing in the West, Latin America's is a continuous struggle to reconcile this tension, occasionally through schizophrenia in individual authors, but more frequently in rival literary factions that, between them, resolve the conflict momentarily until another provocation—political, social, or literary— disturbs the balance and sets the whole process pulsating again. Our focus is on what Latin America became from the discovery forward, not on what it had been. Pre-Columbian poetry and drama, Creation stories, histories, and religious rites are excluded.

The first European word spoken aloud and recorded in connection with the Americas was *Tierra!*, and that shout of relief and anticipation heralded what was to be one of the major themes for years to come: man's relationship to the land and lands of Latin America. American geography first compelled description, then exultation, but it would soon become a social and moral issue—and therefore a literary one.

If New World writing was born in wonder, conflict, and questioning, it would be well to remember too that the Americas became a world for Europe at the same time that Europe itself was at a crossroads. The development of this hemisphere began and was forever caught between the rigid conservatism of the Middle Ages and the thrill of discovery and inviting newness that was to be the Renaissance: numbing credulity, dread, and caution on the one hand; promise, curiosity, and exhilarating recklessness on the other. In the shadow of both of them Latin American writing would emerge.

■ Discovery, Conquest, and Colonization

Four principal literary forms were adapted by the conquerors and colonists of the sixteenth century: 1) the medieval chronicles that often celebrated the glory of the doer without caring overmuch about the documentary accuracy of the deeds; 2) the medieval and popular *auto,* a brief religious play that dramatized points of Christian dŏctrine while entertaining the faithful; 3) the fantasy-world novels of chivalry that were the popular reading of the day; and 4) Renaissance epic poetry (in the style of Boiardo, Ariosto, Camões, and Tasso.) Latin America's literary roots are found in these transported genres, among others, which served to inventory the discoveries, to praise the conquests and the conquerors, to convert the Indians to the One True Faith, and to elevate the adventure of all these events to a wonderful, heroic enterprise on behalf of God, king, country, and self. In large measure, literature during the whole colonial period was seen as fostering church activity or else as a leisurely privilege of the aristocracy. Subsequently this notion of an intellectual elite would involve more than the strictly social-class connotation of nobility. It came to include a sense of special responsibility attached to learning and writing. In more modern times this helps explain the social involvement of many authors who felt themselves in possession of a national trust and under a duty to speak for those less fortunate.

As Renaissance humanism spread across Europe and to the Americas in the early- to mid-sixteenth century and the proper study of mankind became man, the self-serving and occasionally propagandistic chroniclers yielded to those genuinely interested in the natural history of this hemisphere and in its inhabitants. The wholesale appropriation of lands—and Indians to work them under enforced labor—was the first ethical dilemma to plague Europeans after the discovery, and it would continue as the major moral issue until the rise of Protestantism and the Counter-Reformation crowded it out. Virtual annihilation of great pre-Columbian civilizations was the heavy moral price paid for Christianizing the Indians, and many priests challenged the devastating effects of that aggression, both from the pulpit and in their writings. By the end of the sixteenth century, the self-styled "Inca" Garcilaso de la Vega would attempt to rescue the fast-fading culture of the southern empire in his *Comentarios reales de los Incas (Royal Commentaries of the Incas).* It was the first distinguished work of a *mestizo* writer when to be a mestizo, let alone a learned one, was still remarkable. He was also the first to show clearly the struggle that results from dual ethnic allegiances, and in the tenuous poise between the values of his native mother's world and those of his Spanish father's, we see the prototype of the "marginal man" so important as a poignant symbol of exclusion and loneliness in the nineteenth and twentieth centuries.

■ The Baroque

The hierarchical social and economic structures of colonial Latin America encouraged—indeed required—looking to Europe for ideas and styles. Thus, ironically, the "New" World found itself looking back eastward for novelty and innovation, setting a pattern for centuries to come. By the seventeenth century this practice was further intensified through Spain's endorsement of the Counter-Reformation as a virtually national accomplishment. Spain could neither contain the rising humanistic heresies of northern Europe nor match the growing prosperity of the Protestant world, and both she and her territories were cast into a profoundly paranoid spiritual crisis. Isolationism became the last line of defense; as the nation contracted and sealed itself off, so did its artists and writers, disillusioned with life's fleeting rewards. The world seemed a huge and capricious fraud, reversal of fortunes and death the only promises kept on earth. In seventeenth-century Latin America, as much as or more than in Spain, intellectual and artistic activity was closely scrutinized from above through the Inquisition and the Index of Forbidden Books; writers vigorously censored their own work to assure the orthodoxy of its content. Authors shied away from unorthodox ideas and methods, and the exuberant elaboration of form itself became the primary imaginative activity. And it was a safe activity. No matter how profusely detailed the ornamentation, how tortured or hermetic the meaning, or how riotously complex the conceits and the syntax, the most severe censure authors now risked was to be judged stylistically extravagant and difficult to read and comprehend. These thematic and formal tensions provide a remarkable insight into the anxious literary spirit of the times.

Of all the baroque writers of seventeenth-century Spanish America, none stands out more than the Mexican nun, Sor Juana Inés de la Cruz. Her life and works make up a concentrated symbol for the whole period. Her precocious interest in learning was to be her obsession—and her cross. She abandoned the viceregal court because she found it too distracting, and she took religious vows in the expectation that the less worldly life would provide her the time and contemplation she needed to continue her studies. But the glitter and gaiety of the court was replaced by the whiny and trivial bedlam of colonial convent life. Sor Juana's anguish and struggle are candidly revealed in her famous letter of 1691, the "Respuesta a Sor Filotea" (Reply to Sister Filotea). It is a succinct but penetrating autobiography and a profoundly

moving commentary on the limited options available to a woman of the seventeenth century, for whom marriage or the veil were the only respectable choices. Unsuited to matrimony, Sor Juana chose a vocation of humility, obedience, and devotion, yet her spirit was clearly proud, defiant, and curious. She sought but failed to achieve a harmony of intellect and faith, of reason and emotion in her own life at a time and in a society in which reason and intellectual activity were suspect. But she did succeed admirably in her imaginative works where these otherwise impossible reconciliations are conveyed in images of both connection and exhaustion. She caught her polarized world in poetry that still communicates poise on the verge of collapse, oscillation between need and duty, submission and self-affirmation.

■ Neoclassicism

Sor Juana's society discouraged open inquiry and made it dangerous, but the ascension of the French house of Bourbon to the Spanish throne in 1700 eventually opened the colonies to the dazzling panorama of the European Enlightenment and to a relaxation of the most obscurantist features of the Spanish Church. The founding of newspapers and the rise of historical, geographic, scientific, and literary societies in the eighteenth century had a noticeable effect all over Latin America, but nowhere was their impact more profound than in Brazil. Spanish-American neoclassicism, like its Spanish counterpart, was relatively arid in its esthetic results if not in its programs and ideas. Brazil, on the other hand, was in the midst of a major renaissance, not only of thought and expectation, but of accomplishment as well.

The discovery of gold and diamonds in Minas Gerais in the late seventeenth century made the province and its capital Vila Rica a center of lively literary activity for a group of poets known collectively as Arcadians. The movement's chief contribution initially was that it brought Europe's modern literary ideas to Brazil and promoted them throughout the country. Arcadianism took its lead from the other neo-classical writing of the time by strict adherence to classical Greek and Roman models. Clarity of concept and style was cultivated; the last vestiges of baroque excess and complexity were purged. But Arcadianism's ultimate legacy was a clear sense of Brazilian national literature. Its poets produced a large body of good writing about Brazil by Brazilians. In the sixteenth and seventeenth centuries the American landscape had been celebrated as exotic and bizarre because its unruly and unfamiliar flora and fauna did not fit into the accepted classical bucolic idiom. The Brazilian neoclassicists legitimized American nature and incorporated local customs, terms, and even climatology into an expanded vision of Western culture. It would be a full century and more before Spanish America would find the same literary self-assurance in its movement known as *modernismo*.

■ **Romanticism**

Spanish-American revolt and ultimate independence in the period between 1808 and 1825 came at the very moment that neoclassicism and romanticism were locked into a struggle of their own in both Europe and America. Romanticism prevailed, in this hemisphere as in the other. Yet its utter sympathy for change, freedom, novelty, originality, and a nearly infinite play of the imagination in every sphere of life soon put writers at odds with more commonplace political, social, religious, and artistic realities. The often brutish rural feudalism to which the Americas were heir and which the church and the military helped sustain in their own self-interest was a source of anguish and despair for many writers hopeful of change. They passionately contested this renewed but now domesticated tyranny. Intellectual activity, and literature in particular, was thus bound to the conflicts of civic life: the will to combat through writing often led to a will to exile for writing.

Andrés Bello is perhaps the best example of a writer torn between neoclassicism and romanticism. His horror of ignorance, disorder, and fragmentation led him to found and preside over the University of Chile (1843) and to publish *Gramática de la lengua castellana (Grammar of the Spanish Language)* to preserve the Spanish language from degeneration into local dialects in this hemisphere. Bello urged classical tranquility and emotional self-control on a younger generation of writers that was chafing at the outmoded. What the emerging writers sought, however, was novelty, and they found it in cultured France and in impassioned romanticism.

Argentina first provided fertile ground for the romantic imagination, one tempered in the heat of political conflict. President Bernardino Rivadavia's attempt to have a centralist, "unitarian" constitution ratified and implemented was opposed by the provincial overlords, who wanted to govern their vast ranching empires without interference from Buenos Aires. Two of these *gauchos*, Juan Manuel de Rosas and Juan Facundo Quiroga, were to become not only important political figures, but literary models as well: National demons to be exorcised first in fiction, then in fact.

By 1829 Rosas had become the virtual dictator of Argentina in a reign of terror that was to last until 1852. The young intellectuals railed against his violence, brutality, ignorance, and oligarchic rule; the best minds in Argentina were driven from the country as a result of this opposition, producing in exile the most powerful writing of the generation.

One of the most important works of the whole romantic period was *Civilización y barbarie: Vida de Juan Facundo Quiroga* (1845) (*Civilization and Barbarity: The Life of Juan Facundo Quiroga*), published in Chile by Domingo Faustino Sarmiento. While its ostensible purpose is to trace the violent biography of the petty tyrant Quiroga, and through him to excoriate Rosas, Sarmiento turns the project into a wide-ranging analysis of the whole geographic and social fabric of Argentina. He concludes that, since Facundo is a natural product of the barbarity that nurtured him, only when the *pampa* (Argentine plain) is civilized will primitive and dangerous sorts like him be obliterated.

Facundo comes to life in Sarmiento's work not as an inconsequential albeit dangerous local bandit, but as the personification of the pampa's primitive, unchecked power and unpredictability. Sarmiento instinctively admires some of the very qualities he disparages, especially Facundo's independence, self-reliance, and strength. One closes the book believing that all the marvelous power and resources embodied in Argentina and its rural people are merely misdirected, desperately in need of a guiding hand. Sarmiento himself became that hand as president from 1868 to 1874. By the 1870s the power of the gauchos was broken, and immigration was bringing in new blood. With the city and civilization as Argentina's modern symbol, both the gaucho and the pampa had become safe for nostalgia. No longer a menace, they were now themselves endangered, and Sarmiento's own grudging admiration of them was to become a song of national recuperation and a cry for justice in the narrative poem *Martín Fierro*.

El gaucho Martín Fierro by José Hernández appeared in 1872; it attempted to reconcile the conflict between European and American values, the former now seen in terms of cultural power. Hernández's noble gaucho, driven from his home and family by a tyrannical government, spoke equally well to the refined taste of Buenos Aires and to the cowboys victimized by civilization's determination to improve them at any cost. *Martín Fierro* was a smash success from the outset. It sold nearly eighty thousand copies at a time when a successful book might sell five hundred. Seven years later, Hernández published *La vuelta de Martín Fierro (The Return of Martín Fierro)*, which portrayed an older, wiser, and less romantic Martín now in search of reintegration into the society he had justly fled. The tone of "Return" was not up to the political rebelliousness and the moral vigor of the earlier

work. Nevertheless, it helped set the stage for a perennial theme in Argentine literature, one that finds its most finely drawn expression in the works of Jorge Luis Borges: that of the Argentine with two pasts, two heritages—one *criollo*, one European; one violently active and imposing its dynamic mark on the land, the other sedately contemplative and intellectual. It is in fact a Latin American dichotomy never quite resolved in all these years.

The Argentine romantics' enthusiasm for revitalizing the past, as Hernández had done with his justification of the discredited and persecuted gaucho, found its counterpart in the prose sketches called *tradiciones* (issued in series from 1872 to 1911) by Ricardo Palma, director of the Peruvian National Library. What is more, in Palma the notion of a noteworthy past—of a "tradition" in that sense—comes alive as he scours the documentary evidence of Peru's colonial period to reveal a thread of historical and spiritual continuity for an emerging nation at a time of great trial. Palma rescued a Hispanic past previously ignored or vilified and made it a vital part of the national partrimony of Peru.

Brazilian romanticism had a distinctly esthetic rather than political cast. Politics entered in, of course, as did other sides of life, but not as anti-Portuguese sentiment. Portugal's tolerant colonial policy, the early development of Brazil's racial "democracy," and a peaceful transition of independence made such rejection unwarranted. When political thought was turned to literary use it betrayed a fervent sense of nationalism that sprang from the special geography and ethnic background of Brazil or, toward the end of the romantic period, from strong abolitionist convictions.

■ Realism

In the most faithful romantic vision of life, nothing had been conclusive: not things, not time, not states of mind. Prose realism countered that disturbing vagueness, and from the 1860s on, the influence of European realism was increasingly felt in Latin America. For the realist, mere observation by the senses supplied a valid picture of the everyday world, and the writer's task was to report those facts with sufficient detail to permit readers to participate in their actuality. The rise of philosophical positivism in the nineteenth century and its wide adoption throughout Latin America established "sociology" as the highest science of all. Under positivism's banner of "Peace, Order, and Progress," mankind would be carried to ever-higher material and cultural improvement. The realist stressed social setting as the proper one for his characters, since character in real life was assumed to be molded by social and historical environment. Some were more interested in the subjective aspect, which led them to develop "psychological realism." Realist fiction was an entertainment aptly suited to the rising middle class, which wanted a self-assured literature set in a familiar world like the one they lived in. But the cozy and satisfying world could not produce the best that realism had to offer. Instead, out of this movement came an author who saw the worm in the works: Latin America's first world-class novelist, the Brazilian Joaquim Maria Machado de Assis.

Machado de Assis brought to the Latin American novel a penetrating insight into the soul of urban man living in a highly structured society and bound by a complicated network of personal and social relationships. Yet at the heart of this complex web of duties and responsibilities, of ties and supports, emerges solitary man, the individual alone with his own moral flaws and facing a destiny as unknown and unknowable as his societal links are firm and verifiable. Machado's best works are poised on the fulcrum of this paradoxical equation, and like Henry James's, his great talent is for finding maximum expression in the minimum gesture.

Machado's books—*Dom Casmurro* (1899) is his best known—are both built on and propelled by ambiguity and understatement. His most successful technique, that of first-person narration, pits obsessively subjective and unreliable narrators against a pitilessly real world, and in the struggle universal truth is lost to their selfish version of it. In telling us their story they are, as one critic has insightfully noted, telling us the story of storytelling: fiction that "talks about itself." This is a degree of self-consciousness in literature that reappears many years later, first in Borges, then in the writing of what has been termed the recent "boom" in Latin American letters, but Machado was the first to articulate it, just as the nineteenth century came to a close.

■ Naturalism

Realism's objective methods and commonplace themes and characters eventually yielded a tendency known in fiction as naturalism. Underlying it was a pessimistic, materialistic determinism whose sources were multiple. What realism had seen as historical and social factors in the development of the individual, naturalism had construed as irresistible external forces, both social and natural, that thwarted human freedom. There were also internal forces at work in man that restricted his rationality and his moral conduct: specifically, hereditary and subconscious drives. The naturalistic writer portrayed life as a struggle for existence (on Darwin's biological model) or subsistence (on Marx's economic one), and he peopled his works with nature's or society's outcasts.

Latin American naturalism echoes the love-hate relationship between man and nature heard at the outset of romanticism, when the Spanish-American romantics had had a hard time domesticating the Europeans' easy admiration of their infinitely tamer countryside. As the century drew to a close, the awesome and overpowering American landscape loomed more formidable as a raw danger opposing man's designs for it, confirming the latent sense that man was an unwelcome, inconsequential intruder in the vast, natural world of the Americas.

Euclides da Cunha's monumental *Os Sertões* (1902) was not really a work of fiction, but a vast sociological analysis with striking literary merit in its language and its imaginative perception and re-creation of Brazil's special reality. Da Cunha portrays the effect of living in the jungle on a whole class of men whose violent and rebellious lives, like those of Sarmiento's gauchos years earlier, are shaped and determined by their environment. *Os Sertões* was to serve as an inspiration and source for Brazil's later "Novel of the Northeast" and for João Guimarães Rosa's twentieth century masterpiece, *Grande Sertão: Veredas*.

The greatest of all the naturalistic writers, precisely because he transcends naturalism, was the Uruguayan "father" of the Spanish American short story, Horacio Quiroga. He was the first Spanish American to write fiction of international stature. His best known stories leave the reader gasping for breath from the tension created when paltry man dares set foot into the domain of unforgiving nature.

■ **Spanish-American Modernismo**

Positivism's optimistic promises had already begun to go sour by the 1880s. Where there was progress, it was purely material and quite restricted: statues, parks, docks, and tramways. Poverty and misery continued largely unabated, and the few beneficiaries of change were a new class of bourgeois philistines in pursuit of ostentatious prosperity. One literary response to that had been the mechanistic world-view of the naturalistic writers. Still others turned their backs entirely on the crass, material world of commerce and engineering and sought in universal art the finest works of the spirit itself. In the process they explored a new language of literary expression. A partial model for the admiration of beauty in and of itself had been offered by the objective detachment and formal precision of French Parnassianism. Admirers of the Greek and Roman classics as well as of the exotic Orient, the Parnassians strove to achieve an unambiguous artifactlike quality in verse as perfect as statuary or as carefully crafted as jewelry. At the same time in France another movement had de-

veloped. It was known as symbolism and was more directly heir to the romantics in its preference for suggestive images and symbols rather than direct statement, and for finding the hidden correspondences among otherwise dissimilar sensations of sight, sound, aroma, taste, and touch. Abandoning the ugly reality of vulgar, ordinary life, the symbolists sought to equate the poetic imagination itself with the ultimate, ephemeral reality, and as a result they were often called morbid, escapist, or decadent. Like the impressionists in painting, they preferred to capture the impression of things in their works rather than the things themselves, and to achieve that end they constantly challenged the restrictions of conventional versification. They valued music above all other arts and sought its suggestiveness in a poetry of evocative verbal alchemy.

In France the schools of Parnassianism and symbolism had been alternative and frequently contentious ways of viewing the world and the task of the poet, and that separation was maintained in Brazil. In Spanish America, however, these tendencies as well as others were reconciled in a movement of innovation in poetry and prose that came to be known as *modernismo*. Out of the most varied contemporary French sources, the Spanish-American *modernistas* forged an integrated if highly eclectic literature in the last two decades of the nineteenth century. The result was a radical change in the Spanish literary language on both continents. In broad terms, *modernismo* challenged positivistic utilitarianism—which evaluated social institutions and artistic creativity alike in terms of their usefulness in promoting the greatest happiness for the greatest number—by deliberately cultivating the beauty of the useless. Furthermore, their enthusiastic metrical experimentation led modernista poets, through the accentual tonalities of French verse, back to the original rhythms long forgotten or neglected in Spanish. By the time modernismo had run its course, it had also made an invaluable contribution to the craft and profession of writing and to the elevation of the Spanish American writer as a self-assured citizen of the literary world at large.

The figure who best represents modernismo in its development, growth, and decline is the Nicaraguan Rubén Darío. Travel made Darío the apostle of modernismo. He considered himself and the new literature cosmopolitan in intent and appeal, and in his visits to the major capitals of the Hispanic world, including Madrid, he was able to foster and confirm the change he advocated: a virtual reelaboration of literary tradition. Darío and his colleagues discovered, adopted, or invented new meters and cadences. They resuscitated medieval and Golden Age Spanish verse rhythms, adopted all the schools of French postromanticism, and made room for Edgar Allan Poe and Walt Whitman. They sought to capture the wonders of the Far East in China and Japan, the fairytale delicacy of the Middle Ages, and the pomp and circumstance of the court of Louis XIV. Darío's three major books are a concentrated internal history of the movement. The most sensational of them, *Prosas profanas* (1896) (*Secular Poems*) became the touchstone of *modernismo* in its fantasy-world exoticism, its exquisite delicacy, and its profusion of symbols of perfection: swans, peacocks, gems, palaces, and the insistently evocative color blue. The book was a celebration of art and beauty, of erotic hedonism, of the vibrancy and vitality of far-flung places and distant times.

The Uruguayan critic José Enrique Rodó, on reviewing *Prosas profanas*, had said that Darío was "not the poet of America," and the aristocratic otherworldliness of Darío's settings, characters, and voices clearly set him apart from the ugly realities of Latin America. But at least one perceptive reader saw Darío's estheticism not as an ivory-tower evasion of reality, but as a logical expression of disaffection through poetic protest and rebellion. In fact, in *Cantos de vida y esperanza*, 1905 (*Songs of Life and Hope*), he gave full voice to the anguish of living in the real world of age, decay, and death as well as to a continental uneasiness at the aggressive presence of the United States in Latin America.

■ The Avant-Garde

The horrors of World War I lay waste the myth of civilized behavior and of Western culture as the impregnable fortress of mankind's finest achievements. Darwin had destroyed forever the comforting concept of a changeless physical universe. Freud's theories further weakened confidence in the ability of intellect to understand that universe. Einstein struck the final blow to the old order when he represented the physical universe as one in which the only constant was the speed of light, and the old notions of time and space evaporated into relativity. It is no wonder, then, that the former authority of the artist to speak for humanity was undermined.

The reaction to a revolutionized view of the world and to the artist's ambiguous place in its was not uniform, but the period between 1907 and 1924 can be broadly characterized by the profusion of "isms" it spawned in art and literature, a congeries known as the avant-garde. The avant-garde movements sought to address the profound changes previously noted. They were international in outlook, united in their rejection of the past, and — as the name *avant-garde* suggests — militantly aggressive in their programs. Absence of narrative content and a radical dissolution of form were common to all of them.

Out of all that swirl and programmatic poetry came highly experimental verse that tested the limits of language itself — and of the reader's ability to penetrate the new poetry's often hermetic nature. Of the many poets who joined in the effort to make poetry relevant and alive for the modern world, two stand out as superbly representative of the avant-garde and as the best Spanish-American poets of the twentieth century. They are the Peruvian César Vallejo and the Chilean Nobel Prize winner, Pablo Neruda.

Vallejo's work is a poetry of loss, absence, and despair, of something essentially ruinous at the heart of existence itself and shared by all mankind. Loneliness is the natural state of Vallejo, and the dread of its persistence is given concrete form in the broken syntax and ragged grammar of his most famous work, *Trilce* (1922). Vallejo's wretchedness is that of the orphan whose involuntary solitude has become a sign of the world and the poet's place in it: bereft of family and home, God, love, culture, and even human speech itself. Vallejo left Peru in 1923 and never returned. While in Europe, he became a militant Communist, but in general his communism fails to affect his poetry profoundly. Although both personal and intimate, Vallejo's early work had always assumed that humanity everywhere shared a common bond of apprehensiveness and distress. In his latter works he attempts to harmonize his poetry more directly with a now mature sense of solidarity with the world's unfortunates. Formal restraint replaces the nearly total abandon of *Trilce*, and misery speaks in the common language of material want, particularly hunger. What remains of the earlier Vallejo, however, is the nagging suspicion that mankind suffers not because of penury, but because of something in the human condition itself, an incurable ill at the very heart of being. This rejection of the materialist credo is what preserves Vallejo's integrity as man and as poet. His oscillation between doubt and affirmation, between loss and discovery, between language as barrier and as bridge, makes him one of the most profoundly moving and humane of all the Latin American writers.

Vallejo's intimately personal voice and perspective, working out its tortured esthetic of painfully shared loneliness, contrasts with the gigantic and protean figure of Pablo Neruda. The Chilean poet found his first real voice in the somberly erotic *Veinte poemas de amor y una canción desesperada* (1924) *(Twenty Love Poems and a Desperate Song)*, a resounding success for him at the age of twenty. For Vallejo sex was partition confirmed in the unique loneliness of pleasure. For Neruda it was discovery and illumination: a way of knowing and feeling the world and the male poet's incompleteness in it through union with the female, who was the world's true map and surface. But for Neruda union's promise was also ephemeral since even as it united, love

separated, opposing immediacy and distance, presence and absence as preconditions for the gift of knowledge. The instability implied in the sequence seek-find-lose became despairing collapse in *Residencia en la tierra* (1933; 2d ed. revised and expanded, 1935) *(Residence on Earth)*. Here, in pounding, tidal phrasing and forsaken formal restraints rooted in symbolism and surrealism, a visionary Neruda came to grips with the death and destruction that are at the heart of life itself. He finally achieved a harmony with the structures of the world of things: To endure was to do so materially, sharing that persistence with the natural world in an act of poetic faith amid grave doubts.

Neruda's *Tercera residencia* (1947) *(Third Residence)* recognized imperfection as the human condition and affirmed it. Included in this collection were his first political poems, those of *España en el corazón* (1937) *(Spain in My Heart)*, in which he portrays the embattled Spanish socialist republic as the embodiment of the organic, earthy ideal he had pursued and elaborated in the earlier *Residencias*. Later, after joining the Communist party, Neruda undertook in his massive *Canto general* (1950) *(General Song)* to sing of the whole hemisphere, north and south. By the time of its publication Neruda had been stripped of his senatorial seat in Chile and driven into the long exile during which the *Canto* was published in Mexico. Neruda was a late convert to solidarity — unlike Vallejo, whose bond with suffering humanity spans the whole of his work. Neruda subsequently rejected his early works after his political conversion: Their visionary elitism, derived from the romantic tradition of the poet as solitary seer, was uncomfortably narcissistic for a poet of the "people."

In *Canto general* Neruda invoked the continent primeval and the innocence of pre-Columbian America, cruelly but necessarily awakened by the *conquistadores*. The vision of that early indigenous paradise is captured in perhaps the most famous section of the *Canto*, "Alturas de Macchu [sic] Picchu," in which the solitary geomancer of the *Residencias* becomes a spokesman for the Inca dead. In the sequence liberation-betrayal-solidarity, he attributes Latin American liberation to heroic figures from Cuauhtémoc in Mexico in 1520 to Luís Carlos Prestes in Brazil in the 1920s; between the two he posits an emerging mass struggle for an America truly of the people. Betrayal is attributed to foreign capitalists who exploit and plunder America in a second and worse conquest, with the help of their Latin American lackeys, the dictators. Solidarity is achieved as the poet speaks for the living and the dead: the vanished natives and the orphaned, bastard Americans who are the abandoned children of twice-raped America. The *Canto* ends with a song to the sea as a vital, mythic force, whose oracle is Neruda.

Neruda's later poems, especially the *Odas elementales* (1954 and subsequent series), show us a poet captivated and awed by the variety and individuality found in the material world's "unpoetic" substances. He is amazed at the structural uniqueness and complexity of humble onions, artichokes, celery, socks, scissors, liver, and olive oil. Naming them, like Whitman, he gives them poetic life, and he certifies not only their distinctness, but their astonishing vitality as they accompany humanity in its own journey through life.

■ Brazilian Modernism and Latin American Regionalism

In Brazil the origins of the avant-garde can be found as early as 1916–17, but its real confirmation came in February of 1922 in a happening called the Week of Modern Art. The central notion of being above all "modern" gave the movement its name, modernism. This should not be confused with the earlier, Spanish-American *modernismo*. Brazil's modernism began with the intent to scandalize and challenge what its followers saw as outdated and exhausted: the stodgy middle class, the capital at Rio, the literary establishment of gray Parnassians en-

throned there, and the stiff, continental Portuguese they wrote in. The modernists wanted to be thoroughly Brazilian in themes and language, and the movement soon threw off the mantle of a distinctly European avant-garde to seek its authentic character in Brazil alone.

A new folklore and mythology replaced the received culture of Europe, and the previously romanticized Indians (on Rousseau's model) gave way to native cannibals who happily snacked on their European intruders. It was Manuel Bandeira who was to get beyond the pure shock phase of modernism, although he participated in that, too. He and Carlos Drummond de Andrade are the two most significant poets of this modernist period, and also the best Brazilian poets of the twentieth century. In the 1930s Drummond combined a sense of the ironic with a concentrated effort at exorcising the last remnants of the Parnassian tradition from Brazilian poetry. But in the next decade he established positive links with his present in a compromise both with daily life and his fellow man, much in the political manner of Vallejo and Neruda.

The Spanish-American equivalent of Brazil's socially committed regionalism is the Cuban Nicolás Guillén. Guillén sought to identify his own poetic voice with the driving, Afro-Cuban dance and its lyrics, the *son*. To that he added a language enriched with Afro-Cuban dialect and folklore and a violent, and sometimes sardonic, anti-Yankee protest. In the best of his poems he achieves a profoundly moving and spirited fusion of his island's black and white origins, drawing on both popular themes and learned forms.

Among the earliest and most forceful works of Spanish America's prose regionalism was the first novel to result from the turmoil of the Mexican Revolution (1910): Mariano Azuela's *Los de abajo* (1916) *(The Underdogs)*. It echoed the nearly nihilistic view of inevitable change as catastrophe previously heard in naturalistic works. Once unleashed, the violence that began as a means of redressing injustice and abuse becomes an end in itself, and its whirlwind carries off all the participants. A social order is destroyed in *Los de abajo*, but in Azuela's view the price is chaos and the imposition of brute force in place of the hierarchical status quo. The novel stands alone as the best of its kind, a bellwether book whose careful attention to form and structure moved twentieth-century Spanish American fiction toward maturity.

Los de abajo may have seemed a harbinger of the violence and disorder loose in the world generally, but it was also a statement about Mexico as a specific country with a set of problems and a way of speaking all its own. A new Spanish-American regionalism would continue throughout the 1920s and 1930s in the novel, and its style varied considerably. There was the sweating, natural Gothic of Colombian José Eustasio Rivera's *La vorágine* (1924) *(The Vortex)*, a man-eating jungle world; the modernista artistry of Argentine Ricardo Güiraldes in *Don Segundo Sombra* (1926), where the vanishing gaucho was dignified and recast as the nation's mentor in manliness; Venezuelan Rómulo Gallegos' unsubtle novel about the fusion of savagery and civilization for a better tomorrow in *Doña Bárbara* (1929); Ecuadorian Jorge Icaza's portrait of degraded Indians in *Huasipungo* (1934); and Peruvian Ciro Alegría's preachy socialism in *El mundo es ancho y ajeno* (1941) *(Alien and Wide Is the World)*, where an Indian commune is almost saved by Socialist ideology. In all of these works, the underlying theme is man defined by the native soil he occupies.

In Brazil the regionalist strain in fiction was a logical outgrowth of a modernism that began as esthetic anarchy, and after an initial frenzy of nationalism settled rather quickly into a regionalism, for it was a good deal easier to capture and deal with the parts than with the whole sprawling country. The special affection of the Paulistas for their city had already shown the way. Brazilian nationalism was to have two components, one of them abandoned fairly early. Mário de Andrade published *Macunaíma* in 1928; it used Brazilian folklore and myth in a kind of Joycean network with the Amazon instead of Dublin at its heart. That year José Américo de Almeida published *A Bagaceira (The Sugar Mill)*, and a whole school of novelists followed his sociographic lead, not Mário de Andrade's esthetic one. Modernism did not produce the urban regionalism it had seemed to promise; it was the rural northeast that dominated the fiction of the 1930s and 1940s, and on the whole dreary novels of sociology and sentimentalism predominated. They owed much to Gilberto Freyre's immensely popular socioeconomic treatise *Casa Grande & Senzala* (1933) *(The Masters and the Slaves)*. Its theme was class struggle and its setting the drought-ravaged countryside, but in general the "characters" of the novel of the northeast were cardboard types, infinitely transferable from book to book.

■ Jorge Luis Borges

Spanish-American regionalism got most of the attention in the 1930s and early 1940s, but it was the writing of Argentina's Jorge Luis Borges that would endure. Borges began as a poet, and he continued writing concisely evocative "spiritual adventures" set in an intimate and universal Buenos Aires over the years. But it is as a short-story writer that he has developed an international following. From 1925 to 1935 he fashioned the hybrid narrative form that was to become his hallmark. It was both a style and a structure for storytelling grounded in the speculative philosophical essay and refined in the mythic sequence of quest-obstacle-discovery. The novelty of this pattern was further enhanced by Borges's deliberate choice of the experience of life through literature as his working tradition. The sources of his themes, characters, and actions are imaginary, and the setting for every story is the world of the mind.

Borges's protagonists, driven by intellectual curiosity, quest after knowledge, solutions, and answers. His favorite metaphor for the obstacle that hinders them is the labyrinth, whose subtle forms are infinite. Discovery lies within or beyond the labyrinth, and the triumphant intellect frequently breaches the center or breaks free altogether, only to find that the exit toll is annihilation. Borges' mocking insistence on a single, prototypical life lived endlessly over and over in all its variations is an inevitable reenactment of a minor drama with major consequences. In the world of modern fiction, there may be no writer as unpretentiously subversive of individual personality or of discrete historical event as the author of *Ficciones* (1944) and *El aleph* (1949). Borges has been reviled by the documentary realists and worshipped by those who celebrate his rehabilitation of imaginative fiction. And despite the protests of the literary social geographers, no other Spanish-American writer has captured so succinctly or so poignantly the fragmented personality, the multiple legacies, and the torn allegiances of the Latin American intellectual as Borges has. It is not just Borges's sense of tradition and heritage, both social and intellectual, or his profoundly metaphysical themes that determine his importance individually and as an influence on subsequent writing. Perhaps even more important are Borges's sense of craftsmanship and his insistence on self-conscious fiction in the tradition of Machado de Assis.

■ Four Contemporary Poets

The Spanish American poets who came after Neruda had not only to contend with the old polarities of America/Europe, nature/society, solitary intellectual visionary/abject mass man, and what T. S. Eliot called "tradition and the individual talent"; they had also to deal with the imposing presence of Neruda himself. The two who most successfully escaped being smothered were the Mexican Octavio Paz and the Chilean Nicanor Parra.

Octavio Paz has become for his young colleagues in Mexico what Neruda had been for all Spanish-American poets: an institution. His

prolific writing testifies to a searching, cosmopolitan interest in the world and its cultures. At the heart of this quest is identity and voice: what it means to be Mexican, American, Western, and above all a poet. Paz has sought answers to these questions in successive explorations that have highlighted the essentially "baroque" nature of human existence, conditioned as it is by the struggle to reconcile both internal and external oppositions. Paz's initial concern as a visionary poet was to find an expression for that desired harmony in the metaphor of physical love and in the act of writing itself, through their shared properties of creative conjunction, ecstasy, and the abolition of time. The essays of *El laberinto de la soledad* (1950) (*The Labyrinth of Solitude*) constitute one of the most important books on national identity in the twentieth century. He traced the history of Mexican solitude to its source in the rape of the native American mother by Europeans and posited a crisis of identity in which neither parent's heritage was suitable. Seeing the Mexican as a child of nothing, self-beginning yet requiring communion, Paz attempted in *Piedra de sol* (1957) (*Sun Stone*) to harmonize that contradiction in the poetic figure of the sunlit Aztec calendar stone. Paz's poetry and the intellectual concerns of his essays show a continuing need for "getting beyond." The past is superseded by modernity, Mexicanism by cosmopolitanism, and the Western, Catholic, baroque tradition is finally surpassed in the Oriental vision of *Ladera este* (1968) (*Eastern Rampart*) and in its finest poem, "Viento entero" ("Whole Wind").

Another poet who successfully challenged the influence of Neruda was his own countryman Nicanor Parra. Parra responded to the disorder and senselessness of the world, and also to Neruda's surging, oracular style, by flaying poetry alive. In *Poemas y antipoemas* (1954) first, and then in the collected verse of *Obra gruesa* (1969) (*Rough Training*), Parra skinned poetry of its ornamental, "poetic" language. In its place we find jokes, banalities, obscenities scrawled on the page like hysterical graffiti. His verse is scruffy, wrinkled, run-down, and occasionally run over. Parra's is a poetry of anarchy, of reprisal against institutionalized everything, but especially against conventional lyrical verse. This is so much so that in 1972 he published a large carton of postcards called *Artefactos*, in which the antipoems are ungathered into an antibook. But behind this dresser-drawer or shoebox poetry is the same motive that has driven the best poets for nearly five hundred years in the Americas: to come to terms with their impermanent existence between heaven and hell and to find a voice that does justice to their craft.

The works of João Cabral de Melo Neto and Ernesto Cardenal continue the struggle of the Latin American artist and intellectual who seeks to honor his social and political convictions as well as his commitment to a high standard of artistic purity. Cabral's "regionalist" theme is the searing poverty of Brazil's northeast, expressed in a language of the utmost simplicity and concision. Cardenal is a militant Nicaraguan priest whose poetry attempts to reconcile social justice and Christian virtue. His best poems are those in which his biting satire is brought to bear on the rapacious Somoza regime and its United States supporters in commerce and industry. He also excels in the minor heroic genre in which small folk pursue paths of large consequence: decency, liberty, justice, and self-determination.

■ **Postwar Fiction**

Documentary fiction in Latin America, whether rural or urban, had run low on inspiration by the 1930s, but it sputtered along repeating itself inertially until after World War II. Then came an enormous burst of narrative energy that released both new and previously set-aside works. In both cases it was clear that the novel had come of age. In 1946 Guatemalan Nobel Prize winner Miguel Angel Asturias published *El señor presidente*, written in the 1920s and 1930s, but unpublished earlier for political reasons. It was noteworthy because of its surrealistic portrait not so much of a Guatemalan dictator as of the grotesque and anxiety-ridden atmosphere that attends dictatorship itself. What Asturias captured was the disembodied presence of a threat that had no name, only a title, a power, and a nightmare to occupy.

In 1947 Mexico's Agustín Yáñez published *Al filo del agua (The Edge of the Storm)*, a novel that, like Asturias's, substituted atmosphere and mood for character and setting, thereby conveying the sense of an explosive environment ripe for upheaval. Yáñez transforms the fact of the revolution into an evocative symbol of change itself and of the way it challenges stultifying tradition. *Al filo del agua* is a carefully wrought counterpoint to Mariano Azuela's work.

In 1948 two important novels were published in Argentina: Ernesto Sabato's *El túnel* and Leopoldo Marechal's *Adán Buenosayers*. *El túnel* is a tale of alienation told by a homicidal maniac. It immediately became *the* existential novel of Latin American and continues to be a classic. *Adán Buenosayres* was to the capital of Argentina what *Finnegan's Wake* was to Dublin. Like *El Señor presidente*, *Adán Buenosayres* has the flavor of the experimental literary concerns and the surrealistic style of the 1920s in which it was written. It is a raunchy and rollicking parody of Dante's *Divine Comedy* with the city of Buenos Aires as Hell.

In 1949 the Cuban Alejo Carpentier brought out *El reino de este mundo*. Set in Haiti, it is the first of the author's works to interweave the themes and forces that were to define him best: the cyclical nature of time and the cultural incompatibility of the racial groups brought forcibly together in the Americas in discord and dissonance. From the clash of dissimilar peoples occupying the same geography, but having little else in common, comes the vertiginous quality of Carpentier's fiction and of his concept of the special, magical reality of America as incongruity and paradox. Carpentier would later refine his essentially intellectual vision of an hallucinatory American in *Los pasos perdidos*

(1953) *(The Lost Steps)*, and he would rewrite the history of Latin America as a recurrent myth of the forced coexistence of irreconcilable opposites.

The works that appeared between 1946 and 1949 finally embued the most recalcitrant form of Latin American literature, fiction, with the same avant-garde spirit that had reshaped poetry at the beginning of the twentieth century and had already affected drama profoundly by the 1930s and 1940s. The decade of the 1950s provided the necessary bridge between the postwar initiators of the new novel and those who, from the 1960s on, would impose the vitality of Latin American fiction onto the world at large. Three novels in particular had an incalculable effect on what was to come: *Pedro Páramo* (1955), *Grande Sertão: Veredas* (1956) *(The Devil to Pay in the Backlands)*, and *Gabriela, cravo e canela* (1958) *(Gabriela, Clove and Cinnamon)*.

The Mexican Juan Rulfo's *Pedro Páramo* is an almost unbearably spare novel. Its theme and setting are cliches: the disintegration of a vicious rural *caudillo* (dictator) and his fiefdom, Comala, about the time of the revolution. The corrupted character of Pedro Páramo descends directly from Azuela's vision of power as perverse and perverting, and the community's collective withering had been foreshadowed in Yáñez. What is new and original is the way in which Pedro Páramo's personality and history are revealed through the faint sighs and whispers of the town's phantoms, still afraid to raise their voices even though they and their lord have long been dead. Comala lives and dies in Páramo's unmitigated rancour, its infernal persistence conveyed in a fragmentary narration of flashbacks and jump-cuts from their voice to that, from history to eternity, from life to death.

The Brazilian João Guimarães Rosa's masterpiece *Grande Sertão: Veredas* is a vast uninterrupted monologue set in Brazil's boundless outback. The sertão is a grand external symbol of the protagonist's life there years earlier as a *jegunço*—part hired gun and free spirit, part knight-errant with worlds to conquer and wrongs to right. But the sertão as it is recalled by the narrator is also an internal world as well: a searching, spiritual reflection on the meaning and morality of that life of honor, grandeur, mystery, and faith. Guimarães Rosa used the regionalist setting of Brazil's novel and the esthetic freedom of the vanguard for a virtuoso performance of language, memory, and metaphysics in *Grande Sertão*. It is a great baroque fugue, and between its opening word and its final one—*nonada* and *travessia*, a trifle and a traversing—he has captured the paradox of paltriness and passage that is the human condition.

Gabriela, cravo e canela was Brazilian Jorge Amado's first novel after his break with communism. The notoriety occasioned by his politics, the enormous success of his book, and the carnival atmosphere that attended its rendition into television, records, the movies, and even comic books foreshadowed the author-as-celebrity years of the 1960s to 1980s. *Gabriela* is a sweeping panorama of a city whose vibrant humanity seeks to open itself to the promise of the outside world and struggles against the dead weight of its past. Amado told the story of the port city of Ilhéus in 1925, centering his account on the antagonism between modern industrial progress and old-line, feudal conservatism. *Gabriela*'s rollicking comedy, sexual high jinks, withering social and political put-downs, and spellbinding style provided a foretaste of the best works of Gabriel García Márquez and Mario Vargas Llosa. A misreading by at least two administrations even led to the modernization of the port facilities at Ilhéus to assist Amado's characters in their goal of progress. It was a bizarre and hilarious acknowledgment of the "reality" of fiction and an ironic confirmation that Amado as novelist had succeeded where Amado as congressman had failed.

■ The "Boom" in Spanish-American Fiction

In the early 1970s Emir Rodríguez Monegal nicknamed the novelists who had come to maturity in the previous decade as the "boom" generation. Whether the name is apt is less at issue than is the accuracy of his perception that a new and distinct group of powerful writers had taken the field, and that in the aggregate it was reshaping fiction in a decisive way.

The novelists who have dominated the last two decades are united in their common concern for their craft. Their preoccupation with language recalls the sensitivity to its potential for originality and discovery first articulated by the modernista writers of the nineteenth century. They feel a sense of close and easy community not only with their predecessors and among themselves, but with the whole Western tradition of literature. With the writers of the boom, the polarity of America and Europe has finally been resolved and absorbed as a shared artistic heritage, and the earlier "poor relation" complex is gone forever. This sense of belonging and legitimacy may be the single most important factor of the self-confidence that has allowed Latin American novelists to settle comfortably at long last into the role of professional writers.

The authors of the boom challenge their art and its traditions. Positing the creative imagination as the only proper universe of fiction, they probe the outer limits of their genre. Their preoccupation with writing shows not only in the output of the novelist and short-story writer, but in that of theorist and critic as well. Continuing along the path opened by Borges and explored by Octavio Paz, the creative writer often becomes his own interpreter. This happens both in novels whose theme is the writing of novels and in critical essays about one's own work or that of colleagues. A self-indulgence that might at first seem insufferably clannish finds its explanation in novelists' own unquestioned expertise in fiction, but more important, in their initial frustration at the inadequacies of prevailing Hispanic criticism.

The new novelists clearly felt banished at home and missed the stimulation of like-minded writers as well as informed and perceptive critics. The mere arrogance of self-interpretation

alone might not fully address these problems, but a deliberate strategy of internationalization of the writer and his works would. Novelists went to live abroad in England, France, and Spain. They acquired literary agents who placed manuscripts with publishers that would promote them. Translation rights were negotiated for books already circulating, and simultaneous publication in several languages was secured for works even before their completion. Latin America's previous press runs of one thousand to three thousand copies in fiction paled before the onslaught of novels that now sold tens and even hundreds of thousands. These novelists were now sought for interviews in newspapers and on radio and television. The new writers became "personalities."

The road-show atmosphere that occasionally attends the phenomenon of the boom makes it easy to forget that what counts is the quality of the fiction these writers produce. And in their defense it must be said that literary quality has not suffered the potential distractions of fame and material success. If anything, the voluntary exile and frenzied international activity of these displaced writers has quickened their sense of the homelands they left and provided them with the kind of sojourner's truth that comes with distance. No earlier novel has ever conveyed the sense of being in America as fully or as convincingly as Carlos Fuentes's *La muerte de Artemio Cruz* (1962) *(The Death of Artemio Cruz)*, Julio Cortázar's *Rayuela* (1963) *(Hopscotch)*, or Gabriel García Márquez's *Cien años de soledad* (1967) *(One Hundred Years of Solitude)*. And the geographic origin of each writer—Mexico, Argentina, and Colombia, respectively—shows the extent to which their vision is truly a sustained continental phenomenon, not a mere fluke.

Fuentes has been a prolific writer of both fiction and essays and an active participant in the boom. *La región más transparente* (1959) *(Where the Air Is Clear)* was the first serious Spanish-American attempt to work out in novel-length prose the avant-garde's preoccupation with simultaneism. *La región más transparente*, heavily indebted to the technique of John Dos Passos, is a collage or pastiche of interwoven times, places, events, and figures that press the past on the present, summarizing the contemporary life of a nation without the imposition of sequence, order, or apparent cause.

La muerte de Artemio Cruz is generally regarded as Fuentes's masterpiece. In it, the novel's dying protagonist recalls, with emotional rather than chronological priority, the events and his responses to them that have shaped his biblically allotted time of seventy years. Artemio Cruz is the flint-hard, self-made man who has risen out of the turmoil of the revolution to mold its as-yet formless aftermath to his own will. He forges a secular theology that makes survival its first article of faith, power its second, and death the negation of both. Because life is the only reality and the afterlife is its repudiation, the dying man's memory is a vision of both heaven and hell on earth, and the man is at once his own messiah and the Antichrist. This underlying duality pervades the novel, and it is embodied narratively in the author's technique of revealing Artemio Cruz's true self as a profane trinity. His story is told in a fragmented way by three alternating voices, each with its necessary if one-sided perspective, each with its own grammatical "person."

In *La muerte de Artemio Cruz* Fuentes brought the techniques and effects of kaleidoscopic fragmentation to near-perfection in the creation of a complex personality. The book is also an effective and iconoclastic response to national myth about the revolution and its heroes. Yáñez had set the stage for coming to terms with the impending confrontation. Azuela portrayed a man—and a class of men—unequal to the forces that they had helped unleash. But Fuentes's integrated vision of Mexico shows fate to be in the hands of those who, like Artemio Cruz, can tame the revolutionary chaos and shape a nation.

The Argentine Julio Cortázar is justly admired for his short stories, but his greatest re-

nown attaches to *Rayuela* (1963). This novel initiated the boom of Latin American fiction, if any single work can be said to have done so. Its theme is the need to fight free of the smothering effect of received culture, ideas, and attitudes. The protagonist is an Argentine poised between Paris and Buenos Aires in an attempt to give meaning to his life, to liberate himself from a robotic existence that subverts everything—humanity, love, art, politics, and religion—through the endless and meaningless repetition of clichéd formulas. In *Rayuela* the struggle for freedom becomes revolt verging on anarchy, and the foremost target is the novelistic form itself. Cortázar does away with such traditional storytelling devices as causal plot, psychological characterization, point of view, and the omniscient narrator. The book is a huge warehouse of "fictionable" parts with a set of instructions for two possible readings. One is chapters 1 to 56, read in sequence, the economy model sarcastically suggested by the author for the fainthearted. The other is a hopscotch reading of all 155 chapters—out of numerical sequence but in a specified order. In retrospect *Rayuela* may not have been all it purported to be literarily, but as a seductive experience it was unquestionably original, one of a kind. Cortázar's iconoclasm was near total in *Rayuela*, and there was no way the Latin American novel would ever be the same after its general debunking of everything and everybody (including the author himself).

Cortázar will also be remembered for his provocative essays, but his major strength is unquestionably the short story. His best ones involve moments of conjunction and revelation; short-circuitry between distinct realities or between unperceived realms of the commonplace. Cortázar deals with the deceptiveness of sensory perception. Lulled into confidence that they see, hear, and feel the world around them accurately, his characters are often shattered by the revelation that they have failed to do so or that there is a world or worlds beyond their senses. Cortázar later took a new direction in his story "El perseguidor" ("The Pursuer"), which mercilessly examines the perfectionist who deliberately ignores humanity in favor of the highly crafted work his art demands. The story explores but does not really answer the troublesome problem of what, if anything, the writer owes to others besides his writing. It was a concern that would torment Cortázar all his life; it surfaced in *Rayuela* and in his unsuccessful political novel, *Libro de Manuel* (1973). The question is one intimately connected with the old dilemma of the Latin American intellectual's civic and humanitarian duties, and it consistently plagues the writers of the boom.

Gabriel García Márquez is best known for his novel *Cien años de soledad*, the culmination of a cycle of works that were a kind of cartography of Macondo. This fictional locale was first treated as a tense center in which social and political confrontations were knotted and cramped until some catalyst caused their violent release. Later books introduced the Rabelaisian exaggeration that eventually found its fullest expression in *Cien años de soledad*.

The novel is the [hi]story of the Buendía family from the moment their patriarch, José Arcadio, leads them away from civilization in the "pre history" of the nineteenth century. He founds the village of Macondo in the promised land that no one promised him, and for a hundred years we follow the shenanigans of the family and the town as both grow and prosper under the ancestral curse of incest set loose when José Arcadio marries his cousin Úrsula Iguarán. As the life of the town winds down and the last Aureliano falls madly in love with his aunt and she with him, the old textual prophesies surface. The last thundering sexual marathons finally engender messiah or monster, and with a shudder the novel comes to its foretold end. It closes on itself like the Buendía family or the city limits of Macondo. And like Ishmael in *Moby Dick*, García Márquez alone is left to tell the tale.

Cien años de soledad was an end in itself and an end for a kind of writing that García Márquez had cultivated for nearly a decade. His next book, *El otoño del patriarca* (1975) *(The Autumn of the Patriarch)* was a tour de force portrayal of a dictator who had ruled his country for some two hundred years. The book's atmosphere is colored by the presence of the nearly eternal *caudillo*, finally gone to dust but still pressing relentlessly down on his hapless subjects. The narrative point of view oscillates surrealistically between the hallucinatory and disembodied consciousness of the dictator, still hovering in the presidential mansion, and the cautious and tentative perspective of those who have broken down the palace door to verify the patriarch's alleged death.

■ Conclusion

The triumph of Latin American literature, despite its achievements, marks not a culmination but a crossroads. From Sor Juana to Paz, from Machado to Fuentes, many of the old paradoxes have been outgrown. Yet the most persistent unfinished business that frets the writer in Latin America is a problem of long standing, noted earlier. Since colonial days, the Latin American intellectual has felt a debt of responsibility to less fortunate compatriots and a moral compulsion to oppose the society responsible for their misfortune. Latin American writers carry an enormous freight of guilt for having more in common with their European and North American counterparts than with their own populations at large. Urban, cosmopolitan, cultured, and well off, they are haunted by the knowledge that a majority of their compatriots are rural, illiterate, poor, and abject.

The intruder in paradise; the American writer and the European tradition; the struggle with nature; harmonizing the past with the present: these have all become intellectual concerns demanding to be thought out and resolved. Hunger, exposure, illness, and oppression are not just memories from an earlier age, but a painful reality witnessed daily or recurrent in the exile's nightmares. Social and political commitment gnaw at the soul of Latin American writers, sap their imaginative reserves, and goad them to genuine solidarity for masses of people whose metaphysical problems they are better suited to solving than physical ones. Latin American artists, like those everywhere, are an elite by definition, yet there they suffer at least one guilt their foreign comrades need not share. This dichotomy endures, and with it the paradox of all literature of commitment: As the one prevails, the other fails.

12 | *Art and Architecture of Latin America*

JOHN F. SCOTT

The implantation of Iberian culture in the Americas with relatively little resistance must be seen as the most complete "spiritual conquest," to use Robert Ricard's phrase,[1] in the history of the world. Although there was an initial period of racial intermixture — call it *mestizaje* — between the existent Indian population and the Spanish *conquistadores,* the Indian cultural component was thoroughly eliminated in subsequent generations among the ruling classes. It is only in the lower levels of society, especially among the agricultural peasantry, that the Indian racial and cultural inheritance remains strong. The arts produced by Indian groups were considered marginal in the Iberian cultures that supplanted them, relegated at best to the status of minor arts and at worst dismissed as folk crafts.

Not coincidentally, the areas of the greatest artistic production in colonial times were those of the highest pre-Columbian civilizations. Two reasons for this can be offered: The Spanish administration took over control of the Inca and the Aztec empires because they were the best organized and were the center of inflowing tribute. Second, both Mesoamerica and the Central Andes had long traditions of fine artistic craftsmanship in all media and were the only areas in the Americas to produce permanent stone architecture. Thus, in the mid-sixteenth century the two viceroyalties — New Spain and Peru — took over these long-standing pre-Columbian artistic and craft traditions.

■ Renaissance with Gothic Survivals

The revival of ancient Roman forms of the visual arts, which began in Italy in the early fifteenth century, did not affect the rest of Europe until the sixteenth century, contemporary with the colonial expansion of European culture into the rest of the world. Prior to that era, art was dominated by medieval styles, which did not stress naturalism in representation, carefully measured proportions, or clear load-support relationship in architecture. Art in the Middle Ages culminated in the Gothic style of northern Europe, which Spain adopted to a considerable extent. Medieval Spain had been uniquely preoccupied with the reconquest of its territories from the Islamic "Moors," so called for Morocco, whence they came. Spain's art included a blend of Islamic and Christian styles: blank-walled exteriors and richly decorated portals leading to paradisiacally flowering interior patios decorated with geometrically patterned woodwork and tile.

When Columbus set sail, the inquisitive, self-confident Renaissance spirit was in the human heart, but the waning Gothic style provided the architectural backdrop for their actions. The first European settlement in America that provided more than mere shelter, Santo Domingo, was established in 1502 at its present location on the southern coast of the island of Hispaniola. The plan of the city, a grid modified

Photo: John F. Scott

FIGURE 1
Bishop Alejandro Geraldini. Cathedral of Santa Maria la Menor, Santo Domingo, Dominican Republic, 1521–1540. North portal, carved stone.

by the irregularity of the sloping site, later would become required of all new cities by the Laws of the Indies of 1573. Individual buildings in Santo Domingo reveal aspects of the fast-disappearing Gothic style in flame-shaped window divisions, richly sculpted portals with slender colonnettes supporting ribbed arches (Figure 1), and ribbed vaulted ceilings. Vaulting in Latin America retained the ribbed Gothic style into the seventeenth century.

On the mainland the first permanent buildings were usually walled residences for the friars sent to convert the Indians. These buildings, called *conventos* in Spanish, were not at all monastic retreats from the world but springboards into it. At first built in late Gothic style, these conventos quickly show a shift to Renaissance design. The high, notched profile of the walls of the church connected to the convento at Acolmán (Figure 2) recalls the image of the reconquest and the establishment of fortress churches among the heathen Moors in Spain. Around the main entrance to the Acolmán church is carved beautiful Plateresque decoration, suggesting the appearance of ornate silver candelabras instead of columns revived from ancient Rome. Spain acquired the Renaissance late, and her architects were never much concerned about the structural logic of the columns. Wrapped garlands and sashes hide the column shafts; their bases appear to be a series of stacked pots. This decorative early form of Renaissance ornament known as Plateresque continued well into the second half of the sixteenth century in the Spanish colonies.

The reconstructed secular headquarters of

FIGURE 2
Maestro Palomira (and others?). San Agustín church and monastic building, Acolmán, Mexico, 1539–1571.

Photo: John F. Scott

Santo Domingo, known as the Alcázar of Diego Columbus (Figure 3), was in part the fortified stronghold implied by its Arabic name, *alcázar:* It has heavy walls and a fortified roof line; in the two end blocks its openings are small. In the middle, however, it opens up on both stories and on both sides to graceful arcades that shelter porches overlooking the river and the new city. The building combines the medieval military style of reconquest headquarters with the grace of an Italian Renaissance palace. A nearly identical building was erected for Hernán Cortés's palace in Cuernavaca, Mexico, built as the manor house for his newly bestowed marquisate. Undoubtedly the builders in Mexico had already seen the Santo Domingo construction of Columbus's son Diego and wished to emulate it.

The necessity of handling large masses of potential converts stimulated a unique kind of church architecture in Latin America. The buildings centered on a large enclosed forecourt, called an atrium after those in front of the early Christian churches in Italy. The interiors of the new churches created vast covered spaces unknown to pre-Columbian builders, who were restricted to creating narrow chambers or to a forest of short stone columns. The rich exterior decoration of Mexican churches, however, corresponds to some pre-Columbian traditions of dense low-relief designs. And the large enclosed atrium, rectangular in plan and bounded on all sides by walls and shrines but focusing on the soaring façade of the church, recalled preconquest ceremonial spaces. In prehispanic religious observance most of the Indians stood in four-sided plazas to observe rituals that generally took place at the top of a steep pyramid. Just as they built many churches on the site of former pagan temples, so the early friars chose an architectural form that related the Indians' prior religious experience to the new Christian one by creating the same kind of ceremonial space.

Crucial to this substitution was the inclusion

FIGURE **3**
Diego Columbus. Alcázar de Colón, Santo Domingo, Dominican Republic, 1509–1523. Reconstructed west façade.

Photo: John F. Scott

of open-air chapels in the atrium spaces. Although their location varied considerably, ideally the chapels were raised above the worshippers' heads and were framed by architecture, much as the pagan temples had provided a backdrop for the ritual performed in front. The *convento* of Acolmán has such a chapel to the right of the church. For the low platform once placed in the center of pre-Columbian plazas the friars substituted a heavy square base supporting a massive cross. The crosses placed in atriums were an ingenious mix of representation and symbol; they merged the image of the crucified Christ with that of the pre-Columbian World Tree. Christ is represented only by the face in high relief at the center of the cross, but by implication the rest of the cross becomes his outstretched arms and hanging trunk. Other symbols of the Passion story appear on the cross itself in the low relief common in pre-Columbian carvings (Figure 4). Finally, the atriums had small rest stops called *posas*, open at the sides, in each corner; processions around the atrium paused briefly at each posa.

Painting within the cloisters, where the friars lived, was primarily in black and gray on the white plaster ground of the walls. The resulting murals resemble blown-up versions of the Flemish prints imported into Spain from the Netherlands, another possession of the Hapsburg King Carlos I. Retrained Indian artists were given such prints to copy. Pre-Columbian mural painting had often been monochrome, so the Indians undoubtedly felt no compunction about retaining the black-and-white scheme. Most of the images were familiar to Europeans, since they copy Renaissance precedents closely.

The decorative bands painted in such profusion to decorate early colonial buildings are in the tradition derived from first-century A.D. Roman frescoes seen in buried rooms unearthed in the early sixteenth century. Renaissance observers were reminded of grottoes; hence our stylistic term *grotesque* (from the French). Such designs, which defy structural logic, became

popular during the later Renaissance, particularly when used by Flemish wood engravers as space fillers or border decoration in their books. From this source they served as models for the walls of structures in New Spain.

An exceptional cycle of paintings mixing European and Indian styles was uncovered in a small church in Ixmiquilpan, northeast of Mexico City. There a series of battle scenes show men with Indian battle dress and weapons fight-

FIGURE **4**

Anonymous Indian. Atrium cross, stone, c. 2.25 m. high, 16th century. San Agustín, Acolman, Mexico.

Photo: John F. Scott

ing monsters blown up from *grotesque* ornament. These are clearly original compositions by Indian painters directed toward their own people, who were by then converted Christians but who would understand the struggle between Christians and pagans better if presented in these terms.[2] This mural, unlike most of those in cloisters, was rendered in color, featuring

vibrant oranges and blues. The style is European, with figures in their natural proportions and seen at three-quarter angle, a technique unknown to pre-Columbian artists.

The complete assimilation of a known Indian artist is revealed in Tecamachalco, southeast of Puebla, Mexico. Oil paintings in full color on cloth attached to the vaulted ceiling below the

Photo: John F. Scott

FIGURE 5
Baltasar de Echave Orio.
Porziuncola, **oil on canvas,**
2.52 × 1.60 m., 1609. Pinacoteca
Virreinal de San Diego, Mexico
City.

choir loft are dated 1562 and signed Joannes Gersón; it was assumed by the Flemish name and the relatively skilled northern Renaissance style that they were the works of a Fleming. Archival research revealed that Gersón, who adopted the name in honor of a then-famous cleric, was in fact an Indian.[3] Gersón used the black-and-white woodcut compositions in a sixteenth-century Bible as the inspiration for fully modeled — that is, shaded and given the illusion of existing in space — and colored oil paintings, which shows how brilliantly some Indians had assimilated the European style.

By the latter sixteenth century European artists were arriving in Mexico from Europe to accept new commissions and to fulfill the stricter requirements for religious painting imposed by an ecclesiastical council in 1555 and reinforced by the establishment of an artists' guild in 1557. The Fleming Simón Pereyns, who arrived in 1556, gathered around him an impressive group of professionals. Due to their skill and the increasing prejudice of the authorities against Indians, these artists began to supplant native competitors for important civil and ecclesiastical projects. Pereyns's paintings were incorporated in *retablos,* large framed structures that filled the walls behind altars. Assembling these enormous retablos demanded considerable cooperation among painters, sculptors, architectural woodcarvers, and gilders. The earliest fully documented retablo, erected in 1586 in the convento church at Huejotzingo, can serve as a model for these major artistic undertakings. It had eight paintings by Pereyns placed in the frames created by the rectangular wooden architectural grid, much like ancient Roman stage designs. Fourteen heavily robed figures carved out of wood, possibly by Luis de Arciniega, in a style that is still High Renaissance in its balance, strength, and stability, emerge from niches beneath conch-shell arches that appear to be sunburst halos behind the figures' heads. A gilder applied the gold leaf and the enameled skin tones as well as painting the clothing. The great retablos were a major artistic undertaking of colonial Latin America, important both for their high quality and for their quantity. Many of the significant artistic advances in colonial arts appeared in retablos before spreading to more independent sculpture and painting. The very integration of the arts demanded by the retablos may have stimulated each artist to produce his finest works to be seen next to those of his colleagues.

These early artists often established workshops in which other members of their families assisted in the execution of large commissions. Baltasar de Echave Orio founded a dynasty of painters that virtually monopolized official commissions in Mexico for over a century. Although Echave Orio was a painter of the early seventeenth century, like El Greco in Spain he continued the shimmering style of unnatural idealism called Mannerism well after it had died out in other parts of Europe. His major commission was to make fourteen paintings for the retablo of Santiago Tlatelolco in Mexico City; three of these, dated to 1609, have survived. In one, *Porziuncola,* the figures of Christ and the Virgin hover on clouds in front of a kneeling Saint Francis of Assisi (Figure 5). The holy figures' elongated bodies and stylized fingers, and the crackling highlights of their drapery, clearly betray the spirit of late Mannerism, as does the unreal perspective of the scene.

■ Baroque

The Baroque style, which was introduced in Europe around the year 1600, stressed dramatic presentation through active forms, diagonal composition, spotlighting, and deep space. In painting the Baroque style reached the Americas only around the middle of the seventeenth century. Artists working in this mode rejected the fantastic colors, impossible proportions, and illogical and extreme spatial and structural relationships preferred by Mannerist artists of the sixteenth and early seventeenth centuries in favor of realistic directness and clarity. They wanted to make the religious events depicted in their paintings as believable as possible, so that viewers could relate directly to the event and feel as if they were participants. Most popular in the early development of Baroque painting was the dramatically spotlit scene that showed un-idealized, large-scale figures placed close to the viewer. This style, originated by Caravaggio in Italy, became immensely popular with Spanish artists such as Francisco Zurbarán, who was active in Seville, from which most settlers departed for Spanish America. The style appears suddenly in Mexico with the monumental canvas of Sebastián López de Arteaga, *Doubting Thomas*, painted in 1643. The aims of the Baroque subject coincide beautifully with the need to feel the presence of Christ and experience His suffering, which the Apostle Thomas does by inserting his finger in the wound in Christ's side. Those portrayed, whose life-sized torsos fill the canvas, are believable in their ordinariness — disheveled old men with wrinkled brows — except for Christ, Thomas, and a figure in the upper left, which may be the artist's self-portrait.[6] The single source of light shines brightly from the left, eliminating nonessential elements in the background by the deep shadows and spotlighting the wound, emphasizing Christ's fleshiness. The Word is made flesh and dwells among us.

Even more important than Caravaggio as an inspiration to Latin American painters was Peter Paul Rubens. The reason for Rubens's popularity lies in his combination of the immediacy of Caravaggio with sumptuous colors and pictorial effects. Rubens's paintings soften the shocking realism of Caravaggio while retaining his compelling physical presence through large scale (seen in the way in which the figures fill the frame) and sensuous naturalism (seen in the fleshy skin tones and illusionistic textures). His work reappears in innumerable copies, from small painted marble slabs to huge canvases. The handsome canvas of *The Adoration of the Magi* (Figure 6) by Baltasar de Echave Rioja, grandson of the founder of the Echave line of painters, is ultimately derived from Rubens's various engraved versions of that subject.[5]

Echave's painting is a work of great power, rich color, and lush texture.

In Latin America, Baroque painting — painting in the grand manner so suitable to the propaganda needs of church and court alike — was placed above all in the service of the church, since viceroys were transient appointments of the kings in far-off Spain. In the Rubensian tradition, painting expanded from its previous position within architectural frames of retablos to colossal canvases independent of them. The best example of this new scale is seen in the work of Cristóbal de Villalpando in two great cathedrals of Mexico. Between 1684 and 1686 he attached paintings illustrating Roman Catholic dogma to all the walls of the sacristy of Mexico City Cathedral. The paintings were mounted on curved frames, which causes them to echo the vaults of the ceiling, themselves becoming part of the architecture. In the sixteenth century fresco painting had occupied the same position, but rarely was it so large in scale. One of Villalpando's visionary scenes, *The Triumph of the Eucharist*, is derived from sketches by Rubens. It has a sweep unmatched in any Renaissance-style work in America, characterized as it is by more compartmentalized compositions. The colossal chariot, figures, and horses painted by Villalpando have a physical reality that marks them as Baroque: their fluid brush stroke communicates the dashing urgency of the event. Even the light coming through the window in the upper center of the composition is incorporated into the scene as a sunburst from which archangels emerge. The most totally Baroque program, illusionistic ceiling painting, was undertaken by Villalpando in 1688 to represent a celestial Glory for the dome of Puebla Cathedral. He treated the entire surface as one billowing composition of clouds filled with angels and saints, culminating in the Dove of the Holy Spirit descending directly next to the intense light of the cupola, which thus becomes the real light of God's grace. By their grand manner, Latin American painters were trying to capture the emotions and hearts of their viewers, to catch them up in the church's mission.

In Cuzco, Peru, an anonymous artist domesticated these Rubensian spectacles to commemorate the more earthly Corpus Christi processions, which took place in June. He used the large-scale and scintillating color of Europe, yet depicted—for perhaps the first time—contemporary Latin American events. Included are all segments of colonial society, from the aristocratic Spaniards observing from their balconies to the *mestizo* lower classes standing at curbside, but the painting focuses on the leaders of the processions. These are portraits of specific individuals; one is apparently a descendant of the noble Inca, for he wears the distinctive Inca poncho shirt.

In wooden sculpture, the fine, balanced Renaissance carving of the sixteenth century was replaced by more compelling carvings energetically reaching into space. Some works attributed to Spanish masters such as Juan Martínez Montañés are found in the Americas. Their Baroque qualities reside in their full life size, their stunningly realistic fleshtones (achieved by a careful enameling process called *encarnación*—putting on the flesh), and the simulation of rich, gold-threaded tapestry garments by *estofado*, the application of color over gold leaf. Sculptors chose emotionally charged subjects to depict, such as the bleeding Christ on the way to His crucifixion; the reality of the life-sized image, often with real garments, is powerfully felt by every viewer. The masterful sculpture of the Virgin of the Apocalypse carved by Bernardo Legarda in 1734 shows the spatial expansion of the baroque sculpture, which can no longer be confined to a small niche in a retablo. The deeply carved, large folds of the drapery emphasize the figure's dynamic motion as the crowned Virgin plunges her lightning bolt into the writhing serpent, symbolizing Satan, below. Legarda is at the pinnacle of the Quito School of sculpture, the most esteemed in the Spanish-American world.

The reality of sculpture is dramatized by the

FIGURE **6**
Baltasar de Echave Rioja.
Adoration of the Magi, **oil on canvas, 1.54 × 1.98 m., 1659.**

new architectural setting provided for it. In many churches in Spanish America the statues of the Virgin are not only often dressed in real clothing but may be provided a separate room, called a *camarín,* behind the altar. And in Portuguese America the mulatto sculptor known as Aleijadinho carved a whole series of life-size wooden figures from 1797 to 1799. The statues were placed in scenes from the Passion of Christ housed in independent structures lining a zigzag pathway up a hill to the church of Bom Jesús de Matozinhos in Congonhas do Campo, Brazil.

The spatial assertiveness found in Baroque sculpture is also characteristic of Baroque architecture. The calm stability and structural clarity

Photo: John F. Scott

FIGURE 7
Diego Martínez de Oviedo. La Compañía de Jesús, Cuzco, Peru, 1651–1668. Interior of nave with gilded wooden retablo.

of the Renaissance style is supplanted by seemingly active, moving surfaces and visual complexity. The hallmark of this new style is the Solomonic column, characterized by its spiral twist and so named because the form supposedly originated in Solomon's temple in Jerusalem. Its more immediate ancestor is the enormous bronze canopy over the high altar of Saint Peter's Cathedral in the Vatican, created by the Italian sculptor–architect Gianlorenzo Bernini from 1627 to 1633. In Latin America the form first appears around the midcentury in retablos. The great Jesuit church of La Compañía de Jesús in Cuzco, rebuilt immediately after the earthquake of 1650 and finished by 1668, has a main retablo (Figure 7) that Harold Wethey considered "the greatest masterpiece among the altarpieces of colonial Peru."[6] The central section of the retablo rushes upward, breaking the horizontal continuity that had been characteristic of Renaissance retablos. The movement of the columns and the projecting cornices result in a visual unification of the altar wall. Retablo designs, first executed by sculptors, soon inspired architects to apply similar multitiered compositions to the façades of their churches. Parts merge in overall surface ornament and one level penetrates the other. This visual unity is the ultimate aim of the Baroque, as opposed to the Renaissance aim of clarity.

During the Baroque era, artists of the provincial areas in both New Spain and the Viceroyalty of Peru produced church façades and interiors that shared the metropolitan Baroque features of overall richness of color and relief, but that are composed of close planes, which has led many to call their style "mestizo." Especially characteristic is a two-level relief that does not depend on sculptural modeling but rather on drilling into the surface to create a screenlike effect. Pre-Columbian stone- and wood-carving techniques often resulted in dense, bilevel relief designs. In fact, most of the sites of such churches — the southern Peruvian highlands and Alto Perú (now Bolivia), southern and western Mexico, and Guatemala — were centers of high pre-Columbian Indian civilizations and still contain a large percentage of Indians or mestizos. Certainly many of the craftsmen who carved these seventeenth- and eighteenth-century church reliefs were of Indian descent, but how much of the old, pre-Spanish, or even pre-Inca styles could they possibly retain? Artistic style cannot be inherited; it is a cultural phenomenon that must be learned. The flat relief derives from transferring two-dimensional graphic designs into architectural relief, not from any pre-Columbian tradition of carving.

Dramatic sculptural and coloristic effects are achieved by the use of painted and gilt stucco in southern Mexico, especially the states of Puebla and Oaxaca. In the cities, stucco is used as skillfully as in southern Spain to achieve sculptural movement and curves. The little parish church of Santa María Tonantzintla, a mestizo village outside of Puebla, uses the same techniques in a folk idiom, filling the surface of the vaults, domes, and vertical walls with charming angels. The teeming little floral and figural motifs overload the eye and make dispassionate analysis impossible. The stuccoed surface vibrates with a riot of color and high-relief modeling. Church surfaces in Puebla are enriched by dazzlingly intricate glazed tiles, part of the Arabic tradition of Spain. Domes especially herald the church's presence by their bright yellow blue oval forms, easily seen from a distance.

■ Rococo

Riotous forms in dazzling polychromy characterize the most exuberant phase of the Baroque style, often called Ultrabaroque or Churrigueresque after the Churriguera family, important retablo designers in Madrid. More deserving of mention as the founder, especially for Mexico (where the style had its greatest flowering), is Jerónimo de Balbás of Seville. He designed what is known as the Retablo de los Reyes for the high altar of the Mexico City Cathedral. Here columns are abandoned and replaced by *estípites,* composed of upward-flaring pedestals supporting a teetering pile of horizontal blocks. The sources of this motif may well be the long-lived Mannerist woodcuts that bordered the title pages of so many books; their small scallops and scrolls parallel contemporary French Rococo wall surfaces without actually copying them. The deep curve of the half-dome and the soaring verticality of the estípites manipulate the space of the Retablo de los Reyes in a manner that is seldom found in native Mexican designers who followed Balbás. In contrast, they produced flattened versions of his estípites

Photo: John F. Scott

FIGURE **8**
Fray José de la Cruz and Felipe Ureña. La Compañía (La Trinidad), Guanajuato, Mexico, 1747–1765. Façade.

in the numerous gilded wooden retablos and carved stone façades of churches throughout Mexico. The wealth of New Spain in the eighteenth century unleased a frenzy of building, especially notable in the mining districts in north-central Mexico. In that area, an early, heavy version of the estípite facade was built in 1747 for La Compañía de Guanajuato. (Figure 8). Later retablos become more delicate than this early, heavy façade, and some lose both columns and estípites altogether. Such retablo designs in fact overwhelm the paintings and reliefs they are supposed to frame and the sculpture they are supposed to support. The interiors become a feast for the senses: sight, through glittering gold leaf and painted wood; touch, by inference in the sensuous curves; smell, due to incense; and hearing, from the great wooden pipe organs, which are an important part of most churches.

Throughout Spanish America in the eighteenth century the wealthy aristocracy built palaces taking up much of a square block in the urban centers, with grandiose Baroque entrances (as in the Torre Tagle Palace in Lima) and exuberant interior courtyards, like that of the palace of the Marquis of San Mateo de Valparaíso in Mexico City, designed in 1769 by Francisco Guerrero y Torres.

In Europe the Rococo style is more typically one of intimacy and delicacy, as exemplified by the delightful Mexican interior of Santa Rosa in Querétaro (Figure 9). Oval medallions, executed in gilded wood, frame busts of the saints on the great choir screen, which is topped by delicate filigree wood and ironwork. Simulated drapery held back by baby angels provide a canopy over angled glass cases containing statues of saints. Despite the considerable size of the vaulted space, its scale is small and its effect charming, not overwhelming as in the Ultrabaroque retablos, which stress their towering (even apparently uncomfortably teetering) vertical height.

Rococo spirit can be found in another, rarer type of eighteenth-century structure, the curvilinear churches such as the small oval chapel called the Pocito (Figure 10), built between 1777 and 1791 by the aforementioned architect Francisco Guerrero y Torres. On the exterior this delightful building downplays its size by providing a half-oval entrance with a low door. The exploding interior space bites into the mass of the walls to create niches and bursts out through the six-pointed star windows in the upper story.

Brazilian architecture of the last half of the eighteenth century developed this Rococo type more fully than did Spanish America. Although very close to northern Portuguese designs, these colonial buildings display a variety and quantity that reflect the financial prosperity brought about by mining activity, in this instance in the state of Minas Gerais. In the picturesque town of Ouro Preto, with its many extant churches, the Rosário Chapel designed by Manuel Francisco de Araújo in 1784 carries this Rococo approach the furthest. The oval-plan sanctuary links with the oval altar space, although the latter is both smaller and lower. The curving, open nature of the façade, so different from the contemporary Spanish flat façade, prepares the viewer for the curving interior. The small scale and thinness of the parts, especially the little oval windows, creates a delicacy unknown to most Spanish exteriors. In the Americas only Brazilian designs consistently open the façade and the interior of the structures to the flow of space.

The standard Rococo doll-like sculpture of the eighteenth century was best executed in the School of Quito, which Legarda had brought to a pinnacle. The soft, pink-toned encarnación of the infant Christ child seems the very epitome of the Rococo world. Unless we look at the signed and dated (1792) inscription on a tendon of the hand, the figure betrays no hint that the carving was done by an Indian, Manuel Chil, nicknamed Caspicara. Quito served as the sculpural center of northwestern South America, which in 1717 became the independent Viceroyalty of New Granada. Guatemala played a similar role as sculptural center in the southern part of the Viceroyalty of New Spain; the Indian and mulatto origins of its sculptors are equally imperceptible.

The Cuzco School of painting, established in the seventeenth century, was primarily composed of Indian and mestizo artists. Some find in the flat, ornamental painting of the cotton and wooden surfaces they used a continuation of the pre-Columbian design tradition in textiles and pottery. The Inca culture lived on in eighteenth-century Cuzco in painted wooden beakers, folk weavings, and portraits of Indian dignitaries; the Tupac Amaru rebellion of 1780 showed that Inca royalty also survived. By the eighteenth century, Cuzco painting embodied many of the stylistic features of the Rococo:

Photo: John F. Scott

FIGURE 9
Mariano de las Casas or Francisco Martínez Gudiño. Santa Rosa, Querétaro, Mexico, 1752. Interior of nave with gilded wooden screen and oils on canvas.

small scale; doll-like features; a tender, intimate expression; and soft colors, often powdery versions of reds, blues, and ochres, with a surface application of gold leaf that does not follow the contour of the painted drapery on which it is stenciled. The Virgin Mary is often dressed in a Spanish peasant costume, adding an informal touch that is also typical of the Rococo. The tropical landscape in many Cuzco works seems primarily imaginary, based on European conceptions of Egypt rather than the Cuzqueños' direct observation of the nearby Amazonian forest.

Although commissioned portraits of the aristocracy are stiff and haughty, foreshadowing the Neoclassic, self-portraits of painters in Mexico reveal a more informal humanity. The best of

FIGURE **10**
Francisco Guerrero y Torres.
Pocito de Guadalupe, Mexico City,
Mexico, 1777–1791. Exterior.

this tradition is the pastel—itself a very informal, spontaneous medium much favored by Rococo artists—done by José Luis Rodríguez de Alconedo in 1811: It reveals him as a mestizo with tousled hair and wearing an open-necked shirt, in the act of placing a garland of flowers on the head of a classical bust. The informality comes not only through the disheveled dress but also by the choice of a half-length image whose body is angled in one direction but whose head turns to look spontaneously out of the canvas in another direction. It is a completely captivating glimpse of a man who was soon to be executed for his participation in the war of independence.

Some portrayals of everyday life in New Spain on the eve of independence come from new subjects treated by colonial painters who reveal a willingness to go beyond the subject matter commissioned by church and state. An anonymous landscape painting of a wooden glen and rushing stream was probably done from nature, although its specific location has not been determined. No pretext is necessary here to justify the landscape; no religious characters inhabit it, as was typically the case in the seventeenth century. The fruit of the land is revealed in kitchen still-lifes such as those by Antonio Pérez de Aguilar. The different strata of colonial society are best shown in series of small paintings called *Castas* (Castes), that represent intermarriage of different races and assign terms to each mixture. The farther removed from pure Spanish lineage the individual, the humbler the surroundings. Although these paintings may be more allegorical than factual, the backdrops, clothing, and life-styles seem very true to eighteenth-century life.

■ Neoclassicism

Spain made an attempt in 1783 to exert control over the arts by establishing the Royal Academy of San Carlos in Mexico City. Spaniards were dispatched to Mexico to head each of its sections. The most impressive of the newcomers was Manuel Tolsá, who taught sculpture and

later served as director of the academy. His main surviving sculpture is the noble equestrian bronze statue of King Carlos IV of 1803. In the tradition of an antique equestrian ruler portrait, this monumental work, cast in a size never before attempted in the colonies, conveys the pride and power of the king transformed into a Roman emperor dressed in a toga. The term *neoclassic* is applied to this style in part because of the conscious Roman references but also because of its return to calmer, more stable, more rational, and simplified forms. Such qualities can best be seen in the architecture executed by Tolsá, which returns to sober right angles and white color. Graceful touches of curves add a quality of elegance to Tolsá's work, such as the low arches in the courtyard of the College of Mines in the capital (Figure 11).

Architecture in the Mexican mining state of Guanajuato at the turn of the nineteenth century shows the talented stamp of Francisco Eduardo Tresguerras, native-born and self-taught from classical treatises. Tresguerras was also a painter of considerable talent; his self-portrait recalls the work of his Spanish contemporary Francisco Goya in its unflattering realism, severe coloration, and lack of background. He contributed his own fresco decoration to a chapel in the church of El Carmen he designed in his birthplace, Celaya. The airy figures and pale colors recall the now destroyed frescoes in the dome of Mexico City Cathedral executed by the head of painting in the academy, Rafael Ximeno y Planes, whose sharp, firm portraits show great technical skill and remarkable powers of observation.

Most building activity stopped when the wars of independence broke out against Spain in 1810. During this period Brazil became the seat of the Portuguese king, in exile because the homeland was menaced by Napoleonic troops. In 1816 the monarchy established proper training in the rules and practice of art in Rio de Janeiro by founding the Imperial Academy of Fine Arts, the instructors for which were supplied by a French artistic mission. The design of the academy building itself, by Grandjean de

Montigny, is a clear statement of Neoclassic architecture. The Taunay brothers were responsible for sculpture (Auguste) and painting (Nicolas): Nicolas Taunay's picture of Rio is a realistic depiction of a local scene with emphasis on the great expanse of space of this New World.

In the new republics carved out of the old Spanish Empire after 1821, self-taught artists commemorated their heroes and the great events of their recent history in a straightforward Neoclassic idiom: strong, clear delineation in quite vivid colors, and blank gray background. Historical scenes such as battles were rendered from a normal human vantage point, with little rhetorical emphasis either by size or by lighting; Neoclassic lighting is usually very

FIGURE 11
**Manuel Tolsá. Palacio de Minería,
Mexico City, Mexico, 1797–1813.**

even and flat, and small figures are subordinate to the dominant horizontals of the land and the architecture.

■ Romanticism

After independence a number of Europeans came to the Americas in their Romantic search for the unusual and the dramatic. Jean Baptiste Debret, of the French artistic mission, drew sketches of the varied inhabitants of Brazil, which he published via lithographs from 1834 to 1839. Also beginning his South American journey in Brazil was the Bavarian artist Johann Moritz Rugendas, who went to Mexico from 1831 to 1834, to Chile between 1833 and 1845, Argentina from 1837 to 1838, and Peru from 1842 to 1844. Although perhaps extreme in his constant movement from country to country, Rugendas is no different from other foreign travelers in his search for the unusual, the dramatic, and the picturesque. His quick brush strokes and sketchy execution plus his vibrant colors strongly reflect the Romantic style then in vogue in Europe. Although these extant small oils of Rugendas are best considered sketches in preparation for never-realized major canvases, they embody the true spirit of the Romantic movement and brought to the attention of native Latin Americans the beauty, excitement, and distinctiveness of their own newly independent countries.

Native-born artists from affluent families soon began to contribute their versions of the newly independent lands. Typical of the educated artists of the nineteenth century, they studied in Paris and were cosmopolitan but returned to Latin America to paint scenes of its distinctive life. Like many other painters called *costumbristas*, they focused primarily on local traditions *(costumbres)* that distinguished each region. They are more than costume painters; they focus on actions within a naturalistic setting. Artists in the new republics of Latin America were intensely interested in the region's quaint and picturesque sights, yet viewed them from a cultural perspective more European than Latin American. Meanwhile, self-taught artists, especially in provincial areas, produced flattened images of the local bourgeoisie and scenes of important events of the battles of independence and thanks for religious miracles.

Rulers of the new Latin American republics often showed disdain for native artists, preferring instead to award commissions to Europeans and hire them as teachers. Even if they were somewhat second-rate in their own countries, they could give a veneer of elegant European civilization to the new capitals, which until recently had been only provincial outposts of great colonial empires. The administration of General López de Santa Anna, the sometime president and longtime dictator of Mexico, clearly demonstrated its prejudice in this matter when reestablishing the National Academy of San Carlos in 1847. Instead of hiring capable Mexicans like Juan Cordero, then studying in Rome, his agents hired a distinguished but conservative faculty in Spain and Italy. As head of sculpture, the Catalán Manuel Vilar was first to manifest the indigenist fascination with Indian themes. His sculpture of the Tlaxcaltecan Indian warrior Tlahuicale (Figure 12) was executed in plaster in 1851 using an overly muscular style reminiscent of late Greek groups. Thus even if the subject is pre-Columbian, the technique classicizes.

Painters seeking to achieve a re-creation of Aztec times via realistic illusionism portrayed believable settings populated with Indians clearly posed by live models in the studio; their costumes followed sixteenth-century depictions such as those published by Lord Kingsborough between 1831 and 1848 from manuscripts spread throughout Europe. The architecture represented in the painting *The Discovery of Pulque* (1869) by José Obregón is adapted from pre-Columbian Mixtec codices by converting their cross-sectioned diagrams of temples into a very literal design for a throne. Obregón and his academic colleagues trying to re-create ancient events were unable to comprehend that the pre-Columbian artist did not intend to represent the external appearance of his architecture but rather wanted to convey its essence.

In South America artists of the latter nineteenth century also attempted to render in realistic academic style subjects that incorporated their national traditions. These artists were more concerned with representing essential aspects of their own countries than were the artists of the early independence period, who had been more cosmopolitan and European in taste and style. Rodolfo Amoêdo of Brazil, for example, was not high-born; he first learned his craft

FIGURE **12**
Manuel Vilar. *Tiahuicale,* plaster, 2.14 m., 1851. Museo de San Carlos, Mexico City.

Photo: John F. Scott

in the Rio Academy. Only later did he win a scholarship in Paris and then return in 1890 to execute major paintings in public halls. He used a female nude allegorical figure lounging in a tropical rain forest to capture the essence of *Marabá,* a town on the Amazon. The painting is as lush as its subject. In the painting *Indian Potter,* by Francisco Laso of Peru, an early exponent of indigenist themes who died in 1869, an Indian model in stark black costume carries a pre-Columbian Mochica human effigy vessel, obviously painted from an archaeological piece.

Two excellent artists of the end of the nineteenth century transcend the *costumbrista* and *indigenista* traditions of the early national era by making their subjects no longer exotic but universal. Juan Manuel Blanes of Uruguay, sent by his government to study in Florence, returned to document historical events and typical genre scenes throughout the southern cone. His realism, however, goes beyond earlier Romantic treatment of such themes and allows us to identify with the people portrayed in the atmospheric scenes. Realism, as a nineteenth-century artistic movement, swept aside sentimentality as objects, space, and the paint that created and emphasized physical nature. Although José María Velasco of Mexico did paint indigenist themes such as *Aztec Hunters* and *The Pyramid of Teotihuacán,* these oils focus on the tangible feeling of atmosphere and place rather than responses to past times and ruined monuments. His great series of panoramic vistas of the Valley of Mexico analyze the structure of nature as profoundly as his French contemporary Cézanne's series of Mont St. Victoire, although in a more literal style.

In contrast to the meticulous style of the classicists in the academies, a looser, more spontaneous style was developing to express greater emotion. Originally employed by the Romantic painters such as Rugendas for oil sketches done on the spot, this approach began to be consciously sought after by well-trained Latin American painters toward the end of the century in order to express scintillating animation, both of people and of nature. The most admired movement in art that used this technique, the European Impressionists, had originally intended to capture the optical sensation of light on the retina. One of the creators of Impressionism in Paris, Camille Pissarro, had been born and spent his early maturity in the Caribbean. A native of St. Thomas in the then–Danish West Indies, he made his first important studies of landscape painting in Caracas from 1852 to 1855. He was still a Realist then, as was Francisco Oller of Puerto Rico, later his friend, who after studying with Courbet, switched to an impressionist style. Also converted to Impressionism while in Europe during the 1890s was the Mexican lawyer Joaquín Clausell. His beautifully colored works are composed of separate splotches of very intense colors, which, when seen next to each other, create more vibrancy than if they were mixed on the palette. In the early years of the twentieth century, the Impressionist technique had become so accepted that it was used by stylish society painters, among the best of whom are two Peruvians, Carlos Baca-Flor and Teófilo Castillo.

■ Mexican Mural Renaissance

Reaction against academic realism took more political overtones in Mexico, where on the eve of the great political revolution of 1910, the anarchist Dr. Atl organized a dissident exhibition in the Centro Artístico of Mexico City. His own work of volcanic landscapes used exaggerated colors and nontraditional waxy paints, following postimpressionist tendencies he had learned in Europe. In their desire to communicate more directly with the uneducated Mexican masses, many artists admired the gripping, satirical graphics of José Guadalupe Posada, done to illustrate popular broadsides such as the couplets that mockingly eulogized public figures on the Day of the Dead (November 2). Posada's illustrations, whether woodcuts or zinc etchings, show very lively skeletons that caricature the foibles of the living.

After the tumult of the revolution had died down in 1920, the new secretary of education, José Vasconcelos, invited many Mexican artists, some working in Europe, to participate in government-sponsored projects to turn the walls of public buildings into didactic inspiration for the populace. The first major project was the National Preparatory School for Boys in Mexico City, a colonial Jesuit building with three floors of arcades and monumental stairs with vaulted ceilings. Diego Rivera, a young radical studying in Paris and working in such avant-garde styles as Cubism, leapt at the chance to put into practice the theories that he and his fellow Mexican student David Alfaro Siqueiros had discussed: to have art express the life of the people. He greatly admired the way the Italian Renaissance muralists had communicated the important elements of their faith to the illiterate. Rivera adapted their method to his own task, via fresco painting directly on the freshly plastered walls of public buildings. In the Teatro Bolívar of the Preparatory School, Rivera painted an allegorical scene much in the style of Renaissance religious frescoes — except that his angels had mestizo features. He had abandoned Cubism in the belief that it could not be understood by the masses, but soon decided that such allegories in the European tradition were equally irrelevant.

Rivera's greatest artistic success is the fresco decoration for the National Agricultural School in Chapingo, executed between 1924 and 1927, which presents an integrated vision brilliantly related to the architectural shapes on which he painted. The chapel especially recalls the Sistine Chapel, painted by Michelangelo and other Renaissance artists, by the frames painted following the ceiling faults. The subjects are mainly allegorical, but are conveyed in images recognizable to laymen. The side panels present a generalized history of the revolution: the abuses before, the suffering during, and the popular reformation after. Human figures buried in the earth become seeds from which new life can spring. Most important, the forms are smoothly stylized to enhance their accessibility and symbolic content, retaining the simplified outline he had admired in the Italian Renaissance. The forms are neither crowded nor do they bear excessively rhetorical content, excesses of Rivera's later work such as that in the National Palace.

The career of the second major figure of the Mexican mural renaissance, José Clemente Orozco, takes a pattern opposite to that of Diego Rivera: After an initial abortive essay into Italianate allegory, Orozco's work in the Preparatory School is far angrier than Rivera's, expressed in drab colors, bristling diagonals, and a pessimistic vision of unending brutality. Only the beautiful stairway mural of a Franciscan friar succoring an emaciated Indian reveals underlying human compassion; interestingly, the brotherly love illustrated here comes from a Spaniard, the traditional target of the muralists' hate because Spaniards destroyed the genuine Mexican pre-Columbian civilizations. This stairway mural provides early evidence of Orozco's ability to rise above propaganda, a talent later nurtured in the United States (1930–1934).

On his return home to Guadalajara, Orozco produced his finest murals, which transcend their Mexican themes to achieve a universal communication of man's struggle and achievement. Of the three state-owned buildings on which he worked concurrently, his frescoes for the Hospicio Cabañas must be considered his and the whole movement's masterpiece. The beautiful clean lines and curves of the interior, designed by Manuel Tolsá, provide a triumphal setting to the allegorized story of the conquest of Mexico. The Spaniards and their horses are represented as machines, thus linking the brutality of the conquest to injustices experienced in the contemporary era. The cycle culminates in the dome fresco, the composition of which is based on a Dutch Mannerist print by Golzius — a surprising return to colonial traditions of compositional borrowing. Orozco has transformed the print's Ixion — who in Greek mythology was bound to a fiery wheel in the sky for his sin of attempting to possess the divine — into the man on fire, consumed while he strides upward in foreshortened perspective. Recumbent allegorical figures of the elements symbolize other aspects of man's past, transformed into an allegory of his future. The expressive lines, colors, and brush strokes that help communicate the emotional content of the murals relate Orozco's work to the Expressionist movement in twentieth-century art, yet his return to recognizable imagery was then seen as a reaction against the more abstract currents of modernism.

The last of the triumvirate of great Mexican muralists, David Alfaro Siqueiros, was the most radical of the group. A more dedicated Communist than Rivera, he expended much of his energy in writing polemics. His paintings of masses of humanity unfortunately show the interchangeability of each proletarian. His art uses new media such as pyroxylin paint applied with air guns (a commercial technique). He often transcends the traditional limitations of media, integrating sculpture and painting with architecture in a more total conception than the other muralists (Figure 13). He transforms the architectural space provided by adding panels and even plastered lath so as to link the composition over the entire space. Some early works of his mature style were commissioned in the southern cone: In the Escuela México in Chillán, Chile, of 1941, his murals tie together the histories of Mexico and Chile by means of similar groupings of Indian rulers, *conquistadores*, and liberators on opposite walls linked by a rocketlike sweep of colors across the ceiling. Siqueiros's dramatic emphasis on movement by means of extreme foreshortening and power lines derives from Italian Futurist style, but its monumental scale involves the viewer even more.

In publicly commissioned sculptures throughout the nation, bulky figures exhort the Mexican proletariat to continue the revolution; an example is the colossal hilltop sculpture of the worker-hero Pípila overlooking Guanajuato. Large-proportioned, mantle-cloaked Indian women convey an eternal earth-mother expression in the smaller stone and bronze sculpture and drawing by Francisco Zúñiga, a Costa Rican living in Mexico.

The muralist renaissance in the 1920s and 1930s profoundly affected the history of Western art—the first time that Latin American art can be said to have done so. The exciting example that Mexico provided of art deeply involved in redirecting society by its spirit and its images helped moderate the headlong rush toward nonrepresentational abstraction after World War I. Naturally, enthusiasm for public-spirited murals spread to other nations of the hemisphere, both north and south. The works and the example of Carlos Mérida, an essential participant in many Mexican art projects, were influential in his native Guatemala. South Amer-

ican countries with strong pre-Columbian traditions were the first to pick up the exaltation of Indian cultures through art: José Sabogal led the indigenist movement in Peru; Osvaldo Guayasamín heads it in Ecuador; Ignacio Gómez Jaramillo and Pedro Nel Gómez received important mural commissions in Colombia. The encouragement by Americans of self-taught painters in Haiti engendered a lively school of primitive art focusing on typical Haitian scenes and subjects. Although most were easel paintings for sale to tourists, some murals were commissioned, notably for the Episcopal Cathedral in Port-au-Prince. And in Brazil, Cândido Portinari integrated his murals into the modern architecture there; on the wall of the church of São

FIGURE 13

Enrique del Moral and Mario Pani, with mural by David Alfaro Siqueiros. Rectory, with library behind by Juan O'Gorman, National Autonomous University of Mexico, Mexico City, Mexico, 1949–1954.

Photo: John F. Scott

Francisco in Pampulha, he executed paintings on a mosaic of glazed tiles which recalled Portuguese colonial traditions as well as providing a durable exterior (Figure 14).

■ Modernism

Non-Indian South America east of the Andes and in the southern cone, meanwhile, had been receptive to avant-garde European modernism. Whereas Diego Rivera had quickly abandoned Cubism upon returning to Mexico, Emilio Pettoruti of Argentina remained firmly wedded to that style, which he had learned in Paris from the Spaniard Juan Gris, a founder of the movement. When Pettoruti returned to Buenos Aires

in 1924, his first exhibition of Cubist paintings received a cold reception, but he persisted long enough to see Argentina become a major center of the international abstract art movement in the 1960s. Before returning to Montevideo in 1932, Joaquín Torres García of Uruguay had been firmly entrenched in the modern art scene in Europe, first in Barcelona, then in Paris. It was in Paris that he perfected his Constructivist style — deriving from the collages of Synthetic Cubism — flattening the objects of this world into even-colored, geometric shapes separated by thick black lines. While not as abstract as Mondrian's, his Dutch contemporary, his work reveals the same underlying unity in the design of the world. Such a philosophy does not en-

FIGURE **14**
Oscar Niemeyer, with tile mural by Cândido Portinari.
São Francisco church, Pampulha, Brazil, 1943.

Photo: Roy C. Craven, Jr.

courage regionalism, nationalism, or stylistic uniqueness.

The organizers of Modern Art Week in São Paulo in 1922, although interested in the modern movements in European art such as Cubism and Expressionism, were also very concerned with "the use of Brazilian themes for a national art."[7] In fact the leading Cubist painter of the group, Tarsila do Amaral, returned to Brazil from Paris in 1924 to rediscover Brazil and incorporate it into her art; she soon was painting abstracted images of tropical landscapes and geometrically rounded black women. However avant-garde Brazilian art might be, it always reflected an awareness that it was distinctively Brazilian, not some homogenized international style.

The same approach is found in Brazilian modern architecture, definitely the strongest and most creative national style in Latin America today. Although the few modern buildings during the 1920s derived from the Purist version of modernism, emphasizing abstract geometry, it was not until Le Corbusier, the French-Swiss architect who coined the term *Purism*, came to visit Rio de Janeiro in 1936 that a truly national style coalesced. It was based on functional modernism, an architectural style in which a building's structure and materials are clearly revealed. This modernism was softened by the curved forms made familiar from Brazilian Rococo churches. Anathema to Northern-Hemisphere functional modernist architects because of its irrationality, the sensuous curve became the hallmark of this distinctive Brazilian adaptation. Oscar Niemeyer became the darling of the movement; his church of São Francisco in Pampulha, already mentioned for the colorful tile decoration by Portinari, has a façade composed of catenary curves formed out of reinforced concrete shells (see Figure 14). Latin American designers, less restricted by building codes than North Americans, loved reinforced concrete because it could be manipulated into almost any shape. Félix Candela, a Spanish engineer who emigrated to Mexico to escape Franco's dictatorship, designed astonishingly thin and beautifully soaring forms out of concrete even without reinforcing steel. The world was amazed by Latin American thin-shell concrete design, so similar in spirit to the earlier Baroque age of greatness.

City planning, virtually ignored in Latin America since the sixteenth-century Laws of the Indies, showed a sudden burst of creativity in two impressive projects. Brazil constructed a new capital city named Brasília in its sparsely inhabited central plateau, fulfilling what had been dreamed of since 1822: to place a capital in the center of the country. Lúcio Costa won the competition for the design in 1956. This project was amazingly incomplete compared to other entries, but it had a gestural sweep and bold conception reminiscent of the contemporary Action Painting of the New York School, visible in São Paulo during its important biennial international exhibitions begun in 1951. The axis of the monumental government buildings crosses the swept-back wings containing the residential blocks to make a form like a jet airplane, a modern invention necessary to cover Brazil's vast distances. The main buildings, all designed by Niemeyer, stress their importance by dramatic curves.

Like a city on a smaller scale is the new campus of the National Autonomous University of Mexico, constructed between 1949 and 1954. Its buildings favor nonfunctional curves, angles, and textures, not to mention mosaics, which often recall the pre-Columbian past. The focal point of the largest space is the library building by Juan O'Gorman (see Figure 13). The lower circulation area stretches out by means of rough-textured walls with feathered serpent designs in relief; the upper stack area, a sealed treasure box covered with brilliant mosaics using dense pre-Columbian motifs, is visible from all corners of the campus. The same O'Gorman surprisingly had been the most severe exponent of functional modernism in the 1930s, deferring neither to Mexican culture nor to the tropical sun. His own house, designed shortly after the library, seems completely irrational: a free-form structure that does not express its material or construction, much less represent a "machine for living," (Le Corbusier's criterion for modern housing). O'Gorman thus represents the Latin American conversion from international abstraction to regional emotionalism, as Latins attempt to translate international movements into their own visual idiom.

The one European modern style of painting that has found particular affinity in Hispanic America is Surrealism. The stress it places on the irrational, the emotional, and the personal seems especially congenial to the Latin temperament. The French poet–philosopher André Breton's visit to Mexico in 1938 proved a catalyst for the flowering of this style in America. Frida Kahlo, who with her husband Diego Rivera hosted Breton in Mexico, rendered intense portrayals of herself in various transformations, as if her imagination were superimposed on visual reality. Folk arts were examined in search of the instinctive spirit of Mexico, and pre-Columbian art was exploited for the same purpose. Fascination with personal transformation of received culture, such as that exemplified by the great paintings of Europe, is characteristic of Alberto Gironella and José Luis Cuevas in Mexico and Fernando Botero in Colombia. Cuevas — one of Latin America's outstanding draftsmen — often includes his self-portrait in these borrowed scenes, recalling Kahlo's focus on her fantasies. Rufino Tamayo, although sometimes working as a muralist, has made his most potent statements since 1940 by combining ancestral references to Mexican identity with surrealistic abstraction and shocking, non-naturalistic colors. His preference for easel painting is symbolic of the more private vision that surrealist works communicate.

Other Latin Americans have made important contributions after coming in contact with Breton and his surrealist circle: Roberto Matta left Chile permanently in 1934 for Paris, where he abandoned architecture for Surrealist painting under the inspiration of Breton and others; his renderings of abstracted biomorphic forms have made him the best-known Latin American surrealist. Wifredo Lam joined the Breton group in Marseilles just before it fled the Nazi-subservient Vichy government for exile in Martinique, after which Lam returned to his native Cuba. Tropical fantasies abound in Lam's paintings; some forms in them are reminiscent of African sculpture, a phenomenon the Surrealists explain as a surfacing of Lam's black heritage. (One must remember, however, that Lam's first artistic contact in Paris had been Picasso, who at the beginning of the century had used African sculpture as an important source of Cubism.)

Economic necessity as well as artistic stimulus led many into being expatriates. While these reasons have lessened, politics can still make exile prudent, as attested by the Argentine School's dispersal following establishment of a military dictatorship in 1966.

Out of Surrealism has grown the modern Abstract Expressionist movement. Centered in New York, it has many adherents in Latin America. These artists often refer in their work to the primordial natural forces of their homelands. Fernando de Szyszlo of Peru seems to capture the turbulent forces of creation; his titles refer to Inca mythology, here expressed not as literal pictures but as emotional abstractions. Pedro Coronel of Mexico has canvases full of intense, blossoming color reminiscent of Tamayo but completely abstract. Perhaps Alejandro Obregón of Colombia best exemplifies the surrealist trend in Latin America by his lush, broad-brushed canvases, at first apparently abstract, then, through suggestions of the titles or naturalistic fragments, references to nature: the condor, the cock, the tropical flora. They erupt like the fantastic images in the novels of his Colombian contemporary, Gabriel García Márquez, also set in the lush Caribbean jungle; naturalistic images come in and go out of focus in favor of totally imaginary ones. The best of Latin American art refers to inner emotional reality: religious visions in colonial times, the shared soul of a nation in the period after independence.

■ Notes

1. Robert Ricard, *The Spiritual Conquest of Mexico: Essay on the Apostolate and the Evangelizing Methods of the Mendicant Orders in New Spain, 1523–1572,* trans. Leslie Byrd Simpson (1933; reprint, Berkeley: University of California Press, 1966).
2. Donna L. Pierce, "Identification of the Warriors in the Frescoes of Ixmiquilpan," *Review of the Research Center for the Arts* 4, no. 4 (San Antonio, October 1981): 7.
3. Rosa Camelo Arredondo, J. Gurría Lacroix, and Constantino Reyes Valerio, *Juan Gersón: Tlacuilo de Tecamachalco* (México: Instituto Nacional de Antropología e historia, Departamento de Monumentos Coloniales 16, 1964), 28.
4. George Kubler and Martín Soria, *Art and Architecture in Spain and Portugal and Their American Dominions, 1500–1800* (Baltimore: Penguin Books, 1959), 87.
5. Marcus Burke and Linda Bantel, *Spain and New Spain* (Corpus Christi: Art Museum of South Texas, 1979), 25–26, 33–35, and 89–90.
6. Harold Wethey, *Colonial Architecture and Sculpture in Peru* (Cambridge: Harvard University Press, 1949), 219.
7. Gilbert Chase, *Contemporary Art in Latin America* (New York: The Free Press, 1970), 184.

■ Suggested Readings

Angulo Iñiguez, Diego. *Historia del arte hispanoamericano.* 3 vols. Barcelona: Ediciones Calpe, 1945–1956.

Bayón, Damián. *Artistas contemporáneos de América Latina.* Barcelona: Serbal/UNESCO, 1981.

Burke, Marcus. "Introduction: Mexican Colonial Painting in Its European Context," in *Spain and New Spain.* Corpus Christi: Art Museum of South Texas, 1979, 15–59.

Castedo, Leopoldo. *A History of Latin American Art and Architecture.* New York: Praeger, 1969.

Catlin, Stanton Loomis, and Terence Grieder. *Art of Latin America Since Independence.* New Haven: Yale University Art Gallery and The University of Texas Art Museum, 1966.

Charlot, Jean. *Mexican Art and the Academy of San Carlos, 1785–1915.* Austin: University of Texas Press, 1962.

Chase, Gilbert. *Contemporary Art in Latin America.* New York: The Free Press, 1970.

Edwards, Emily, and Manuel Álvarez Bravo. *Painted Walls of Mexico from Prehistoric Times until Today.* Austin: University of Texas Press, 1966.

Fernández, Justino. *A Guide to Mexican Art.* Translated by Joshua C. Taylor. Chicago: University of Chicago Press, 1969.

Kelemen, Pál. *Baroque and Rococo in Latin America.* 2d ed. 2 vols. New York: Dover Publications, 1967 (orig. 1943).

Kubler, George, and Martín Soria. *Art and Architecture in Spain and Portugal and Their American Dominions, 1500–1800.* Baltimore: Penguin Books, 1959.

McAndrew, John. *The Open-Air Churches of Sixteenth-Century Mexico.* Cambridge: Harvard University Press, 1965.

Messer, Thomas M., and Cornell Capa. *The Emergent Decade; Latin American Painters and Painting in the 1960s.* Ithaca: Cornell University Press, 1966.

Palm, Erwin Walter. *Los monumentos arquitectónicos de la Española.* 2 vols. Ciudad Trujillo (Santo Domingo): Universidad de Santo Domingo, 1955.

Robertson, Donald. *Mexican Manuscript Painting of the Early Colonial Period: The Metropolitan Schools.* New Haven: Yale University Press, 1959.

Rodríguez Prampolini, Ida. *El Surrealismo y el arte fantástico de México.* México: Universidad Nacional Autónoma de México, 1969.

Toussaint, Manuel. *Colonial Art in Mexico.* Translated and edited by Elizabeth Wilder Wiesman. Austin: University of Texas Press, 1967.

Weisman, Elizabeth Wilder. *Art and Time in Mexico from the Conquest to the Revolution.* Photographs by Judith Hancock Sandoval. New York: Harper and Row, 1985.

Wethey, Harold. *Colonial Architecture and Sculpture in Peru.* Cambridge: Harvard University Press, 1949.

13 | Music, Dance, and Drama: An Anthropological Perspective

ANYA PETERSON ROYCE
ANTHONY SEEGER

You have arrived in a Latin American capital city, and you want to know what the political climate is. You could interview members of the government. You could read the columns of the major daily. Or you could attend a play by a national playwright, dance and watch a show at a nightclub, and see the sunrise from inside a small bar on the outskirts of the city while listening to two men duel with songs. Do the night activities sound like a frivolous waste of time? They are not. You would be wise to interview, read, and then go out on the town as well, because each provides different perspectives on the country and its social, political, and cultural processes. The government official will usually repeat the government position. The newspaper may criticize the government, but it depends on advertising to survive and is run by a board of directors with close ties to important economic and social groups. The play will present a different perspective; at the nightclub the humor may dwell on the political as well as the racy, and the dancing will show you how people move; the verses sung by the two men express popular sentiments quite distant in style and content from the editorial pages or official government views. The arts are part of the social and political processes of any society or country, and they are important to anyone who would understand the history and current events of Latin America.

It may seem strange to argue for the importance of art forms in countries with the social and economic problems outlined in this volume, but Latin American governments have often been the first to recognize how powerful the arts are as expressions of opinion and formulators of action. On the negative side this is expressed through a long history of censorship and repression. In 1569 an Aztec stone around which many blacks often danced and played music in the heart of Mexico City was buried by order of the viceroy, and the blacks allowed to sing only on Sundays and feast-day afternoons.[1] Censorship of the arts has continued through the centuries, right down to the military regimes of Chile, Brazil, and Argentina, which all censored popular music, banning many songs from the radio and closing down nightclub acts in the 1970s. (The McCarthy period of the 1950s saw similar persecution of artists in the United States.) On the positive side, most Latin American countries have government organizations for the patronage of the arts. These include programs for the collection and dissemination of folklore, the protection of national music and film industries, and the sponsorship of national dance, theater, and musical groups.

In countries where only a small part of the population can read, music, dance, and drama may move more people to action than editorials. Artistic power resides in an ability to express through form and content sentiments and attitudes in a language that can be made accessible to any sector of the population. The arts may also support or criticize values that are stronger and more enduring than those of political allegiance. They often present very basic ideas and sentiments about the body, the self, important social relationships, and about life in ways that both express common values and help develop them.

Anthropologists study the arts as part of what they call culture. Culture is defined as a system of symbols and values that both orient and are defined by people's actions. What people do is strongly influenced by vaguely formulated but nonetheless very strong ideas about what is "right" or "wrong," "good" or "bad," "possible" and "impossible." These ideas, values, and symbols are not the same in every society. Human beings do not share the same perceptions of events or the same values. Nor are ideas and values static: They relate to specific situations and often are themselves transformed with and by the society. Specific contexts, ideas, and values have changed over the five hundred years since the European conquest began, but the role of the arts in orienting action remains as strong as ever.

It is difficult to separate music, dance, and drama, since many groups in Latin America mix them together: Traditional Indian music is usually accompanied by dance; some Afro–Latin American saints' celebrations combine music, dance, and dramatic performances; and even contemporary popular music is a phenomenon of the discotheques, bars, or streets. It is danced to as well as heard. More recently, Music Television (MTV) and similar shows, which are widely aired in parts of Latin America, have combined short dramatic presentations with popular music and dance.

■ Music, Dance, and Trance

Music affects the body in many ways — among them its rhythms, its intensity, and the hyperventilation that may accompany singing or dancing. Music often plays an essential role in contact with a spirit world. Thus the Mapuche shaman (priest-doctor) in Chile will sing for a long period of time to contact the spirits, similarly to a Tupi shaman in Brazil, a Warau in Venezuela, or a Cuna in Panama. Rhythm and repetition induce an altered state of consciousness, a heightened awareness in which the spirits are accessible. It is often believed that the spirits speak musically, through whistles, flutes, or song. The shaman's spirit may make a long trip in the sky or the underworld, and learn songs, cures for a sick person, or simply find his or her spirit and bring it back. Shamanism is an important feature of the music and drama of the native Americans of both North and South America.

Native Americans introduced Europeans to tobacco, and in addition to that narcotic they were familiar with others such as yaje, ebene, peyote, and many others.[2] All of these plants alter the normal state of consciousness. Some of them may be particularly stimulating to the auditory canal; others stimulate visual perceptions. Music that accompanies the use of hallucinogens has been described as a means to order the hallucinogenic experience by telling people what they should be seeing or by providing a basic structuring of experience through rhythm.[3]

Not all altered states are reached through

narcotic use. Just as music plays an important part in organizing the experiences of hallucinogenic drugs, so music and dance can provide a vehicle for altered states. The Afro-American possession cults found in Brazil and Venezuela, as well as throughout much of the Caribbean, involve the achievement of "possession" by a spirit through dance and rhythm. Drumming and dancing are extremely important in achieving possession. The intricacies of Latin American drumming have been extensively studied and are renowned for their beauty and intensity.

In the case of the Afro-Brazilian cults, various intricate rhythms are employed; the drummer often plays a specific beat that will induce trance in certain members when introduced at the appropriate point in the cult. Many of the Afro-Latin cult traditions are clearly derived from African cults — for example, the Yoruba or Gege-nago cults of Bahia — but they have inevitably undergone transformation in their host countries. Afro-Brazilian cults attract not only the descendants of African slaves; they are on their way to becoming a national phenomenon, recruiting members from all social classes and ethnic groups. Many Afro-American rhythms have been incorporated into hugely popular song styles such as the Brazilian samba, Afro-Cuban music, reggae, and other forms.

Dance and music thus not only use the body for expression, but affect the perceptions and experiences of the body itself. This is one of the reasons they are so important to their participants. To sing or dance together is often a symbolic statement of belonging to a group. To have a national dance style or dance troupe is often a symbol of national identity. Indeed, music and dance are intimately linked to the identity of the social groups that perform them.

■ Music, Dance, and Identity

Music and dance are inextricably bound up with other aspects of human behavior that together we call culture. Virtually all societies dance, make music, or have dramatic presentations that involve dance and music. To understand the values and behaviors of these societies, we must also understand these expressive phenomena. Dance has a very high potential for communicating something about how people feel about themselves. This potential gives dance great power and at the same time makes it very threatening. Monica Wilson once lamented, "One of the ironies of culture contact is that each group regards the art, and particularly the dancing, of the other as *immoral*, as well as distasteful."[4] In postclassic Mesoamerica, the Aztec would burlesque the dancing of other groups as a way of humiliating them. And music, dance, and dance drama were among the first aspects of preconquest Latin American culture to be banned or changed by the Spaniards.

We should consider the reasons for the power of music and dance for communication — especially communication in situations of conflict or contact. Dance employs no instrument apart from the human body, and, further, it has no product separable from the dance performance itself. Some music uses only human capabilities; some relies on instruments; most has the same immediacy as dance. This means that we must confront dance and music on the spot, without the leisure of contemplation or absorption at our own pace. We are, in fact, caught up in these communicative forms whether we like it or not. Because the human body creates this sense of helplessness in the face of performance, we react with all our prejudices about the relative values of body and soul, physical manifestations, and mind.

Given the power of music and dance to engender strong feelings in both participants and observers, it is not surprising to see these forms used by groups that have a need to express their identity in situations of contact or conflict. The Isthmus Zapotec of southern Mexico use dance in precisely this way.[5]

Dance Style and Zapotec Identity

The city of Juchitán is the largest city in the southern half of the Isthmus of Tehuantepec and has a population of about thirty-seven thousand, a diverse lot including Isthmus Zapotec, Mexicans, Spaniards, Italians, Japanese, Lebanese, and other Indian groups such as the Huave, Mixe, and Zoque. The Zapotec, who have been there since before the Spanish Conquest in 1521, are four-fifths of the total. In terms of identification with particular dance styles, we can divide Juchitán into two groups: the four-fifths of the population who adhere to Zapotec style, and the remaining fifth, which, although heterogeneous in background, follows Mexican national style to the exclusion of any other. The greatest degree of elaboration for both styles, but especially for the Zapotec, is evidenced by the upper classes, who alone have the wealth required to display its distinctive elements. These include a facility in the Zapotec language; the regional costume and gold jewelry that must accompany Zapotec music, songs, and dances; and the social round of parties and festive occasions highlighted by the more than twenty-six major *velas* (complexes of daytime parties, masses in the parish church, parades, and an all-night dance under a canvas tent).

Not one of these indicators of Zapotec identity approaches what one might call "pure" Zapotec in origin and composition. In fact, the very complex of these elements seems to have become elaborated as late as the mid-nineteenth century. At that time a propitious combination of factors allowed the inhabitants of Juchitán to give concrete form to their fervent sense of cultural identity, a trait that had characterized them for at least the preceding three centuries. These factors included the prosperity brought by speculators connected with the transisthmian railroad and the ever-increasing rivalry with the city of Tehuantepec. Many of the elements of Zapotec style were already part of Juchitán life and simply became elaborated and more important. Other elements were added, especially those of French and Spanish origin.

Zapotec dance has undergone foreign, particulary French, influences. The *son,* regarded as

Zapotec rather than Mexican, as it developed in the mid-nineteenth century and as it is danced today by members of the old Zapotec families of Juchitán, combines a variety of elements. It is an open-couple dance, which makes it of a later vintage than round dances or line dances. The woman's part incorporates the erect, almost arched-back posture reminiscent of the Andalusian fandango, while the steps themselves remind one of nineteenth-century waltzes. The effect is to show off the costume with its heavily embroidered, full velvet skirt and multiple starched white lacy petticoats while giving the dancers that languid, haughty, restrained quality that suits the Juchiteco character so well.

Both in costume and choreography, the woman conveys a thoroughly European quality. The man, on the contrary, is thoroughly Indian. His traditional costume of white cotton shirt and baggy pants, sandals, sombrero, and red neckerchief is like that of almost every other Indian or peasant group in Mexico. His posture, bent slightly forward from the waist with knees relaxed and one or both hands clasped behind his back, is the posture typical of Mexican Indian dance. His steps, too, are the typical modified *zapateado* found all over rural Mexico.

It is difficult to describe the impact that a performance of *sones* has upon non-Zapotec. Zapotec dancers are unique and unexpected. They are unexpected because they are not out of the Oaxaca Indian mold of homespun cotton or woolen costumes and heavy, earthbound, repetitious dances that are done by men and women in the bent-from-the-waist posture with downcast eyes. A sense of wealth and pride is conveyed by the Zapotec women striding regally onto the dance floor with enormous starched and pleated white lace headdresses set back from their faces and lush, flower-embroidered velvet skirts and blouses that provide a background for thousands of pesos' worth of gold jewelry hanging heavily from ears, necks, and wrists. Nothing in the dances that follow contradicts this first impression; rather, it is strengthened as the dancers glide through the sones with arrogant graciousness. The whole performance conjures up and reaffirms the image of the proud, fierce, wealthy Zapotec who manage through their wealth and shrewdness to maintain Juchitán as a Zapotec city.

Most fiestas in Juchitán are characterized by the dancing of sones. There are some occasions when sones seem almost mandatory, usually whenever there is a threat felt from outsiders. Most often this occurs within the context of a Zapotec–non-Zapotec marriage. At the Sunday celebration of mixed marriages it is not unusual for the women guests to be requested to wear the regional costume rather than the long dresses or pantsuits they might otherwise wear. Often the hosts will hire flute and drum players to play the oldest form of music still heard in Juchitán, not normally played at weddings. Many more sones are danced than usual; in fact, they outnumber the popular Mexican social dances that generally predominate at weddings. Zapotec style is explicitly displayed so that the friends and relatives of the outsider spouse will be impressed with the extravagance and richness of the Zapotec heritage, which can more than hold its own in competition with anything else Mexico has to offer.

Any occasion at which non-Zapotec are present may call forth this same display of style. There are also displays of Zapotec identity when no outsiders are in evidence. One occurred in 1971 at a victory dance given to celebrate a local candidate's winning the municipal presidency on a Juchitán-for-the-Juchitecos ticket. The women came in their finest costumes hung about with fortunes in gold. Two of the five bands hired for the occasion played nothing but sones, and the other three alternated between sones and *piezas,* the modern popular music.

One also sees magnificent exhibitions of Zapotec style during the velas sponsored by two of the oldest families of Juchitán. Each of the families would like to be considered the finest embodiment of all that is Zapotec, and they attempt to outdo each other in their respective velas.

Zapotec identity is also a primary feature of celebrations associated with important events in local history. For example, the victory of the Juchiteco forces over the French army with its regiment of traitors from Tehuantepec on 5 September 1866 is celebrated each year with a municipal dance in which Zapotec dress is de rigueur, and those who come in Western dress must sit in the back rows.

Otherwise, one is quite as likely to see piezas being danced as sones. Many of the Zapotec pride themselves on being excellent performers of the latest social dances. Latest, however, usually implies a time lag, so that at the beginning of the twentieth century the waltz was popular; this was followed by the *danzon* (a slow Cuban dance) in the 1930s and 1940s, which was superseded in the 1950s and 1960s by the *cumbia* (dance of Black origins) and the twist; and today *música tropical* (Latin music) and the dances that accompany it such as the cha cha, samba, and mambo enjoy preeminence. Being expert in the two distinct dance traditions is a source of pride, and it certainly causes no conflict of loyalties. Both the reasons and occasions for doing each form of dance are different, and the Zapotec are accustomed to making the appropriate selection for each situation.

Zapotec dance is an effective symbol of pride in a Zapotec heritage mainly because in all respects it connotes aristocracy. The choreography and posture are regal and unhurried; the required costume is lavish and costly; finally, the skill required to dance well in the Zapotec fashion can be acquired only through imitation and practice. Fine dancers belong to the Zapotec elite because it is those families who began the tradition and who have the money to maintain it. Any Zapotec can dance sones, but only those few with access to the tradition can dance them well.

■ Adaptation and Religious Drama

One of the predominant characteristics of Latin American society is its blend of indigenous and

European cultures. Survival for many of the indigenous groups depends on their flexibility and selectivity in adapting those aspects of European culture that enhance and strengthen the indigenous culture. For many groups, this kind of selective adaptation took place at the time of the Spanish Conquest of the New World. The Catholic ritual calendar was superimposed on the indigenous one; some Catholic festivals corresponded to indigenous rituals, but some were entirely new. Whichever the case, the result was a blend of the two traditions. Major Catholic contributions to ritual and dance occasions included three dance-dramas, the *Moriscas* [Moorish dramas] (including *Moros y Cristianos* (Moors & Christians), *Santiagos,* and *Matachines*), the Passion plays, and the Christmas *posadas.* Moriscas were and are frequently performed during Carnival, Corpus Christi, or on 26 July, the day of Santiago. Like their preconquest counterparts, these dances reenact mock combat, usually between Christians and Moors. Santiagos and Matachines also include battle mime, with the dancers themselves organized into quasi-military cadres. All three types of Moriscas have a clown figure most often danced by a young boy in female attire.

The Passion plays all tell the Passion of Christ more or less faithfully. One example comes from Catacaos on the north coast of Peru. Holy Week begins on Palm Sunday. In the morning there is a mass and blessing of the palms. The images of the Virgin and Saint John the Baptist are dressed and later in the day figure in a procession to the parish church together with *Señor Triunfante* (one of the images of Christ), who is carried on a white donkey. The priest knocks on the doors of the church and he, the images, and the members of the *cofradías* (religious societies) enter in triumph. On Monday, Tuesday, and Wednesday there are processions with images of different saints each evening. On Wednesday, the image of Jesus of Nazarene makes its first appearance, and, on meeting, the other images all bow to *El Señor Jesús.* On Thursday there is a replica built of the Last Supper. On Good Friday, the Cofradía Jurada del Santo Cristo takes over responsibility for the proceedings. They place three crosses in front of the church, and the images of Jesus Christ of Calvary and the two thieves are placed on them. In the evening there is a banquet and a three-hour sermon, after which the image of Christ is removed from the cross and placed in the sacred coffin. The procession with the coffin lasts all night, returning to the church at midday on Saturday. On Easter Sunday there is a Resurrection mass, a *Misa de Resurrección* at 4:00 A.M., timed to coincide with the sunrise. After more processions around the plaza, the images are returned to the church and, after several hours of display, are returned to their glass cases for the rest of the year. This is a much more strictly Catholic interpretation than the one described below for the Yaqui.

Processions are also the key element in the Christmas posadas. These go from house to house, where they beg entrance, are admitted for refreshments, and continue until they finally reach the parish church.

In addition to these dance dramas, another blend arose out of Catholic influence and indigenous custom, the dances and pilgrimages of the *Concheros.* Concheros groups are found all over central Mexico. The major features include vow-taking pilgrimages, some kind of Christian emblem (usually Christ, Mary, or the Virgin of Guadelupe), organization into brotherhoods, a plumed headdress such as was common among the Aztecs, and accompaniment by the *concha,* an instrument with five double strings made from the shell of an armadillo. The dance itself has both indigenous and postconquest elements. A Concheros performance begins with a procession to the church followed immediately by the singing of a praise song *(alabanza).* The group's leader initiates the dance by playing the first tune of his concha. The other dancers then join him. The steps themselves are both aboriginal, the flat-footed stamping, and European, pas de basques, skips, and jigs. There is no dance formation as such; rather the dancers dance in place and accompany themselves individually.

Similar selective adaptation characterizes the Yaqui of northwest Mexico. Spanish elements were selectively incorporated into Yaqui values and ritual so that today it is difficult to imagine what the pre-Spanish Yaqui world might have been.[6] The Yaqui are important because, like the Isthmus Zapotec, they have maintained a fierce sense of their identity as Yaqui while partaking of selected elements of the Mexican world.

In order to understand the significance of most of Yaqui ritual, one has to examine events and structures that constitute the yearly cycle. Yaqui divide the year into two seasons: the dry (January to May) and the wet (May to December). This basically ecological division is paralleled in both social and ritual structure. The dry season is associated with Jesus, whose devotions are carried out by two male groups, the *Fariseos* (Pharisees) and the *Caballeros*.[7] The wet season belongs to the Virgin Mary, or Our Mother, who is celebrated by the *Matachines,* a group of men and young boys who pledge themselves to this activity for a period of years. The two points of change in the yearly cycle are marked by especially important sets of rituals. In December, when the wet season with its emphasis on Mary, the female principle, fertility, and benevolence is coming to a close, the Yaqui celebrate their military patroness, the Virgin of Guadalupe. The military brotherhoods, all with Spanish military titles, are responsible for the festive activities. During the times of war, all too frequent in Yaqui history, these same groups fought in defense of Yaqui independence, with the Virgin of Guadalupe as their protectress.

The end of the dry season in April is marked by probably the most significant ritual in the Yaqui year, Easter. The Fariseos and Caballeros who have dominated ritual life for the preceding six months give way to the Matachines, who embody the forces of life. The weapons that characterize the dry season festivities fall before the flowers and ribbons representing Christ's blood and the principle of goodness.

In the following abbreviated description of Yaqui Easter ritual and drama, the mixture of Catholicism and indigenous religious beliefs, Spanish and Yaqui, is apparent.

Beginning with Ash Wednesday and for every Friday in Lent, the rituals are primarily Spanish and Catholic. The Friday processions, for example, are an enactment of the traditional Catholic Way of the Cross as Jesus is pursued by his enemies. Holy Week itself begins on Palm Sunday with the dramatization of the entry of Jesus into Jerusalem. The cottonwood twigs decorating the path to the church, however, are symbolic of the Yaqui belief in the association of flowers with the forces of good. On Holy Thursday an Old Man standing for Jesus is pursued by the *Chapayekas*. Later that night the figure of Jesus is captured by the Fariseos, yet another of the enemies of the Christ. Good Friday rituals are a combination of foreign and native symbolism and values. The Crucifixion is enacted in the afternoon and is followed by a watch and offerings of flowers and candles. At midnight there is a procession representing the Resurrection. In that, the figure of Jesus is taken from the evil forces by a trick on the part of the church group. Afterward, the Chapayekas have a mock fiesta in which cultural values and symbols are reversed.

It is on Holy Saturday and, to a lesser extent, Easter Sunday, that the rituals stress the native beliefs and symbolism. But because those beliefs are consonant with much of Western Christianity, the whole set of activities takes on doubly powerful meanings. Early on Holy Saturday, the church altar and the holy figures are decorated with flowers symbolizing rebirth and goodness. In the middle of the morning the New Fire ceremony takes place, again, an ancient Mesoamerican ritual designed to renew the world. The Chapayekas appear again parading with Judas, their leader. The high point of the day's activities occurs at noon with the "Gloria." The Fariseos attack the church three times trying to get back the figure of Jesus. They are ritually "killed" by flowers thrown at them by the church group and the *Pascolas* (holy clowns), by the switches of the angels, and by the dancing of the Matachines, Pascolas, and the deer dancer. The evil forces are destroyed by the blood of Jesus transformed into flowers. Judas is burned, and the masks and weapons of the Fariseos burn with him. In the early evening, the Matachines celebrate their triumph with a maypole dance.

Events on Easter Sunday simply reaffirm the triumph of good over evil and that part of the year associated with birth and fertility. Symbolically, this is represented by the green twigs that the Fariseos now carry instead of weapons.

While much of the outward symbolism here is Spanish, from the concept of Easter itself to the names of many of the participants, celebrations that marked the beginning of spring are widespread throughout the indigenous populations of Latin America, especially among those groups that both hunted and farmed, such as the Yaqui. The Virgin Mary is an overlay on the Yaqui Our Mother; the New Fire ceremony on Holy Saturday is clearly a continuation of Mesoamerican fire ceremonies that periodically renewed civilization. Flower symbolism is as ancient as human habitation in Latin America, and in the Yaqui case, the antiquity is overlaid with Catholic symbolism, giving it double strength; the Deer dancers and Pascolas date back to an earlier hunting and gathering society when it was important to mediate between human society and nature. In keeping with this earlier relationship, these dancers dance as a result of a dreamed vision rather than a vow. In the contemporary Easter celebration, these figures are linked with the Matachines and the side of good.

Outside of the Easter season — but also an example of the blend of cultures — are the societies responsible for the festival of the patron saint and for funerals. Pre-Columbian villages and towns in many parts of Mesoamerica had deities closely associated with them. The patron saint was simply a different kind of deity. Funerals, too, were often the responsibility of certain

groups within society. In the Yaqui case, the Spanish influence is clear in the names of the two groups responsible for both these functions — the Moors and the Christians. The former dress in red, the latter in blue, and both engage in a ritual battle during the feast of the patron saint.

The strands of indigenous versus European content may be separated out for the Yaqui, just as for the Zapotec or many other groups in Latin America. And because dance and drama are discrete, performance-oriented forms that call attention to themselves, it is often easier to analyze them in their context. However, both these examples demonstrate the kind of mutual reinforcement of core values that occurred in the selection and blending of diverse cultural elements. Both Yaqui and Zapotec cultures are stronger and more resistant to outside forces because of this adaptive syncretism.

■ The Social Context

Music, dance, and drama are always parts of specific social contexts, which have economic, political, and ideological features. While music and dance retain a certain degree of autonomy in style and form from their social contexts, there is always an initial decision as to whether to sing or to remain silent, to dance or to sit still. This is coupled with a decision of what specific form will be used. A good example of the importance of context is the decision by the Kiriri Indians in Bahia, Brazil, as to when and where to perform the *Toré* ceremony in 1983.

The Kiriri Indians had been decreed the perpetual use of "one square league"(perhaps 15 square miles) of land in the interior of the state of Bahia in the seventeenth century. Much of that parcel had been invaded by 1982, and the Kiriri were reduced to living on only a part of their traditional territory. They no longer speak their native language and look and live much like most of the regional population. Over a decade ago they began to perform a native ceremony called the Toré, which they learned from another group of Indians in the northeast. Then, in a political move timed to coincide with the 1982 Brazilian elections, they invaded one of the non-Indian ranches and took possession of it.

This repossession of their lands took much of the regional population by surprise. The Kiriri cleared a large community garden plot at the top of the highest hill on the repossessed ranch and built a shelter for the Toré ceremony. This they performed at night, in full view of much of the surrounding area, illuminated by fires. Their decision to dance the Toré where they did expressed (1) their control of the top of the mountain which had for many years been claimed by a non-Indian, and (2) their "Indianness" through the performance of an indigenous religious ceremony.

A similar musical expression of a political stance occurred in Rio de Janeiro at the time of the Brazilian elections in 1980. For a while there was a direct correlation between the type of music played at parties and the political affiliation of the person or group giving the party. One group liked to play urban popular music of Brazilian origin — associated with the proletariat and radical bohemia. Another liked to play rural music associated with the Brazilian peasantry. A third liked to play urban popular music largely inspired by North American forms. These three tastes in music were paralleled by political affiliations and concern with the future of the proletariat, the peasantry, or the middle class. The distinctiveness of musical taste went so far that groups of friends might argue loudly over the type of music to be played at a party, and then not visit each other again for months afterward. The issue was political; the medium was music. While the identity produced by the music was not ethnic, music did serve — however briefly — as a catalyst of allegiances.

Music and dance are thus sometimes direct, concrete expressions of political intentions and alliances, but this will depend on the specific context within which they are performed. At one moment the Toré will be of interest only to its adepts, and Brazilian popular music will be considered a matter of individual taste. At another moment these musical and dance forms will crystallize the aspirations and identity of an entire group.

■ The Urban Transformation

The transformation of the Latin American countries from predominantly rural societies to countries with large urban populations has been accompanied by some important changes in their music and dance. While the exchange and mutual influence of art forms between the cities and the rural areas has always occurred, a number of forms once popular in rural areas are virtually disappearing before new forms that originate in the cities and that are disseminated by the nearly ubiquitous battery-operated radios and by television (where there is electric power). Migration and urbanization have led to the development of new musical and dance institutions partly as a result of changes in people's lives. When small landholders are removed from lands developed by large corporations for other ends, many of the local art forms also vanish. Or they may vanish from the rural regions but reappear in the poorer corners of a city to which the residents have migrated. Change in art forms may also result partly from strong pressure by multi-national recording companies to sell their products.

Carnaval in Rio de Janeiro is an example of an international holiday that has become a massive spectacle involving hundreds of thousands of participants, a huge influx of tourism, large commercial interests, and a multi-faceted outlet for popular arts. Traditionally, Carnaval — known as Mardi Gras in the United States — is a festival related to the Catholic church calendar, in which believers have one last party before the somber days of Lent, which begins on Ash Wednesday and continues through Easter. Carnaval is a kind of "last chance for revelry," ignored or discouraged by Church officials. There are celebrations in Germany, New Orleans, and around the world.

In Rio de Janeiro Carnaval mobilizes an entire city. During the brief pre-Lenten exuberance many usual behaviors are inverted: the days are devoted to sleeping, the nights to drinking and dancing; the business district is paralyzed and becomes a center of revelry; nudity and physical intimacy, usually typical of the house or the beach, are found in the central avenues and public places. The body, its shapes, movements, and dress are celebrated during consecutive nights of revelry. Many of the urban poor wear the elaborate costumes of nobility; many men dress as women; groups of old men parade with rubber baby pacifiers; groups of masked dancers play practical jokes and take sweet revenge for some indignity suffered during the year. The everyday behavior of the rest of the year is in some way inverted and transformed, and appears in unusual places and times.[8]

The Carnaval in Rio de Janeiro comes at the culmination of the hot tropical summer, shortly before the school year begins again. The whole city moves at a different pace during the summer months. People look different, the air is filled with damp perfume, noise, and industrial pollution. The beautiful beaches are crowded with people, and the local groups that produce the informal *blocos,* or music and dance associations, or the more formal and elaborate samba schools (*escolas de samba*) rehearse regularly on weekends while hundreds of seamstresses prepare the elaborate costumes. Carnaval mobilizes huge numbers of people—hundreds of thousands of people dance and parade during the four days. Hundreds of thousands of costumes are prepared. New songs are written, special lights are strung, and special viewing stands are built. Tons of confetti are made, thousands of gallons of beer are brewed, hundreds of thousands of records are sold. Carnaval is a moment of creativity, consumption, indulgence, and performance.

The complex, hierarchical groups found in large cities celebrate Carnaval in distinctly different ways. There is no single way to celebrate Carnaval in Rio de Janeiro. The different groups in the city's social hierarchy celebrate in distinctly different ways. The less wealthy spend Carnaval in the streets. Neighborhood-based associations, typical of large cities, often arrange to parade together in some kind of organized fashion. The most famous of these are the samba schools, which appeared in the 1930s. Each of them prepares an elaborate theme, with its own song, floats, costumes, and allegory. These is a mixture of music, dance, and drama into an integrated theme that is the subject of a specially composed samba, expressed through floats, costumes, and banners, which moves through the streets with the driving force of percussion bands and thousands of dancers. Escolas de samba parade down a major avenue competing with each other for prizes of money and prestige. While Carnaval is a moment of collective abandon, these samba schools are examples of careful, controlled, popular organization in which people who in the larger society have little control over their own affairs exercise rigid control over all aspects of the tremendously complex task of getting thousands of people to parade down the avenue at the right time with the correct costume and singing in the correct way.[9]

Many Brazilians celebrate Carnaval in private clubs, where there are several women for every man. Other clubs are restricted to transvestites. The celebrations in the private clubs vary in emphasis: some are elaborate costume balls; others are more like a nightlong orgy of drinking, dancing, and display. Yet other residents, usually wealthier, leave for their country houses. There they either give parties for small groups of friends or grumble about the waste and inefficiency of Carnaval and watch the parades on television.

There have always been different attitudes toward this pre-Lenten festival. Members of the intellectual groups have almost always frowned upon it or wished the older forms could come back.[10] But new musical forms, new allegories, new dances, and new trends are constant in Carnaval. They influence the rest of the country, and draw tourists from around the world.

Tourism has dramatically altered many aspects of music and dance in Latin America. In many countries there are special places in the cities and towns where tourists may see the traditional Latin American arts. What they see, however, is usually subtly altered in order to be more palatable or easily understood. The anarchy of earlier Carnaval has become a parade, with bleachers reserved by the tourist agencies. The attitude of business and the Brazilian state toward Carnaval has also changed. Today, Carnaval is a means of obtaining scarce foreign currency. Hotels, travel agencies, the city of Rio de Janeiro, and the central government of the country all promote Carnaval, stage competitions, and try to ensure that the encounter with Brazilian exuberance will not be fatal to the visitors. These moves have certainly affected Carnaval, and in some ways injected a great deal of government control into the popular festival. But Carnaval has not been deprived of its innovation and controversy. Transformed into a kind of Macy's Thanksgiving Day parade in one place, it breaks out in full disarray and spontaneity in others.

Carnaval is a huge, dynamic, and constantly transforming event. A spectacle for tourists, a brief interruption in the daily routine for most Brazilians, it is a good example of the tremendous economic, cultural, and personal importance of music, dance, and drama today, even in the heart of highly industrialized urban societies, and of the kinds of continuities and transformations found in popular art forms in Latin America.

The Urban Scene and the Rise of Popular Performers

The urban scene has affected popular art forms in other ways. The professional popular performer is largely an urban phenomenon. Urban popular music in Latin America is often part of musical trends that exist outside the continent but that have important musical roots in the traditions of the respective countries. Thus the improvisational style of the Brazilian *choro* is

similar to jazz and developed at approximately the same period. The tango, a dance of Argentina and Uruguayan origins, became immensely popular not only in Latin America but in the United States and Europe. The radio, phonograph, and television have all enhanced the diffusion of urban forms to the rest of the country. A Brazilian film that was distributed widely in the United States, *Bye Bye Brazil,* illustrated the results of these processes in a humorous way. Only with the advent of the inexpensive cassette recorder have the people in the rural areas begun to preserve and disseminate their own traditions instead of merely consuming those of the major urban centers.

Most Latin American countries are tremendously concerned about the domination of mass media by the United States and Europe. On many radio stations it is impossible to hear anything besides British and North American rock music. It is less expensive to show "canned films" (programs made in the United States) than to produce new ones. Thus old United States programs, dubbed into Spanish or Portuguese, may dominate television in some countries. Many countries in Latin America are attempting to develop programs that reflect a national identity, and often go to rural or popular urban forms for their inspiration.

In Mexico, for example, the *Ballet Folklórico* brings performances of traditional and contemporary dances to the people of Mexico and most other nations of the world. The repertoire of the company, founded in 1961 by Amalia Hernández, spans the entire breadth of Mexican dance. It includes the Yaqui deer dance, Veracruz *huapangos* (couple dance with zapateados), reconstructions of Aztec and Mayan ceremonial dance, and modern versions of the old dramas portraying good and evil, life and death. The Ballet Folklórico is a a crystallization of Mexico's past and present in its heritage of dance. At regional levels, there are annual performances of music and dance. One that attracts thousands of spectators each year is the *Guelaguetza* of the state of Oaxaca. For six hours on two consecutive Sundays in July, representatives of all the indigenous groups in the state present their music and dance traditions to appreciative audiences from the state, nation, and from abroad.

One of the reasons Latin American governments are so active in sustaining national art forms today is that they want to establish or maintain artistic independence from the United States. Some countries have passed laws that require a certain percentage of national films, records, or shows to be played on radio, over television stations, or in movie houses. The issues confronted, however, transcend the issue of sound or movement, and are an intricate part of national aspirations and international relations. Even where economic dependence is strong, cultural independence can be declared and may be an indicator of hopes and intentions for a different kind of future.

Today Latin American music, dance, and drama are among the world's most experimental and avant-garde. Composers, choreographers, dramatists, and popular musicians are preparing works that are presented in New York, Paris, London, and Africa as well as in their home countries. There is an effervescence to the artistic life of many countries in Latin America that reflects the profound social and political transformations that are occurring, yet also exhibit profound continuities with past movements.

■ Conclusion

Throughout this essay, we have viewed the arts of music, dance, and drama in terms of their complex relationships with the cultures and societies that produce and enjoy them. While art is not synonymous with the everyday because all art involves stylization, selection, and transformation, there is nonetheless a relationship between the world of art and the world of the everyday.[13]

Art, especially music and dance, is also an excellent vehicle for people's feelings about their own identity. At the individual level, there is the opportunity to express personal style in music or dance, both in the variations on the general choreography or musical text and in the decision about whether to participate at all. For groups, whether ethnic, village, neighborhood, region or nation, music and dance provide a way to make a statement about group identity. Sometimes the statement is for the benefit of the group itself, as in the case of the Yaqui Easter cycle where it functions as a symbolic condensation of what it means to be a Yaqui and is the more powerful because all the meanings of Yaqui are concentrated into one week of highly dramatic forms of music, dance, and ritual. Sometimes the statement of identity contained in these forms is directed toward other groups. We have seen this kind of use by the Isthmus Zapotec. Nations, too, exemplify themselves in music and dance, sending companies around the world as representatives and using indigenous dance forms on posters and brochures for the tourist trade. In contemporary Latin American drama, nationalism is promoted at the same time that antinorthern, especially anti-United States, sentiments are expressed.

Music and dance also comment on changing social contexts. In Latin America one can distinguish styles in these performing arts that derive from Spain, Portugal, and Africa — the Catholic dance-dramas, congadas, all the couple dances, and many more. Again, it is important to note the blending of indigenous and imported elements.

Another feature of the Latin American context is the rural-urban contrast. In cultural terms, the cities and the countryside have developed different kinds of music, dance, and drama. However, it would be inaccurate to say that these remain separate and uninfluenced by each other. The city imports rural elements periodically as a way of invigorating its own forms. The impetus for the importation often results from a need felt by urban dwellers to get in touch with their roots, to validate their heritage again. The country, through the media of radio, television, stereos, records, tape cassettes, and movies, is well aware of urban styles and borrows selectively. Discotheques spring up in provincial towns with tape selections featuring Michael Jackson as well as Latin American singers and groups.

The arts, then, are at once of the world and separate from it. The separation allows them to articulate perspectives on social and cultural processes. Statements in music, dance, and drama are condensed and powerful and reach their audience in both emotional and intellectual ways. At the same time, because they are intimately of the world, we learn through them about other aspects of culture and society.[11] The arts have always been a vital part of Latin American society, changing with changed contexts, an instrument of identity, and a way to carve out moments of peace and exhilaration in an often chaotic world. To ignore them in a quest for understanding Latin America leads to an unfortunate kind of myopia. Through them one can see Latin America through a different and powerful lens that brings us glimpses of what Latin Americans themselves deem vital elements of their own society.

■ Notes

1. Robert M. Stevenson, "Latin America III: Afro-American Music," in *The New Grove Dictionary of Music and Musicians,* ed. Stanley Sadie (London: Macmillan, 1980).
2. See Peter Furst, *Flesh of the Gods* (New York: Praeger, 1972).
3. Gerardo Reichel-Dolmatoff, *The Shaman and the Jaguar: A Study of Narcotic Drugs among the Indians of Colombia* (Philadelphia: Temple University Press, 1975); and M. Dobkin de Rios, "Some Relationships between Music and Hallucinogenic Ritual: The 'Jungle Gym' of Consciousness," in *Ethos* 3: 64–76.
4. J. S. Fontaine, *The Interpretation of Ritual: Essays in Honor of I. I. Richards* (London: Tavistock Publications, Ltd., 1972), 194.
5. For further reading on the Isthmus Zapotec see Anya Peterson Royce, *Prestigio y Afiliación en una Comunidad Urbana: Inchitán, Oaxaca.* (Serie de Antropología Social 37) (México: D. F.: SepSetentas and Instituto Nacional Indigenista, 1975); *The Anthropology of Dance* (Bloomington and London: Indiana University Press, 1977); *Ethnic Identity: Strategies of Diversity* (Bloomington: Indiana University Press, 1977); and "Dance as an Indicator of Social Class and Identity in Juchitán, Oaxaca," CORD Research Annual VI (New York: Committee on Research in Dance, 1974); and Miguel Covarrubias, *Mexico South* (New York: Alfred Knopf, 1946).
6. For more about the Yaqui and Yaqui ceremonialism see Edward Spicer's many works, various publications of the Instituto Nacional Indigenista, Murial Thayer Painter's *Yaqui Easter* (1971), and Francis Densmore's *Yuman and Yaqui Music* (1933).
7. Terms such as Fariseos, Caballeros, Chapayekas, and Matachines take on different meanings depending upon the culture that uses them. In general, they identify groups associated with the Easter Passion plays, but in the case of Matachines may depict the dances and music of that group at Christmas, the day of the Virgin of Guadelupe (December 12) and other saints' days. The Fariseos (Pharisees), Caballeros, and Chapayekas are the male societies that persecute Christ during the Easter dramas. Pontius Pilate is their leader. Of these three, the Chapayekas are the most linked to pre-Spanish Yaqui tradition. They are in the tradition of native American clowns who, by doing everything the reverse of what is usual, reaffirm the established pattern. The name literally means "long, slender noses."

    Matachin comes from the Arabic word that means "those who put on a face" or "those who face each other." The dance done by this society comes out of Renaissance Europe and was brought to the New World by the Europeans. The musical accompaniment and dance formations are European while the steps and much of the costume are indigenous. For the Yaqui, the dance has become thoroughly integrated in the Catholic ritual and has a complex votive organization devoted to the Virgin.
8. Roberto Da Matta, *Carnarais, Malandros e Herois* (Rio de Janeiro: Editora Zahar, 1979); and *Universo de Carnaval Carioca* (Rio de Janeiro: Ediçoes Pinakotheke, 1981).
9. Maria Julia Goldwasser, *O Palacio do Samba: Estudo*

Antropológico de Escola de Samba Estaçao Primeira de Mangueira (Rio de Janeiro: Editora Zahar, 1975).

10. See Luis D. Gardel, *Escolas de Samba, An Affectionate Descriptive Account of the Carnival Guilds of Rio de Janeiro* (Rio de Janeiro: Livraria Kosmos Ltda., 1967); and Eneida [Eneida de Morais] *Historia do Carnaval Carioca* (Rio de Janeiro: Editora Letras e Artes Ltda., 1958).

11. Anya Peterson Royce, *Movement and Meaning: Creativity and Interpretation in Ballet and Mime* (Bloomington: Indiana University Press, 1984); Anthony Seeger, *Os Indios e Nos* (Rio de Janeiro: Editora Campus, 1980).

■ Suggested Readings

Behague, Gerard. *Music in Latin America: An Introduction.* Englewood Cliffs, N.J.: Prentice-Hall, 1979.

Chase, Gilbert. *A Guide to the Music of Latin America.* 2d ed. Washington: Pan American Union, 1962.

Lekis, Lisa. *Folk Dances of Latin America.* New York: The Scarecrow Press, 1959.

List, George, and Juan Orrego-Salas, eds. *Music in the Americas.* The Hague: Mouton, 1967.

Marco, Guy A., Ann Garfield, and Sharon Ferris. *Information on Music: A Handbook of Reference Sources in European Languages: Volume II, The Americas.* Littleton, Colo.: Libraries Unlimited, 1977.

Nettl, Bruno. *Folk and Traditional Music of the Western Continents.* 2d ed. Englewood Cliffs, N.J.: Prentice-Hall, 1973.

Royce, Anya Peterson. *The Anthropology of Dance.* Bloomington and London: Indiana University Press, 1977.

Sadie, Stanley ed. *The New Grove Dictionary of Music and Musicians.* 20 vols. London: Macmillan, 1980.

Seeger, Anthony. *Nature and Society in Central Brazil: The Suya Indians of Mato Grosso.* Cambridge: Harvard University Press, 1981.

Toor, Francis. *A Treasury of Mexican Folkways.* New York: Crown Publishers, 1947.

14 | *The Economics of Latin America*

DARREL YOUNG

The economic history of Latin America consists largely of efforts to find an appropriate stance within the context of international trade. This external fixation is unsurprising given that Latin America, in almost all facets of its internal life, has had to contend with strong outside influences. This chapter attempts to explain its two major responses to the international scene: primary-export orientation and import-substitution industrialization. Then these and related strategies will be probed in order to assess Latin America's economic prospects.

■ Primary Export Orientation

Policy

Latin America's export orientation has its roots in the conquest. The Spaniards and Portuguese came in the sixteenth century, for God and gold—although not necessarily in that order. The Iberians desired not to enrich the lives of the Indians they encountered, but rather to enrich themselves. As a consequence the conquered lands and peoples were organized with almost exclusive emphasis on the extraction of wealth to be sent to the "mother" country.[1] This policy led to the formation of large landed estates, which became the basis for producing sugar, cotton, hides, and other agricultural goods aimed at the European market. In all forms, then, the colonial era skewed the economic structures of Latin America toward exportation.

Independence did not alter this arrangement in any substantial manner. The list of raw materials from agriculture and mining changed and grew, and an increasing proportion of Latin American output in the nineteenth century went to the United States. By the early twentieth century there was some industrial capacity in the region, but primary exports continued to dominate Latin America economies.

Problems

Concentration on primary exports created problems for Latin America in several ways. Internally, it reinforced maldistribution of wealth and income, for land remained concentrated in a few hands. Labor had no bargaining power, and owners had little reason to raise wages above a

215

minimal level. Landowners had no interest in creating a greater domestic market via higher wages; they expected to sell their product abroad, not at home. Their interest lay in keeping costs, including labor, low. Moreover, the high level of activity in the export sector was largely self-contained and induced little growth in the rest of the economy.

Primary goods have certain characteristics that put Latin America at a disadvantage internationally. These negative traits include price inelasticity, income elasticity, and susceptibility to substitution.

Price inelasticity refers to those markets in which the customer's decision whether to buy is not influenced, to any great degree, by the price of the article; that is, pretty much the same quantity of the good will be bought no matter what the price. This phenomenon tends to apply to agricultural goods in general, but particularly to products such as sugar and coffee, with which strong habits are involved. Even if prices increase or decrease greatly, demand for these items changes only slightly. This inelastic demand becomes significant when coupled with fluctuating supply; and agricultural production, since it is dependent upon the weather, is especially subject to fluctuations. Harvests vary from year to year because of flood, drought, freeze, or pests. As can be seen in Figure 1, the result is frequent variation in price.

With coffee at $3.00 a pound, 8 million

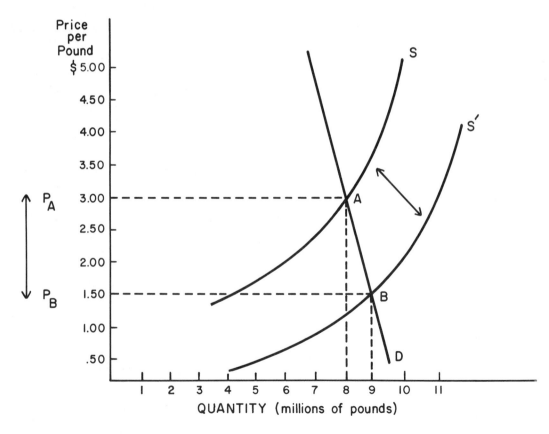

FIGURE 1
Coffee

pounds are purchased (point A). However, suppose that growing conditions become very favorable; the resulting bonanza would cause the supply of coffee to increase from S to S'. As a consequence, the price must fall to $1.50 a pound in order to persuade present coffee drinkers to drink enough additional cups per day (or to induce a sufficient number of those presently not drinking coffee to do so) to absorb the extra million pounds produced by the bumper crop (point B). If the following years are not as favorable, supply will shift back from S' to S (or beyond) with price rising to $3.00 per pound (or more). With minerals, such as copper or tin, changes originate more often on the demand side, depending on whether boom or recession prevails in the industrialized countries, but the impact on price is much the same.

These markets, then, are subject to fluctuations in price, and this is a negative factor for several reasons. First, when an economy depends upon export earnings that change greatly from year to year, future revenues cannot be estimated with any certainty, and this makes developmental planning difficult. Even when a given country experiences high earnings from its product, the good times are likely to be at the expense of some other country that has been hit by drought, flood, freeze, or the like.

Second, if a country attempting to develop improves its efficiency and productivity in turning out these price-inelastic goods, supply moves out from S to S', thereby reducing price and revenues (the increase in sales is not enough to offset the decrease in price). This phenomenon is sometimes called immiserizing growth.

Third, constant fluctuations expose primary-export countries to the possibility that terms of trade may deteriorate. Suppose that those in industrialized countries who purchase primary goods in order to turn them into finished goods, because of their advantage in bargaining power, pay less than what the market calls for in times of high prices but do require exporters to bear the full brunt of low prices. In this case, the average price received for commodities, over time, may not keep pace with increases in the price of manufactured products. The more frequent the fluctuations, the greater the chance of balance-of-payments problems.

Income inelasticity refers to demand for a product not matching increases in income. Once again, agricultural goods are seen as being inelastic. As incomes double, for example, people — at least those above the subsistence level — do not eat twice as much food as previously. They might eat more in absolute terms, but not proportionately more; that is, a smaller percentage of income is spent on these items.

Income inelasticity, therefore, is disadvantageous as regards international terms of trade. If, as world income grows, demand for primary goods decreases as a percentage of income, while relative demand for finished goods (which tend to be more income-elastic) increases, then the prices of the former vis-à-vis the latter will deteriorate. The tendency for raw materials to be more susceptible than manufactured products to substitutes also contributes to terms-of-trade vulnerability.

Studies regarding actual changes in terms of trade for Latin America vary according to country and time period. However, in general, comparisons for periods prior to 1940 show manafactures, not commodities, to be the more dynamic.

■ Import-Substitution Industrialization

Policy

Although doubts were raised from time to time about the wisdom of heavy reliance on primary exports, it required the combination of the Great Depression and World War II to bring about a major policy shift in Latin American economics. In the 1930s the demand for raw materials plummeted, causing a sharp decrease in Latin America's capacity to import. Since its ability to pay for processed goods was limited, the region began to look to its own fledgling industry to meet its needs.

World War II reinforced this inclination. Demand for primary goods rose dramatically during this time, but the industrialized countries were too occupied producing military items to provide Latin America with enough manufactured goods. As a consequence, national producers were called on to service the increased demand for manufactures within the region.

In the postwar years, countries in Latin America began to implement policies of economic growth based on import substitution. Faced with the return of the industrialized nations to full-scale production of consumer articles, Latin American states erected protective tariff barriers on such goods in order to reserve their internal markets for local industry. By doing so, leaders hoped to lessen their economies' dependence on fluctuating export markets and take advantage of the more dynamic growth and employment that industrialization seemed to offer.

As a result of this policy change the state came to play an increasing role in Latin American economic life. It did this indirectly by providing low-interest loans, cheap energy rates, low tariffs on machinery and intermediate imports needed by national producers (overvalued exchange rates maintained by the state served the same purpose), and other such assistance to encourage industrialization. The state also acted directly through state-owned firms that produced items previously imported. During these years multinational corporations (MNCs) also became a significant presence in Latin America. Companies wanted to locate in the area because tariff barriers limited their ability to export to these markets; the Latin American countries needed MNC expertise to help bring about rapid industrialization.

Latin America had an impressive average economic growth rate of more than 5 percent annually during the 1950–1970 period. Production for the manufacturing sector of Latin America as a whole grew at an average rate of approximately 6 percent per year from 1945 to 1961 and at an even faster pace during the 1960s; industry based on import substitution grew fastest.[2]

Problems

Import-substitution industrialization (ISI) provided Latin America with a considerable period of economic expansion, but by the 1970s several problems became evident. First, local manufactures tended to be of high price and low quality. This was due in part to the inclination of national producers not to focus their energies on becoming more efficient and productive, but rather on ensuring that high tariffs would continue to shield them from competition (a large number of state enterprises seem to have acted this way). High prices were also attributable to the fact that the limited size of most domestic markets would not allow the manufacture of many goods on a scale large enough to permit the lower per-unit costs associated with mass production.

Second, whereas ISI was intended to alleviate balance-of-payments problems by reducing imports, the policy in fact aggravated trade deficits. Imports of consumer items did decrease, but in most countries this decrease was more than offset by an increase in the import of capital goods (i.e., machinery needed for industrialization). ISI programs promoted the production of articles formerly imported, that is to say, finished consumer items, but ISI growth never generated domestic capital-goods enterprises on a large scale.

The underdevelopment of national capital-goods industries was due in part to the fact that to be profitable, production of capital goods requires markets even larger than those of consumer goods. In addition, development of capital-goods sectors was thwarted by conflicts within the ISI process itself. If tariff barriers were erected to encourage the local manufacture of machinery, this would raise the cost, and possibly lower the quality, of such goods, something that national producers of consumer items were not prepared to accept.[3] Whatever the explanation for this gap in the production chain, it remains true that ISI-based growth locks Latin America into high levels of capital-goods imports, a fact that has contributed to the region's current debt problems.

Third, overvalued exchange rates and low tariffs on capital goods not only facilitated machinery imports, but—along with the subsidized loans, cheap energy, and other ISI inducements that lowered the cost of capital— they skewed the process toward automation, thereby limiting employment creation. Statistics show, in general, that manufacturing employment in Latin America grew at only about half the rate of growth in manufacturing output.[4]

Fourth, the underside of the emphasis on industrialization was inattention to agriculture. With resources being concentrated in industry, agricultural productivity in many countries stagnated, sometimes resulting in increased food imports. This combination of industrial movement and agricultural stagnation was a major factor in the strong rural-to-urban migration, and resulting urban congestion, that Latin America continues to experience.

Fifth, multinational corporations during this period seemed to create as many problems as they solved. The hoped-for benefits in terms of increased capital formation, employment, technology transfer, and tax revenues for Latin American economies did not materialize to the degree expected, largely because of MNC use of local credit, of capital-intensive (i.e., automated) production methods, of imported executives and techniques, and of transfer pricing (manipulating internal prices of sales and purchases across different national divisions of the same company in such a way as to show low profit in high-tax countries and vice versa).[5]

Lastly, ISI did not serve to rectify maldistribution of income. Partially, its failure to do so resulted from the capital-intensive nature of ISI production, which in turn kept labor income down. In cases such as Brazil, where import-

substitution industrialization centered on the manufacture of middle- and upper-class consumer goods, a conscious skewing of national income by means of wage constraints became necessary. This was done in order to raise the incomes of the upper classes so that they might buy increased amounts of the goods being produced, thereby stimulating continued economic growth.

■ Status of Related Strategies

Several approaches have been used to counter the negative aspects of the two major economic strategies, primary-export orientation and import-substitution industrialization. In broad terms, these related policies can be categorized as attempts at commodity-price stabilization, economic integration, export diversification, and expansion of internal markets. A look at the current status of these alternatives will permit an evaluation of Latin America's prospects.

Commodity Price Stabilization

Fluctuations in the price of primary goods can be minimized if supply can be controlled. Although weather conditions remain beyond human manipulation, there are other means of regulating the amount of product entering the market at a given time. One way is through the maintenance of buffer stocks. In bumper years when production is high, purchases to build up the buffer stock will keep prices from falling as much as they would otherwise. In periods of poor crops, the accumulated reserves can be sold in order to restrain price increases. The same actions can be taken in mineral markets to offset changes in demand.

Buffer stocks can be manipulated in such a manner that price changes are restricted within a targeted range, thereby reducing fluctuations to an acceptable level. However, this requires not only the compliance of all major producers of the commodity, but, just as importantly, funding adequate for buying and storage on a large scale. A similar sort of control over supply, at least as regards downward fluctuation, is possible by means of export-quota agreements among producing countries.

Latin American countries have been involved in several attempts to stabilize the prices of primary exports, but with limited success. The International Tin Council, of which Bolivia has been a member, established a buffer-stock arrangement in 1956. However, the group has been largely ineffective, unable at times (1970 and 1977), because of insufficient stock, to control soaring prices and unable at other times (1957) to defend its minimum price because of insufficient funds.[6] A new agreement was reached in 1982; it called for a higher level of tin reserves, but Bolivia, wanting higher target prices, refused to sign it.

The International Coffee Agreement, important to fifteen Latin American economies, is an export-quota system, initiated in 1962, which has had some difficulties, particularly vis-à-vis cheaper African coffee, but it has limited downward pressures on price. The arrangement, however, did not keep prices from soaring (a 600 percent jump!) in the years following the 1975 frost in Brazil. The present agreement, signed in 1976, calls for price maintainenance within a range of $1.15 to $1.55 per pound, but a possible glut makes it questionable whether this range can be defended in the coming years.[7]

International sugar agreements date back to 1902 and have since undergone various transformations. Pacts have been primarily export-quota arrangements, but some attempts at creation of buffer stocks have been made. Sugar is an important export for Brazil, Cuba, the Dominican Republic, Haiti, Paraguay, and Peru, but these efforts have not controlled prices, mainly because industrialized countries can increase production of beet sugar as desired. Prospects for the current agreement, which utilizes both buffer reserves and export quotas, do not appear any brighter.

The first International Wheat Agreement was signed in 1933. Wheat pacts have been of interest principally to developed countries such as Australia, Canada, and the United States, but are also important to Argentina. In their more recent forms the arrangements have centered around ceiling (maximum) and floor (minimum) prices. During the 1970s, however, attempts at stabilization were swamped by wild market fluctuations brought on by the development of "miracle wheat" and by huge purchases by the Soviet Union. Present arrangements call for a wheat buffer stock.

Attempts to stabilize the prices of other primary products from Latin America, such as cocoa and copper, are in various stages of discussion or development, but none plays a significant role in today's market. The success of OPEC, which heavily damaged most Latin American economies in the 1970s, did at the same time inspire all primary-product groups. However, now even OPEC (which has benefitted Ecuador and Venezuela, who are members, as well as nonmember Mexico) finds itself incapable of controlling its own market. (Price stabilized at too high a level invites substitution and conservation.)

Despite this gloomy picture of current price-stabilization efforts, it should be noted that although prices have fluctuated, terms of trade for commodities in relation to manufactured goods have improved over the last two decades. Moreover, they probably will continue to do so in the foreseeable future as world population growth and rising standards of living cause raw materials to become dearer and dearer. However, even though the long-term trend of prices may be upward, frequent fluctuations are disruptive of development, and Latin America, despite all price-stabilization schemes, remains a captive of constant changes in export earnings.

Economic Integration

One of the problems with import-substitution industrialization is that the limited size of the national market may not permit production on a scale large enough to achieve low per-unit costs. Economic integration offers a possible solution within the ISI context.

Economic integration is the agreement among several nations to allow all members access to one another's markets while maintaining barriers against nonmembers. Thus, economic integration provides larger but still protected markets, permitting import substitution to take place on a regional, not just national, basis. Integration attempts in Latin America include the Latin American Free Trade Association, the Latin American Integration Association, the Central American Common Market, and the Andean Common Market.

Latin American Free Trade Association. The Latin American Free Trade Association (LAFTA), consisting of Argentina, Bolivia, Brazil, Chile, Colombia, Ecuador, Mexico, Paraguay, Peru, Uruguay, and Venezuela, began in 1960. Although established with high hopes, LAFTA contributed little to Latin American economic development, for the members never had a sufficiently strong commitment to trade liberalization.

Member countries promised to lower tariffs on articles they were already importing in quantity from one another, but this obligation did not cover many items; reductions on other products were not automatic. Domestic protectionist pressure kept governments from granting concessions on most ISI goods; consequently there was no blossoming of interregional trade. Almost 90 percent of members' exports was still going outside LAFTA in the 1970s.[8]

Of the LAFTA trade that did take place, exports from Argentina, Brazil, and Mexico dominated. These were the economies that were relatively industrialized and in a position, therefore, to take advantage of new market opportunities. Most other members ran deficits on intra-LAFTA trade during the 1960s. By the end of its first decade, LAFTA was no longer a force in Latin America, and it remained stagnant throughout the 1970s.

Latin American Integration Association. Recently, however, LAFTA has been re-organized as the Latin American Integration Association (LAIA). Formed in 1981, LAIA comprises the same nations as LAFTA. The new organization does make provisions to reduce big-country economic supremacy. In trade agreements with either Argentina, Brazil, or Mexico, other members are not called upon to lower their tariff barriers to the same degree as the bigger countries. The least-developed economies of LAIA — Bolivia, Ecuador, and Paraguay — receive the same economic concessions granted to other members in any LAIA negotiation.

In the main, however, LAIA has even lower ambitions regarding trade liberalization than LAFTA did. LAIA does not provide for region-wide tariff reduction; rather, it depends on "partial agreements" for specific industries to be negotiated among those member states that choose to participate. Such lowered sights do not raise much hope for increased integration among Latin American economies.

Central American Common Market. Costa Rica, El Salvador, Guatemala, Honduras, and Nicaragua signed the Treaty of Managua in 1961 to form the Central American Common Market (CACM). The treaty required the immediate elimination of restrictions on 50 percent of all trade articles and the removal of remaining intra-CACM barriers by 1966. A uniform tariff schedule for nonmember goods was to apply to all member countries, and in order that five economies might develop at an even pace, the agreement also called for the development of "integration industries" (large-scale plants with unrestricted access to the entire regional market), which would be located in an equitable manner in each of the CACM countries.

By the mid-1960s the Central American Common Market was regarded as a successful example of economic integration. Exports were growing at annual rates above 30 percent, intra-CACM trade was accounting for approximately 25 percent of the region's total exports, and more than two-thirds of the products traded among the participating nations were industrial.[9]

However, not all countries shared equally in the growth, and this caused discontent. Nicaragua and Honduras felt that Guatemala and El Salvador, the more advanced economies within the pact, were reaping disproportionate benefits, particularly with respect to the location of integration industries. The resentment erupted in a short-lived war between Honduras and El Salvador in 1969. Honduras's temporary withdrawal from the common market in early 1971 placed further strains on intraregional trade balances, causing Costa Rica to reimpose duties on certain CACM articles at the end of the same year. Ensuing events led to the effective dissolution of the agreement.

Although CACM remains nominally intact, at present it is a mere shadow of its former self. Free trade has not been restored within the group, nor has there been any agreement on a common external tariff. Import reduction measures by CACM nations during the current economic crisis generally include no exceptions for intraregional trade.[10]

The five countries are involved in ongoing discussions regarding the revitalization of CACM, but growing economic and political differences among member states seem to preclude significant integration in Central America for some years to come.

Andean Common Market. The Andean Common Market (ANCOM) was formed in 1969 as a subregional pact by some of the "have-nots" of LAFTA: Bolivia, Chile, Colombia, Ecuador, and Peru (Venezuela joined in 1973). The ANCOM arrangement included a schedule of automatic tariff reductions aimed at freeing intra-ANCOM trade for most items over a ten-year period, plus a timetable for establishing a common external tariff. In addition, in order to avoid the skewed-benefits syndrome that they had suffered in LAFTA, the ANCOM members agreed to more lenient provisions for the two least-developed nations in the pact, Bolivia and Ecuador; the members also devised programs of sectoral allotment.

Sectoral allotment involves measures somewhat similar to those of the Central American Common Market's integration industries. More specifically, Andean sectoral allotment meant the parcelling out of given industries — automobiles, metalworking, and petrochemicals — among member countries. That is to say, exclusive rights to manufacture certain specified products were granted to each nation within ANCOM. The respective governments then decided which domestic companies would carry out the actual production for each allotment. It was hoped that sectoral allotment, by guaranteeing a regional market to a firm, would not only help to harmonize regional development, but also would permit manufacture on a scale not possible with limited national markets.

Another aspect of the Andean agreement worth mentioning is its provisions concerning multinational corporations. Decision 24 and other related steps taken by the Andean Pact represent one of the first less developed country (LDC) attempts at curbing the power of MNCs. Strict limits were imposed on profit remittance, reinvestment of profits, the use of host-country credit, and majority foreign ownership.[11] Although the terms were relaxed somewhat in later years, ANCOM's actions did signal a change in LDC–MNC relations.

Decision 24 was indirectly a factor in the stagnation of the Andean Common Market. In 1976 Chile, having undergone a dramatic change in economic philosophy, withdrew from ANCOM; limits on foreign investment and high external tariffs had no place in the "open economy" Chile planned to establish. A more fundamental cause, however, of the breakdown of the ANCOM process was the difference in aims among individual members. Colombia, and to a lesser degree Venezuela, were most interested in the tariff-reduction aspects of ANCOM; since they were relatively more industrialized, these two countries were in a better position to take advantage of subregional markets. On the other hand Peru, Bolivia, and Ecuador looked to the sectoral-allotment programs to spur industrialization and growth in their economies.

These differences were vividly revealed in the mid-1970s attempt to construct a common external-tariff structure. Colombia and Venezuela pushed for strong tariff protection on non-alloted intraregional trade, but sought low external tariffs on sectoral-allotment production since they did not wish to be bound to regional suppliers whose costs and prices tended to be higher than those of similar imports from the outside world. The other ANCOM members, of course, wanted quite the reverse.

The Andean Common Market has yet to agree on a common external tariff, and the failure to do so has cast a pall over ANCOM transactions in general. Although trade still continues under its auspices (over a billion dollars a year in 1981 and 1982), the dynamism of the group has been checked.[12] Economic nationalism has impeded any new agreement on trade liberalization or sectoral allotment; moreover, in the face of present economic difficulties such attitudes seem to be growing, not ebbing, in strength.

Overall. In sum, the present status of economic integration in Latin America does not seem to offer an avenue of escape from the limits of import-substitution industrialization. Although intraregional trade did increase from the early 1960s to the late 1970s, most of those gains have been wiped out during the 1980s as Latin American countries reacted to the economic crisis of recent years not by working to expand regional markets, but rather by limiting imports from neighboring nations.

Latin American economies have similar resource bases and patterns of development, so they tend to be competitive, not complementary, entities. This is not the best basis for cooperation, and though some gradual advances

may be forthcoming, at present it appears that there is insufficient political will to give much more than lip service to the idea of vibrant economic integration within the region.

Export Diversification

Another possible way around the problems of primary-export orientation and import-substitution industrialization is through diversification of exports. If Latin America were to export significant amounts of manufactured goods, dependency on fluctuating commodity exports would be lessened. Manufactured exports would also allow ISI firms to overcome the limitations of the domestic market.

The nations of Latin America have attempted to promote nontraditional, or manufactured, exports, not just to economic integration partners but also to the world as a whole, particularly to the industrialized countries. Various incentives have been utilized, including direct subsidies (usually a 5 percent to 15 percent government rebate on the price of each nontraditional export) as well as low-interest loans, cheaper energy rates, and reduced taxes for export-oriented firms.

Efforts to diversify exports, however, have encountered difficulties. Domestic producers, accustomed to the protected world of import-substitution industrialization, have been reluctant to become involved in competitive export production. Furthermore, the tariff structures of the industrialized economies seem to discriminate against imported manufactures. While duties on raw materials may be low or nonexistent, tariffs tend to escalate as the schedule progresses through intermediate to finished goods. This pattern of tariff escalation may fit the needs of the already industrialized, but it works to skew Latin American exports away from manufactures back toward primary products.

In 1971 the members of GATT (General Agreement on Trade and Tariffs), the world trade organization, agreed to a Generalized System of Preferences (GSP), an arrangement that allows LDC manufacturers duty-free access to markets within the industrialized economies. Western Europe and Japan established their versions of GSP in 1971–1972; the United States and Canada did so in 1976.

GSP has had minimal impact, however, principally because of restrictions on its implementation. Europe and Japan placed ceilings on duty-free entry. The United States excludes vital sectors, such as textiles, shoes, steel, glassware, and watches, from GSP treatment.[13] Those items included in the United States system are subject to strict limitations. Once the GSP imports from a given country amount to more than $55 million annually, or if they account for more than 50 percent of the total United States market, no matter how small total sales, they no longer qualify for tariff exemption.

Whatever the reasons, raw materials still dominate Latin American exports. According to the Inter-American Development Bank, for the period of 1976–1980 almost 90 percent of the region's total exports was in the form of primary products.[14] The figure is currently somewhat lower, but only because of the general collapse of commodity markets in the 1980s.

Because of the oil shocks, the 1970s may not have been the best of times for export diversification. However, given the current cry in the United States for countervailing tariffs to offset foreign export subsidies, along with rising protectionism in the industrialized world in general, the 1980s do not promise to be any more favorable toward nontraditional Latin American exports.

Expansion of Internal Markets

If internal markets can be enlarged, import-substitution industrialization faces fewer limits. Market size depends on population, but just as importantly on what percentage of the population has the wherewithal to participate in a money economy. Given the large number of those at low levels of material existence in Latin America, the opportunities for market expansion are great, but expansion entails redistribution of income. Many actions affect the distribu-

tion of purchasing power within a society; this section takes a brief look at some of them.

The major attempt at redistribution in Latin America has been through land reform. Breaking up large estates changes power relationships; formerly landless peasants have the opportunity to capture more of the fruits of their labor. Faced with the colonial legacy of highly concentrated land ownership, most Latin American societies have initiated reforms to one degree or another, with Mexico, Bolivia, Cuba, Chile, and Peru being the more prominent examples.[15]

Although these efforts have generated impressive numbers of new owners, the lot of subsistence farmers has changed very little in overall terms. This is attributable partly to the fact that the great majority of Latin American peasant farmers have never shared in land redistribution. Moreover, the welfare of those who have received land has not improved as much as it might have because of the limited provision of credit, agricultural extension services, and economic infrastructure (farm-to-market roads, marketing facilities, irrigation systems, for example) needed to increase rural incomes.

The 1970s and 1980s have seen a renewed interest in agriculture. In order to overcome the agricultural stagnation resulting from the ISI emphasis on industry, there has been a movement in recent years to allocate more resources to the agrarian sector. However, a major portion of this effort has been directed at agribusiness as a means for increasing productivity. Some distribution of land continues under existing programs, but aside from Nicaragua and El Salvador, land reform is not a dynamic factor in Latin America today.

Other actions in the region that bear on income distribution include programs for comanagement, employment generation, and tax reform. Comanagement is worker participation in the ownership and management of the firm. Peru's efforts in the early 1970s represent the only significant example in Latin America, but even there, comanagement was introduced only to a limited degree and has been deemphasized by later governments.

Some countries, such as Brazil and Mexico, have sought to counter ISI stagnation by heavy government investment in infrastructure and the production of capital goods. However, the employment generated by these policies has not caused a more equitable distribution (most studies show that already high income concentration in Brazil and Mexico became even worse in the 1970s), in part because wages were held down to promote investment and also because unemployment remains high in any case.

Tax reform and more efficient tax collection are increasing fiscal revenues in Latin America. Unfortunately, tax systems are still overwhelmingly dependent on indirect (export/import duties and sales taxes), as opposed to direct (income and property taxes) levies. The degree to which this is true varies somewhat from country to country, but the overall pattern is clear. In a typical Latin American economy, sales taxes account for more than 40 percent of total government revenue, with income and property taxes less than 25 percent. The problem with this arrangement is that direct taxes can be progressive (the wealthy pay more) in nature and therefore redistributive of income, whereas indirect taxes tend to be regressive (the poor are harder hit). Given this mix (along with the fact that even income taxes might not be very progressive because of loopholes open to the rich), taxes are not presently a vehicle for redistribution of income in Latin America.

In the mid-1970s the poorest 40 percent of the region's population received only about 10 percent of the total income. Given what has been said above regarding land reform, comanagement, employment creation, and tax structure, there is little reason to believe that the current distribution of income works to expand internal markets.[16]

■ Present Tasks

The tasks before Latin America continue to be those of commodity-price stabilization, export diversification, and expansion of internal markets. All of these depend to some degree upon the international community for solution. Price stabilization requires agreement among countries, possibly between both producing and consuming nations of the primary goods, whereas export diversification depends on access to foreign markets. Even internal market expansion has an international aspect, if only as regards the financing of needed programs. Because it is a capital-scarce region (low standards of living do not permit sufficient domestic savings), Latin America must look abroad—to trade, aid, or loans—for funds. To increase production for internal and external markets, these economies need financing for substantial investments in infrastructure, both economic (transportation, communications, energy) and social (education, health).

■ New International Economic Order

In 1974 the United Nations General Assembly adopted the "Declaration on the Establishment of a New International Economic Order" (NIEO).[17] This call sprang from the concerns of the developing nations. Many LDCs find that international economic relationships leave them no role other than that of suppliers of raw materials. If they are to close the gap that separates them from the developed countries, a restructuring of the international economic order is needed.

Latin American countries have played a major role in the push for NIEO. A look at the principal proposals reveals why NIEO is of such importance to the region.

Commodity Price Stabilization

In order to combat price fluctuations, NIEO proposes that producing and consuming nations arrive at international agreements on eighteen major export commodities (all of Latin America's principal primary exports except petroleum are included in the list). The expansion of raw-material processing within LDCs is emphasized. Also mentioned is the idea of indexing (typing the prices of primary products to changes in the prices of manufactured goods in order to avoid terms-of-trade deterioration). LDCs wanted a $6 billion Common Fund, under United Nations auspices, from which to finance buffer-stock arrangements. The Common Fund was established in 1980; however, its capital base was set at only $750 million.[18]

The International Monetary Fund (IMF) has offered since 1963 a compensatory financing scheme that allows member nations with a temporary decline in export sales to borrow funds to be repaid when exports recover. Such a program allows its beneficiaries to achieve some stability in annual inflows without the problems and pitfalls of buffer-stock management. However, compensatory financing has a rather serious pitfall of its own; developing countries have found it much easier to borrow than to repay. In 1979 the IMF set up a Buffer Stock Financing Facility through which countries can draw up to 50 percent of their respective quotas to finance buffer-stock arrangements.

Market Access

Another NIEO objective is that LDC manufactures obtain preferential access to developed countries' markets. In the main, this calls for an amplification of GSP—more years, fewer exclusions, higher monetary limits, and non-reciprocal treatment. Reduction of tariff barriers by both developing and industrialized economies would tend to benefit the latter, not the former: LDC markets would be awash with developed countries' products, but not vice versa. NIEO also favors the strengthening of regional integration organizations.

Flow of Capital

NIEO calls for renegotiating the debt of developing nations through some combination of forgiveness, moratorium, and rescheduling of payment over longer periods at softer terms. This is a topic of particular concern to Latin America. During the last decade the hard-pressed economies of the region eagerly accepted the easy credit made available by the abundance of petrodollars in international finance. As a result Latin America's total foreign debt now stands at approximately $385 billion, more than that of any other part of the world. As matters now stand, the debt-service burdens of many Latin American countries can be met, if at all, only by forfeiting all hope of economic development for years to come.

In view of this, some sort of accommodation must be reached, one that not only reduces current payments but that also ensures continuing credit as needed for recovery and growth. Although some rescheduling has taken place, further renegotiation will be needed.

Regarding other possible sources of capital, NIEO advocates request each economically advanced nation to increase its aid to the developing world until reaching a level at least equal to 0.7 percent of the donor's GNP. (In 1979 First World countries were averaging about one-half of that amount.[19]) Moreover, the aid is to be "untied"; grants are not to require the recipient to use them for the purchase of goods from the donor country. Along the same lines, NIEO wants greater LDC participation in the decision-making process of the IMF and other international agencies.

As a part of NIEO, monopolistic practices in the sale of technology, such as obligatory service contracts, limits on exports, or insistence that only the complete package may be purchased, are to be eliminated. This would contribute to a lower cost of technology for LDCs.

NIEO supporters favor more control over multinational corporations. There are indications that some shift in bargaining power has occurred and that LDC governments are learning to deal more effectively with MNCs.[20] All the same, relations with multinationals continue to be a problem for developing countries: In some cases, global sales of a multinational corporation are greater than the GNP of the country in which the MNC is located. NIEO would require a code of conduct to prevent MNC interference in the internal affairs of LDC societies and to ensure that MNC operations do result in an increased flow of capital, technology, and taxes to LDCs.

Because the NIEO idea proposes more equitable income distribution, higher levels of health and education, and more labor-intensive industry and employment creation within LDCs, it is clear that the call for a new international economic order touches matters of major importance to Latin America.

▪ Conclusion

The two major strategies of economic development in Latin America, primary-export orientation and import-substitution industrialization, have resulted in a regional need for the stabilization of commodity prices, the diversification of exports, and the expansion of internal markets. Because the United Nation's call for a New International Economic Order addresses these concerns, the progress of Latin America depends, in large part, on the degree to which the NIEO program is carried out.

▪ Notes

1. For a detailed description of these times, see Celso Furtado's *Economic Development of Latin America*, 2d ed. (Cambridge: Cambridge University Press, 1976), parts I and II.
2. Werner Baer and Michael E. Herve, "Employment Industrialization in Developing Countries," *Quarterly Journal of Economics* 80: 88–89; David Morawetz, "Employment Implications of Industrialization in Developing Countries: A Survey," *The Economic Journal* (September 1974): 494–95.
3. Albert O. Hirschman, *Strategy of Economic Development* (New Haven: Yale University Press, 1958), 118.
4. Baer and Herve, op. cit., and Morawetz, op. cit.
5. Richard Barnet and Ronald Mueller, *Global Reach* (New York: Simon & Schuster, 1974), 152–72.
6. Jan S. Hogendorn and Wilson B. Brown, *The New International Economics* (Reading, Mass.: Addison-Wesley Publishing Co., 1979), 427.
7. Franklin R. Root, *International Trade and Investment* 5th ed. (Cincinnati: South-Western Publishing Co., 1984), 402.

8. Root, ibid., 409.
9. See Root, ibid., 408 on export rates; Michael P. Todaro, *Economic Development in the Third World*, 2d ed. (New York and London: Longman, 1981), 390 for intra-CACM trade; and Root, op. cit., 408 for proportion of industrial goods exchanged.
10. Inter-American Development Bank, *Economic and Social Progress in Latin America, Natural Resources, 1983 Report*, Washington, D.C., 1983, 141.
11. Acerdo de Cartagena, *Regimen Comun De Tratamiento A Los Capitales Extranjeros* (Decisiones 24, 37, y 37a), Lima, 1971. For later limits, see Decisión 103.
12. Aggregate trade figures in Inter-American Development Bank, *op. cit.*, 140.
13. Alan Batchelder and Kanji Haitani, *International Economics, Theory and Practice* (Columbus, Ohio: Grid Publishing, 1981), 445.
14. Inter-American Development Bank, op. cit., 392.
15. See Furtado, op. cit., chapters 23–24.
16. Montek Ahluwalia, et al., "Growth and Poverty in Developing Countries," *Journal of Developmental Economics* (September, 1979): Table 2, 342. Figures based on estimates for eight countries— Argentina, Brazil, Chile, Colombia, Guatemala, Mexico, Peru, and Venezuela. It is interesting to note that Cuba, for all its redistributive accomplishments, is still dependent on sugar exports.
17. The NIEO document is reprinted in John Adams, ed., *The Contemporary International Economy* (New York: St. Martin's Press, 1979), chapter 31.
18. Todaro, op. cit., 504.
19. Todaro, op. cit., 505.
20. Paul Streeten, "Multinationals Revisited," *Finance and Development* 16 (June 1979): 39–42.

▪ Suggested Readings

Adams, John, ed. *The Contemporary International Economy*. New York: St. Martin's Press, 1979.

Anderson, Charles W. *Politics and Economic Change in Latin America*. Princeton: Van Nostrand Reinhold, 1967.

Farley, Rawle. *The Economics of Latin America: Development Problems in Perspective*. New York: Harper & Row, 1972.

Foxley, Alejandro. *Latin American Experiments in Neoconservative Economics*. Berkeley: University of California Press, 1983.

Furtado, Celso. *Obstacles to Development in Latin America*. New York: Doubleday, 1970.

Hirschman, Albert O. *Strategy of Economic Development*. New Haven: Yale University Press, 1958.

———. *Journeys toward Progress: Studies of Economic Policy-Making in Latin America*. New York: Twentieth Century Fund, 1963.

Hogendorn, S. Jan and Wilson B. Brown. *The New International Economics*. Reading, Mass.: Addison-Wesley Publishing Co., 1979.

Mesa-Lago, Carmelo. *The Economy of Socialist Cuba: A Two-Decade Appraisal*. Albuquerque: University of New Mexico Press, 1981.

Loup, Jacques. *Can the Third World Survive?* Baltimore: Johns Hopkins University Press, 1983.

Lozoya, Jorge, and Jaime Estévez. *Latin America and the New International Economic Order*. Elmsford, N.Y.: Pergamon, 1982.

Puyana de Palacios, Alicia. *Economic Integration among Unequal Partners*. Elmsford, N.Y.: Pergamon, 1982.

Salazar-Carillo, Antonio Jorge, and Rene Higonnet. *Foreign Debt and Latin American Economic Development*. Elmsford, N.Y.: Pergamon, 1982.

Todara, Michael P. *Economic Development in The Third World*. 2d ed. New York and London: Longman, 1981.

15 | *Urbanization in Latin American Development*

ROBERT V. KEMPER

When you think of the world's largest cities, do you think of New York City, Tokyo, Paris, or Los Angeles? What about Mexico City, São Paulo, Buenos Aires, or Rio de Janeiro? In 1950 none of these Latin American cities was among the world's ten largest, but their positions changed dramatically by the 1980s. According to current estimates, Mexico City (14 million) and São Paulo (12.6 million) are now the second- and third-largest urban agglomerations in the world, trailing only New York City (16.1 million); Buenos Aires (9.8 million) and Rio de Janeiro (9 million) now rank seventh and eighth among the world's largest cities. Thus, when we speak of the great metropolitan areas of the contemporary world, Latin America—despite its relatively low level of economic development—now ranks with the United States and Europe, far surpassing other developing regions such as sub-Saharan Africa.

This chapter first examines the history of urbanization in Latin America and then turns to the role of urbanization in shaping contemporary Latin America. It describes how the prevailing high rates of population growth and city-ward migration affect both cities and countryside. The chapter discusses the many problems confronting great metropolitan centers as well as smaller areas of urban settlement. The increasing participation of Latin America in the international urban system is emphasized throughout. The economic, political, and social dimensions of contemporary Latin American urbanization emerge as part of the broader transformation of Latin American societies since the voyages of Columbus.

■ Historical Overview

Urbanization is one of the great themes in the transformation of the native cultures of the Americas into the contemporary nation-states of Latin America. Some define urbanization in terms of changes in population concentration, but it seems best understood more broadly. The many components of urbanization must be examined within a framework that reflects the diversity of the Latin American experience.[1]

Before Independence

The most magnificent example of pre-Columbian urbanization may have been the island city of Tenochtitlán, founded in 1325 and by the late 1400s the dominant force in Mesoamerica. (See chapter 2, "Pre-Columbian Cultures.") Although it was virtually destroyed by the Spanish Conquest, recent excavations of the Great Temple give some idea of what the *conquistadores* saw when they entered the Valley of Mexico for the first time in 1519. As Bernal Diaz del Castillo, a soldier in the company of Hernán Cortés, described the event:

> We were amazed. . . . It was like the enchantments they tell of in the legend of Amadis, on account of the great towers and temples and buildings rising from the water, and all built of masonry. And some of our soldiers even asked whether the things that we saw were not a dream. . . . I do not know how to describe it, seeing things as we did that had never been heard of or seen before, not even dreamed about. Some . . . among us who had been in many parts of the world, in Constantinople, all over Italy, and in Rome, said that so large a market and so full of people and so well-regulated and arranged, they had never beheld before.[2]

The fall of Tenochtitlán in 1521 and Cuzco in 1536 ushered in a new era in Latin America urbanization. Between 1521 and 1820 the Spaniards and the Portuguese created hundreds of cities and towns, both on and near established indigenous sites and in newly conquered lands beyond the limits of the former Aztec and Inca empires. This considerable urban expansion was not carried out just to assure military and political control of the vast reaches of Latin America, but to create a system for exploiting its human, mineral, and agricultural resources for the benefit of the home countries. The colonial urban system was designed to expedite the flow of goods between the hinterlands and the major ports of trade and then onward to the Iberian

peninsula — as well as to improve the counterflow of goods and immigrants from Spain and Portugal to the New World.

The consequences of the Spanish and Portuguese urban policies may be summarized as follows: (1) the colonies were economically dependent on Europe and suffered from restrictive trade practices that hampered their economic development; (2) the cities and their hinterlands were dominated by a bureaucratic–political system that was tied to the needs of Spain and Portugal rather than to local conditions; (3) the establishment of cities and towns essentially ignored the boundaries recognized by the indigenous populations; and (4) the cities and towns were the focus of a fairly rigid caste system.

The New States

Just as the conquest had profoundly transformed the pre-Columbian urban systems, so the fierce fighting between loyalists and *independentistas* (those seeking independence from Europe) had significant consequences for the colonial urban system. Mining and agricultural productivity declined sharply, throwing the entire economy into disarray. Many people abandoned their villages and towns as unsafe; their cityward migrations temporarily swelled the populations of the larger urban centers. Although the period of violence and revolution lasted from about 1810 to the late 1820s, it did not result in a population decline comparable to that following the conquest. Ultimately, independence simply took earlier administrative and economic reforms one step further: The restrictive chain laid on the colonies by Spain and Portugal was broken, and the colonial urban system and the hierarchy of power it represented could be reorganized.

Nevertheless, Latin America's urban system changed relatively little in the first half of the nineteenth century. Few new cities were established; those of the colonial period continued their desultory growth. The continent was dominated by large rural landholders whose estates assumed a central place in the economic and political struggles between liberal and conservative forces. In midcentury, when Latin America as a whole had 30 million inhabitants, only four cities — Rio de Janeiro, Salvador (Bahia), Mexico City, and Havana — had more than a hundred thousand residents, and only six other cities — Lima, Buenos Aires, Santiago, Recife, Caracas, and Montevideo — had more than fifty thousand. This relatively slow urban growth was in marked contrast to the rapid growth experienced by cities in Europe and in the United States during the same period. In effect, the Latin American nations were saddled with highly regionalized, weakly articulated urban systems in which the cities were consumers rather than producers.[3]

As the well-known historian Jorge Hardoy has pointed out, between the 1850s and the 1890s a new stage in Latin America urban development began. The national capitals and port cities grew rapidly as a result of domestic migration and immigration from European countries, especially to Argentina, Uruguay, Brazil, and Cuba. The millions of immigrants included Jews, Russians, Poles, Italians, Swiss, Germans, and Spaniards. Because of their generally better education and greater business experience, many immigrants began to control the petty and medium-scale commerce of the expanding cities. Moreover, the immigrants played an important role in bringing European experience with labor unions and political movements to bear on the Latin American urban scene. Thus, the newcomers made a major contribution to urban and industrial growth at a time when their contribution was vitally needed to supplement the relatively unskilled indigenous work force.

By 1900 Buenos Aires had a population of 867,000 inhabitants; Rio de Janeiro had 691,000; Mexico City, 541,000; Montevideo, 309,000; Santiago, 287,000; São Paulo, 239,000; Havana, 236,000; Salvador (Bahia), 208,000; Lima, 130,000; and Recife, 113,000. With the exception of Mexico City, these ten most populous cities of Latin America were critical cogs in the city–port

complex that linked their nations to European and United States markets.

The policies followed by governments from Mexico to Argentina promoted strong ties between local agricultural interests and foreign capitalists; the growing interchange of raw materials (exported from Latin America) and finished goods (imported into Latin America) was concentrated in one or two ports in each country. A vital aspect of this interchange network was the establishment and expansion of railroads. This development greatly affected existing cities. Those that were thereby connected with the capital and the major ports greatly benefited, those that were bypassed were fated to decline. In addition, the railroad networks tended to reinforce the primacy of one or two urban centers in each country.

As in the United States, the railroads opened vast territories for agricultural and mining development and created new urban frontiers.[4] Thousands of new towns and cities were built. The majority were simple service centers and transportation hubs, but some — such as La Plata and Belo Horizonte — were shining examples of European-influenced urban design.

Not since the sixteenth century had so many new urban settlements been founded in Latin America. However, very few of the new cities achieved the population and importance of urban centers forming the old network inherited from the colonial period. Indeed, the pattern of dependent urban development of the late nineteenth and early twentieth centuries merely preserved the old colonial pattern of external domination in another guise.

The Emergence of Primate Cities

Latin American economic and demographic growth was increasingly characterized toward the end of the nineteenth century by growing primacy in the urban system — the situation in which the largest (the "primate") city is many times larger than the second biggest city. According to Bryan Roberts, the major city acts as a nodal point in the nation's economic and political affairs and serves as the link to the foreign metropolis that dominates the international export-import relationship.[4] As a place of government, the major city attracts elite groups and becomes the place of residence for the landowning and merchant class. Consequently the purchasing power of the nation becomes concentrated in the primate city, stimulating further commercial and service activity, construction, and local industrial production. This growth attracts migration from less prosperous agricultural regions and also draws the bulk of foreign immigrants. Once the primate city emerges, the process of urban agglomeration tends to become cumulative because other places are starved of the resources needed to compete. For example, by the end of the nineteenth century, as a result of the centralization produced by the development of a railroad network based on the capital, Mexico City had become three times as large as the next biggest city in the country, whereas in midcentury it had been only twice as large.

The extreme degree of urban primacy in Latin America seems to be related to the region's dependent role in the world economy. By 1920 most Latin American countries had primate urban systems, with the highest primacy rates found in Argentina, Cuba, Mexico, Chile, Peru, and Uruguay. Brazil was a special case in which the two largest cities, Rio de Janeiro and São Paulo, emerged as a biprimate urban node. Foreign investments, dominated by Britain and the United States, were focused on these same countries in the late nineteenth and early twentieth centuries. Indeed, the absence of pronounced urban primacy in Venezuela and Colombia may be due to their relatively weak incorporation into the world economy during this period.

By the period of the economic crises of the 1930s, the pattern of urban primacy was firmly entrenched throughout most of Latin America. The annual growth rates of the principal metropolitan areas were higher than the annual growth rates of national population. The urban population by 1930 included some twenty-eight cities with more than a hundred thousand inhabitants although, as Hardoy points out, these were not evenly distributed throughout the region.[5] Seven of the hundred-thousand-plus cities were in Brazil, six in Argentina, four in Mexico, three in Colombia, two each in Chile and Ecuador, and only one each in Bolivia, Cuba, Peru, and Venezuela. There were none in Haiti, the Dominican Republic, or the majority of Central American countries. In sum, urbanization during this period reinforced the politico-administrative structure formed during the nineteenth century and reflected the growing economic dependence of the relatively underdeveloped Latin American countries upon industrialized countries such as the United States, Britain, Germany, and France.

Latin American Reactions to Dependency after World War I

The dangers of relying on the export of primary products became increasingly obvious to many in government and in the private sector during the period after World War I. European demand declined sharply, and supplies of manufactured products from abroad were similarly reduced. Other world regions, with even lower labor and production costs, also began to compete with Latin American countries for the world markets of many primary commodities, including rubber, sugar, coffee, cacao, and copper. The Depression struck another serious blow to the relationship between urban centers in Latin American and foreign markets. Not only international exchange but also internal economic growth suffered.

Not surprisingly, nationalist sentiment advocated diminished local dependence on foreign economic forces. As a result, by the 1940s most Latin American countries were producing basic consumer goods, construction materials, and tools needed to further economic development in the postwar era. Some such as Argentina,

Brazil, and Mexico, were even able to establish national industries in rubber, steel, cement, and petroleum refining as part of the broader effort to substitute domestic products for foreign imports.

Expansion of industry provided a great impetus for urban growth and began to transform the economic linkage between countryside and city. As a result, the metropolitan areas where local industrial development was centered witnessed dramatic population growth by the 1940s, which continued unabated through the 1970s. Thus the path of economic development taken by Latin American governments in recent decades has had a direct impact on population distribution, migration rates, and levels of urbanization. In a few cases governmental policies dictated the creation of new towns, especially in previously marginal regions. Ciudad Sahagun in Mexico, Brasilia in Brazil, Ciudad Guayana in Venezuela, and Chimbote in Peru are well-known instances of urban centers created during the 1950s and 1960s to expand the urban-industrial network and stimulate regional economic development.

In sum, Latin American reactions to dependence on external capital have speeded urbanization even where economic development has remained uneven. As the flow of foreign immigrants has declined, the stream of rural-urban migrants has assumed enormous proportions, so that overall rates of urban population growth have remained high in most cases. The fundamental economic and political dominance of the major cities has not been challenged by the growth of numerous secondary and tertiary urban centers. This historical-structural background is essential for understanding the urbanization of Latin America during the contemporary period.

■ Population Growth and Urbanization in Contemporary Latin America

The remarkable growth of the Latin American population since World War II has no parallel in the history of the world. In 1950 the region's total population was about 156 million; in 1960, 206 million; in 1970, 274 million; and in 1980, 365 million. In other words, Latin America increased in population by almost the equivalent of the entire population of the United States in just thirty years. Table 1 provides basic data on total, urban, and rural population trends for the 1950–1980 period.

In recent decades the average rate of growth for the population of Latin America taken as a whole has been about 2.7 percent per annum, although the range is from lows under 1 percent per annum to highs above 3.5 percent per annum. According to the Inter-American Development Bank, for the period 1970–1979 in the lower range of demographic growth were countries as diverse in size and economic structure as Barbados (0.3 percent), Uruguay (0.9 percent), Trinidad and Tobago (1.1 percent), Argentina (1.3 percent), and Jamaica (1.5 percent). A middle range of population expansion included such countries as Colombia (2.1 percent); Chile, Cuba, Haiti, and Honduras (all at 1.7 percent). Most fell into the high growth rate category, led by Mexico and the Bahamas (both at 3.6 percent), and followed by such countries as Honduras (3.4 percent); Ecuador and Paraguay (both at 3.3 percent); Venezuela (3.2 percent); Nicaragua and Panama (both at 3.1 percent); the Dominican Republic (3.0 percent); El Salvador, Guatemala, and Peru (all at 2.9 percent); Brazil (2.8 percent), and Bolivia and Costa Rica (both at 2.6 percent).

This population expansion is staggering, yet its implications for economic and social development take on special significance in the context of the urbanization process. The very high rates of overall population growth (due especially to declines in infant mortality and increased longevity) have been combined with substantial flows of rural-urban migration since the 1940s. As a result, even though the rural population has been expanding in absolute terms, the cities have been growing at rates that are sometimes twice as high as those for the nations as a whole.

TABLE 1

Urban and Rural Population of Latin American Countries: 1950–1980 (In thousands)

Country	1950	1960	1970	1980
Argentina	17,189	20,956	24,937	29,334
Urban	11,038	14,161	17,431	21,043
Rural	6,151	6,795	7,506	8,291
% Urban	64.2	67.6	69.9	71.7
Bolivia	3,013	3,696	4,658	6,000
Urban	778	1,104	1,652	2,514
Rural	2,235	2,592	3,006	3,486
% Urban	25.8	29.9	35.5	41.9
Brazil	52,178	70,309	93,752	123,566
Urban	16,083	28,329	44,926	66,779
Rural	36,095	41,980	48,826	56,787
% Urban	30.8	40.3	47.9	54.0
Chile	6,073	7,627	9,636	12,300
Urban	3,327	4,861	6,850	9,274
Rural	2,746	2,766	2,786	3,026
% Urban	54.8	63.7	71.1	75.4
Colombia	11,679	15,468	20,514	27,691
Urban	4,253	7,134	11,161	17,193
Rural	7,426	8,334	9,353	10,498
% Urban	36.4	46.1	54.4	62.1
Costa Rica	801	1,206	1,769	2,491
Urban	232	377	647	1,071
Rural	569	829	1,122	1,420
% Urban	29.9	31.3	36.6	43.0
Cuba	5,508	6,797	8,307	10,034
Urban	2,753	3,816	5,083	6,546
Rural	2,755	2,981	3,224	3,488
% Urban	50.0	56.1	61.2	65.2
Dominican Republic	2,243	3,030	4,277	6,174
Urban	482	834	1,435	2,444
Rural	1,761	2,196	2,842	3,730
% Urban	21.5	27.5	33.6	39.6
Ecuador	3,197	4,317	5,909	8,080
Urban	878	1,423	2,297	3,573
Rural	2,319	2,894	3,612	4,507
% Urban	27.5	33.0	38.9	44.2
El Salvador	1,868	2,490	3,417	4,730
Urban	515	721	1,105	1,708
Rural	1,353	1,769	2,312	3,022
% Urban	27.6	29.0	32.3	36.1
Guatemala	2,805	3,765	5,053	6,942
Urban	674	1,124	1,780	2,885
Rural	2,131	2,641	3,273	4,057
% Urban	24.0	29.9	35.2	41.6

Urban and Rural Population of Latin American Countries: 1950–1980 (In thousands) *(cont.)*

Country	1950	1960	1970	1980
Haiti	3,380	4,140	5,255	6,912
Urban	340	513	927	1,749
Rural	3,040	3,627	4,328	5,163
% Urban	10.1	12.4	17.6	25.3
Honduras	1,428	1,950	2,750	3,879
Urban	249	432	797	1,367
Rural	1,181	1,518	1,953	2,512
% Urban	17.3	22.2	29.0	35.2
Mexico	26,366	36,018	50,733	72,659
Urban	12,144	19,741	32,105	51,340
Rural	14,222	16,277	18,628	21,319
% Urban	46.1	54.8	63.3	70.7
Nicaragua	1,060	1,477	2,083	2,938
Urban	297	502	819	1,343
Rural	763	975	1,264	1,595
% Urban	28.0	34.0	39.3	45.7
Panama	797	1,055	1,387	1,823
Urban	282	447	669	975
Rural	515	608	718	848
% Urban	35.4	42.4	48.2	53.5
Paraguay	1,397	1,768	2,296	3,065
Urban	392	508	674	920
Rural	1,005	1,260	1,622	2,145
% Urban	28.1	28.7	29.4	30.0
Peru	7,969	10,025	13,586	18,527
Urban	2,498	3,904	6,345	9,782
Rural	5,471	6,121	7,241	8,745
% Urban	31.3	38.9	46.7	52.8
Uruguay	2,195	2,491	2,802	3,126
Urban	1,734	2,030	2,341	2,665
Rural	461	461	461	461
% Urban	79.0	81.5	83.5	85.3
Venezuela	4,974	7,331	10,399	14,827
Urban	2,422	4,611	7,300	11,031
Rural	2,552	2,720	3,099	3,796
% Urban	48.7	62.9	70.2	74.4
Latin America	156,120	205,916	273,520	365,098
Urban	61,369	96,572	146,344	216,202
Rural	94,751	109,344	127,176	148,896
% Urban	39.3	46.9	53.5	59.2

Source: Walter D. Harris, Jr., *The Growth of Latin American Cities* (Athens: Ohio University Press, 1971), Table 2.1, 45–47.

TABLE 2
Yearly Growth Rates for Total, Urban, and Rural Population: 1980–1985

Country	Total	Urban	Rural
Argentina	1.2%	1.5%	−0.3%
Bolivia	2.7	5.1	0.5
Brazil	2.3	3.3	0.4
Chile	1.7	2.1	0.1
Colombia	2.1	3.1	0.2
Costa Rica	2.3	3.8	1.0
Cuba	0.6	1.6	−1.6
Dominican Republic	2.4	4.1	0.9
Ecuador	3.1	4.3	2.1
El Salvador	2.9	4.0	2.0
Guatemala	2.9	3.6	2.5
Haiti	2.5	4.1	2.0
Honduras	3.4	5.0	2.3
Mexico	2.9	3.8	1.0
Nicaragua	3.3	4.5	1.7
Panama	2.2	3.5	0.5
Paraguay	3.0	3.7	2.6
Peru	2.8	3.6	1.4
Uruguay	0.7	0.9	0.4
Venezuela	3.3	3.7	1.7
Latin America	2.4	3.2	0.9

Source: James Wilkie, ed., *Statistical Abstract of Latin America*, vol. 22 (Los Angeles: UCLA Latin American Studies Center, 1982).

In 1980 approximately 216 million people lived in areas defined as "urban," according to Latin American censuses. This represents some 59 percent of the total population. The proportion of "urban" population ranges from a high of 84 percent in Uruguay and 82 percent in Argentina to a low of just 23 percent in Haiti. For Latin America as a whole, the estimated growth rate of urban areas for the period 1980–1985 is 3.2 percent per annum, whereas it is just 0.9 percent per annum for rural areas. As the data in Table 2 demonstrate, for every Latin American country the growth rate for cities is higher than that for rural areas.

The Primacy Problem

All Latin American countries have at least one city, also the political capital except in the cases of Ecuador and Brazil, that is disproportionately larger than other cities and that represents a large share of the national population. The primacy problem, as seen earlier in this chapter, is a result of nineteenth-century economic and political forces. Nevertheless, in many nations, the problems of hyperurbanization have been exacerbated by the population explosion of recent decades. Table 3 provides data on the percentage of national population residing in the largest city for Latin American countries.

As this table reveals, most of the cities continue to expand their share of national population, some cities seem to have stabilized their share, and a few cities have suffered a decline in their share. In almost every instance the population distribution in these large metropolitan

TABLE 3
Percentage of National Population in Largest City: 1940, 1960, and 1980

Country/Largest City	1940	1960	1980
Uruguay (Montevideo)	27.3	37.9	43.4
Costa Rica (San José)	10.6	20.6	37.7
Panama (Panama City)	18.1	25.8	34.5
Argentina (Buenos Aires)	17.0	35.1	34.3
Chile (Santiago)	18.8	25.2	29.6
Dominican Republic (Santo Domingo)	4.8	12.1	22.8
Peru (Lima)	7.4	15.1	21.5
Nicaragua (Managna)	7.6	14.0	21.2
Mexico (Mexico City)	7.9	14.1	19.6
Colombia (Bogotá)	4.1	8.0	17.6
Guatemala (Guatemala City)	8.5	12.4	16.9
Bolivia (La Paz)	8.5	10.8	15.7
Ecuador (Guayaquil)	5.2	10.3	15.3
Paraguay (Asunción)	8.7	17.6	14.6
Venezuela (Caracas)	9.3	17.4	14.4
Haiti (Port-au-Prince)	4.0	6.2	12.3
Honduras (Tegucigalpa)	4.4	8.6	11.8
Cuba (Havana)	19.6	22.0	10.2
Brazil (Rio de Janeiro for 1940 and 1960; São Paulo for 1980)	3.7	6.7	9.8
El Salvador (San Salvador)	6.3	9.8	8.0

Source: For 1940 and 1960 data, James Wilkie, ed., *Statistical Abstract of Latin America*, vol. 22 (Los Angeles: UCLA Latin American Studies Center, 1982), Table 641; for 1980 data, Hama Umlauf Lane, ed., *The World Almanac and Book of Facts 1984* (New York: Newspaper Enterprise Association, Inc., 1983).

areas has resulted from the failure of government to regulate the geographic mobility of people living in the countryside and in small cities. Only in the Cuban case does the decline in primacy seem to be due to active urban planning.

These figures may taken on more meaning when they are compared with a non–Latin American situation. In the United States, for example, New York City has about 16 million inhabitants, which represents about 7 percent of the national population. This proportion is lower than that for any city included in Table 3. Moreover, unlike the Latin American cases, New York City is not disproportionately larger than the next largest cities in the United States. Los Angeles, with more than 11 million inhabitants, is some 3 million persons above the figure that would fit the rank: size rule (i.e., the largest city should be twice as large as the second city, three times as large as the third city, and so on). To invert the situation, if New York had the same share of national population as Mexico City does, then then New York would have about 45 million inhabitants, and if it had the same share as Montevideo does, then it would have almost 100 million.

Such comparisons become even more significant since Latin American population growth is not coming to a halt in the 1980s. In general terms, it is anticipated that the urban share of the population will reach 73 percent by the year 2000 and will continue to rise to over 80 percent by 2025. Most projections suggest that Latin American cities will gain nearly twice as much population in the period from 1975 to 2000 as they gained in the 1950–1970 period. To give just one example, this means that Mexico City might reach about 32 million inhabitants by the year 2000. And, of course, the effects of current governmental and private efforts to slow the population growth rate will not be apparent until early in the next century, so there is little reason to expect that the figures projected for the year 2000 will not be surpassed in subsequent decades.

Cityward Migration and the Urbanization Process

The integration of people and places tied to the urban system has increased from the largest metropolitan areas to the smallest hamlets. The flow of population to and from the cities is not just a demographic phenomenon; it is a significant feature of the social, cultural, and economic matrix of Latin America's continued development. Urbanization is not restricted to cities; the extension of urban institutions and the imposition of urban standards in the countryside confirms the truism that the highways carrying migrants to cities are not one-way streets. Thus cities, towns, and villages become part of a national (even international) network in which urban processes affect people today.

Millions continue to migrate from the countryside to the major cities and secondary towns of Latin America. Their movements may be temporary or permanent, entail short or long distances, involve individuals or groups, and be characterized by certain sociodemographic features related to the migrants' age, sex, education, employment, social class, ethnicity, and even personality. Given the volume and diversity of the migration stream, it is not surprising that social scientists have had difficulty generalizing about the qualities of individual migrants. Furthermore, it has proven a considerable challenge to link individual aspects of migration to the broader historical-structural factors beyond individual control, though such factors influence or even force people into decisions about why, where, when, and how to migrate. Finally, as socioeconomic circumstances change in both rural and urban areas, the causes and effects of migration change too, and migrant characteristics are transformed.

At the risk of overgeneralization, the following statements regarding cityward migration seem valid:

1. Migrants are overwhelmingly young adults.

2. Females tend to migrate more often than men do.

3. Ethnicity can facilitate the migration process since ethnic enclaves may assist new arrivals to adjust to their cities.

4. The presence of relatives or friends in specific cities often influences the migrant's choice of destination.

5. Migrants to large cities tend to come from smaller urban centers and from higher-status families in towns and villages.

6. Migrants tend to have higher levels of education and more appropriate job skills than do those who remain behind.

7. Migrants from rural areas may travel directly to large cities or they may travel by stages (i.e., from village to town to city).

8. Some cityward migration is an intergenerational process in which parents leave the village, but their children eventually settle in the large cities.

9. Migration is highly selective of those individuals who are risk takers, adventuresome, dynamic, and responsive to perceived opportunities beyond their place of origin.

The substantial volume of emigration from the rural areas of Latin America influences conditions in villages of origin as well as in cities of destination. The tendency for young women and men to leave their villages sometimes depletes the local community of its potential future parents. Although most rural areas have been able at least to maintain their size in recent decades (through high birthrates and lower death rates), some of them are suffering a net loss of population because of the high rates of emigration. For example, Douglas Butterworth and John Chance describe the situation for the Mexican community of Tilantongo: "Marital infidelity, temporary sexual liaisons, and marriage dissolution are becoming more frequent largely as a result of the breakup of the immediate and extended family through out-migration and the exodus of potential marriage partners."[6]

Another consequence of substantial emigration is the loss of the local community's young and middle-class inhabitants — those most likely to become innovators and leaders. This "rural brain drain" mirrors the international movement of well-educated and talented people from underdeveloped regions to Europe and the United States. When and if the village offers its emigrants the chance to practice their newly acquired skills (e.g., as doctors, dentists, pharmacists, veterinarians) some will probably move back to the community.

Villagers who return to their communities of origin, either permanently or temporarily, bring back new ideas, new aspirations, and new consumer goods. They know that their village is not isolated from the outside world, and others witness this. Some migrants visit relatives and friends for the holidays or for vacations. Others return to attend to local responsibilities, whether familial, economic, or religious. Still others abandon the city because they have lost their jobs or homes.

Even those migrants who seldom or never return to their home communities may have profound effects on the lives of those who remained there. They often send money to their relatives to help with the economic problems that caused (at least in part) the emigrants to leave in the first place. Migrants also provide their fellow villagers with assistance in looking for jobs and housing in the city. As a result, complex social networks bridge the geographic and cultural gap between village and metropolis, transforming what were once individual migration itineraries into a continuing and expanding social process. Finally, migrants provide valuable information about city life and about the economic and political events that are shaping village affairs. For example, the migrants often serve as intermediaries when villagers need assistance in dealing with businesses, government agencies, or with admissions to higher educational institutions in the city.

In many rural or semirural communities village-oriented migrant associations play an important role in local religious and educational activities. Migrants join with those who stayed behind to improve circumstances in the community (e.g., by building a new wing for the school) or by affirming the historical solidarity of the community (e.g., by sponsoring dances and fireworks displays at the annual patron-saint festival). Such migrant associations may also provoke social conflict in the community of origin by highlighting the success of some families (to the chagrin of other families) or by attempting to gain control of the local political system for private gain.

Urbanization of the Countryside

Aside from the obvious impact on rural areas of returning migrants and remittances from migrants, other aspects of the urbanization process are played out in the countryside, including the diffusion of government programs, business activity and individual decisions. Along the same lines, in many rural zones of Latin America, federal and state governments are building systems of transportation and mass communication to integrate the population with urban priorities. Building schools is also a high priority in the national development schemes of most countries. Health care can be improved through the establishment of rural clinics, the dissemination of health-related information, campaigns for immunization, and programs for population control and family planning. In many countries government and private-sector corporations are trying to attract tourists to economically depressed rural areas that offer some combination of archaeological, environmental, and cultural or ethnic attractions. These tourist development projects often have mixed results for the village economy and culture, precisely because they are more focused on meeting the "needs" of urban-based tourists than they are on ensuring that the local residents maintain control of their lives and their lands. Similar problems arise with other development projects, such as hydro-electric schemes whose purpose is to bring electric power or water to the growing cities — often at the expense of rural areas.

These examples of urban bias could be multiplied endlessly, but the central point remains: The rural sector contains most of the poverty, whereas the urban sector contains most of the power. In general, it appears that national development policies have slighted the countryside in their attempt to deal with the enormous problems visible in the cities. This is not just a matter of where one lives, but also a function of one's involvement in agriculture or industry and of one's position in the class hierarchy. For example, government policies promoting large-scale irrigation-based agriculture may do little to improve the situation of small farmers who have little or no access to irrigation or mechanization. Indeed, there is some evidence to show that the Green Revolution and other efforts to raise agricultural productivity through the use of improved seeds and fertilizers may have accentuated landlessness and has probably stimulated, rather than reduced, the flow of cityward migrants. Even the vaunted schemes of the Brazilian government in recent decades to develop the Amazon Basin have created problems for indigenous populations, for the rain forest environment, and for the thousands of poor people expected to join in this population movement. As Alan Gilbert and Josef Gugler have argued: "Spectacular the Amazon program may well be, but it demonstrates most of the faults of uncontrolled capitalist development; it generates economic growth, without improving the extreme maldistribution of wealth and income. [I]t clearly demonstrates the paramount importance of the style of national development on the formulation of subsidiary policies."[7] And, it might be added, the style of Brazilian "national" development is formulated by elite members of the urban-industrial society dominated by Rio de Janeiro, São Paulo, and Brasilia.

Urban Problems

The problems of cityward migration and the urbanization of the countryside are only two sides of the problem facing urban planners and government agencies as the twentieth century draws to a close. The cities themselves, especially those with a hundred thousand or more inhabitants, face a wide range of serious difficulties related to the fundamentally unequal distribution of income, resources, and goods and services among the urban population. Housing shortages, transportation problems, environmental pollution, unemployment and underemployment, and the unavailability or inadequacy of government services such as health care delivery are evident throughout Latin America. The issue of equitable income distribution however, is most apparent in the cities, where enormous wealth and abject poverty confront each other every day.

Perhaps the most obvious and serious set of urban problems is related to housing and land use. Because conventional housing and land are increasingly beyond the means of most city residents, and because the only affordable housing involves renting apartments, rooms, or shacks in the overcrowded, deteriorating central-city slums, millions of urban residents (including migrants and the city-born) have established urban peripheral settlements. They may join "invasions" to occupy unoccupied land, or they may purchase lots in unplanned, unauthorized subdivisions. In most metropolitan areas about half of the people now live in such irregular or uncontrolled settlements.

Squatter settlements have been the object of numerous studies by social scientists and government planners. The earliest studies suggested that such aggregations were "festering sores" or "cancers" on the urban system; most of the recent investigations conclude that the residents of squatter settlements have taken the only realistic approach to the housing and land-use problems of most Latin American cities. One of the prevailing myths about the squatter

settlements claims that they are "marginal" to the larger city. On the basis of her extensive fieldwork among squatters in Rio de Janeiro, Janice Perlman concluded:

> Socially, they are well organized and cohesive and make wide use of the urban milieu and its institutions. Culturally, they are highly optimistic and aspire to better education for their children and to improving the condition of their houses. . . . Economically, they work hard, they consume their share of the products of others (often paying more since they have to buy where they can get credit), and they build — not only their own houses but also much of the overall community and urban infrastructure. They also place a high value on hard work, and take great pride in a job well done. Politically, they are neither apathetic nor radical. . . . [They] are generally system-supportive and see the government not as evil but as doing its best to understand and help people like themselves. . . .
>
> In short, *they have the aspirations of the bourgeoisie, the perseverance of pioneers, and the values of patriots.*

Unfortunately, few people in the squatter settlements have a chance to realize their dreams. They get the worst jobs with the lowest pay; their children seldom enjoy the benefit of public schooling or adequate health services; they are often politically manipulated by government agencies or by strong-armed police officials; and they usually suffer from the worst environmental problems of urban dwellers, including inadequate water and sewage systems, high levels of air pollution, and dangerous exposure to pests and vermin. Despite arduous conditions, the resiliency of their social support systems, involving families, friends, and *compadres* (fictive kin), makes possible the "survival of the unfittest" — as Larissa Lomnitz has referred to the residents of a squatter settlement in Mexico City.[9]

Governmental responses to the phenomenon have ranged from brutal evictions to benign acceptance of a social reality. In Lima the proliferation of squatter settlements has been followed by government programs to help residents install basic urban services and to help them legalize land titles. Government attempts to repress squatter settlements by relocating their residents to housing projects have failed to meet their objectives. As a result, government housing programs are now usually designed for the middle classes rather than for the poor. One problem underlying the proliferation of squatter settlements and the failure of urban and national governments to offer viable alternatives to them is rampant land speculation by individuals and companies of the middle and upper classes. Cuba stands out as a significant exception to the general miasma in which the housing problems of the urban poor generate huge profits for the urban elite.

Unequal distribution of resources such as land and housing among urban residents is a continuing problem for Latin American countries. The region's wide range of wealth and poverty is responsible. For instance, more than 70 percent of Port-au-Prince (Haiti) households have incomes of less than forty dollars per month.[10] In many nations, extremely high rates of inflation, coupled with continuing devaluation, have made poverty more desperate in the 1980s than it was a decade ago. Migrants from the countryside may see cities as places of opportunity, but far fewer jobs are created there than necessary to accommodate the economically active population. In this sense Latin America is overurbanized and underindustrialized. And many of the new jobs belong to the tertiary or services sector rather than to the secondary or manufacturing sector in any case.

Most new entrants into the urban job market find an opportunity in the so-called informal economy rather than in the standard categories defined by government economists and protected by government social security programs. The informal sector of the economy includes a wide range of low-paying, labor-intensive activities that often involve families (including women and children) in small-scale enterprises.

A young boy selling chewing gum to motorists at a stop sign, a women with a few pears for sale on the street corner, a family gathering trash and garbage for resale — all are participating in the untaxed, uncensused, unmeasurable informal economy. The informal economy involves a great deal of entrepreneurship and individual initiative, especially in central-city slums and peripheral squatter settlements. The informal sector meets the subsistence needs of perhaps one-third of Latin Americas's urban population. Even successful middle- and upper-class businessmen are often engaged in informal activities (including bribery and contract "incentives") that they hope will escape taxation or official notice.

Many analysts suggest that the inability of government or private enterprise to create enough jobs in the formal sector of the economy will mean continued expansion of its informal sector. Moreover, because informal-sector activities tend to be small-scale, family-oriented, labor-intensive, and highly competitive, they are an appropriate indigenous response to the dependency that marks formal-sector activities dominated by multinational corporations or elite national firms. Thus, for diverse reasons, the informal sector of the urban economy is likely to prosper — both in terms of the number of households that participate in it and in terms of economic activities outside of large-scale, high-technology, capital-intensive enterprises. Such a pattern of urban economic development promises to fragment the already highly diversified labor market still further. As a result, the economic strategies of urban residents begin to resemble the traditional practices of villagers in the countryside at the same time that villagers increasingly emulate urban consumption patterns. Thus the urban system continues to be transformed.

■ **Toward the Future**

This brief examination of urbanization in Latin American development shows that both past and present offer important lessons for the future. Ever since the European conquest, the unequal relationship between Latin America and the industrialized North (i.e., Europe and the United States) has been a hallmark of urbanization. The exploitation and dependency inherent in this long-term relationship is further reflected in the ties between the city and countryside within Latin American nations. In this sense, the capital cities and port cities of Latin America have served as intermediate points in the international urban system.

The sheer magnitude of the problems facing Latin American cities offers little hope that the twenty-first century will see real solutions to the dilemma of population growth and urban expansion. Assuming that the population of Latin America continues to grow at rates even close to those of recent decades, and that the metropolitan areas continue to expand at high rates through rural–urban migration, the challenge of the next few decades will be clear. Can nearly half a millennium of dependent urban development be transformed into greater economic equity and social well-being for all, whether in the largest city or the smallest hamlet, whether rich or poor, whether well educated or illiterate — and whether they remain in their home country or migrate to another nation such as the United States?

■ **Notes**

1. Robert V. Kemper and Anya P. Royce, "Urbanization in Mexico: Beyond the Heritage of Conquest," in *Heritage of Conquest: Thirty Years Later,* ed. Carl Kendall, John Hawkins, and Laurel Bossen (Albuquerque: University of New Mexico Press, 1983).
2. Bernal Díaz del Castillo, *The Discovery and Conquest of Mexico* (New York: Farrar, Strauss, and Cudahy, 1956), 218–19.
3. Jorge Hardoy, "Two Thousand Years of Latin American Urbanization," in *Urbanization in Latin America: Approaches and Issues,* ed. Jorge Hardoy. (Garden City, N.Y.: Anchor Press/Doubleday, 1975), 46–49.

4. Bryan Roberts, *Cities of Peasants: The Political Economy of Urbanization in the Third World* (Beverly Hills: Sage, 1978), 47–48.
5. Hardoy, op. cit., 51.
6. Douglas Butterworth and John K. Chance, *Latin American Urbanization* (New York: Cambridge University Press, 1981), 82–83.
7. Alan Gilbert and Josef Gugler, *Cities, Poverty, and Development: Urbanization in The Third World* (Oxford: Oxford University Press, 1982), 184.
8. Janice E. Perlman, *The Myth of Marginality: Urban Poverty and Politics in Rio de Janeiro* (Berkeley: University of California Press, 1976), 242–243.
9. Larissa Lommitz, *Networks and Marginality: Life in a Mexican Shanty Town* (New York: Academic Press, 1977).
10. Wayne A. Cornelius, "Introduction," in *Metropolitan Latin America: The Challenge and the Response,* ed. Wayne A. Cornelius and Robert V. Kemper (Beverly Hills: Sage, 1978), 11.

■ **Suggested Readings**

Butterworth, Douglas, and John K. Chance. *Latin American Urbanization.* New York: Cambridge University Press, 1981.

Cornelius, Wayne A., and Robert V. Kemper, eds. *Metropolitan Latin America: The Challenge and the Response.* Beverly Hills: Sage, 1978.

Cornelius, Wayne A., and Felicity M. Trueblood, eds. *Urbanization and Inequality: The Political Economy of Urban and Rural Development in Latin America.* Beverly Hills: Sage, 1975.

Gilbert, Alan, and Josef Gugler. *Cities, Poverty, and Development: Urbanization in the Third World.* Oxford: Oxford University Press, 1982.

Hardoy, Jorge, ed. *Urbanization in Latin America: Approaches and Issues.* Garden City, N.Y.: Anchor Press, Doubleday, 1975.

Harris, Walter D., Jr. *The Growth of Latin American Cities.* Athens: Ohio University Press, 1971.

Portes, Alejandro, and Harley L. Browning, eds. *Current Perspectives in Latin American Urban Research.* Austin: University of Texas Press, 1976.

Portes, A., and J. Walton. *Urban Latin America: The Political Condition from Above and Below.* Austin: University of Texas Press, 1976.

Roberts, Bryan. *Cities of Peasants: The Political Economy of Urbanization in the Third World.* Beverly Hills: Sage, 1978.

16 | *The Political Systems of Latin America: Developmental Models and a Typology of Regimes*

HOWARD J. WIARDA

The nations of Latin America share a common language (Spanish, or in the Brazilian case, Portuguese), a common religion (Catholicism), a common history dating back to the discovery of the Americas in 1492, and many other political, economic, cultural, and sociological features. Yet they are also very different countries—and increasingly so. Paraguay is very different from Argentina, Venezuela different from Colombia, Costa Rica different from the other Central American countries, and so on. This theme of diversity amidst unity is the first fact we must understand in coming to grips with the political systems of Latin America.

A second point requiring emphasis is the *systematic* nature of Latin American politics. That is often difficult for North Americans to understand. We frequently think the area is so unstable that it is devoid of any system. In fact, Latin

American politics is quite regular and systematic. Even instability has a rationale and logic, constituting a normal, recurring, almost everyday fact of political life. It is not that Latin American politics is unsystematic; rather, the problem is that its *system* of politics is quite a bit different from ours and that we in the United States seldom understand what that system is and how it works.

A third point to remember, related to the previous one, is that Latin America is increasingly following its own developmental routes. In its quest to modernize, Latin America does not appear to conform very closely—except in the broadest of terms—to familiar developmental models drawn from the experience of Western Europe and the United States. Yes, there is industrialization, class changes, growing pluralism, and so forth in Latin America; but the precise nature of these changes, the institutional arrangements for dealing with them, and the developmental results do not quite fit the expectations we have based on the record of the already industrialized nations. Hence, while one may wish to employ *some* of the categories familiar from the general development literature, one also needs to be aware of the nuances and distinct patterns of the Latin American countries. The discussion returns to these themes later.

■ The Historic Pattern of Latin American Development

Colonial Spain and Portugal bequeathed to their American colonies a form of government that was authoritarian and hierarchical. This form was superimposed on indigenous Indian institutions that were often authoritarian and hierarchical themselves. In this way the indigenous and the imposed colonial institutions complemented and reinforced each other. The pre-Columbian Indian civilizations and the Iberian colonizers organized their rule in an organic (highly unified and centralized) manner, involving the unity of civil and religious authority and a segmented or corporate system of social groups (military, oligarchy, and religion or priesthood). The lower orders in such a corporate system also were organized as part of the organic whole, though they were clearly assigned a subordinate role.

What was remarkable was not that the colonial systems established by Spain and Portugal should be founded on an authoritarian, hierarchical, organic, and corporatist basis; that was the dominant European pattern in the early sixteenth century. Truly remarkable was instead the longevity of these institutional arrangements in the Iberian colonies. The system survived not only three centuries of colonial rule but also the transition to independence early in the nineteenth century. There is abundant evidence, furthermore, that these same oligarchic and authoritarian traditions are alive and persistent today throughout Latin America, although now undergoing transition.

Five distinct periods may be identified in the overall historical process since independence. The first, from the 1820s to the 1850s, was marked by general instability and some social and economic retrogression. The rule of Portugal and Spain had ended (except in Cuba and Puerto Rico), leaving an institutional vacuum. The new states adopted liberal and democratic constitutions, but underlying social and political institutions remained authoritarian and aristocratic. Landed oligarchies alternated in power with the leaders of newly created armies that had emerged from the wars of independence, producing anarchy and chaos. Local economies also suffered from the political disruption and the separation from Portugal and Spain.

The second period, from the 1850s to the 1890s, saw greater order brought out of the prevailing chaos. Some of the vexing political problems of the first thirty years (church-state issues, federalism, boundary controversies) were resolved. The first generation of *caudillos* (military dictators) passed from the scene. New political parties were organized. Foreign capital (chiefly British at this time; later, it would be American) began to come in, and the pace of economic life quickened. Population increased and governments, bureaucracies, and armies were better organized. Although coups were still frequent, the political system became somewhat more settled and regular. New organizations and interest associations helped fill the previous institutional vacuum. The preconditions for an economic takeoff were established.

That takeoff occurred in the third period, which ran from the 1890s to 1929. This period has been widely referred to as the heyday of oligarchic rule in Latin America. By this point the landed elites had consolidated their power, often with the help of new and more centralized armies. In a number of the Central American and Caribbean countries during this same period, military occupation by the U.S. Marines established stability and contributed to institutional development, while also provoking some nationalistic resentment. Foreign capital helped develop roads and port facilities so that the primary products of the area—sugar, coffee, bananas, tin, copper, and rubber—could be shipped to Europe and the United States. Large estates were consolidated; more and more peasants were correspondingly relegated to an even more marginal position. Stability and prosperity reigned in Latin America—but prosperity was reserved for the very few. This stable, oligarchic system began to unravel following the world market crash of 1929.

The period from the 1930s until the 1960s, with variations from country to country, was one of reordering. By this time a new middle class had grown sufficiently in size and influence to challenge, or rule alongside of, the traditional elites. Trade unions sprang up, as did a variety of new political parties. Industrialization was stimulated and social change began to accelerate. Government bureaucracy grew, and new social services were created. The economies of Latin America experienced modernization and new growth. Under both military and civilian auspices, an older oligarchic system began to give way to a newer urban and middle-class-dominated system, yet this was accomplished without a radical or revolutionary transformation of society.

A fifth period began in the 1960s; neither its precise contours nor its outcome can yet be described exactly. In general, this was and remains a time of increased societal fragmentation, revolutionary challenges to the status quo, and widening division over social and political issues. In several of the more advanced and important countries—Argentina, Brazil, Chile—an authoritarian regime, responding to increased revolutionary militance, replaced civilian government. The Latin American systems had proved more or less capable of adapting to the earlier, middle-class challenges, but they began to unravel when faced with rising mass challenges. The growing economic crisis of the late 1970s and 1980s also made it more difficult to maintain the older accommodative system. Political cloture or sclerosis set in in several regimes—Guatemala, Nicaragua, and El Salvador—which, instead of bending to change,

became more brutal, corrupt, and repressive. Fragmentation and polarization became endemic.

This brief survey shows that Latin American political systems have not historically been as rigid and unchanging as is often thought. Instead, they have proved quite flexible and accommodative—at least to a point. That point seems to have come after 1960, when a new period of instability set in. Since then the societies and polities of Latin America have frequently proved incapable of dealing with accelerated change, and a situation of crisis and polarization has arisen in many countries. That is the context in which Latin America now finds itself.

■ A Typology of Latin American Political Systems

Although the Latin American political systems have all gone through roughly the same or parallel processes of change in the last 175 years, the patterns vary. Some nations have lagged behind while others have forged ahead. Some had large Indian populations, others did not; some had rich natural resources, whereas others had meager endowments. Thus, not only was the starting point of development different for the several nations of the area, but the routes to and end points of development varied as well. Latin American nations have no single, inevitable, or unlinear path to development; instead there are multiple starting points, various outcomes, and several crisscrossing routes.[1]

Recognizing that any classificatory scheme involves some oversimplificaton, one may nevertheless divide Latin American political systems into five distinct categories.[2] What is needed is a typology that reflects Latin America's own history and traditions, not artificial categories imposed from the outside. The five types are: (1) traditional authoritarian regimes, (2) closed corporatist regimes, (3) open corporatist regimes, (4) democratic regimes, and (5) revolutionary, or what one scholar has called "Trotsko-Populist," regimes.[3]

Traditional Authoritarian Regimes

This type of rule used to be dominant throughout Latin America and corresponds to many ancient stereotypes about the area. This kind of regime was particularly prevalent in the nineteenth and early twentieth centuries; today, however, only vestiges of the type remain— Alfredo Stroessner's government (Paraguay) and that of Jean-Claude ("Bébé Doc") Duvalier (Haiti).

The traditional authoritarian regime is characteristic of a "sleepier" and more traditional society, and there are few of these left in Latin America. That is, traditional authoritarian regimes tend to arise in countries where wealth and power are concentrated in a small landed elite, where the mass of the population is poor and apathetic, where the middle class is small, and where there are few competing groups besides the military and the oligarchy. Obviously these conditions no longer apply in most of Latin America, where major economic, social, and political changes have been under way during the twentieth century. Traditional, "sleepy" authoritarianism is largely a category of the past.

Closed and Open Corporatist Regimes

These two categories of regimes are considered together for a number of reasons. First, the lines between them are not always clear-cut, which is unfortunate for purposes of neat classification but does reflect the realities of Latin American politics. Second, several Latin American nations have oscillated between these two types in recent decades and therefore may fall under one category at one moment and under the other at another. Third, treating these categories in conjunction, almost as mirror images of the same phenomena, enables one to say some general things about Latin American politics, the process of change in this region, and about how politics and change often differ from the United States's experience.

At one level, the differences between closed and open corporatist regimes may be viewed as corresponding to the differences between dictatorship and democracy. The trouble with this formulation is that it paints the differences in stark, either-or terms; it derives more from Anglo-American than Latin American criteria; and it ignores the fact that most Latin American regimes consist of complex mixes halfway between dictatorship and democracy or involve rapid alternations between these two forms. The closed vs. open corporatist system of classification provides a more satisfactory means for understanding these dynamics than does the dictatorship–democracy dichotomy; it also corresponds more closely to Latin American realities.

The pattern of oscillation between open and closed corporatist systems in Latin America has its origins in the 1930s, precisely at the time when the traditional oligarchic and authoritarian regimes of the region began to break down and politics became more complex as a consequence. The question facing the elites and middle sectors at that time was: How can we preserve the authority, hierarchy, and order of the past while also responding to, even accommodating, the new forces of change? Although Latin American countries experimented with several formulas in the 1930s and on into the postwar period, most of them eventually settled on an updated form of corporatism, in both its open and its closed varieties.

By "corporatism" is meant the tendency to view the political community as consisting of the *functional interests* in the society, with each of these interests deemed to have a defined role and legitimate rights to participate in the political society.[4] Under a corporatist system, however, political participation is determined largely by sector or social role rather than on the egalitarian, liberal, and United States calculations of elections based on one-man-one-vote. The typical "corporations" or "corporate interests" in such a system are the landowners, armed forces, Church, businessmen and industrialists, professionals, and, more recently, organized labor. In practice most corporatist states in

Latin America have combined this kind of functional representation with one form or another of electoral representation.

The corporatist system still leaves much of the population in Latin America — chiefly unorganized peasant and indigenous elements — un- or under represented. That, of course, was the purpose of those elites and middle sectors who designed the system and who have never been convinced that all men are created equal and therefore deserve an equal say in the selection of their leaders. Corporatism also limits participation in the government to those whom the state itself recognizes as having a legitimate right to bargain in the political process. Those not so recognized are generally excluded from participation. In addition, the vertical, hierarchical, and usually personalist (based on personal loyalty) principles on which the separate "corporations" — and indeed the entire national system — are organized means that real decision makers are few in number. Corporatism is frankly undemocratic, at least as North Americans understand that term. In fact it was designed to keep the masses "in check" and to prevent them, in the new era of mass society, from overwhelming the political system from below.

Although corporatist regimes were undemocratic — often antidemocratic in nature — they were not necessarily entirely insensitive to change. Indeed, it was largely to deal with new popular demands, spiraling up in the inter-war period — from the rising commercial class, from the middle class, and from the emerging trade unions — that corporatist and semicorporatist schemes were developed in the first place. Rather than stand fast against all change, these regimes tried to adjust to it — but without allowing it to get out of hand.

Since the 1930s, therefore, Latin American corporatist regimes have been dominated no longer just by one (elite) class, as was the case earlier. Rather the tendency has been (with some usually temporary reversals) to incorporate more and more "corporations" into the system: first the rising commercial class, then the middle sectors, and finally organized labor. An effort was thus made both to accommodate to the new forces while leaving intact much of the traditional, hierarchic order. As Mark Falcoff has written, a great deal of Latin American political activity hence involves the effort to put a "Western," "modern," and "democratic" gloss (United States–style elections, political parties, and the like) on indigenous and corporatist systems that operate according to their own logic.[5]

Corporatism or semicorporatism in Latin America took many different forms, divided here into "open" and "closed" types with many variations in between. Closed corporatist systems keep the number of groups that rule and are allowed to participate small ("closed") with power concentrated in the hands of landed and business elites, the armed forces, and perhaps some middle-class professionals and technicians. Peasants, workers, students, and the lower middle class are generally excluded or at best manipulated from above. Open corporatist systems generally include these latter groups in one form or another, but usually under state or elite auspices and regulation.

Examples of closed corporatist regimes include the dictatorships of Rafael Trujillo in the Dominican Republic, Anastasio Somoza in Nicaragua, Jorge Ubico in Guatemala, Carlos Ibáñez in Chile, Fulgencio Batista in Cuba (especially during his second administration in the 1950s; during his earlier presidency Batista's rule was more open), Getulio Vargas in Brazil (1930–1945), and Juan Perón in Argentina (1946–1955; later Perón came back and won a democratic election — as did Brazil's Vargas). Such closed corporatist regimes often evolved from the traditional authoritarian form; they represented updated, "modernized" versions of the earlier type.

There were, to be sure, major differences among these regimes. Trujillo's regime was probably the bloodiest and most repressive; the others embodied somewhat milder forms of authoritarianism. The differences were also great between the smaller, less well-articulated systems of the Caribbean and Central America and the larger, better-organized systems of Argentina and Brazil. In both of the latter, the corporatist systems were sufficiently well articulated to conjure up memories of Italian-style fascism.

The open corporatist systems were at least equally diverse. Precise categorization is even more difficult for them because they frequently coexisted with more democratic forms. Included in this category would be the Mexican political system: one-party dominated but with elections every six years, corporately organized *within* that single party but providing some degree of choice rather like a primary election in a United States one-party state; authoritarian in many ways — but not entirely unrepresentative or undemocratic either.

Colombia provides another example. Colombia may be described as an elite-directed democracy. Unlike Mexico, Colombia has two parties that have long alternated in power according to informal gentlemen's agreements or formal pacts. The principle of alternation and coparticipation in power operates in the bureaucracy as well; appointments are divided up on a quasicorporatist basis. Venezuela provides another example of a system that is democratic at some levels and in some areas but paternalist and corporatist in others.

The same applies to Costa Rica and Chile. Both these countries have (or had, in the Chilean case) well-articulated political party systems and regular elections. They have managed to incorporate the middle classes and, to some degree, the lower classes into what might be called the "participatory nation" — those who actively take part in national social, economic, and political life. But much of the political life in these countries (which, along with Uruguay before the military takeover in the mid-1970s, were the most democratic of the Latin American nations) was still dominated by elites. Corporatist or semicorporatist features pervaded the structure of labor relations, social security, peasant participation, and business activity.

The differences between the open corporatist

regimes and the closed corporatist regimes are not always as clear-cut as desirable for a precise regime typology. But that is exactly the point here: The lines in Latin America between "democracy" and "dictatorship" are often fuzzy and vague; indeed, the various halfway houses the Latin Americans ingeniously improvise are precisely what makes their political systems so interesting and gives them their special dynamism. Classification is further complicated by the fact that a number of the Latin American countries have alternated between these two types of corporatist political organization, while others have evolved toward pluralist democracy along the lines of Western Europe or the United States.

First the alternations. Argentina has gone back and forth repeatedly since the 1930s between military and civilian rule, between relatively open and closed forms of corporatism — none of which has been able to resolve that country's massive problems. In Brazil after Vargas, a more open form of corporatism prevailed from 1945 until 1964, when the military took power and reinstituted a closed and authoritarian form of corporatism. Peru, Ecuador, Bolivia, and Panama have similarly alternated between military and civilian forms, between closed and open corporatist regimes. In both Chile and Uruguay — countries that had long and strong democratic traditions, albeit with powerful vestiges of authoritarianism and corporatism that were usually unacknowledged by either scholars or the peoples of these two countries — highly repressive corporatist regimes returned to power in the early 1970s. In quite a number of these closed corporatist regimes (Argentina, Brazil, Peru, Ecuador, Panama, Uruguay) there has been renewed movement back toward democracy and a more open system.

Now let us examine the evolving regimes. Two types command attention. The first includes those regimes especially in Central America that seemed for a time to be moving from closed to open forms of corporatism. The second involves those regimes that are moving away from all forms of corporatism and toward genuine democracy; in some cases this evolution has proceeded far enough that they now are full-fledged democracies. Both trends have had important implications not only for the countries affected but also for United States policy.

El Salvador provides the best example of a transition, between 1948 and 1972, from a closed to a more open corporatist form—and back again, with disastrous consequences. In that country a more or less nationalistic and progressive military regime came to power in 1948. Modeling itself in part after Mexico's corporatist regime (by no means democratic in the conventional sense of the term), El Salvador's government over this twenty-four year period nevertheless carried out a number of reforms, allowed some trade unions to organize, generally respected human rights, aligned itself with the U.S. Alliance for Progress, and ruled in an open, not entirely undemocratic way. The origins of the present crisis in El Salvador can be traced back to 1972, when a brutal and repressive regime replaced the more open one that had gone before, thus providing a fertile breeding ground for radical and revolutionary movements to flourish in the late 1970s and making democratic compromise almost impossible.

Much the same thing—although not quite so clear-cut—occurred in the other two crisis countries of the area, Guatemala and Nicaragua. Guatemala's two more or less centrist regimes of the 1960s, one military and one civilian, gave way in the 1970s to a viciously brutal regime that closed off all possibility for peaceful change and sought to turn the clock back to an earlier and "sleepier" stage. In Nicaragua the relatively mild authoritarianism of Anastasio Somoza, Sr., and his son Luis gave way in the 1970s to the violent, corrupt rule of Anastasio Somoza, Jr., which precluded the development of a more open form of corporatism. This helps to explain the precipitate radical shift in a Marxist direction when the Sandinistas overthrew Somoza in 1979.

In all these cases, had a more open system of corporatism been allowed to prevail, we would not now be encountering the degree of prob-

lems in that area that we presently face. An open corporatist system had earlier maintained stability while also adjusting to change. A closed corporatist system in contrast, in the charged political atmosphere of the present, no longer provided for stability but precipitated its own downfall by making the conditions ripe in which guerrilla movements would flourish. It is not coincidental that it is in precisely those countries that reverted from an open to a closed corporatist regime in the 1970s that the greatest conflict and upheaval has occurred and that present the most difficulties for U.S. policy.

Democratic Regimes

While the precise line between closed and more open corporatist systems is often fuzzy and sometimes reversible, so too is the line between open corporatism of the type practiced in, let us say, Mexico or El Salvador in the 1960s *and* full-fledged democracy. Nevertheless, because some Latin American countries are making this transition or have made it already, the category merits separate consideration.

In countries such as Costa Rica, Venezuela, and perhaps even the Dominican Republic, there has been a definite transition to democracy. This means not just the importation of democracy's institutional paraphernalia—elections, electoral commissions, and political parties—but the implantation of a genuinely democratic civic consciousness. Public opinion research in all these countries indicates that a fundamental shift is under way: A mentality of corporatism (elitism, hierarchy, sectoral organization of society) is changing into a civic political culture appropriate to democracy. Indeed, it may be that in these countries by now the democratic strain is the dominant one, rather than the ideology and consciousness of corporatism. If that is and continues to be the case, a sea change in public opinion has transpired, marking the arrival of true democracy in Latin America.

The shift is of course more pronounced in some countries than in others. It seems to be strongest in Costa Rica and Venezuela but growing in the Dominican Republic, Colombia, Peru, and elsewhere. The democratic political culture was also strong in Chile and Uruguay, but that was reversed in the 1970s — and now may again be going back the other way, towards democracy. Argentina installed a new, democratically elected government in 1983, accompanied by a widespread public outpouring of democratic sentiment; some parallel trends have been under way in Brazil. Mexico may also reform its aging corporatist regime to make it more democratic. So far, in some of these transitional regimes, democratic sentiment is often inchoate and may still be reversed, but there does seem to be growing sentiment not for the values of the past, but for those of a democratic political culture.

Revolutionary Regimes

To this point there are only two genuinely revolutionary governments in Latin America: Cuba and now Nicaragua. Grenada appeared to have joined this group, but in 1983 that seemed to have been reversed by a United States military intervention. Guyana and Suriname have moved in some parallel trajectories but the transition to a revolutionary regime in these two countries remains incomplete. Bolivia had a true social revolution in 1952 and may be again headed in a radical direction; and early in the century Mexico also had a profound social revolution that for a time seemed quite radical.

The causes for the coming to power of these radical-revolutionary, or "Trotsko–Populist," regimes are clear. In both the Cuban and Nicaraguan cases, revolution had its roots in the transition backward from an open to a closed corporatist regime. There is no record of an open corporatist regime in Latin America ever giving way to radical revolution; rather, it is the closed kind that provides the breeding grounds for revolutionary upheaval. In the cases of both Batista in Cuba and Somoza in Nicaragua, the regime sought to revert to a more closed and repressive form of corporatism and au-

thoritarianism after an initial opening, but their people had come to expect something better. Revolution soon followed.

Several lessons may be learned from these experiences. First, one cannot turn the clock back in Latin America — unless one is willing to use brutal repression, which, however, may in the long run provide just the kind of conditions that will cause revolutionary sentiment to grow and expand. Second, an open corporatist system is much to be preferred to a closed one, from the points of view both of the peoples affected and for the long-term foreign policy interests of the United States. The third lesson is that mixed closed-and-open systems — such as those in El Salvador, Guatemala, or Honduras — bear especially close watching. Should the pendulum in any of these three countries swing away definitively from more open forms toward a closed one, then radicalism will almost certainly spread, and a revolutionary upheaval inimical to United States interests is likely. On the other hand, if openness can be maintained and expanded, both the interests of the peoples of these countries and United States policy will likely be enhanced.

There are three main difficulties with the revolutionary regimes in Latin America. First, they (especially Cuba) have opted for an alliance, or close ties, with the Soviet Union, substituting one form of external dependence for another and quite possibly leaving themselves and their peoples worse off than when they were closely tied to the United States. Second, political liberty and freedom have been curtailed in the face of what seems to be a rising tide of sentiment in favor of democracy throughout Latin America.

Third, the economies of these two countries have not proved very successful: The Cuban and Nicaraguan economies are both in trouble: Nicaragua has been living on borrowed capital since 1979 and now faces the prospect of shortages, food lines, rationing, and a lowered standard of living. The Cuban economy, some twenty-five years after the revolution, has reached almost the same level it had in the late 1950s. Not only are the Cubans no better off now in per capita terms than many of their capitalist or semicapitalist neighbors whom they once ranked ahead of, but alone among the Socialist countries of the world, Cuba has shown no economic progress since 1960.

True, these two regimes have improved education, housing, and health care: therein lies the case for judging them successful. The social programs of these revolutionary governments are impressive, but their economic accomplishments have been far less so. Eventually, it would seem that these regimes must produce concrete accomplishments in the way of material goods and economic development, not just rhetoric, if they are to succeed, if their peoples are to remain contented, and if the revolutionary option they offer is to be attractive elsewhere in Latin America.

■ Explanatory Paradigms and Models

The history and mechanisms of the political system of Latin America are fairly clear to those who study the area, but the explanatory models and paradigms that we use to interpret the region are far less clear. Let us review the major interpretations to sort out what is useful and what is not so useful in each.

Marxism

The Marxist framework is useful, at its most general level, in helping one to understand the broad course of Latin American development since the nineteenth century. But many scholars find it less useful as a guide to the more specific events, movements, and regimes of today. That is, one can say that there has been in Latin America since the last century a long-term process in which feudalism has come to be supplanted by more capitalistic structures and, in some countries at least, a further transition from capitalistic to more social-democratic and socialist forms.

Moreover, the motor force in these transformations has been economic development. Economic development helped undermine the old landowning class, stimulated the rise of a new business-entrepreneurial elite, paved the way for the growth of the middle class, and eventually gave rise to trade unionism. These changes in the class structure, in turn, wreaked a profound transformation in the political structures as well, particularly from the 1920s and 1930s on when the pace of change accelerated.

The Marxist-Leninist thesis about imperialism also has a certain validity. In colonial times it was Spain and Portugal that milked Latin America of its wealth for their own advantage; in the nineteenth century Great Britain was a major imperial presence; in the twentieth century the United States has played that role. United States investments in Latin America are considerable, the area depends on the United States for capital and markets, and the United States has repeatedly intervened in Latin America. To some, this is a definition of "imperialism." The Marxist paradigm thus helps provide a large map, a set of contours, for the understanding of the broad sweep of Latin American history from the past to the present.

The Marxist framework proves less useful, however, (1) the closer one moves to the present, and (2) the more specific one seeks to become. For example, though virtually all Latin American clerics as well as armed forces officers are now from the middle class—and that is useful to know—the Marxist class categories do not reveal much about why one officer corps or group of clerics moves to the left and the other goes to the right, or about the divisions *within* their respective ranks. Nor do these categories go far to clarify some aspects of Latin American bureaucratic behavior, political party machinations, the role of the state, circulations in power by various groups, and so forth. Although the Marxist explanation is useful up to a point in all these areas, it tends to ignore both the strong force of cultural continuity in Latin America and the degree to which political variables are independent of class structure. These should not simply be subordinated to economic determinants. Hence, the Marxist explanation carries us only so far, leaving a great deal of Latin American political phenomena unexplained and unaccounted for.

The Developmentalist Approach

The developmentalist approach derives from the literature on social, economic, and political development of the 1960s; it has strongly influenced such United States assistance programs as the Alliance for Progress. The developmentalist approach offered a non-Communist route to development, and was presented as an alternative to Marxism. The approach was based on the developmental experiences of the United States and Western Europe and assumed that these processes were unilinear, inevitable, universal, and repeatable. The "developing nations" of Latin America were thus viewed as somewhat backward versions of the United States, but fated inevitably to follow our footsteps if only enough economic assistance and technological know-how could be applied.

Hence the United States, through the Alliance for Progress, supported economic pump-priming in Latin America with the hope that this would lead to development and a higher standard of living. Economic growth, it was also presumed, would lead to a stable middle class, a more moderate, apolitical trade unionism, and a military establishment characterized by professionalism and less inclination to meddle in civilian politics. The ultimate goal was a stable, democratic, socially just political order that would closely resemble that of the United States.

These assumptions were not borne out in the Latin American setting. The middle class did not become a bulwark of stability, trade unions remained highly politicized or even revolutionary, greater professionalism led frequently to *more* military intervention rather than less, and stability and democracy remained elusive. To be sure, considerable economic growth did occur

under the Alliance for Progress during the 1960s, but the social and political concomitants that were supposed to follow did not, in fact, do so.

The developmentalist approach had several weaknesses. The greatest problem was that the grand universal categories put forth in the literature had but limited relevance to Latin America. Latin America is not non-Western, but it does represent a special (Iberian) fragment of the West to which the experiences of the United States and northern Europe had only partial relevance. The reverse side of this coin was the fact that the developmentalist approach betrayed an appalling ignorance about Latin America — its middle class, military, trade unions, and so on. Indeed, what was said above about the Marxist paradigm could also be said about the developmentalist theory: Both were based on a grand universal model that had only limited utility for Latin America.

The Andersonian "Power Contenders" Approach

To help remedy these deficiencies in both the Marxist and the developmentalist approaches, Charles W. Anderson of the University of Wisconsin and one of the nation's leading Latin Americanists, formulated a new theory of Latin American politics.[5] He based his formulation on the actual experiences of Latin America, not on models imported from the outside and only partially applicable there. For a long time Anderson's theory was the dominant one in the field.

Anderson argued that in Latin America the political system consists of a variety of rival power contenders — Church, army, oligarchy, and the like — roughly comparable to the "corporate" groups discussed earlier. These groups vie for influence and political power in accord with fairly specific rules of the game—rules that are quite different from those prevailing in the United States but not entirely unviable or unworkable in Latin America. Anderson suggested that elections there are tentative rather than definitive and constitute only one among several routes to power; that coups are a rather normal part of the political process; and that politics often involves the circulation of several elites in and out of power. In these regards, Anderson's model corresponds rather closely to the alternation between closed and open corporatist regimes described above.

The *system* of Latin American politics Anderson described was not rigid but in fact quite flexible. It could admit new groups into the system provided they met two conditions: (1) They had to demonstrate sufficient strength to threaten the system itself, and (2) they had to agree to moderate their demands so as to allow the old elites to continue in power while also getting something (but not *all*, which would mean a revolutionary transformation) for themselves.

The Andersonian model was particularly useful where the Marxist and developmentalist frameworks left off, in enabling one to understand better the dynamics of specifically *political* change in Latin America and the continuous overlap (even now) of traditional with modern aspects. But the Andersonian model proved excessively optimistic, a product of the hopeful early 1960s. It pictured the Latin American political systems as almost infinitely flexible and accommodative, but did not adequately account for the reversal of these processes and the return to more authoritarian practices in the mid-to-late 1960s. It demonstrated that the Latin American middle sectors could be assimilated in the time-honored way the area had long dealt with change, but it was not able to account for the breakdowns of these systems under rising mass pressures in the late 1960s and 1970s. Nor did it take deal adequately with international forces. These elements would be factored into the newer models that arose subsequently.

The Corporatist Approach

The corporatist approach, as outlined previously, served as a complement and extension of the Andersonian model. It derived from dissatisfaction with the incompleteness of the Marxist categories and the inadequacies of the developmentalist approach, and from a need to update and modify Anderson. It sought to understand Latin America in its own (corporatist) terms rather than in the ethnocentric terms of United States social science and political preferences.[6]

The corporatist approach was meant not as an all-encompassing and complete explanation of Latin American politics but, more modestly, as a partial explanation designed to shed light on phenomena not adequately explained by other approaches. It sought to explain the almost inherently corporate and sectoral organization of Latin American social and political life, as contrasted with the interest-group pluralism of the United States. It was useful also in enabling us to understand better the structure of Latin American labor relations, the role of the state, the nature of group interaction, the special position of the church and the army, the system of social security, and the functions of the bureaucracy.

The corporatist paradigm caused considerable controversy, particularly because some critics interpreted corporatism as identical with fascism. Actually, fascism is only one particularly venal form of corporatism; in Latin America corporatism took more benign, less totalitarian forms. There was also some objection because the corporatist explanation seemed excessively pessimistic about democracy's chances of ever taking firm root in Latin America. But stripped of these often emotional overtones, there is little doubt the corporatist canon of interpretation, especially when used in conjunction with other approaches, added to the understanding of Latin American politics.

The Bureaucratic-Authoritarian Approach

The bureaucratic-authoritarian approach arose at about the same time as the corporatist model, and for several of the same reasons. It too sought to explain why Latin America failed to correspond to the developmental models of the already industrialized nations and more particularly why the most advanced of Latin American nations — Argentina, Brazil, and Chile — reverted in the 1960s and early 1970s to a system of authoritarian rule. It should be emphasized that this was modernized *bureaucratic*-authoritarian rule, as distinct from the often unsophisticated one-man or traditional dictatorships of the past. Bureaucratic authoritarianism is a system close to the description and category of closed corporatism described earlier.

The basic cause for the growth of bureaucratic authoritarianism, leading theorists of this position argued, was the failure of Latin America's development strategy of import substitution — that is, the strategy of fomenting manufactures by producing locally what had previously been imported.* The result had been rising unemployment, economic stagnation, growing balance of payments problems, and rising mass unrest. To stem the unrest from below, the military (the "bureaucratic authoritarians") had been obliged to step into power to prevent revolutionary upheaval and to forge a new and more conservative developmental strategy.

This interpretation has its uses, but it is not without problems. First of all, in the writings of some of its best-known proponents, it took on a quasi-Marxist form that seemed overly rigid and deterministic. Second, questions arose over whether the import-substitution strategy had been analyzed correctly. Third, it failed to fit all countries equally well. And fourth, renewed political liberalization in the later 1970s made it imperative to rethink the inevitability of bureaucratic authoritarianism.

Dependency Theory

The dependency approach, largely formulated by Latin Americans themselves, holds that the fundamental problem of the area's underdevelopment derived from its dependency on the outside world—especially in the United States. It suggests that development in the United States came at the cost of leaving Latin America underdeveloped. Rather than the two parts of the Americas pursuing development in tandem, this approach suggests they were fundamentally antagonistic.

Now there are vulgar as well as sophisticated writers in the dependency school—as is the case for all the approaches reviewed here. Certain facts emphasized by dependency theorists are incontrovertible: Latin America *is* excessively dependent on the outside world, the United States *does* get involved inordinately in its internal politics, United States multinational corporations *do* sometimes engage in some nefarious practices in Latin America, the international banks *do* have a major role in determining the rhythms of Latin American development.

Excessive enthusiasm for such explanations should be tempered with caution, however. Dependency is by no means the only cause of Latin American underdevelopment; and too often the dependency argument is used by Latin Americans to blame all their problems on the United States rather than looking inward to their own societies for the causes. Furthermore, some writers use the dependency approach as a shorthand for Marxist-Leninist arguments about United States imperialism and as a justification for guerrilla war. Rather like the corporatist paradigm, if dependency analysis is stripped of some of this excess ideological baggage, it offers a worthwhile approach, particularly if used in conjunction with other approaches. But again, one needs to beware of elevating a useful but still partial explanation into a single, all-encompassing one.

The Struggle-for-Democracy Approach

The struggle-for-democracy approach is an updated version, with new features, of the developmentalist approach. It holds that the United States model still has considerable relevance for other nations. It tends to view Latin America as locked in a constant struggle be-

---

*Editor's Note: For more on import substitution see Chapter 14, "The Economics of Latin America."

tween democracy and dictatorship. If only we can get rid of the repressive oligarchies and the military, the argument runs, then Latin America's naturally democratic inclinations can triumph. The more enthusiastic backers of this position believe that United States democratic institutions can be exported to Latin America and that United States capital, technology, and know-how can accomplish these goals.

Others are skeptical. They doubt that United States institutions can be transplanted to other nations where the culture and history are so different. They doubt that the United States has the will, capacity, or resources to effect these goals, or that the Latin American nations necessarily want to replicate the United States model. The typology given earlier showed that the political problem in Latin America usually involves a continuous effort to devise formulas that combine and reconcile diverse features in its political tradition, rather than the either-or choice between dictatorship and democracy.

Still, there is a democratic opening in Latin America that merits attention and support. This discussion has portrayed it, however, not so much as a "struggle for democracy" but as a trend from closed to open corporatism in some countries and from open corporatism to a genuine civic culture in others. That, we have felt, is a more accurate rendering and enables us to avoid some of the exaggerated expectations — and the frustrated hopes — that the dictatorship-versus-democracy dichotomy gives rise to.

■ **Conclusions and Implications**

Latin America has a system of politics uniquely its own. Some parts are borrowed from abroad (the United States constitutional tradition, the French system of legal codification) but the most salient features are indigenous. These have developed, even "modernized," over time into complex patterns, processes, and institutional arrangements. Corporatism (the sectoral organization of society) as well as representative government, have been incorporated into the Latin

American systems as part of the dominant social and political structure.

The classification of Latin American political systems used here includes traditional authoritarian regimes, closed corporatist regimes, open corporatist regimes, democratic or "civic" regimes, and radical-revolutionary regimes. The traditional authoritarian regimes are becoming anachronisms, with only one left in Latin America. Genuinely democratic and radical revolutionary regimes have also been relatively rare in the hemisphere.

The real political struggle and dynamic, therefore, has generally involved closed and open corporatist regimes and the combinations and oscillations between them. One may prefer the genuinely democratic ones, but for many Latin American countries that is not now a very realistic possibility. Open corporatist regimes have the additional advantage of being close to the region's historical traditions while also presenting an opening *toward* democracy. Particularly in the strife-torn nations of Central America, and maybe some of those in South America as well, an open corporatist regime may be about the best that can realistically be hoped for in the present circumstances.

Also surveyed were the various models and paradigms that scholars and policy analysts have used to interpret Latin America. Both the Marxist and the developmentalist approaches offer useful broad categories, but they become less helpful when applied in very specific circumstances. For understanding Latin America on its own terms and in its own context, many scholars find a combination of the Andersonian, corporatist, bureaucratic-authoritarian, and dependency approaches most useful — especially if these are shorn of their ideological baggage and employed pragmatically and eclectically. Even the struggle-for-democracy paradigm has its utility in the appropriate circumstances.

A synthesis of these various approaches has yet to be achieved. Most open-minded students of the area see no reason why one cannot combine a Marxist or a developmentalist perspective with the corporatist approach, with dependency theory, and with the bureaucratic-authoritarian or struggle-for-democracy approaches. We now have considerable literature on each approach; what is now required is both further testing and refinement of these theories and a building of bridges between them. Such a grand synthesis is required as a way of broadening and enriching our understanding of Latin America and the interpretations we use to comprehend the area.

■ Notes

1. Philippe C. Schmitter, "Paths to Political Development in Latin America," in *Changing Latin America*, ed. Douglas Chalmers (New York: Academy of Political Science, Columbia University, 1972).
2. These formulations derive from the author's own writings, *Politics and Social Change in Latin America*, 2d rev. ed. (Amherst: University of Massachusetts Press, 1982), and *Corporatism and National Development in Latin America* (Boulder, Colo.: Westview Press, 1981); and from Mark Falcoff, "The Politics of Latin America," in *Western Hemisphere Stability — The Latin American Connection* ed. R. Daniel McMichael and John D. Paulus (Pittsburgh: World Afffairs Council of Pittsburgh, 19th World Affairs Forum, 1982).
3. Falcoff, op. cit.
4. The definition and discussion derive from Falcoff; also Wiarda, *Corporatism and National Development*.
5. Falcoff, op. cit., 56.
6. Charles W. Anderson, *Politics and Economic Change in Latin America: The Governing of Restless Nations* (Princeton: D. Van Nostrand, 1967).
7. Howard J. Wiarda, "Toward a Framework for the Study of Political Change in the Iberic-Latin Tradition: The Corporative Model," *World Politics* 25 (January 1973): 206–35.

■ Suggested Readings

Anderson, Charles W. *Politics and Economic Change in Latin America: The Governing of Restless Nations.* Princeton: D. Van Nostrand, 1967.

Cardoso, F. H., and E. Faletto. *Dependency and Development in Latin America.* Berkeley: University of California Press, 1978.

Collier, David, ed. *The New Authoritarianism in Latin America.* Princeton: Princeton University Press, 1979.

Duncan, R. W. *Latin American Politics: A Developmental Approach.* New York: Praeger, 1976.

Einaudi, Luigi, ed. *Beyond Cuba: Latin America Takes Charge of Its Future.* New York: Carne, Russak,1974.

Mander, John. *The Unrevolutionary Society: The Power of Latin American Conservatism in a Changing World.* New York: Knopf, 1969.

Mercier Vega, Luis. *Roads to Power in Latin America.* New York: Praeger, 1969.

O'Donnell, Guillermo. *Modernization and Bureaucratic Authoritarianism: Studies in South American Politics.* Berkeley: University of California, Institute of International Studies, 1973.

Petras, James. *Politics and Social Structure in Latin America.* New York: Monthly Review Press, 1970.

Pike, Fredrick, and Thomas Stritch, eds. *The New Corporatism: Social and Political Structures in the Iberian World.* Notre Dame, Ind.: University of Notre Dame Press, 1974.

Rostow, W. W. *The Stages of Economic Growth: A Non-Communist Manifesto.* Cambridge: Cambridge University Press, 1960.

Schmitter, Philippe C. "Paths to Political Development in Latin America." In *Changing Latin America*, edited by Douglas Chalmers. New York: Academy of Political Science, Columbia University, 1972.

Silvert, Kalman. *The Conflict Society: Reaction and Revolution in Latin America.* New York: American Universities Field Staff, 1966.

Véliz, Claudio. *The Centralist Tradition in Latin America.* Princeton: Princeton University Press, 1980.

Wiarda, Howard J., ed. *The Continuing Struggle for Democracy in Latin America.* Boulder, Colo.: Westview Press, 1980.

———. *Corporatism and Development in Latin America.* Boulder, Colo.: Westview Press, 1981.

———. *Critical Elections and Critical Coups: State, Society, and the Military in the Processes of Latin American Development.* Athens: Center for International Studies, Ohio University, 1979.

Wiarda, Howard J., and Harvey F. Kline, eds., *Latin American Politics and Development.* Boulder, Colo.: Westview Press, 1985.

Williams, E. J., and F. J. Wright. *Latin American Politics: A Developmental Approach.* Palo Alto: Mayfield, 1979.

17 | *The Military in Latin America*

DAVID SCOTT PALMER

Military establishments have been important features of the Latin American landscape since the colonial period. Independence for most countries would have been long delayed without the rebel armies to fight against the Spanish forces. Protection or expansion of national boundaries after independence often required the military's attention, as did the internal conflict in many countries over the nature, orientation, and direction of their political institutions. These two distinct roles — national defense and national politics — have played themselves out in many ways over the past 150 years in every Spanish- and Portuguese-American country of Latin America.

The military's defense role, for example, included the establishment, protection, and enhancement of the new nations in the nineteenth century. In the twentieth century, boundary protection needs have continued for most countries, but this has occurred in the context of growing professionalization of the military through training and specialization, the insertion of Latin American nations into regional and international defense systems, and internal security concerns. The political role of the mili-

tary has also changed; from involvement with one elite faction or another in civil wars and *caudillo* (military dictator) rule in the nineteenth and early twentieth centuries, to a growing willingness to play an independent political role. Through the 1940s this often meant supporting either reformist governments on behalf of the middle class or backing status quo governments for the elites. Beginning in the 1960s it frequently involved the military as the primary political actor in governments of reform or reaction. The task of this chapter is to describe and analyze the principal features of these two major roles, both in terms of the broad patterns that apply to the region as a whole and to variations within individual countries.

From a United States perspective, the basic security needs of individual Latin American countries are usually viewed as quite small in the international scheme of things. From the same vantage point, the frequent military takeovers, or *golpes de estado*, of the countries' governing institutions are often seen a a sign that Latin American nations are incapable of governing themselves. Many Latin Americans perceive the two major roles of their military establishments quite differently. In their view, most countries do have important security problems of maintaining or defending national boundaries and, in many cases, of protecting domestic institutions from internal subversion. Often these security problems are of long standing and are believed to require constant vigilance and military preparedness. The political role of the military, in turn, is often seen as a legitimate alternative to civilian rule under certain circumstances, even as constitutional norms and a commitment to open, pluralist politics are championed. Only Costa Rica, among Latin American nations, has concluded that a military establishment is not required for security and not needed for politics. Therefore, its government eliminated the military institution in 1948. Since then, Costa Rica has relied on the force of world opinion and international organizations to help maintain its security, and on the twin strengths of well-institutionalized, responsible parties and an educated citizenry to uphold an effective political system.

■ The Military's Defense Role

The defense role of the military has involved various concerns. Most of the newly independent states had early problems in defining and establishing their boundaries. This was understandable and even to be expected, given the fact that sixteen independent countries emerged from one colonial master and four vice-royalties of the Spanish Empire by 1840. Military force was often needed to assert and maintain control. The fact that many of the ill-defined boundaries existed in quite underpopulated areas, often difficult of access, kept boundary problems and conflicts from being even more serious in the nineteenth century—but insured their frequent reemergence in the twentieth. Examples of contested boundaries that continued unresolved for decades, include those between El Salvador and Honduras, Honduras and Nicaragua, Venezuela and Guyana, Ecuador and

Peru, Bolivia and Paraguay, Brazil and virtually all its neighbors, and Argentina and Chile.

Besides the problem of border establishment and maintenance, which required and justified a military establishment, there were numerous conflicts within most countries after independence to determine the nature of the institutions and, in many cases, the individuals who would be in charge. Military forces were needed to assert rival claims. Although most of these early forces bore little resemblance to the well-disciplined and well-trained institutions that eventually evolved from them, their regional bases and personalist ties to leading individual officers, or caudillos, often led them to acquit themselves well.

There were, in addition, occasional regional conflicts in the nineteenth century in which the participating armed forces' preparedness and competence affected both the outcome and served as a stimulus for better training. Uruguay was created as a buffer state between rival Brazil and Argentina under pressure from the British after inconclusive battles between the countries in the 1820s. Paraguay lost substantial portions of its national territory to Brazil and Argentina, as well as almost 90 percent of its male population, in the long and bloody War of the Triple Alliance in the 1860s (to which Uruguay was also a party). Bolivia lost its coastline and Peru was forced to give up the nitrate-rich province of Tarapacá when defeated by Chile in the War of the Pacific (1879–1883). To this day both nations' armed forces rue their loss and base much of their military strategy on the means by which they might regain "the lost provinces."

Several twentieth-century disputes, usually related to the old problem of ill-defined boundaries, demonstrated to the participants the need for a well-trained and professional military. For example, the Chaco War (1932–1935) between Bolivia and Paraguay dragged on, in spite of numerous efforts by international commissions to halt the conflict, until Paraguay defeated

Bolivia and then secured by international award most of the territory it had conquered by military action.[1] The Peru-Ecuador war of 1941 was brief but equally decisive and secured for Peru under the Rio Protocol of 1942 virtually all of the land in dispute — almost half of Ecuador's former territory. Some conflicts remain troublesome, like those between Guatemala and Belize (formerly British Honduras, which Guatemala claims in its entirety); Venezuela and Guyana (formerly British Guiana, of which Venezuela claims almost two-thirds); Ecuador and Peru (Ecuador has renounced the Rio Protocol and has reasserted its claim over Amazonia, with armed incidents almost every year); Argentina and Great Britain (over the Malvinas/Falkland Islands, which erupted into war in 1982); and Chile and Argentina (over the Beagle Channel and islands to the south of Tierra del Fuego, which almost came to war in 1978, and is now being resolved through papal mediation). The boundary disputes issue as a basic element of national defense strategy has been considerably complicated by international acceptance in the 1970s of the Latin American-inspired Law of the Sea proposal, which established sovereign economic exploitation rights out to a two-hundred-mile limit from a country's coastline.

Given the number, variety, and duration of disputes, it is not surprising that the governments of many Latin American countries would eventually place a high priority on making the military a more professional institution. Beginning in the last decades of the nineteenth century, Latin American governments and their armed forces increasingly turned to foreign assistance. Before World War I (1914–1918), for example, six of the ten South American countries asked French or German military missions to improve the quality of military education and combat training.[2] In many cases this was continued or expanded after World War I to include not only the French and the Germans but also missions from Italy, Spain, and the United States.

With the outbreak of World War II (1939–1945) and in the years immediately following, United States training missions came to dominate in the region. In fact, between 1947 and 1967 the United States armed forces had a virtual monopoly on training their Latin American counterparts. United States military assistance of all kinds during the period totaled about $2.6 billion, with about thirty-three thousand officers and enlisted men from every Latin American country trained by United States counterparts in their own countries, at facilities in the Panama Canal Zone, or in the United States.[3] In the 1940s and 1950s, the Inter-American Defense System for common efforts against an external threat — first anti-Fascist, then anti-Communist — provided the underlying rationale. From the 1960s onward the threat was seen to be an internal one, in the form of guerrilla warfare. Consequently, United States training programs emphasized counterinsurgency tactics and civic action. With the decline of United States military assistance, arms sales, and military missions in the 1970s, other countries stepped in. These included France, Germany, Italy, Great Britain, the Soviet Union, and Israel. But the majority of Latin American armed forces, particularly the larger ones, had by this time acquired a strong base of professional training, with their own autonomous educational institutions. Thus, much of what foreign military personnel provided was quite technical and specialized training, closely related to teaching Latin American personnel how to use the equipment they had purchased.

The seventy-to-ninety-five-year span during which foreign military missions have worked with their Latin American counterparts has had an important impact, although its precise nature is difficult to determine. Military training facilities, content, and technical orientation were often foreign-inspired and -directed. They clearly increased the professionalism of the armed forces, i.e., the capacity of military institutions to defend the nation. But foreign military training also contributed, after a certain time lag, to more rather than less active military involvement in the political life of the nation — whether as a result of German or French training by the 1920s and 1930s or United States training by the 1960s and 1970s.[4] This was due partly to the resultant increase in the overall capacity, élan, and discipline of military officers, and partly to the way this training strengthened military institutions more rapidly than their civilian counterparts, such as political parties and labor unions, advanced.

A review of government expenditures on the military and their trends is one way to get some perspective on the relative importance of the

military's defense role — and perhaps of its political role as well (see Table 1). The overall average percentages of government budgets spent on the armed forces decline through time, from 25 percent for those countries for which data were available in the 1880s to just under 11 percent for the late 1970s. Broad generalizations are risky, given the wide variety of specific country situations. However, these overall figures seem to suggest either that defense issues became less salient for the region over the years, or that competing priorities and new demands for central government resources claimed a larger share of them, or both. The substantial fluctuations in individual countries also indicate that

TABLE **1**
Military Expenditures in Latin America, 1880–1980
(Percentages of National Budgets)

	ca. 1880	ca. 1900	ca. 1920	ca. 1940	ca. 1960	ca. 1970	ca. 1980
Argentina	24.5	29.3	17.6	19.1	18.6	15.2	30.2
Bolivia	21.6	35.0	20.0	29.9	N/A	11.3	8.3
Brazil	20.5	26.1	25.0	26.0	26.4	21.9	9.4
Chile	59.1	22.1	8.4	24.4	12.7	11.5	12.6
Colombia	15.7	8.4	14.0	16.9	17.1	13.9	8.5
Costa Rica	13.1	8.7	2.0	7.9	3.9	0.0	0.0
Cuba	—	N/A	N/A	N/A	N/A	N/A	N/A
Domin. Rep.	29.2	N/A	N/A	9.8	20.3	11.9	12.1
Ecuador	29.8	19.3	27.1	20.7	20.8	9.6	15.1
El Salvador	23.5	19.8	25.0	17.5	8.9	9.1	9.3
Guatemala	28.2	20.8	24.9	13.6	9.9	15.4	8.0
Haiti	N/A	N/A	N/A	20.6	23.6	17.6	7.5
Honduras	N/A	33.7	20.4	23.8	10.0	5.9	8.6
Mexico	34.3	22.9	46.4	20.0	11.2	6.8	3.2
Nicaragua	N/A	16.6	N/A	N/A	N/A	12.1	10.6
Panama	—	—	N/A	N/A	N/A	3.8	2.9
Paraguay	N/A	8.0	18.2	32.9	N/A	14.9	12.2
Peru	18.8	22.5	29.0	21.4	16.0	18.2	26.5
Uruguay	23.8	10.8	17.7	12.0	N/A	13.1	13.1
Venezuela	8.5	27.7	19.0	10.0	9.5	9.0	5.7
Average:	25.0	20.7	21.0	19.2	14.9	11.6	10.7

N/A = not available

Sources: 1880–1980 figures from Arthur S. Banks, *Cross-Polity Time-Series Data* (Cambridge: MIT Press, 1971) Segment 3, Field e, "National Defense Expenditure/National Government Expenditure," nearest year of real rather than extrapolated data. 1970 and ca. 1980 figures from ACDA, *World Military Expenditures and Arms Transfers, 1969–1978* Washington, USGPO), Take I.

political, economic, or defense priorities can and do change frequently. A country such as Ecuador can show a rather low level of military expenditure under civilian rule (e.g., 9.6 percent in 1970, or thirteenth of nineteen countries) and quite high military expenditure under military rule (e.g., 15.1 percent in 1978, or third of nineteen). Brazil shows precisely the reverse (26.4 percent in 1960, or first of fourteen; 9.4 percent in 1978, or ninth of nineteen). As a general rule, though, military regimes tend to look out for their own institutional needs a bit more assiduously than their civilian counterparts (e.g., Argentina, Chile, Peru, and Uruguay in the 1970s) do.

Although military governments were widespread during the 1970s, this period saw no massive changes in defense spending patterns. This pattern prevailed in spite of decreasing United States military sales and assistance, with its concomitant loss of control over balanced defense spending for the countries of the region. Military expenditures for Latin America, as a percentage of central government revenues, are lower than for any other major world region (except Africa) — 14.2 percent in 1970 and 10.9 percent in 1978.[5] These are well under world totals of 31.6 percent for 1970 and 22.4 percent for 1978. It appears, then, that the size of Latin American military establishments, in terms of government resources consumed, is not disproportionate to the level of security threats most of these countries face. In the most recent period, only Argentina and Peru seem to be considerably out of line.

■ The Military's Political Role

A true understanding of what the armed forces do or of their political role in Latin America has to recognize that the political context in which they have evolved is basically an authoritarian one. The military emerged from an almost three-hundred-year colonial experience in which authority emanated down from the crown rather than up from the people, and the military was an integral rather than a subordinate part of government. Democratic procedures and practices were not part of the colonial experience. Therefore it should not be surprising that the constitutions of newly independent Latin American nations retained many of the authoritarian features of past experience (though without the crown, except in Brazil), including careful limits to citizen participation. The military was still called upon to protect the state and guard the system; in most countries it seemed necessary or expedient to intervene politically from time to time in order to carry out these responsibilities.[6]

In "core regions" of the former Spanish Empire such as those now encompassed by the independent nations of Mexico, Peru, and Bolivia (where Spanish influence had been greatest in order to protect its control over substantial mineral resources and large numbers of people), civilians had considerable difficulty establishing legitimate republican institutions. Regular intervention by the military soon became the nineteenth-century norm. Between independence and 1870, for example, these three core countries experienced thirty *golpes de estado*, or coups, among them, or 42 percent of all coups of the sixteen independent countries carved from the former Spanish Empire by that time. In another "core region," which became Guatemala, and in such "peripheral regions" as Paraguay and Venezuela, personalist military dictatorships were established, acquired legitimacy, and endured — in some cases well into the twentieth century. Golpes de estado were few in number (only one before 1870 in the three countries), but authoritarian political structures prevailed. Even in such exceptional cases as Chile, a former "peripheral region" in which civilian rule was established and institutionalized after 1833, authoritarian principles were enshrined in the constitution as the basis for that nation's political legitimacy. They included the following:

1. Centralization of authority
2. Hierarchical rule through administrative

(nonparliamentary) agencies at the provincial and local levels

3. A "flexible" constitution that offered little effective constraint on the exercise of government authority
4. Official recognition of possible governance through a state of siege[7]

These principles, or a variant of them, reflect the historical, cultural, and legal bases for legitimating the political role of the military in every Latin American country. They function somewhat differently in specific nations, depending on many factors. These include the "core–periphery" distinction noted above, such economic resources as extensive mineral deposits and good soils, the strength and capacity of civilian political leaders and organizations, the degree and rate of incorporation of a country's population into the national system, international markets and prices, strategic concerns of the larger powers outside the region, and levels of military training, leadership, and internal dynamics. Clearly, then, "the political role of the military is a function of the interaction of variables operating both within the military institutions and in its societal environment."[8]

Building Political Legitimacy in New States

In most countries during the fifty years following independence, the military was highly involved in the struggle to build domestic consensus and political legitimacy. Elites were usually divided between conservatives and liberals, and both sides enlisted corresponding factions of a poorly institutionalized military in the many civil wars. [The problems of nation building are discussed at length in Chapter 6.]

Even though the military might have been expected to follow conservative principles because of its own internal organization and institutional interests, such was often not the case. The wars for independence contributed to the dissociation of many armies from the more conservative ideological basis of Spanish rule and fostered their identification with liberalism. Mil-

itary establishments frequently followed the lead of the strongest and most charismatic officers. Civilian leaders lacked both strong organizational backing — because political parties were just beginning to be formed — and experience in governing — because this was not a feature of Spanish colonial rule. Continued political turmoil often resulted.

In this period of independence and national consolidation, then, the military was almost always intimately involved. In the fluid postindependence political situation, legitimacy through force often prevailed. Very early the golpe de estado became a common mechanism for bringing a government to power, and the caudillo often became head of state. In most countries neither elections nor liberal ideas were any match for a coup or for three hundred years of conservative tradition. They had to await growing economic prosperity, better organized civilian political parties, the routinization of political processes, and recognition by elites that their interests could actually be enhanced by adherence to liberal principles.

The 1870s through the 1920s mark a period of gradually declining numbers of military coups for each succeeding decade and an increase in the number of countries that go for longer periods of time without such military takeovers. After peaking at twenty-nine in the 1860s, golpes de estado gradually decline over the succeeding decades, from twenty-six in the 1870s to seventeen in the 1920s. The number of countries that do not have golpes for entire decades at a time increases from just four of eighteen in the 1870s to twelve of twenty in the 1910s (and eleven of twenty in the 1920s; see Table 2). Somewhat more elaborate data on degrees of instability and extent of authoritarianism for the Spanish-American countries show similar trends. These include such information as the number of constitutions and changes in executive, as indicators of the degree of instability; and years of nonelected governments, a weak or absent legislature, and military rule as indicators of authoritarianism.

TABLE 2

Golpes de Estado in Latin America by Decade 1810–1980

	1810	1820	1830	1840	1850	1860	1870	1880	1890	1900	1910	1920	1930	1940	1950	1960	1970	Total by Country
Argentina	1	0	0	0	1	0	0	1	0	0	0	0	1	1	2	2	3	12
Bolivia	—	1	0	2	1	3	2	2	2	0	0	1	4	2	1	2	5	28
Brazil	—	0	1	1	0	0	0	1	1	0	0	0	1	1	2	2	0	10
Chile	0	2	1	0	0	0	0	1	1	0	0	5	1	0	0	0	1	12
Colombia	0	0	1	0	2	2	0	0	0	2	1	1	0	0	2	0	0	11
Costa Rica	—	—	0	0	1	1	2	0	1	0	2	0	0	1	0	0	0	8
Cuba	—	—	—	—	—	1	—	—	1	1	0	0	2	0	0	0	0	5
Domin. Rep.	—	—	2	2	3	6	3	2	1	0	4	0	1	1	0	3	0	28
Ecuador	—	—	0	1	1	2	2	1	1	1	0	1	3	3	0	3	2	21
El Salvador	—	—	0	0	1	2	2	1	2	1	0	0	2	3	0	2	1	17
Guatemala	—	—	0	0	0	0	1	1	0	0	0	1	2	2	2	1	0	10
Haiti	—	0	0	7	1	2	2	2	1	2	7	0	0	1	3	0	0	28
Honduras	—	—	0	0	1	2	3	0	2	3	1	3	0	0	1	1	3	20
Mexico	—	1	3	4	3	3	2	2	0	0	2	1	0	0	0	0	0	21
Nicaragua	—	—	0	1	1	0	1	1	1	1	0	2	1	1	0	0	0	10
Panama	—	—	—	—	—	—	—	—	—	0	0	0	1	1	0	0	1	3
Paraguay	0	0	0	0	0	1	2	2	1	4	3	2	3	4	1	0	0	23
Peru	—	2	2	1	1	3	2	3	2	1	2	0	3	0	0	2	1	25
Uruguay	—	—	1	0	1	2	1	1	0	0	0	0	0	0	0	0	1	7
Venezuela	—	—	0	0	0	0	1	1	3	1	0	0	0	2	1	0	0	9
Total by Span. Amer.	1	6	8	11	17	27	24	17	18	16	15	17	25	21	12	17	18	
Decade All	1	6	9	19	18	29	26	20	20	18	22	17	26	23	17	19	18	
Countries w/o coups	3	6	11	10	5	6	4	5	5	11	12	11	7	7	10	10	11	
	4	10	17	18	18	18	18	18	18	20	20	20	20	20	20	20	20	

Sources: 1815–1966 data from Arthur S. Banks, *Cross-Polity Time-Series Data*, Segment I, Field e, "Number of Coups d'etat", defined as "the number of successful extra constitutional or forced changes in the top government elite and/or its effective control of the nation's power structure in a given year." 1966–1979 data from newspaper accounts and various country studies.

The number of coups declines only modestly from the 1880s onward, but there is a bit larger decline in the number of new constitutions and a substantial decrease in the number of changes of executive from the 1870s through 1909. The overall index actually increased slightly in the second and third decades of the twentieth century, almost entirely because of a quickening pace of executive turnover. This may be a reflection of the political systems' initial responses to more rapid social and economic change (see Figure 1).

The combined index shows steadily declining levels of authoritarianism throughout the 1870–1929 period, with the sharpest decreases recorded for years of military rule (from 24 in the 1870s to a low of 7 in the 1900–1909 decade), followed by years of nonconstitutional government (53 in the 1870s to 17 in the 1920s) and years of weak or absent legislature (103 years in

FIGURE 1

Levels of Instability in Spanish America by Decade, 1810–1979.

Average Level of Instability per Country
(number of changes)

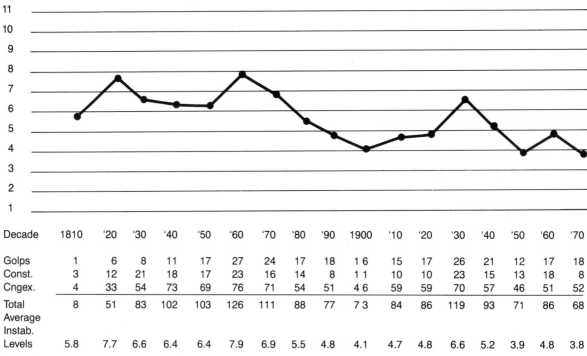

Decade	1810	'20	'30	'40	'50	'60	'70	'80	'90	1900	'10	'20	'30	'40	'50	'60	'70
Golps	1	6	8	11	17	27	24	17	18	1 6	15	17	26	21	12	17	18
Const.	3	12	21	18	17	23	16	14	8	1 1	10	10	23	15	13	18	8
Cngex.	4	33	54	73	69	76	71	54	51	4 6	59	59	70	57	46	51	52
Total	8	51	83	102	103	126	111	88	77	7 3	84	86	119	93	71	86	68
Average Instab. Levels	5.8	7.7	6.6	6.4	6.4	7.9	6.9	5.5	4.8	4.1	4.7	4.8	6.6	5.2	3.9	4.8	3.8

Source: Arthur S. Banks, *Cross Polity Time Series Data*, Segment 1, Fields E, F, and N, supplemented by *Statesman's Yearbook* and the American University, *Area Handbook* series, for missing data in Banks. This figure originally appeared in David Scott Palmer, *Peru: The Authoritarian Tradition*, 21.

Note: Instability level is measured by the number of coups (golpes), the number of times basic changes are made in the country's constitution (const.), and the number of times a change of executive independent of his predecessor occurs (cngex.); 1810–39 data are adjusted by a correction factor to account for countries' becoming independent in the middle of given decades. For the 1810s the factor is 2.4, for the 1820s and 1830s, 1.2.

the 1870s to 67 years in the 1910–1919 decade). While the number of golpes declined less rapidly, the sharp decrease in years of military rule during the 1880–1909 period suggests that these interventions were increasingly of the veto variety. That is, they were short-term in nature and designed to protect the interests of already established civilian groups or to correct modest aberrations. The sharp decline in years of military rule coincided with the period during which foreign military missions were introduced on a substantial scale for the first time (See Figure 2).[9]

Significant developments during this period allowed a number of governments to become more stable and less authoritarian. One factor

FIGURE 2

Levels of Authoritarianism in Spanish America by Decade, 1810–1979.

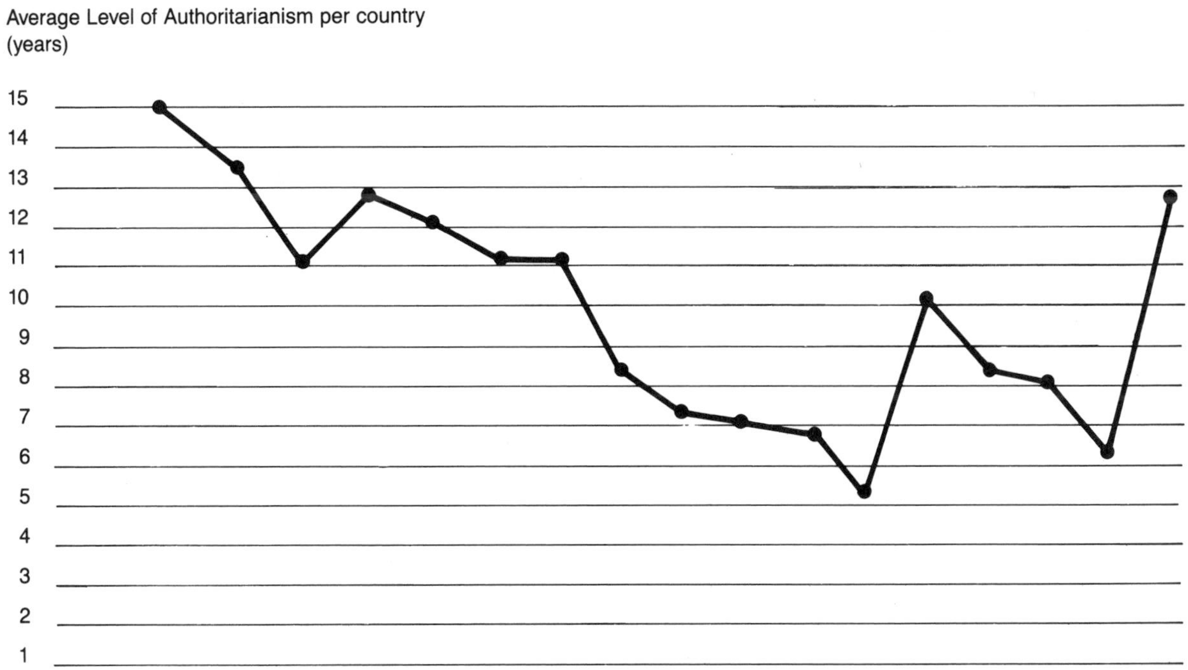

Average Level of Authoritarianism per country
(years)

Decade	1810	'20	'30	'40	'50	'60	'70	'80	'90	1900	'10	'20	'30	'40	'50	'60	'70
NONEL	11	38	49	77	66	57	53	36	23	29	34	17	41	42	40	36	73
MILRL	2	6	0	1	1	21	24	8	4	7	21	11	31	30	32	23	73
NOLEG	12	46	80	127	128	101	103	91	86	92	67	69	114	81	74	55	85
Total	25	90	129	205	195	179	180	135	113	128	122	97	186	153	145	114	230
Ave. auth. Levels	15	13.5	11.1	12.8	12.2	11.2	11.2	8.4	7.4	7.1	6.8	5.4	10.3	8.5	8.1	6.3	12.8

Source: Arthur S. Banks, *Cross-Polity Time Series Data*, Segment 1, Fields D, E, O, supplemented by *Statesman's Yearbook* and the American University, *Area Handbook* series, for missing data in Banks. This figure originally appeared in David Scott Palmer, *Peru: The Authoritarian Tradition*, 22.

Note: Authoritarianism is measured by the number of years of nonconstitutional government (NONEL), military rule (MILRL), and weak or absent legislature (NOLEG). Highest possible score per decade is 30; 1810–39 data are adjusted by a correction factor to account for countries becoming independent in the middle of given decades. For 1810s factor is 2.4, for 1820s and 1830s, 1.2.

was the rapid economic growth for most countries because of growing foreign trade, investment, and loans. Over a thirty- to forty-year period a dramatic number of new opportunities in the modern economy were created, first in the private and then in the public sector.

The presence of new opportunities and new resources contributed to the complex processes of social mobilization, by which more and more individuals began to give up traditional occupations, rural residence, and older life-styles by incorporating themselves into the modern sector. Indicators of urbanization, voting levels, literacy and education levels, as well as communication networks, suggested how quickly this process was occurring. Countries with the largest number of coups during the period tended to have political organizations that lagged behind social mobilization. But declining levels of instability and authoritarianism for the region as a whole during this period indicates that the majority of countries were increasingly able to keep these concerns in balance.

One of the most important areas of political organization was the establishment of civilian political parties. Conservative and liberal parties were well established by the 1870s; radical parties representing the interests of the growing middle class were also being organized in the last decades of the nineteenth and the first decades of the twentieth centuries. By the 1920s, both labor unions and Socialist parties were established as reflections of the growing differentiation of many Latin American societies in response to outside economic infusions to include both mining and urban working-class elements. Along with the growing institutionalization of civilian control and liberal principles was a growing emphasis on the need for professional armed forces. Foreign military missions were invited and national military academies were established. Gradually the standards of discipline, order, and self-sacrifice in the interest of the nation were inculcated into the officer corps, along with a sense of competence and capacity. Thus military establishments developed a

greater sense of mission and corporate identity as they became more institutionalized. The military's experiences paralleled somewhat the growing organization, capacity, and sheer numbers of civilian political institutions. In the short run (between 1880 and 1910), the introduction of foreign training was associated with a sharp decline in military rule.

However, growing professionalization did not necessarily mean a growing willingness to abstain from political activity over the long term. "The overriding impact of fifty years of European military training or orientation on Latin American armies was to stimulate rather than lessen political interest and to motivate elitist professional army officers to assume responsibility for the conduct of national affairs."[10] Nevertheless, up until 1930 at least, as long as civilians seemed to be able to manage their political affairs and did not infringe upon the military's own corporate interests, it was usually willing to stand on the political sidelines, or to intervene only briefly in correction of temporary maladjustments within governing elites. When civilians faltered, though, the army had come to feel sufficiently trained and upgraded to take on the responsibilities of political office. Among the larger countries, direct intervention by this "new" military first occurred in Chile in the 1920s, and in Brazil, Argentina, and Peru in 1930. One legacy of more professional and better-trained armed forces, then, was an increase in both their awareness of political issues and their perceived capacity to intervene when necessary.

From Short-Term to Long-Term Military Rule

During the time from 1930 to the present, an increasingly professional military continued to intervene, often in the midst of social, economic, or political turmoil. In the 1930s and 1940s, the army often served as the crucial ally or willing subordinate of civilian leaders. It intervened either as part of a progressive "New Deal" middle-class opening to an expanded democracy, or as part of a conservative or populist corporatist movement to contain working-class elements.[11] The military lent itself to civilian coalitions or to charismatic individuals of left or right during this period, rather than governing directly. In the 1960s and 1970s, however, the military tended to intervene as an autonomous political actor with its own agenda, which normally excluded civilian political parties and incorporated civilians only as individuals and only on the military's terms. This marked a historic departure. The armed forces entered politics as an institution entitled to rule for an indefinite period. Thus they ushered in the era of long-term military rule. Its political orientation — whether reformist or reactive — depended on particular economic conditions, on social mobilization levels and rates of change in the wider society, and on the specific circumstances leading to the golpe in the first place.

During the 1930s and 1940s, the same factors that had strengthened and legitimated one form or another of liberal democracy now undermined it. The economic prosperity that had benefited both public and private sectors was based on foreign investment, foreign trade, and foreign loans. Therefore, most governments did not control the wellsprings of their own economic destiny. With the Great Depression of the 1930s, both investment and trade dried up. Thus governments were deprived of resources they had come to count on, forcing sharp reductions in services and general defaulting on loans. Unemployment spiraled, social protest increased dramatically, and many established governments rapidly lost their claim to loyalty from the governed. Increasing social mobilization and organizational differentiation, which the economic prosperity and political competition of the liberal state had stimulated, now served as corrosive forces. Military establishments, themselves beneficiaries of systems that had encouraged their growing professionalization, saw intervention as the only way to control the increasing turmoil. Thus, to a large degree, the liberal state was a victim of its own success.

Only a few countries survived the period without military intervention. After Mexico passed through the violence and social chaos of its revolution, it put together—with strong guidance—a one-party grand coalition of the major power contenders (labor, peasantry, middle classes, and military) under a strong executive. The result was a unique synthesis of the traditional and the modern, drawn from Mexican historical experience. This solution has endured under civilian control to the present, with only minor modifications.

Venezuela remained under personalist dictatorships but gradually opened up its political system to new interests. The Venezuelan government had the decided advantage, thanks to its oil resource, of being the only one in Latin America whose revenues actually increased during the depression years of the 1930s. Colombia had a well-established two-party system along with multiple economic centers scattered over a crazy-quilt geography, a rather small central government (in terms of revenue per capita), and one of the lowest levels of economic dependency in Latin America during the 1920s.[12] Haiti and Honduras suffered from extensive United States intervention, while Uruguay maintained high government revenues with only modest fluctuations in its well-established two-party system. Costa Rica's government revenues declined by about 40 percent during the 1930s. (This reduction was less than that affecting most countries.) For the first time in over thirty years, the majority of Latin American countries experienced golpes in the 1930s. Instability and authoritarianism increased to levels not experienced in the region as a whole since the 1870s. As a result, civilian government constantly had to look over its shoulder at possibly adverse military reactions, adjusting its policy to keep the military and its allies from intervening. This was particularly true when such governments tried to deal with the economic crisis of the 1930s or the social demands of the 1940s. In most cases, then, the result was "reigning" rather than "ruling" coalitions, in which civilian governments moderated their policies in order to stay in power, and military establishments cast a veto by way of coup when they thought the civilians were straying beyond the status quo.[13] Such coalitions, whether civilian or military, actually increased tension as well as the likelihood of still further military interventions by postponing difficult choices.

Even so, from the 1940s into the 1960s, authoritarianism and instability in the region declined. This coincided with the period of sharply expanded United States presence, both military and civilian, and with the Allied victory in World War II. It was also a period of expanding foreign investment, growing world markets, and relatively favorable international prices for goods that Latin America sold abroad. Domestic industrialization ("import substitution") policies of the 1930s were also important. Middle-class reformist parties came to power in a number of countries (e.g., Guatemala, Peru, Venezuela, Costa Rica, Bolivia), often with military support—and endured in some of them (e.g., Costa Rica after 1948, Venezuela after 1958, and Bolivia from 1952 to 1964). By 1962 some authors could write that a kind of "New Deal" middle-class democracy was taking hold in Latin America, and that the end of military regimes was at hand.[14]

During this period, however, the very forces that worked against authoritarianism and instability also helped to incorporate new elements of the population into a national system. Urbanization increased by 40.2 percent between 1930 and 1950, and by 54.4 percent between 1950 and 1970. From 1940 to 1960, school enrollments grew on the average by over 63 percent for the region as a whole.[15] The participation of larger and larger segments of the national populations in national economic, social, and political systems meant that new demands were made on governments. Because most of them were run by "reigning" coalitions, it was difficult for many of them to respond effectively. Furthermore, because many of the political parties and unions were relatively new and incompletely institutionalized, many of their demands were

presented in chaotic or irresponsible ways. All of this eroded the tenuous legitimacy enjoyed by the new civilian order of the 1940s and 1950s.

During this same period most Latin American military institutions became more professionalized through better training, fostered both by United States military missions and by the upgrading and expansion of domestic military educational facilities. A number of countries developed specialized facilities to train the most promising officers. The Superior War College (ESG) in Brazil, or the Center for Higher Military Studies (CAEM) in Peru are good examples. These military schools emphasized a broadened definition of national security as national economic, social, and political development. The traditional concern for boundary defense and preparation against potential foreign aggressors was no longer the primary concern. Civic action programs and counterinsurgency training responded to a growing perception that threats to the nation could come from within as well as from without. The Cuban Revolution of 1959 and Cuba's efforts in the early 1960s to export its revolution to other Latin American countries by internal subversion led several military establishments to suppress dissidents. This was particularly the case in Venezuela between 1962 and 1966, in Guatemala after 1960, in Colombia from the mid-1950s, in Peru in 1965, in Bolivia in 1967, in Brazil from 1969 to 1972, in Uruguay from 1965 to 1973, and in Argentina from 1972 through 1977.

Growing military professionalism, specialized training, a redefinition of national security to encompass national development, greater exposure to domestic problems, and counterinsurgency operations gave most Latin American armed forces the capacity to operate more effectively, both in traditional military roles and as political actors. When civilian governments ran into difficulties, the military often felt itself uniquely qualified to take over. Besides the historical tradition of military involvement in politics in times of crisis, the armed forces could now argue that national security was at stake.

This interaction of social and intramilitary forces resulted in a reintroduction of the military into politics by the golpe de estado and its indefinite tenure of power. This new phenomenon of long-term military government occurred in the major countries of Latin America between 1964 and 1976.* Some countries (like Haiti and Paraguay) remained under traditional personalist dictatorships; others — like Mexico, Colombia, Costa Rica, and Venezuela — retained civilian single- or multiparty democracies, but the main trend was back to indefinite military rule. Authoritarianism in the 1970s reached levels equaling the historic highs of the 1840s, but it was of a very different nature and had very different causes.

The "new" military regimes of this period were both reformist and reactionary, depending largely on the circumstances that brought them to power.[16] In the cases of Uruguay, Chile, and Argentina (1976) the polarization of political forces and open guerrilla warfare led army leaders to believe that the salvation of order demanded their action. Once in power, their policies were repressive and directed toward the recreation of a liberal economic order within a conservative political framework. The Brazilian case was special. The takeover in 1964 was provoked by actions of a progressive president who tried to open up the system along socialistic lines but did not really threaten the social order. The real threat came only after the military was in power, in the form of simultaneous rural and urban guerrilla activities between 1969 and 1972. The Brazilian military, once in power, supported economic growth under close state supervision, but also a degree of repression unusual in Brazilian political history. However, the military harbored a long-term commitment to organize a new political order that civilians would eventually control.

The cases of Peru, Panama, Ecuador, and Honduras represented not only the new phe-

nomenon of long-term military rule, but also a commitment to reform the social, political, and economic structures rather than to restore them.[17] The commitment to reform was born from two factors: security doctrines that emphasized development as the best defense, and takeover circumstances that did not include profound social turmoil. In Peru, the precipitating factors for the 1968 golpe included allegations of economic mismanagement amidst growing inflation and debt, corruption scandals, and a botched initiative on foreign company nationalization. For the other reformist military governments, events precipitating the takeovers were either the election of candidates unacceptable to them (Panama), scandals involving high government officials (Honduras), or the actions of a populist but somewhat irresponsible president, with prospects for revenues from new oil exports imminent (Ecuador). Absence of an immediate threat to national security in these four countries gave the military a certain amount of political space within which to try out its reformist programs. With the exception of Panama, they were countries with relatively low levels and rates of social mobilization compared to others in the region.

Each of the reformist governments succeeded in expanding the purview of government, in establishing modest agrarian reforms with cooperatives as a core unit of social and economic organization, and in pursuing somewhat more active foreign policies, often oriented toward objectives of the Third World. The governments were authoritarian, but repression was moderate: Political parties were excluded from power but were not banned, and union organizations actually expanded. The Peruvian case was clearly the most ambitious of all and the most far-reaching in its effects. Nationalization of foreign enterprises and expanded state programs almost doubled the size of the government bureaucracy and dramatically increased its scope. A large-scale agrarian reform turned land over to more than three hundred thousand farm families, mostly in cooperatives. Industrial reforms led to the application of self-management

*Brazil (1964–1985), Argentina (1966–1973 and 1976–1983), Peru (1968–1980), Panama (1968–1978), Ecuador (1972–1979), Honduras (1972–1982), Uruguay (1973–1985) and Chile (1973–).

principles to most larger enterprises, with workers sharing in profits and ownership in some thirty-five hundred establishments. During the period of military rule, Peru became a leader of the Third World movement, hosting major conferences, extending full diplomatic and trade relations to the Socialist bloc, and entering into a major military assistance relationship with the Soviet Union. Economic growth rates were quite high through 1976, though with a tendency to inflation and deficit financing through short-term foreign loans; similar patterns prevailed in the other reformist military regimes.

On balance, these leaders accomplished much less than their rhetoric suggested they wanted to. This resulted from several factors. Once power had been consolidated, internal divisions quickly surfaced. The consensus on the need to take over or the need to accomplish national security objectives broke down on the specifics. Only in Peru up through 1973 and in Panama until 1977 were the key leaders (Gen. Juan Velasco Alvarado of Peru and Col. Omar Torrijos of Panama) strong enough to forge agreement within the military on the specifics of reform. In both Ecuador and Honduras, intra-military squabbling immobilized most reform policies at an early stage.

A second factor was the problem of implementation. The officer corps, however well-prepared professionally for the tasks of ruling, was not large enough to run the government itself. It depended on a civilian bureaucracy and on civilian cadres to carry out its initiatives. Although the military could decree the changes it desired, implementation was frequently another matter. The results often had the appearance without the substance of change—much to the frustration of the leaders.

A third factor included international and environmental constraints. Bad weather reduced crop production, oil discoveries and revenues did not match expectations, market prices for exports were erratic and for energy imports steeply increased, key leaders became ill, or United States policy concerns conflicted with reformist objectives (e.g., nationalizations, the Panama Canal treaties).

These considerations limited the ability of the military to accomplish its objectives and simultaneously gave it a new appreciation for the difficulties of actually carrying out policy when it stayed in power long enough to do so. Civilian political actors, in turn, were chastened by the long hiatus in their access to power; but given the nonrepressive nature of the military regimes, political parties had not been dismantled. The result was both a ready alternative for rule when the military decided it had enough and an increased willingness by both sides to restore the status quo ante expeditiously and fully. Where the military had tried to carry out reform under long-term institutionalized rule, then, civilian actors regained power through the electoral process (Panama, 1978–1984; Ecuador, 1979; Peru, 1980; Honduras, 1982). Furthermore, the threshold for intervention in the future has probably been substantially raised even though the cycle of military intervention may not have been broken.

Even though reactionary military governments pursued quite different policies once in power, the results appear similar to those of the reformist regimes. Despite severe restrictions on key political actors and the banning of normal political activity, civilian political organizations did not lose their capacity to serve as interest aggregators and interest articulators and seem capable of returning to power when the system once again opens up. This is particularly evident in Argentina, where one of the most open elections in that country's history restored a civilian government in 1983 after a very repressive military regime. In this case the armed forces lost considerable prestige by their growing ineffectiveness and by their humiliating loss in the 1982 Malvinas/Falkland Islands War. In Uruguay, political parties returned to power as well in 1984, though in somewhat less dramatic fashion than in Argentina. In Chile a similar erosion of legitimacy for a repressive military government amidst the demonstrable resiliency of civilian political actors is also taking place. The military government of Brazil completed the electoral process that fully turned over power to civilians in 1985.

It is unlikely that the cycle of military intervention is over in Latin America. Nevertheless, the recent experience of long-term military rule has made both sides more aware of how hard it is to govern — and more likely to collaborate rather than confront each other in the future. Golpes can be expected in countries that lack stable civilian political institutions and have yet to experience long-term military rule, and in others when matters are sufficiently grave to suggest a possible collapse of the system. It seems likely that for the balance of the twentieth century the trend in Latin America will be toward less authoritarianism and instability. There are likely to be fewer overt military regimes along with more accommodations among military and civilian political actors over who should govern and how. The danger of reigning (rather than ruling) coalitions will continue — but so will a greater appreciation of the adverse consequences of inappropriate policy responses to the needs of an increasingly aware populace.

■ Notes

1. See J. Lloyd Mecham, *The United States and Inter-American Security* (Austin: University of Texas Press, 1961) 154–50, for discussion of this and other disputes.
2. Frederick M. Nunn, "Effects of European Military Training in Latin America," 1–7.
3. NACLA, "U.S. Training Programs for Foreign Military Personnel," 30–31.
4. Frederick M. Nunn, "Professional Militarism," 406, and John Samuel Fitch, "The Political Consequences of U.S. Military Assistance."
5. ACDA, *World Military Expenditures*, Table I, 33–36.
6. See discussion of the antipolitics of nineteenth century Latin America based on the colonial tradition in Brian Loveman and Thomas Davies, *The Politics of Antipolitics*, 5–6.
7. David Scott Palmer, "The Politics of Authoritarianism in Spanish America"; idem, *Peru: The Authoritarian Tradition*, Table 3.2, 29; for a slightly different approach, see Warren Dean, "Latin American Golpes and Economic Fluctuations"; Loveman and Davies, op. cit., 5.
8. See the useful summary of the theories of military intervention presented by Donald L. Horowitz, *Coup Theories and Officers' Motives*, 3–15. Lyle McAlister, et al., *The Military in Latin America*, 3.
9. This information is intended to be suggestive rather than definitive, not only because of a decline of golpes could simply mean that an individual tyrant clings to office longer, but also because both the decade division is arbitrary and the designation of key political characteristics may hide other significant developments in individual countries. But taken together, it does give a sense of "big picture" developments. See Palmer, *Peru*, for an elaboration of these themes, both for the region as a whole and for Peru as a case study.
10. Nunn, "Effects of European Military Training," 1.
11. Martin Needler, *Political Development in Latin America*, especially Chapter 4.
12. Palmer, *Peru*, Tables 5.1, 5.2, and 5.3, pages 69, 72–73, and 75.
13. Eldon G. Kenworthy, "Coalitions in the Political Development of Latin America." Also see Needler, op. cit., for a different definition of reform and his conclusion that 29 percent of the 56 coups during the period were of a reformist nature.
14. For example, Edwin Lieuwen, *Arms and Politics in Latin America*.
15. Palmer, *Peru*, Table 5.4, 77, and Table 5.5, 78. Urban figures are calculated as the percentage of the total population in cities of more than twenty thousand.
16. See the articles in Robert Wesson, ed., *New Military Politics in Latin America*.
17. David Scott Palmer, "Reformist Military Rule in Latin America," in Wesson, op. cit., 131–49.

■ Suggested Readings

Einaudi, Luigi, and Alfred C. Stepan. *Latin American Institutional Development: Changing Military Perspectives in Peru and Brazil.* Santa Monica: Rand Corporation, April 1971, R-586-DOS.

Horowitz, Donald L. *Coup Theories and Officers'*

Motives. Princeton: Princeton University Press, 1980.

Johnson, John J. *The Military and Society in Latin America.* Stanford: Stanford University Press, 1964.

Lieuwen, Edwin. *Arms and Politics in Latin America.* New York: Praeger, 1961.

Loveman, Brian, and Thomas M. Davis, Jr., eds. *The Politics of Antipolitics: The Military in Latin America.* Lincoln: University of Nebraska Press, 1978.

McAlister, Lyle, et al. *The Military in Latin American Sociopolitical Evolution: Four Case Studies.* Washington, D.C.: Center for Research in Social Systems, 1970.

J. Lloyd Mecham. *The United States and Inter-American Security, 1889–1960.* Austin: University of Texas Press, 1961.

Needler, Martin C. *Political Development in Latin America: Instability, Violence, and Evolutionary Change.* New York: Random House, 1968.

North, Liisa. *Civil-Military Relations in Argentina, Chile, and Peru.* Politics of Modernization Series #2 (Institute of International Studies, University of California, Berkeley, 1966).

Palmer, David Scott. "The Politics of Authoritarianism in Spanish America," in *Authoritarianism and Corporatism in Latin America,* ed. James M. Malloy. Pittsburgh: University of Pittsburgh Press, 1977, 377–412.

———. *Peru: The Authoritarian Tradition.* New York: Praeger, 1980.

Wesson, Robert, ed. *New Military Politics in Latin America.* Politics in Latin America, A Hoover Institution Series. New York: Praeger, 1982.

Wiarda, Howard J. *Critical Elections and Critical Coups: State, Society and the Military in the Processes of Latin American Development.* Athens: Ohio University Center for International Studies, Latin America Program, 1979.

18 | *Latin America in the World*

JACK W. HOPKINS

The preceding chapters have explored a wide variety of the different dimensions that constitute the complex mosaic of Latin American life and civilization. A richly diverse region, Latin America does not lend itself easily to facile generalizations and stereotypes, although frequently it is reduced to such terms. A principal purpose of the chapters to this point has been to sensitize the reader to the complexity of Latin America so that its role in the contemporary world can be appreciated more fully.

In any event, however, one must recognize that generalizations about Latin America's role in the world have to be tempered by an understanding of the separateness of the region's components. Rarely, if ever, have its nations acted or spoken in unison on any really critical issue. This is the case even in the Organization of American States, where the United States has been so powerful as to be described as "the majority of one."[1] For myriad reasons the divergent national interests of the region's countries have prevented a consensus on many substantive matters. Even when potentially unifying situations arise, such as the 1982 Falklands/Malvinas war between Argentina and Great Britain,

a variety of crosscutting interests and pressures make a unified posture for the Latin American countries very difficult and unlikely. However, there is at least a high degree of theoretical consensus on broader questions.

As Davis and Wilson point out, the states of Latin America have arrived at similar positions on a surprisingly large number of issues.[2] These common policies include commitment to the prohibition of intervention by one country in the affairs of another, arbitration and peaceful settlement of international disputes, the granting of asylum to political refugees (although this policy has been restricted severely with the rise of authoritarian governments in the region), hemispheric defense under the Rio Treaty, and the claim to the two-hundred-mile offshore limit. There is no Latin American "bloc" in these policy areas, but the tendency toward unanimity is strong. This must be qualified, however, because most of the principles and policies are subject to definition and differing emphases in individual cases. Despite the tendency toward consistency on these policy areas, in practice particular national interests often lead to departures from a consistent policy.

■ Influences on Latin America's World Role

Several factors, if not determinants of Latin America's role in the world, have at least conditioned its relations with the rest of the world. Although the precise impact of these factors cannot be measured with precision, one could safely assume their influence is strong.

First, Latin America began its international relations as part of two colonial empires. Although colonial status is hardly a unique condition, the longevity of the Spanish and Portuguese empires in America (from approximately 1500 to about 1825) was such that enduring patterns of behavior were set. In many respects the colonies were controlled and administered in a classically mercantilist fashion. As a result, Latin America in general began its international experience ill equipped to stand alone in such relationships. No substantial infrastructure or production capacity existed apart from residues of the colonial apparatus. When that apparatus disappeared (mostly by 1825), there followed a long period of struggle for control by competing personalistic leaders or oligarchies in most countries. The result was an unsettled, frequently chaotic condition in much of Latin America after independence, and the failure of nation-states to emerge throughout much of the region. The colonial legacy was in large part one of inept governments, widespread corruption, anarchy, and warring factions. It is not surprising that Domingo Faustino Sarmiento wrote of the barbarism of the period or that Simón Bolívar lamented that Latin America was ungovernable. In frustration the Great Liberator exclaimed, "From one end to the other, the New World seems an abyss of abomination. . . . There is no good faith in America nor among the nations of America. Treaties are scraps of paper; constitutions, printed matter; elections, battles; freedom, anarchy; and life, a torment."[3] Such problems were aggravated by the generally low level of education and the unassimilated indigenous population throughout most of the region. Both problems have continued to plague much of Latin America to the present day. In spite of substantial progress in raising the level of education and despite the significant racial mixture that has occurred, a high illiteracy rate persists in many countries, and where large Indian populations exist they are largely unintegrated. The resulting dualism in the social structure of many countries inevitably weakens them in their international posture.

The protracted colonial experience, in summary, provided an inadequate foundation for eventually autonomous states in the international arena, established patterns of social relations that weakened the unity of Latin American societies, created economic systems that fostered continuing dependency, and encouraged attitudes toward government legitimacy that undermined stability and made orderly transfers of power difficult.

Second, Latin America achieved independence only in a political sense. The mercantilist colonial system had siphoned the wealth of Latin America, largely in the form of gold and silver, for the benefit of the parent countries. The outlook of most of Latin America was conditioned by the prevailing narrow conception of development that saw colonies as providers of wealth to benefit the imperial powers. It was an easy transition from colonial mercantilism to export dependency. After achieving political independence, the new states came to be simply providers of primary materials for consumption or processing in the more developed countries. Export dependency contained the seeds for many continuing problems.

The region's dependence on exports of a few primary commodities (mainly minerals for processing abroad) led to a variety of pernicious effects. Pressure for production of export crops (chiefly coffee, sugar, cotton, and bananas) encouraged the use of prime agricultural land for that purpose. In turn, such land use, highly profitable and attractive as a means of earning foreign exchange, discouraged the development of agriculture for domestic consumption, much of which would have been carried out by small landholders. Thus the land tenure problem was worsened, and the seeds of later discontent and agitation for land reform were sown.

An accompanying feature was the intrusion of foreign corporations, which became major landowners in many countries and encouraged the production of export crops to the detriment of domestic consumption. Similar effects followed from ownership of much of the mineral wealth by foreign companies. Almost invariably, their investments were for extraction only, with most of the processing and manufacture occurring in the home country, so that the multiplier effect from economic development and the infrastructure that would normally follow such extraction rarely occurred.

These features, combined with Latin America's inheritance of an almost feudal economic system, produced a serious inequity in the ownership of land, degrading income levels for most of the people and resulting in low educational levels, widespread disease, and malnutrition. All in all, the system provided a very weak base for effective participation in the world community, particularly because the critical relations were with far more fully developed countries in the industrialized West.

> All these domestic problems reinforce the tendency of Latin America to remain subject to the influence or control of outside powers and vagaries of the world markets. In many respects, Latin America is a giant without power, torn by its own internal weaknesses. These weaknesses contribute to the vulnerability of the countries of Latin America to penetration by outside powers.[4]

Likewise, the export orientation of many Latin American countries subjected them to overreliance and dependence upon often fickle world markets and their unstable price system. Boom-and-bust cycles often depended on the price and market trends for various commodities, both agricultural and mineral. Even moderate price fluctuations can have disastrous effects. With good reason Latin American countries complained that they were forced to compete at a great disadvantage with the industrialized world, whose manufactures rose in price far faster than did primary commodities.

Third, and following largely from the first two factors, Latin America has been linked closely with external powers (foreign states primarily but also transnational or multinational corporations). The region's economy has been penetrated generally and pervasively by such external agents. Rawle Farley describes the situation as "regionally and technologically dualistic. They are largely enclave economies, peripherally dependent on the highly industrialized countries to which their economic activity is linked." Carlos Astiz calls the political systems of Latin America "penetrated systems."[5] Their freedom in international politics is restricted as a result.

Finally, inter-American affairs have dominated the foreign policies of most Latin American states since the immediate postindependence period. Obviously, Latin America's interests concern far more than its relations with the United States, but this dimension has been a consuming preoccupation. Indeed, much of the history of Latin American foreign relations has been a constant attempt to assert independence from the United States.

The disproportionate power of the United States has affected virtually every aspect of international relations south of the Rio Grande. Gordon Connell-Smith describes the situation as a conflict between "the one and the twenty."[6] For better or worse, Latin America has had to adapt itself to being within the sphere of influence of the United States. The great disparities in wealth, standard of living, and military power have made the coexistence frequently uncomfortable, and conflicts of interest have been a constant.

Simón Bolívar once observed that the "United States appear to be destined by Providence to plague Latin America with misery in the name of liberty."[7] United States pronouncements regarding the Western Hemisphere and United States relations with Latin America have typically been cast as if they were in the interest of Latin America. There are exceptions to this observation, of course, as seen in the bullying attitude of President Theodore Roosevelt and the self-righteousness of Woodrow Wilson toward Mexico. But generally, from the initial declaration of the Monroe Doctrine in December 1823 through the Caribbean Basin Initiative of President Ronald Reagan in 1983, United States hegemony has been justified on the basis of its benefits to Latin America.

■ The Monroe Doctrine and United States Hegemony

Initially, the Monroe Doctrine was justified as a necessity to protect the independence of both the young United States and the newly liberated countries to its south. In effect, the doctrine put Latin America off-limits for European colonization. There were certain clear advantages for Latin America in the doctrine's umbrella, although it can be argued that its effectiveness at first depended more on the strength of the British fleet than the power of the United States. In any case the original pronouncement and its corollaries, including the "no-transfer" resolution of 15 January 1811 and the Polk Corollary of 1845, in effect delineated a sphere of influence for the United States. The no-transfer resolution was intended to prevent transfers of territory in the Western Hemisphere from one foreign power to another; the Polk Corollary extended that concept to include even voluntary cession of territory by Western Hemisphere countries to European states.

In one sense the effect of the Monroe Doctrine, along with its corollaries and interpretations of it by different presidents of the United States, was to create a kind of security dependence for Latin America. Most of the Latin American states, at least tacitly and often explicitly, relied on the United States for hemispheric security, although it was not always clear where the threat lay. However, the price of re-

liance was limits on the freedom to act unilaterally, and the paternalistic attitude of the United States often rankled.

At its worst the Monroe Doctrine served as a pretext for both direct and indirect intervention in the affairs of several Latin American states. United States hegemony in the Western Hemisphere has been characterized by territorial seizures, extended occupations, and many instances of indirect and covert actions to achieve foreign policy objectives.[8] Although the record improved somewhat after the enunciation of the Good Neighbor Policy by President Franklin D. Roosevelt, in recent years the United States has resumed a policy of direct and indirect intervention. The record includes United States assistance in the overthrow of the Jacobo Arbenz government in Guatemala (1954); the attempted invasion of Cuba at the Bay of Pigs (1961) as well as continual harassment and economic embargo of Cuba; intervention in the Dominican Republic (1965, although the action was later "legitimized" by creation of the Inter-American Peace Force); covert action against the government of Salvador Allende in Chile (1973); and armed intervention in Grenada (1983); along with major United States involvement in the Central American conflicts since 1980, including covert and overt assistance to anti-Sandinista forces trying to destabilize the government of Nicaragua.

■ Latin America and Inter-American Organizations

The Organization of American States, which in 1948 succeeded the Pan American Union (created in 1889), represents the major organizational expression of the Pan-American vision. The Latin American countries, in seeking a union of the Western Hemisphere states, sought primarily a mechanism for dealing with political and security questions. However, the early history of the Pan American Union reveals a fairly consistent United States antipathy to the concept of collective security. Part of the slowness in facing that fact derived from the expectation of some Latin American leaders that the PAU would provide protection for their states *against* the United States, an unlikely posture for the latter to support. United States domination of the organization was apparent.

Despite United States resistance to involvement by the Pan American Union with security questions, the organization was able to function reasonably effectively in specialized areas such as health, commercial agreements, communications, and similar problems. So long as sensitive questions involving national interests and the political role of the United States in the region were avoided, the Pan American Union could often reach satisfactory agreement.

The League of Nations, looked to by the Latin American states for protection against the United States, in practice provided no such shield. Indeed, Article 21 of the Covenant of the League of Nations specifically referred to the Monroe Doctrine as a valid international understanding, although the Latin American states had long since forgotten any interest in internationalizing the doctrine. In ratifying the covenant, most of them entered reservations about the reference to the Monroe Doctrine in Article 21.

Only after the enunciation of the Good Neighbor Policy by President Franklin D. Roosevelt did significant change occur in the Pan American Union. At the Seventh Pan American Conference in Montevideo in 1933, the organization finally adopted the Convention on Rights and Duties of the States, which provided that "no state has the right to interfere in the internal or external affairs of other states." United States agreement to that convention represented a substantial change of policy although, as Alonso Aguilar observes, the Good Neighbor Policy was neither the end of United States imperialism nor just an empty phrase.[9] There was a gradual shift in the United States position on security, brought on in large part by the threat of war in Europe and Asia. In-

creasingly, the United States emphasized "joint action" for dealing with continental security questions. As war became imminent, that approach became more obvious, especially at the consultative meetings in Lima (1938), Panama (1939), and then at Havana and Rio de Janeiro during the war. Nevertheless, the Latin Americans were always cautious about surrendering too much of their autonomy in the interest of continental solidarity and security.

The first real collective security system in the Americas was established by the Inter-American Treaty of Reciprocal Assistance (the Rio Treaty), signed at the Rio Conference of 1947. The Rio Treaty represented a very significant change in the traditional insistence of the Latin American states on national sovereignty. Article 3 provides that

> an armed attack by any State against an American State shall be considered as an attack against all the American States, and, consequently, each one of the said Contracting Parties undertakes to assist in meeting the attack. . . .

However, the legitimate concern of many Latin American leaders was that Article 3 could involve their countries in United States conflicts unrelated to the security interests of Latin America. A practical effect of the Rio Treaty was essentially to multilateralize the Monroe Doctrine and make responses to hemispheric threats a matter for joint action. Nevertheless, it would become obvious in time that the treaty left each state wide discretion in judgments regarding threats and the nature of the assistance to be provided. The South Atlantic war of 1982 is a case in point. In that crisis most Latin American states argued that the British action against Argentina was an attack covered by Article 3, and they called for the United States to come to the aid of Argentina. Obviously, the United States interpretation was different, so no action was taken.

The Rio Treaty laid the base for a major reorganization of the inter-American system. The

Organization of American States was created at Bogotá in 1948. Its charter (in Article 15) emphasizes the principle of nonintervention, which had long been championed by the Latin American states.

> No State or group of States has the right to intervene, directly or indirectly, for any reason whatever, in the internal or external affairs of any other State. The foregoing principle prohibits not only armed force but also any other form of interference or attempted threat against the personality of the State or against its political, economic, and cultural elements.

United States agreement to Article 15 amounted to a trade-off to secure Latin American support for Resolution 32, "Preservation and Defense of Democracy in America," part of the United States strategy to contain communism in the Western Hemisphere. In return for that support the Latin American leaders hoped for increased technical and financial aid.

Later experience with the OAS and its peace-keeping machinery was to show that the organization could be reasonably successful in the maintenance of peace and settlement of disputes among the Latin American states, provided that the United States or extracontinental powers were not involved. When United States security interests entered the picture, the OAS proved politically impotent.

■ **Latin America and the Cold War: The First Challenge to United States Hegemony**

The traditional close association between Latin America and the United States, growing from geographical proximity, natural economic ties, and the willingness of the United States to intervene when its interests appeared to be threatened, was rudely shaken by the intrusion of Cold War pressures after 1960. The victory of Fidel Castro in Cuba in 1959 and new Soviet ties with the Castro government subjected the inter-American system to severe stresses. Virtually all issues came to be affected by the subsequent injection of East-West perspectives into what was earlier a region of clear United States hegemony.

Actually the campaign to redefine inter-American issues in Cold War terms began years before the Cuban revolution. From 1948 onward the United States attempted to mobilize the states of Latin America as part of a worldwide containment policy. OAS resolutions in 1948 and 1954, adopted after strong lobbying by the United States, pointed to international communism as a threat to the sovereignty and political independence of states in the hemisphere. The United States intervention in Guatemala in 1954, which overthrew the government of President Jacobo Arbenz, obviated an earlier call for a meeting to consult on the danger under the provisions of the Rio Treaty.

The Guatemalan case raised serious questions about hemispheric security, questions that went far beyond the issue of United States intervention. Also involved was the matter of exclusive regional jurisdiction of the OAS (the grounds on which the United States prevented United Nations action in the case) and the question of the Monroe Doctrine's applicability. The increasing determination of Latin American leaders to act independently of the United States in international affairs, only suggested in the aftermath of the Guatemalan case, was symbolized dramatically by the challenge of Cuba.

Revolutionary victory by Fidel Castro's forces in 1959 marked the beginning of serious challenge to United States hegemony in the Western Hemisphere. Relations between Cuba and the United States deteriorated rapidly after 1960. Though somewhat reluctantly, the OAS adopted the Declaration of San José at the organization's meeting in 1960, holding that "existence of a threat of extracontinental intervention . . . endangers American security" and that totalitarianism is incompatible with the inter-American system. The declaration was not a direct condemnation of Cuba, but its target was obvious.

Cuba saw the San José meeting as "the first

great inter-American fight against Cuba."[10] In retrospect, twenty-five years after the event, the Cuban reaction appears accurate. In that quarter century, except for a short-lived promise of acceptance and peaceful coexistence during the administration of President Jimmy Carter, the record has been one of almost unremitting hostility and tension between Cuba and the United States.

That record was punctuated abruptly by the Bay of Pigs invasion in April 1961. To Latin America, there was little doubt about the United States attitude toward outside intervention in Latin America. President John F. Kennedy very clearly stated the United States determination to protect its vital security interests — through the inter-American system if possible, alone if necessary. The United States persisted in its goal of isolating Cuba as a means of preventing further advances by communism in the hemisphere. The United States, of course, had a difficult argument to win because there was no precedent for expulsion of a government from the OAS. Even in the final vote to expel Cuba at the Punta del Este conference of 1962, six Latin American states (Argentina, Brazil, Chile, Mexico, Bolivia, and Ecuador) voted aginst the move. The vote was a dubious victory for the United States and, to much of Latin America, a clear violation of the principles of self-determination and nonintervention.

The Cuban missile crisis in 1962 appeared at the time to witness a change in Latin American attitudes toward United States resistance to extracontinental intervention. A unanimous OAS vote supported the United States recommendation for a quarantine of Cuba, and several Latin American states even contributed ships, aircraft, and material to support the quarantine operations. However, Latin American willingness to follow United States leadership in the Cuban affair was only a temporary departure from a steadily increasing resistance to United States hegemony. Even at the time of the OAS vote, several of the member countries — Mexico, Brazil, Bolivia, and Uruguay — hedged by making it clear that their support extended only to the quarantine itself. Nevertheless, the record suggests that the United States considered OAS support crucial. President Kennedy would undoubtedly have acted alone if necessary, but he clearly preferred to base his action on OAS concurrence.

What changed the nature of relationships in the Western Hemisphere in the 1960s was the intrusion of external actors in what was previously a "domestic" situation. Before the Cuban revolution there had been no appeal to outside forces. After 1960, in effect, the conflict broadened, an array of new actors entered the scene, and Cuba came to symbolize the growing independence and anti–United States sentiment of Latin America. The election of Salvador Allende in Chile in 1970 represented another challenge. Along with increasing assertions of autonomy by Latin American states came a wider set of economic and political relationships with other countries of the world. Peru, for example, purchased major weapons systems from the Soviet Union in the 1970s.

Fidel Castro made his call for the liberation of Latin America explicit in the Second Declaration of Havana three years after he came to power, and Cuba pledged its support for that liberation. The strident tone of the declaration and Castro's endorsement of violent means to achieve the revolution not only alarmed many Latin American states but led also to severe stresses between Havana and Moscow and Havana and Peking over the nature of change in the region. Both the Havana Conference of November 1964 and the Tri-Continental Conference of January 1966 were attempts to resolve the fundamental differences between the Moscow and Peking approaches. Among its other actions, the Tri-Continental Conference denounced the OAS as having "neither legal nor moral authority to represent the Latin-American continent." Castro proceeded in 1967 to establish the Latin American Solidarity Organization as a means of supporting revolutionary change in the region.

Despite this thrust, however, in the late

1960s and into the 1970s Castro generally retrenched and concentrated his efforts on development of the Cuban economy. Internal economic difficulties and failure of the guerrilla strategy gradually pushed Cuba into deeper dependence and closer cooperation with the Soviet Union. In 1972 Cuba was accepted as a member of COMECON (Council for Mutual Economic Assistance). However, an important long-range effect of Castro's more moderate approach to change was a growing desire to normalize relations with Cuba and to relax the sanctions against it. At the Quito meeting of the OAS in November 1974, a majority of the member states voted in favor of lifting sanctions against Cuba, but the motion was two votes short of the two-thirds majority required for such action. Finally, at the San José meeting in August 1975, the OAS lifted economic and political sanctions. Nevertheless, the United States has maintained its economic restrictions against trade with Cuba and periodically has tightened regulations governing travel there by United States citizens.

■ Cuba in the World Arena

Cuba has defied conventional notions about the role of less-developed countries in international politics and has become an important actor. Fidel Castro has demonstrated both the capability and will to exercise influence far out of proportion to Cuba's size and resource base. Of course, much of that capability is derived from continued heavy economic support from the Soviet Union. In return, Cuba's support for Soviet foreign policy has remained virtually complete.

Of course, interpretations vary as to the degree of Cuban independence in its foreign policy. Jorge Domínquez argues:

> Unlike the perspective common among some that Cuba is simply doing the bidding of the Soviet Union, a more plausible description is that Cuba is the leader within the Soviet-Cuban alliance on Central American matters. . . . Cuba appears to have formulated independently its own foreign policy toward its neighbors, to have fashioned

appropriate instruments, and to have experimented with different approaches. The Soviet role appears to have been more that of a follower than a leader. Thus the success or failure of these policies is more properly attributed to the government in Havana than to the one in Moscow.[11]

Cuban "internationalism" has meant more than expressions of solidarity with the Socialist family of nations; it also has meant concrete support for guerrilla and liberation movements in widely scattered areas.

Under the leadership of Fidel Castro, Cuba has not only upset traditional relationships in the inter-American system. It has also projected its influence far beyond its borders and the Western Hemisphere. Cuba has capitalized on its posture of resistance to United States dominance to raise its credibility with other Third World countries and radical movements. Since 1971 Cuba has participated in the "group of seventy-seven" in the UN Conference on Trade and Development (UNCTAD).

Cuba's "internationalism" has led it to heavy involvement in a variety of countries near and far, beginning with Nicaragua, Grenada, and Suriname. In Africa, Cuban intervention has been substantial in Angola and Ethiopia; earlier Cuba had become involved in Algeria, Zanzibar, Mozambique, the Congo, Guinea, and Yemen. Some reports indicate a Cuban presence also in Afghanistan, Iraq, and Iran.

Such interventions are consistent with Cuba's revolutionary ideology and its close ties with the Soviet Union. Ideologically, Castro has asserted Cuban solidarity with movements struggling against colonialism or imperialism. As a strong Soviet ally, Cuba has served almost as a Soviet proxy in many international ventures. Without continued large-scale aid from the Soviet Union, Cuba's ability to maintain its activist role in international politics would be weakened severely. With such aid, it has become the most heavily armed country in the Caribbean Basin. By any measure, its military strength makes it a powerful regional actor able to assert its influence directly should it choose. However, the danger of United States retaliation undoubtedly has caused Cuba to refrain from direct military intervention in regional conflicts.

■ The Rise of Autonomous Latin American States: The Second Challenge to United States Hegemony

Traditional hemispheric relationships were irrevocably altered by the Cuban revolution and the intrusion of the Soviet Union through its Cuban surrogate. A second challenge to United States hegemony in the region derives from the rise of increasingly autonomous states. No nation, of course, can act with complete autonomy in the world; all, including the superpowers, are constrained by various factors beyond their total control. The concept of autonomy is relative.

Nevertheless, in recent years several Latin American states have achieved levels of population, production, industrial development, or control over certain natural resources that make them factors to be reckoned with in international politics. Their new status has introduced additional stresses in the traditional relationships of the inter-American system. Among such states are Brazil, Venezuela, Mexico, and Colombia. Argentina, which has always aspired to major power status but which has faltered on the route, also clearly has the potential to be a relatively autonomous actor in international politics.

Despite the still-general tendency of Latin American countries to adopt an essentially pro–United States position in international forums, such support is increasingly shaky. The United States has steadily lost the leverage it enjoyed in the past, and the area that can be reasonably described as its sphere of influence has shrunk. This is not to assert that the United States is without major influence: In direct and indirect ways it can still project its will. This ranges from covert efforts, such as the campaign to destablize the government of Salvador Allende in Chile and support of the anti-Sandinista *contras* in Nicaragua, through overt military aid to many countries, to the direct and indirect dependency that arises from economic rela-tionships. But overall the United States influence has waned, and the readiness of Latin American states to assert their autonomy has risen.

During the last quarter century, several countries of Latin America have attempted to chart new, independent directions for themselves. Brazil has resolutely asserted its own role in world politics; that country's burgeoning population (approximately 125 million in 1982) and its rapidly developing and diversifying economy make an independent foreign policy feasible. As the largest and most populous country of South America, it can aspire to and legitimately claim the status of a world power.

Brazil's economy is the tenth largest in the world, with a gross domestic product of $320 billion at the end of 1982. Despite continuing severe economic problems, including runaway inflation and an external debt of some $95 billion in 1983 (the largest of any developing country), Brazil's international influence has increased steadily. Its vast human and natural resources, rapidly expanding productive capacity, and broadly diversifying industrial base hold the potential for an even stronger role. Brazil's growing importance, in and beyond the Western Hemisphere, casts it as a countervailing force to United States hegemony in the region, although relations between Brazil and the United States have traditionally been harmonious.

For many years Argentina also sought to assert a leadership role in South America to counterbalance what it considered excessive United States influence. Argentina's Juan Perón attempted to stake out a "third position" between the United States and the Soviet Union and reached various agreements with other countries of Latin America to solidify Argentina's leadership. The effort failed when Argentina collapsed economically. Nevertheless, it still has the essential features and resources for an economic and political resurgence that could recapture the old promise.

Mexico has combined a principled approach to foreign policy with a pragmatism born of its need to coexist with the United States. Even with a very limited resource base, Mexico fiercely defended its autonomy and generally took a leadership role in international forums. Its foreign policy for many years has demonstrated a remarkable consistency based mainly on three principles: the rule of international law, the right of self-determination, and opposition to all forms of external intervention into the internal affairs of nations. That policy was in large part a defensive reaction to the looming presence of Mexico's neighbor to the north.

Mexico steadfastly defended Cuba's right to self-determination, opposed the exclusion of Castro's government from the Organization of American States, and maintained diplomatic relations with Cuba despite United States objections to that policy. Mexico's new oil wealth greatly strengthened its hand when dealing with other countries, especially the United States (now critically in need of reliable energy imports). It was no accident that United States approaches to Mexico, after the magnitude of its oil reserves became known, were in general more solicitous. With its new income from petroleum, Mexico was also more capable of taking initiatives in the Caribbean Basin. An example was the agreement with Venezuela to establish an oil facility as a means of assisting small countries in the region that were hard hit by the high cost of oil imports. Another example was Mexico's 1984 financial assistance to Argentina, a casualty of severe debt problems.

Venezuela was able earlier than Mexico to bankroll its own rapid economic development and, on the basis of oil production, buttress its international standing (dramatically accelerated by the rapid escalation of petroleum prices in the 1970s). Access to great new wealth was the principal factor in its increasingly independent role in the world.

The new autonomy of these states has forced the United States to make readjustments in its traditional attitude: It has to deal with these states on a more nearly equal level now. However, it clearly has not fully appreciated the changing power contexts in the inter-American

system and often fails to understand or take into account the national interests of newly autonomous states such as Argentina, Brazil, Mexico, Venezuela, and Colombia. Washington frequently persists in its traditional hegemonic approach to Latin American relationships and thus may fail to understand the constructive role these countries could exercise in the region.

As Abraham Lowenthal so well expresses the problem, "Since the early 1960s, U.S. policy has failed to cope with hegemony in decline. . . . The postwar period of virtually unchallenged U.S. dominance in the Western Hemisphere is over." And in the face of that, President Reagan's policy toward Latin America "arises from a fear of hegemony lost, not from a vision of the future of Latin America."[12]

The danger is that the United States will interpret regional conflicts such as those in Central America only in the light of its own national interests, particularly its security interests, and fail to appreciate how this attitude may increase rather than diminish the influence of extracontinental powers such as the Soviet Union. Foreign policy analyses predicated on a world-view that translates all issues into East–West confrontational terms are likely to foster inaccurate diagnoses of primarily local or regional conflicts. However, one possible effect of the rise of more autonomous states in Latin America is a mitigation of this United States tendency. The enhanced power of such countries may be accompanied over the long run by a necessarily more circumspect attitude in Washington.

■ **Latin America in International Organizations**

Latin America's numerical voting strength in the United Nations — twenty members when the "Latin" states are counted — can be misleading. Actually, the block is loose and far from monolithic.

Latin American voting patterns in the United Nations vary substantially according to issue. Although it is difficult to generalize about the overall tendencies, it is clear that the United States cannot command automatic support from Latin America. Just as the Non-Aligned Movement has seen a gradual shift against Washington's policies by Latin American states, the United States had become progressively less able to secure Latin American support in the United Nations. In the General Assembly elections for the Latin American seat on the Security Council in 1982, for example, Nicaragua was elected comfortably in spite of intense United States lobbying in favor of the Dominican Republic. In the same session, however, the Cuban attempt to put the "Question of Puerto Rico" on the agenda of the General Assembly as a decolonization issue was soundly defeated when the Latin American and Caribbean countries failed markedly to support the Cubans.

In the 1982 General Assembly session, indeed, the large majority of Latin American and Caribbean states did not vote with the United States on a wide range of issues. In the debates and votes of the OAS regarding the Falklands/Malvinas issue, the majority clearly felt compelled to show solidarity on the question of Argentine sovereignty over the islands. But individual national interests and special considerations prevented the invocation of sanctions against the United Kingdom. When Argentina, supported by nineteen other Latin American countries, took the dispute to the UN General Assembly, the United States voted for the resolution calling for negotiations between the belligerents.

■ Integration Efforts

Latin America's history, like that of Europe, reveals various efforts toward integration. The results of such attempts are mixed, though certainly not notably successful; the region has moved in fits and starts toward the elusive goal of more fully integrated economies. Political integration has been even less successful; the few political unions and linkages have been generally unstable and short-lived.

Early postindependence unions such as Gran Colombia (northern South America) and the United Provinces of Central America soon disintegrated in the face of strong tensions between competing power centers. Central authorities were constantly challenged in the widespread conflict during the formative period of the Latin American states. The struggle to unite the often factious peripheral areas was long and frequently bitter; "Argentina" emerging from the United Provinces of the Rio de la Plata is a good example.

In recent years several ambitious attempts at economic integration have been made. These include the Latin American Free Trade Association begun in 1960 (reincarnated as the Latin American Integration Association in 1981), the Central American Common Market (growing out of the Treaty of Managua in 1961), and the Andean Common Market, formed in 1969. [Editor's Note: See chapter 14, "The Economics of Latin America."] Suffice it to say that overall these schemes have achieved only limited success in integrating the economies of the Latin American states, breaking down trade barriers, or promoting economic development. Although intraregional trade has increased substantially in recent years, the broad goal of integration has not been accepted fully by any means, and efforts have run aground on conflicting national interests of the member states or peculiar regional problems.

■ The Debt Problem

A host of factors combined during the 1970s to push Latin America into serious economic recession by the early 1980s. Among these were the effects of the rapid escalation of petroleum prices after the 1973 oil embargo, unstable markets for some of the region's most important export products, the severe impact of economic recession in the industrial countries, and a rapid rise in interest rates on loans. In addition several Latin American states, notably Mexico, Brazil, Venezuela, and Argentina, gambled on a continuation of the earlier healthy economic growth and borrowed excessively from the world financial centers.

As Nicholas Bruck describes the situation:

> The private banks saw several advantages in this type of international lending: the absence of regulatory control on external loans, the profitability of international credits resulting from the complex fee structure, low overhead costs, a matched maturity of loans, and the confidence that governments could not become bankrupt as private corporations could.[13]

As a result, several states rapidly accumulated staggering debt burdens, both public and private, and found themselves strapped to service the debts (pay interest and principal). By 1983 the total external debt of Latin America had risen to over $350 billion. Most of that was owed by Brazil, Mexico, and Argentina. Servicing the debts consumed an inordinate share of export earnings. Even oil producers such as Mexico and Venezuela staggered under the load and were forced to take radical steps to handle the problem without resorting to default. Currency devaluations, rampant inflation, and general economic decline led to widespread concern over the worldwide impact of possible default, and several countries were forced to renegotiate the terms of repayment of their debts, among them Brazil, Mexico, Chile, and Argentina. All took steps to slow the increase in external debt and a further deterioration in their international economic position. The debt problem, which reached crisis proportions in the early 1980s, again demonstrated the close linkages between Latin America's and the industrialized states' economic well-being.

■ The Internationalization of Latin American Conflicts

Increasingly, a characteristic feature of the international politics of the Latin American nations is the internationalization of their regional conflicts. To an unprecedented degree, in recent years these have attracted not simply the interest of outside actors but frequently their active involvement. Such heightened interest and engagement have added to the volatility of conflicts that might otherwise have remained local or regional in character.

This internationalization did not spring full-blown on the scene. Long-evolving relationships in the OAS, the activism of Cuba after 1960 and Soviet sponsorship of Cuba's internationalism, and the growth of increasingly autonomous states in the region, among other factors, all contributed to such internationalization. Although numerous conflicts in Latin America in past years have led to the involvement of outside powers, in recent times the character of the involvement has changed radically. Before the 1960s, typically, non-American states became engaged in Latin American disputes for discrete, limited purposes — such as to mediate conflicts, to protect the business interests of a country, or to protect citizens in danger. Rarely did such engagements amount to a threat to the security interests of the United States, and rarely were they cast in confrontational terms or in rhetoric that fundamentally challenged existing power relationships.

The Cuban revolution and Fidel Castro's audacious challenge to the United States virtually insured that future conflicts in the hemisphere would be viewed in East–West confrontational terms. The survival of the Castro government, in spite of continuous United States efforts to destabilize or overthrow it, has kept alive the specter of further Marxist success in the region. The failure of the Bay of Pigs invasion in 1961 did not deter the United States from a direct challenge to further Soviet expansion in the Cuban missile crisis of 1962. It did not discourage President Lyndon Johnson from intervening militarily in the Dominican Republic in 1965, ostensibly to protect that country and the Americas against further Communist expansion. Neither did it dissuade the United States from assisting in the destabilization of the Socialist government of Salvador Allende in Chile in 1973.

Of course, not all United States action has been directed toward Marxist threats. In 1978 the Carter administration indirectly intervened in the elections of the Dominican Republic, making clear by a show of naval force that it would oppose the apparent intention of the Dominican military to interfere in a free election. That action was probably the decisive factor insuring a continuation of the vote count and the election of a civilian president.

In October 1983 United States reaction returned to a more consistent theme when President Reagan ordered the invasion of Grenada with the stated objective of insuring the safety of American students at St. George's University on the island. In the process, the radical Marxist group that shortly before had murdered Premier Maurice Bishop and overthrown his government was deposed, and Cuban personnel on the island were sent packing.

The Grenada invasion was only the most dramatic in a series of United States steps that included a broad campaign against insurgent forces in El Salvador and the Sandinista regime in Nicaragua. All these actions reemphasized Washington's determination to resist further advances by Marxist forces in the hemisphere.

Thus the historical record is clear and rather strongly indicates that, despite the apparently successful Cuban revolution (perhaps in large part *because* of it), the United States government still conceives of Latin America primarily in terms of its sphere of influence. Given sufficient provocation, and under the appropriate conditions, it is highly likely that the United States will intervene, directly if necessary, to protect its perceived interests in the region. To this extent, declarations about the death of the Monroe Doctrine are somewhat premature.

The election of Ronald Reagan to the presidency in 1980 intensified United States concern over further Marxism in the Western Hemisphere, and also led to substantial changes in the nature of inter-American relations. The human rights policy of President Jimmy Carter had created frosty relations with the au-

thoritarian governments of Latin America, all of which had egregious records of violations of human rights. In particular, relations with the military governments of Argentina, Chile, Uruguay, El Salvador, and Guatemala had sunk to new low levels, and relations with Brazil were little better. The Reagan administration, buttressed by the tortuous philosophical reasoning of Jeane Kirkpatrick (Reagan's United Nations ambassador) in regard to the distinction between authoritarian and totalitarian governments, opened warm dialogue with the former. In the grand scheme of Reagan's foreign policy, these governments could provide a bulwark against further Communist expansion in Latin America and the Caribbean Basin. Indeed, before the Falklands/Malvinas war of 1982, the Reagan administration had begun negotiations with the military government of Argentina to arrange Argentine military assistance in the Central American conflict. Once the United States dropped its role as mediator in the South Atlantic war and openly supported Great Britain, the Central American plan for Argentina was canceled abruptly.

Considered in the broader context of internationalization of hemispheric struggle, the successful Cuban revolution was only an opening wedge for a further broadening of conflict. Several situations suggested cracks in the structure of United States hegemony. These included the establishment of the People's Revolutionary Government of Maurice Bishop in Grenada in 1979, the victory of the Sandinistas over the dictatorial regime of Anastasio Somoza Debayle in Nicaragua in July 1979, and much earlier, the Cooperative Republic of Guyana under Forbes Burnham since 1964. Burnham managed to maintain good relations with states in both the East and West camps, sometimes to the discomfiture of the United States, and Guyana became an active member of the Non-Aligned Movement.

The survival of these governments, distinctly independent in their foreign policies and relations with other states outside the Western

Hemisphere, encouraged greater autonomy on the part of other Latin American countries. It also encouraged other states to intervene more freely in the affairs and conflicts of Latin America and the Caribbean Basin. Following the lead of the Soviet Union in Cuba, several states took increasingly active roles in a number of situations in the region.

For example, the hostile attitude of the Reagan administration toward the Bishop regime in Grenada led to a substantial inflow of assistance from Cuba, the Soviet Union, and other Socialist states, as well as some nations in Western Europe. Guyana's independent course attracted considerable aid from a wide range of countries. The conflict in El Salvador led the governments of France and Mexico to recognize the insurgent forces there as "representative political forces," much to the irritation of the Reagan administration, as well as of several Latin American governments, which considered the declaration to be intervention in a Central American concern.

These situations challenge the notion that Latin America and the Caribbean Basin are private preserves of the United States. They also challenge the long-argued stance of the United States that conflicts in the region must be settled through the institutional arrangements of the inter-American system, principally the Organization of American States. For years that principle had been used to prevent United Nations action in disputes and security issues arising in the hemisphere. The increasing readiness of external states to take positions on Latin American questions, combined with the growing autonomy of several countries in Latin America, served to weaken United States hegemony in the region. Thus regional and local conflicts increasingly became international in their implications, the stakes in their outcome became higher, and as the scope of conflict broadened, settlement became more difficult.

As this chapter is written, the observer of Latin America sees a region wracked by the violence of seemingly intractable conflicts, gripped by economic woes and dislocations, and lurching from crisis to crisis. The United States has continued to intervene in Central American and Caribbean affairs in response to perceived Soviet or Soviet-surrogate intervention. Yet there are encouraging signs as well. Several countries have moved to gain control over their debt problems, there has been substantial progress in the transition from authoritarianism, and several nations of the region (such as the Contadora Group) have become increasingly involved in reconciling international differences. Latin America presents a complex face to the world as it seeks to play a more important role in international affairs.

■ Notes

1. See Minerva M. Etzioni, *The Majority of One: Toward a Theory of Regional Compatibility* (Beverly Hills: Sage, 1970).
2. Harold Eugene Davis and Larman C. Wilson, *Latin American Foreign Policies: An Analysis* (Baltimore: Johns Hopkins University Press, 1975), 445–47.
3. Victor Alba, *The Latin Americans* (New York: Praeger, 1969), 103.
4. Jack W. Hopkins, *Latin America in World Affairs: The Politics of Inequality* (Woodbury, N.Y.: Barron's Educational Series, 1976), 42.
5. Rawle Farley, *The Economies of Latin America: Development Problems in Perspective* (New York: Harper and Row, 1972), 34; Carlos Alberto Astiz, ed., *Latin American International Politics: Ambitions, Capabilities, and the National Interest of Mexico, Brazil, and Argentina* (Notre Dame, Ind.: University of Notre Dame Press, 1969), 13–14.
6. Gordon Connell-Smith, *The Inter-American System* (New York: Oxford University Press, 1966), 23.
7. Quoted by James Petras, H. Michael Erisman, and Charles Mills, "The Monroe Doctrine and U.S. Hegemony in Latin America," in *Latin America: From Dependence to Revolution*, ed. James Petras (New York: John Wiley & Sons, 1973), 232.
8. For a detailed listing of military interventions up to 1933, the reader may consult *Intervention in Latin America*, ed. C. Neale Ronning (New York: Knopf, 1970), 25–32.
9. Alonso Aguilar, *Pan-Americanism From Monroe to*

the *Present: A View from the Other Side* (New York: Monthly Review Press, 1968), 69.

10. Aguilar, op. cit., 111.

11. Jorge I. Domínguez, "Cuba's Relations with Caribbean and Central American Countries," *Cuban Studies/Estudios Cubanos* 13 (Summer 1983): 100.

12. Abraham Lowenthal, "Change the Agenda," *Foreign Policy*, no. 52 (Fall 1983), 75; ibid., 77.

13. Nicholas Bruck, "The Continuing External Debt Problem in Latin America," in *Latin America and Caribbean Contemporary Record*, vol. 2, ed. Jack W. Hopkins (New York: Holmes & Meier Publishers, 1984), 225.

■ Suggested Readings

Davis, Harold Eugene, and Larman C. Wilson. *Latin American Foreign Policies: An Analysis.* Baltimore: Johns Hopkins University Press, 1975.

Fagen, Richard, and Olga Pellicer, eds. *The Future of Central America.* Stanford: Stanford University Press, 1983.

Falk, Pamela. *Cuban Foreign Policy in the Twentieth Century.* Lexington, Mass.: Lexington, 1982.

Feinberg, Richard, ed. *Central America: International Dimensions of the Crisis.* New York: Holmes & Meier Publishers, 1982.

Ferris, Elizabeth, ed. *Latin American Foreign Policies: Global and Regional Dimensions.* Boulder, Colo.: Westview Press, 1981.

Martz, John D., ed. *Latin America, the United States, and the Inter-American System.* Boulder, Colo.: Westview Press, 1980.

Múñoz, Heraldo, and Joseph Tulchin, eds. *Latin America in World Politics: Comparative Perspectives.* Boulder, Colo.: Westview Press, 1984.

Schoultz, Lars. *Human Rights and United States Policy Toward Latin America.* Princeton: Princeton University Press, 1981.

PART

IV

APPENDIX

NOTES ON CONTRIBUTORS

INDEX

Appendix: Researching Latin America in the Library

GLENN F. READ, JR.

Just a scant two or three decades ago the student about to commence a bibliographic search on some Latin American topic often found allies mainly in the library's card catalog and a few indexing tools that concentrated on articles published in English-language journals. Two notable exceptions were the *Handbook of Latin American Studies* and the Modern Language Association's *International Bibliography*. In the 1960s a number of specialized bibliographies and reference works designed for use by Latin American researchers in the United States appeared, and other general reference works expanded their coverage of Latin America. Since that time there has been a phenomenal growth in reference materials that offer the user many approaches in the search for information on Latin America and the Caribbean.

This current superabundance of reference aids may confront the library user with a baffling array of research devices. With many library collections offering more than one hundred thousand books and hundreds of thousands of articles on Latin American themes, the card catalog and the old familiar periodical indexes may prove inadequate to finding just that handful of materials that can best satisfy the user's informational needs. The following pages give a representative sampling of these reference aids and suggestions on how best to use them to make library research an efficient and orderly process. In an age of computerized databases, document delivery services, and cooperative acquisitions programs among libraries, it may be advisable to look beyond the holdings of one's own library in order to obtain the best or the most timely information on Latin America.

■ Union Catalogs

If, for example, one needs to identify works of a particular author that cannot be found in the local library's card catalog, one might wish to consult a "union" catalog. A union catalog lists the holdings of several libraries, and the most comprehensive of these is the *National Union Catalog* (NUC). It is essentially a card catalog in book form for the holdings of some eleven hundred libraries in the United States and Canada. The *NUC* is updated at regular intervals with supplements containing the cataloging records of new or recent acquisitions of the various contributing libraries. Millions of books are cited in the several hundred volumes that make up the *NUC*. Since 1983 the supplements have been issued, on a monthly basis, in microfiche format.

Many libraries now offer on-line versions of a union catalog and, through the use of a computer terminal, the local library's reference staff can help library users locate materials in other libraries that may be needed for their research. The national interlibrary loan network makes it possible for most of these materials to be borrowed or photocopied.

Catalogs serve to open up the vast field of Latin American library resources to the more serious student and scholar in dimensions (including electronic databases) that barely existed some twenty years ago.

■ Library Guides

Most students in the early stages of library research will have little occasion to look beyond the resources of their local library in obtaining or identifying wanted materials. All the same, it may be useful to know that there are published guides or directories to library collections of Latin Americana in other parts of the United States, or even the world. These so-called library guides contain narrative descriptions, usually of a paragraph or two, of a particular library's Latin American resources. Some also include directory-type information regarding library hours, loan policies, addresses and telephone numbers, and the names of library staff specialists in the Latin American field. Students spending time away from their local library, but in need of Latin American materials for re-

search, may find them useful. A selection of such guides would include:

Ash, Lee, ed. *Subject Collections: A Guide to Special Book Collections and Subject Emphases as Reported by University, College, Public and Special Libraries and Museums in the United States and Canada.* 6th ed. New York: Bowker, 1985.

Bartley, Russell H., and Stuart L. Wagner. *Latin America in Basic Historical Collections: A Working Guide.* Stanford, Calif.: Hoover Institution Press, 1972.

Grow, Michael. *Scholars' Guide to Washington, D.C., for Latin American and Caribbean Studies.* Washington: Smithsonian Institution Press, 1979.

Haro, Robert P. *Latin Americana Research in the United States and Canada: A Guide and Directory.* Chicago: American Library Association, 1971.

Hilton, Ronald. *Handbook of Hispanic Source Materials and Research Organizations in the United States.* 2d ed. Stanford, Calif.: Stanford University Press, 1956.

Jackson, William Vernon. *Library Guide for Brazilian Studies.* Pittsburgh: Distrib. by the University of Pittsburgh Book Centers, 1964.

■ Reference Guides

Another type of guide is one commonly referred to as a reference guide, an annotated bibliography of reference books, dictionaries, encyclopedias, biographical or institutional directories, statistical sources, and a host of other related reference materials. Most, but not all of them, are arranged according to the particular genre of the reference works they are citing and describing: "periodical indexes," "book review indexes," "audio-visual directories," and so on.

Let us assume, for example, that the research problem is to find a map that would show the New World as it was presumed to exist in 1546. A good reference guide might list and describe an historical atlas that would contain such a map, or it might cite a catalog of sheet maps in a major map library that would include it. Perhaps the research problem deals with locating a color reproduction of a famous mural by Diego Rivera, or another Mexican muralist, that could be found in a book or encyclopedia. A reference guide may cite an index to paintings reproduced in books, journals, museum catalogs, or art encyclopedias.

Several such guides are available to the library user. Two are especially helpful to the Latin Americanist. The first is entitled *Guide to Reference Books,* 9th ed., compiled by Eugene P. Sheehy. The annotations and indexing in this guide are excellent, and it is supplemented or completely revised at regular intervals. The second is *Reference Materials on Latin America in English, the Humanities,* written and compiled by Richard Donovon Woods. It offers an annotated listing of some 1,252 reference books that deal primarily with Latin American themes. Although they are organized in a single alphabetical arrangement by the author's name, as opposed to the "genre" arrangement in the Sheehy guide, the former provides a well-developed subject index.

■ Bibliography of Bibliographies

Often, an initial search of the local library's card catalog and general periodical indexes results in a list of materials that are too few, or too many, to satisfy the needs of the researcher's project. Fortunately, another type of library aid is available, a "bibliography of bibliographies." Such a tool lists bibliographies on very specific topics that have been published in books or journals. The citations are generally grouped in broad subject categories, such as archaeology, economics, or religion. A student researching a topic like "land tenure in highland Peru," "the press in modern Mexico," or "religious orders in colonial Chile" may discover, by consulting a bibliography of bibliographies, that a bibliography describing and evaluating the best and most

authoritative writings on that particular theme has already been published. If the bibliography is well organized and annotated it may save the student valuable time by permitting him to quickly select only those works that are most appropriate to the topic.

The best available tool in the field is *A Bibliography of Latin American Bibliographies* (Metuchen, N.J.: Scarecrow Press, 1968) and its companion *A Bibliography of Latin American Bibliographies Published in Periodicals* (Metuchen, N.J.: Scarecrow Press, 1976), both compiled by Arthur E. Gropp. These basic works are kept up to date with periodic supplements.

■ Current Bibliography

There are two bibliographic aids devoted exclusively to newly published works in the Latin American field. They cite materials published in all languages, including English, appropriate to this field. The *Handbook of Latin American Studies* (HLAS) has been published annually since 1935. It selects and annotates about forty-five hundred to six thousand of the most important books and journal articles published each year in the humanities and social sciences on Latin America and the Caribbean. The *Bibliographic Guide to Latin American Studies* is an annual listing of all books acquired during the year by the University of Texas's Benson Latin American Collection, supplemented by new Latin American acquisitions of the Library of Congress. It has appeared each year since 1978 and organizes its entries in a dictionary arrangement (author, title, and subject), much like a typical library card catalog. It contains no annotations. While *HLAS* is selective in its approach, the *Bibliographic Guide* attempts near completeness in its listing of new books on any subject from or about Latin America.

■ Indexing Services for Periodicals

We move now to another species of library reference aid: the index. A number of these open the way to pertinent journal articles, book reviews, dissertations, and biographical sketches of prominent Latin Americans, both living and deceased. Because these aids are described in the books by Sheehy and Woods, only a few that relate specifically to Latin America need be mentioned. These are:

> *HAPI, Hispanic American Periodicals Index. 1970–present.* Los Angeles: UCLA Latin American Center Publications, University of California.

> Leavitt, Sturgis E. *Revistas hispanoamericanas: índice bibliográfico, 1843–1935.* Santiago de Chile: Fondo Histórico y Bibliográfico José Toribio Medina, 1960.

> Pan American Union. Columbus Memorial Library. *Index to Latin American Periodical Literature, 1929–1960.* Boston: G. K. Hall, 1962. 8 v.

> ———. *Supplement.* 1st–2d, 1961/65–1966/70. Boston: G. K. Hall, 1967–80. 4 v.

HAPI is the indexing tool for current Latin American journals, and approximately three hundred journals from the United States, Latin America, and Europe are indexed in this annual publication. The other two indexes are retrospective in their coverage of journal articles but, taken all together, they offer their user access to journal literature on Latin America covering a span of nearly one hundred and fifty years. The lists of journals indexed are, for the most part, different in each of the tools, and their formats are also quite dissimilar. Nevertheless, the student should have no difficulty in mastering their use, and *HAPI* is a particularly good index in terms of format and organization.

■ Book Review Indexes

There are a number of good indexes that could be used to find reviews of books about Latin America. Tools like the *Book Review Digest* offer indexing or abstracting coverage back to the be-

ginning of this century, but most of them list book reviews found only in English-language journals. Fortunately, there is an index that, since 1960, has abstracted reviews published in journals from Latin America, as well as from those of the United States and Western Europe. The *Guía a las reseñas de libros de y sobre Hispanoamérica (A Guide to Reviews of Books from and about Hispanic America)* is an annual publication, compiled by Antonio Matos, that contains abstracts from over 680 journals, two-thirds of which are in Spanish. One annual volume may contain as many as six thousand reviews that evaluate the contents of nearly four thousand new books.

■ Dissertation Indexes

Doctoral dissertations are frequently used in the course of one's research on Latin America since they generally contain quite detailed and specific information, and because the bibliographies found in them are good selective guides to the literature of a topic. There are a number of general dissertation bibliographies or indexes of interest to the Latin Americanist. Since academic libraries acquire and catalog principally the dissertations submitted for the degree requirements of their parent university, it is best to begin a search for other university dissertations by using such a specialized tool. Most researchers are familiar with *Dissertation Abstracts* and a companion retrospective work entitled *Comprehensive Dissertation Index* (1861–present), but two reference aids that are particularly useful for Latin American research have recently appeared. These are:

> Sims, Michael. *United States Doctoral Dissertations in Third World Studies, 1869–1978.* Waltham, Mass.: Crossroads Press, 1980.

> Deal, Carl W., ed. *Latin America and the Caribbean: a Dissertation Bibliography.* Ann Arbor, Mich.: University Microfilms International, n.d.

The Deal index is regularly updated with supplements, and most of its bibliographic information is extracted from *Dissertation Abstracts.*

■ Biographical Indexes

Indexing services provide access to biographical information on prominent Latin Americans, and on scholars in Latin American studies. Sarah de Mundo Lo is compiling *Index to Spanish American Collective Biography,* a multivolume work begun in 1981 that, when completed, will analyze the contents of about thirty-two hundred collective biographies for Spanish America. *Collective biography* is a term generally applied to reference works, such as biographical dictionaries and encyclopedias, *who's whos,* and genealogies that contain biographical information on a number of individuals. The Mundo Lo work will contain over two hundred thousand citations to biographical sketches of some ninety thousand people from the seventeenth century to the present. Brazil and the non-Spanish-speaking parts of Latin America and the Caribbean will not be included, but these areas are covered for the most part by individual biographies and collective biographies. A biographical index leads the searcher straight to the source of information without a hunt through *who's whos* and similar biographical dictionaries.

Bio-Base is a microfiche index to the contents of 375 biographical dictionaries, *Who's Whos,* and similar works. It also incorporates the listings of the quarterly *Biography Index* and those of over 750 journals, including *Hispanic Review* and the *Journal of Interamerican Studies and World Affairs,* that frequently contain biographical material. Although the biographical sources indexed by *Bio-Base,* such as *Contemporary Authors* and the *Oxford Companion to Spanish Literature,* are intended primarily for English-language users, its scope is worldwide, and it includes many prominent Latin Americans and scholars of Latin America. The information may run from a few dozen words in a *Who's Who* kind of source to a major sketch in something like *Current Biography,* which could encompass several thousand

words. The 1981 cumulation of *Bio-Base* contained 3,800,000 citations, and this index is updated or supplemented on a regular basis.

■ Selecting the Proper Tools of Research

As we have seen, the scope of research tools can vary considerably. Some reference aids may limit *geographic* coverage to materials on or from Latin America, or to a specific country or region. *Subject* coverage can be quite specific, such as a bibliography on constitutional government; or it can be very broad, including all appropriate materials in the humanities and social sciences. A bibliography or index may restrict its *format* to newspaper titles, or articles in newspapers, or it may include just books or parts of books. Other tools may limit coverage to certain forms of writing, or *genre:* book or film reviews, poetry, necrology, essays, travelers' accounts.

Bibliographies frequently restrict their *chronological* coverage as well and may list only materials published over a particular span of years; they may cite only works about a particular historical period, such as the Mexican Revolution. Restrictions on what may, or may not, be included in a bibliographic reference work will collectively define its scope. It is important to understand the limitations of each tool if precious research time is not to be wasted.

Moreover, some bibliographic works may offer the user certain features such as annotations or abstracts of the works they cite. This additional data may enable one to more easily identify those writings that contain information most appropriate to the research topic. Other bibliographies may simply list the relevant bibliographic data — author, title, and imprint — and the user must determine from the limited information provided just which of the writings cited in the bibliography are the ones to examine.

The scope of the *National Union Catalog,* for example, is universal in its subject, geographic, and chronological coverage, but is restricted in terms of format, since virtually all the works cited are books. Like most book catalogs, it does not provide annotations. The *Hispanic American Periodical Index* (HAPI) begins coverage with journal articles written in 1970, focuses on Latin America and the Caribbean, and confines its subject coverage primarily to the humanities and social sciences. The *Handbook of Latin American Studies* contains the same basic subject coverage as *HAPI* but includes both books and articles. Its chronological coverage extends back to 1935.

Before searching the literature of a given field, one should always be careful to define the topic in detail, and then lay out a careful strategy to make use of the best and most appropriate library tools. One should decide in advance if the information is to come only from books and journal articles, or whether it may be necessary to look at maps, photographs, or other nonprint materials. Perhaps one's research will draw on data obtained from government publications. Because many libraries do not catalog such materials even though they have them, it may be necessary to consult specialized bibliographies of government documents in order to locate them.

Finally, some bibliographic aids that restrict their coverage to writings on Latin America may not in fact be as up-to-date, as well organized, or as easy to use as tools that are more universal or worldwide in geographic coverage. The existence of a very specialized Latin American bibliography for a certain subject, a certain genre, a certain period of literary or historical writing, or a certain publishing format does not necessarily imply that it would be more advantageous to use it than another work of broader scope. The more familiar one becomes with the field of reference bibliography, the more discriminating one becomes in choosing the right tool for a particular project, and the more skilled one becomes in its application.

The bibliography or index is a reference aid that offers an *indirect* approach to information contained in books, journals, or other sources. One must first select the appropriate bibliographic tool and then use it to identify the source of the information sought. There are many nonbibliographic reference aids, however, that provide *direct* access to specific bits of information on Latin America. Dictionaries and encyclopedias are handy sources of concise information on people, places, events, and institutions. Most libraries possess single- or multivolume encyclopedias, in English, Spanish, or Portuguese, that have good coverage for Latin America. Atlases that contain either current or historical maps for various parts of the Americas are generally available, and language dictionaries are part of every library's collection of reference works.

Some reference works are often better sources for timely data on the Americas than articles in magazines or books. It would make more sense, for example, to consult a reference tool such as the *Europa Year Book* to learn the names of all the current cabinet ministers in the Nicaraguan government rather than attempt to locate them in a book describing current politics in Central America. The number of female teachers in the public schools of Chile can be easily found in the UNESCO *Statistical Yearbook,* and the United Nations' *Demographic Yearbook* is an excellent source of population statistics for Latin America. Data on the current silver production of Mexico is readily available in the United Nations' *Statistical Yearbook,* and the *Statistical Abstract of Latin America* gathers together all types of data drawn from nearly 150 other yearbooks, statistical journals, and reports. The United Nations' Economic Commission on Latin America publishes *Statistical Yearbook on Latin America* and *Economic Activity in Caribbean Countries,* which provide similar data. All of these are updated annually and are easily accessible in most libraries.

International Financial Statistics and the *Statistical Bulletin of the OAS* appear even more frequently and offer a wealth of data on banking, finance, trade, and consumerism in the Americas. If these sources do not supply enough hard data on certain trades or industries, or on segments of the population or economy of a country, then perhaps a very special tool like the *Index to International Statistics* can help. It locates information in publications by organizations like the Organization of American States. It appears quarterly, with annual cumulations, and both indexes and abstracts the contents of international agency publications.

Remember, too, that nonbibliographic reference aids, just as the bibliographic ones, should also be carefully evaluated in terms of what they include or exclude in their coverage. The authoritative quality of reference works that purport to cover the same field of information may vary considerably. The care given to organizing the information in a reference book, its factual correctness, its access to information through complete and well-constructed indexes, its timeliness, and the degree to which its information is comprehensive—all of these things need to be considered. A good annotated "reference guide," such as those compiled by Sheehy or Woods, can be of enormous help in selecting the right bibliographic and nonbibliographic tools for the initial stages of library research.

It often happens that when one begins to study a new subject or an unfamiliar part of the world, one loses direction in the course of delving into the literature. When one is relatively unacquainted with the scholarly literature and does not generally understand the important aspects of a country's culture, it is easy to falter in the attempt to evaluate the importance of various books or articles.

If this is the first time one writes on a topic, it may be useful to have read some general background information before commencing a search of the literature. Such background data can provide a road map or skeletal framework to guide the search. Most disciplines associated with Latin American studies — history, literature, politics, economics — offer the background necessary to research a specific topic.

Examples of recently published background studies might include:

Burns, E. Bradford. *Latin America: A Concise Interpretive History*. 3rd ed. Englewood Cliffs, N.J.: Prentice-Hall, 1982.

Skidmore, Thomas E., and Peter H. Smith. *Modern Latin America*. New York: Oxford University Press, 1984.

There are a number of excellent journals that regularly publish articles on Latin America in English. Students should be aware of them, as they contain some of the most up-to-date and authoritative writing in the field. In history the list would include *The Americas: a Quarterly Review of Inter-American Cultural History, HAHR* (Hispanic American Historical Review) and the *Journal of Latin American Studies*. Literature includes *Hispania* and the *Latin American Literary Review*. *Inter-American Economic Affairs* has long been a major journal in the field of economics. For articles on Latin American foreign affairs one should consult the *Journal of Interamerican Studies and World Affairs,* and the *Latin American Research Review* is a reliable source for writings on almost any subject relating to Latin America. These journals take no particular political or editorial stance, but try to provide their readers with a balanced, objective interpretation of Latin American life and culture. Two very good journals that do reflect a particular social or political point of view are the *NACLA Report on the Americas* and *Latin American Perspectives*. These two concentrate their attention on the "political economy" of Latin America and offer their readers a certain perspective on events in the hemisphere.

If the topic cuts across traditional disciplinary lines, however, such as "poetry of political revolution," then one may wish to find a book that deals with several aspects of Latin American life and culture for background reading. Fortunately, material is available to provide basic knowledge about a number of related subjects, much as the earlier chapters of this book address Latin American studies from a variety of perspectives.

For lack of a better term these introductory works may be called *handbooks*. Often there are whole families or series of handbooks that focus on Latin America and the Caribbean, and each handbook touches on many facets of the history and people of a particular country or region of the Americas. A good example of such works is the *Area Handbook* series prepared by the American University in Washington, D.C. The series covers the whole world, but twenty-three volumes are devoted to individual countries of Latin America and the Caribbean. A typical volume contains 275 to 400 pages and will provide a useful digest of information on a country's history, governmental and educational institutions, economy, society, and national security. Each volume is revised and updated at regular intervals, and all are illustrated with valuable maps, photographs, and tables. They are to be found in the library's card catalog, or in its government publications department, under such titles as *Peru: A Country Study.*

■ Two Exercises in Library Research

To illustrate how we might use some of the reference tools described in the preceding pages, let us select a topic or two that might be the subject of a short term paper, perhaps ten to fifteen pages in length. We can then outline the steps that might be taken to identify the best information available. We do not need an exhaustive search of the literature, only enough to provide a few well-selected sources of information. To further limit the scope of our search, let us restrict ourselves to writings in English.

Researching the Humanities

First, let us pick a topic in the humanities, perhaps one that involves research on contemporary writers of Latin America, say, twentieth-century women writers of Argentina, from the perspective of literary history and criticism. Since most of our sources are likely to be books and journal articles, we should concentrate our initial search on them. We can now plan our search strategy by first setting its parameters:

1. Our sources should be in English
2. They should be mainly found in books and journals

3. The search should be for writings dealing with at least one of three elements: (a) literature, (b) women, and (c) Argentina
4. A fourth element, that of chronology (i.e., the twentieth century), will have considerably less importance in our search strategy than the other three

We have to check our own library's card catalog (or computerized catalog) for books on this subject, so let us begin our search by looking under some likely headings. The most specific will probably be something like: "Argentine Literature — Women Authors — History and Criticism." If we are working in a library with strong Latin American resources, we may even wish to qualify the literary genre a little further, for instance, "Argentine Drama," "Argentine Fiction," or "Argentine Poetry — Women Authors — History and Criticism." If this fails to produce much, we can try a less specific approach along two separate lines: "Spanish-American Literarure — Women Authors — History and Criticism," or "Argentine Literature — History and Criticism."

Let us also watch for bibliographic tools to help us identify more books and articles on the topic. Look for the further subdivision "Bibliography" after the words *History and Criticism* in the subject heading. Thus far our search for bibliographies may have turned up something like David William Foster's *Argentine Literature: A Research Guide,* 2d ed. and two more general guides: the *Manual of Hispanic Bibliography,* 2d ed., compiled by David and Virginia Ramos Foster, and Donald W. Bleznick's *A Sourcebook for Hispanic Literature and Language,* 2d ed.

Of those three elements in our search parameters, we have pretty well exhausted the literature approach, including literature subdivided by women, so let us turn next to the term *Women,* used not as the subdivision of another term, but as the main term itself. This subject heading emphasizes the sociological aspect of women's studies, and we can further qualify our search by looking under "Women — Argentina" or "Women Authors, Argentinian." The latter heading emphasizes the role of women in society as writers, as opposed to the heading of "Argentine Literature — Women Authors," which examines and evaluates the literary works of women writers. The further subdivision of "Bibliography" can also be applied to these headings under "Women."

A search of the third element, that is to say, looking in the catalog under "Argentine Republic," becomes unnecessary because we have already qualified our search for literature and women with a geographic descriptor. A term like *Argentine Republic — Women,* if it existed, would have the same meaning as "Women — Argentina." Our fourth element, chronology, is always treated in subject headings as a subdivision — for instance, "Argentine Poetry — Twentieth Century — History and Criticism" — so we do not have to make an additional check for this element of our search parameters.

Other subject headings might be tried, such as "Women's Periodicals, Argentinian"; but if you have trouble thinking of new ones, ask a reference librarian to show you a printed list of subject headings used by your library. Such lists usually have many cross-references to guide you from subject words or descriptors not used by the library to those that are.

Most catalog cards have information on the botton of each card called "tracings." This is a record of additional subjects, or "entries," under which the book may be found in the catalog. If you are looking under one subject heading, and you find the card for a book that looks as though it contains the information you seek, look for tracings at the bottom of the card, for they may suggest additional subjects to look under. Then look under those subject headings until you find another book that seems appropriate, check its tracings, and continue your search under these new headings. In this way you can use the subject part of the card catalog as a set of chain references to guide you through a complete search.

Having completed our search of the catalog,

it is time to use one of the reference guides mentioned earlier. Sheehy's *Guide to Reference Books* has a subject arrangement, so look over the table of contents to familiarize yourself with its organization. There is a subsection for "Sociology–Women" in the "Social Sciences" section but, from this point on, our search will be concentrated on the literary aspects of our topic, so we can bypass this approach.

Turn now to the section "Humanities" and scan the pages under "Literature–Romance Languages–Spanish" and "Spanish America." There you will find descriptions of the reference aids that can facilitate your search. The two Foster guides are listed there, as well as an index that will be particularly useful in our search for journal articles. It is the *MLA International Bibliography of Books and Articles on the Modern Languages and Literatures.* This Modern Language Association annual publication includes excellent coverage for Latin American literature. Select the subject index volume of the *MLA* and look under "Women." Indexing for women in literature has two aspects, and we need to bear this in mind when researching a topic such as women writers of Argentina: There is a distinction between women as writers and women as the subject of writers. Because our interest is in the former, we want to look under subject headings like: "Women Writers," "Women Novelists," "Women Poets," subdivided by the phrase "Argentine literature, 1900–1999" or "Spanish-American literature, 1900–1999." Now we can see all four elements of our research strategy coming into play. A careful survey of several years of *MLA* will undoubtedly turn up a number of articles and a few books that will prove useful. If more articles are needed, we could also search through such basic tools as *HAPI (Hispanic American Periodicals Index)* and the humanities volumes of the *Handbook of Latin American Studies* (HLAS). *HAPI* has a subject arrangement, so we can look under "Women Authors" with subdivisions for "Latin America" and "Argentina." Although *HLAS* has a subject arrangement as well, it might be preferable to use a separate subject index at the end of each volume, again looking under the heading "Women Authors." Remember that *HLAS* includes both books and articles in its listings.

More books on the topic can be identified by consulting the subject portion of the *National Union Catalog* and the *Bibliographic Guide to Latin American Studies*, and we can look under the same subject headings in these that we used to search the card catalog. Women writers of Latin America could conceivably be a dissertation topic as well, so if we wished to expand our search further, we could look for these works under key words, such as *Argentina* and *women* in the "Language and Literature" section of the *Comprehensive Dissertation Index*.

Now let us return to those guides by Foster and Bleznick. The *Manual* and *Sourcebook* cover the entire field of Hispanic literature. The former is an annotated bibliography of bibliographic reference works, somewhat similar to Sheehy in this respect. The latter describes the important bibliographic reference works on Hispanic literature but also cites many valuable anthologies and histories on the same topic. A few minutes' time spent on these two works might reveal additional sources, particularly writings on Argentine literary history and criticism that provide useful background information.

This brings us to Foster's *Argentine Literature: A Research Guide*. By this point our search has probably turned up a respectable group of books and articles on our topic. We need to pause now, look over our search results, and then select a few titles to read. Our reading at this point is mainly to familiarize ourselves with the topic: to learn the names of the important women writers of Argentina and some of their major contributions. Choose the titles that appear to offer the broadest overview of the topic, and as you read them, form a mental picture of the structure for your term paper. Having done this, you are now ready to look at Foster's guide. Although it lists all the important general books, articles, and dissertations on Argentine literature, its chief value at this point is that part of

the guide that cites the important books and articles of literary criticism about specific writers. We can now turn to the section, for example, on Sylvina Bullrich Palenque—one of our major women writers—and find a sizeable number of titles dealing with that author and her writings. To supplement this list we may wish to return to the more recent volumes of *MLA*, but looking now in the subject index under the name of Bullrich and other women writers in search of works that will lend more depth and substance to our paper. With our list of books and articles in hand we are now ready to begin our reading and note taking, bearing in mind the framework devised in our earlier reading.

The field of Latin American literary history and criticism is enormous, and its associated reference bibliography is quite extensive. But we have seen that by using a few well-selected tools and a modest expenditure of search time one can find sufficient information, on almost any topic, to write a modest-sized term paper. Let us turn now to the problem of researching another hypothetical topic—one that requires a somewhat different approach.

Researching Contemporary Events

Let us assume that we have been asked to write a short paper on a current events topic. Again, we will restrict our search to materials in English. The topic we have been assigned is President Ronald Reagan's Caribbean Basin Initiative. Unlike news events such as wars, natural disasters, elections, or international conferences that have a clear beginning and an end, the word *initiative* suggests only a beginning, an introductory step, that is then followed by a period of development. The goals of the initiative may be articulated, but the timetable for reaching them may be vaguely defined. Just as with President Kennedy's Alliance for Progress, any assessment of the program's success or failure may be conditioned by the point at which we choose to examine its progress.

To simplify our approach, let us assume that our study of the initiative will begin about a year after its inception. It is unlikely that any books will have been published on the topic during this time, so a search of the card catalog will probably prove fruitless. Most of our information will have to come from government publications, newspapers, and news magazines.

Unlike the previous exercise, in which we knew from the beginning that our subject dealt with women writers and that the geographic and chronological scope of our research would be confined to twentieth-century Argentina, the phrase *Caribbean Basin Initiative* does not evoke any clear images about the nature of the topic. We may know its geographic locale, but whether it deals with foreign relations, international trade, regional economic development, investment, military security, or whatever, we do not yet know.

Most of us are familiar with newspaper indexes and their use, and we could conceivably scan the *New York Times Index* for the early 1980s in search of a feature article on the initiative. Using the *Index*, however, means an expenditure of valuable time in the attempt to identify just the right article, and more time in loading microfilm into a "reader" and turning wheels or pushing buttons until the text of the article appears on screen. Perhaps there is a better way.

Let's look at Sheehy again, this time under the heading "History and Area Studies–General History–General Works–Annuals and Current Surveys." There we find listed two valuable loose-leaf services: *Facts on File* and *Keesing's Contemporary Archives*. Both of these reference tools contain weekly digests or summaries of major news events. These pamphlet-type summaries are collected in special binders until a full year's worth has been accumulated. Both contain cumulative indexes, so one index will cover events for an entire year. Unlike a newspaper index, these are "direct" sources. Akin to an encyclopedia yearbook, they contain the information itself in capsulized form.

We know that the first Reagan administration

began in 1981, so the initiative would have been announced sometime after that date. So let us start with the 1982 volumes of the two services. In *Facts on File* the index refers us from "Caribbean Basin" to "Latin America," and under a subheading of "U.S. Relations" we find several relevant citations, including one that says, "Reagan proposes Carib aid plan." The organization of *Facts on File* is chronological, and we are referred to the section containing news summaries for the week ending February 26, 1982. On the front page of that section we find nearly half a printed page devoted to Reagan's forty-minute address to the Organization of American States, in which he outlined his plan of trade and investment incentives and technical assistance for the Caribbean Basin and Central America that would be aimed at improving economic conditions and ensuring military security in the area. The remainder of the first page and most of the following page are devoted to verbatim excerpts from that address. This is the first announcement of the Caribbean Basin Initiative. The index also refers us to further related developments in 1982, including an aid package, voted on by Congress in September, that authorized $355 million in funds for several nations of the Caribbean.

Turning to the index in the 1982 volume of *Keesing's*, we find "Caribbean Basin Initiative" and are referred to a seven-page résumé of the initiative (in the July 2, 1982 section), including a description of the events that led up to it, beginning with the Nassau Four meeting of July 1981. We now have all the necessary background information on President Reagan's plan and, in fact, have almost enough information to write a good descriptive paper. But let us continue a little further. We can now define our search parameters:

1. Our sources will be in English
2. Our search will concentrate on government publications, newspaper, and journal articles
3. Search elements will include: (a) United

States—foreign economic relations, (b) economic conditions, and (c) the Caribbean area

4. The search will be concerned primarily with events in the years 1981 to 1983, as well as with materials published during those years

Now to review some of those tools that were described earlier in the chapter and see if any of them can help. Catalogs of books, including the *National Union Catalog,* are of little value for current events topics. Annual bibliographies or indexes, such as *HLAS* and *HAPI,* are not much help either because one must often wait for a year or longer after the publication of a book or article before it is indexed in one of these annuals. Back we must go to the ever-useful "reference guide." Because United States government publications are one of our targets, we may wish to check Sheehy for a current bibliography of such materials. Under the heading "General Reference Works–Government Publications–United States–Catalogs and Indexes" we find a detailed description of the U.S. Superintendent of Documents' *Monthly Catalog of United States Government Publications.* This tool seems ideally suited to our needs: It provides an up-to-date catalog of current federal documents, including those authored by the executive and legislative branches of government, and it is well indexed. (Entries are in chronological order of publication, so an index is the only practical way to access it.) The monthly indexes cumulate at six- and twelve-month intervals, and they fall into four separate parts: (1) author, (2) title, (3) subject terms, and (4) "key" word subject.

By looking in the annual subject indexes for 1982 under terms like *Caribbean Basin Initiative,* or by key words such as *Caribbean* or *Initiative,* we find several publications of the State Department and House committees that deal with the initiative. The House documents are committee reports, and these usually contain voluminous amounts of background information. If our li-

brary is a depository for federal documents, then we should have more than enough information from this group of materials. Many libraries do not catalog their United States or foreign documents, so we should ask one of the librarians to help us locate them on the shelves.

Now to the matter of locating newspaper articles on the topic. One of the types of information we are looking for is the reaction of legislators and the business and academic communities to the president's plan, so the newspaper is frequently a good source for this. Most libraries will have the *New York Times* on microfilm, and a check of the newspaper's index for 1982 will reveal numerous articles relating to the Caribbean plan. If the library also has a film file of the *Washington Post,* the *Wall Street Journal,* and the *Christian Science Monitor,* these should be consulted as well. A few libraries may have one of the more recent technological innovations: the *National Newspaper Index.* This is a joint index to the four newspapers named above plus the *Los Angeles Times.* The index is on microfilm, mounted in a power-driven film reader. The flip of a switch and the press of a button will take the user right to the section of the index for the Caribbean Basin Initiative. A particularly nice feature of this index is that it clearly indicates which citations are editorials and gives the number of column inches (i.e., the length) of each article cited.

By now more than enough sources for a short term paper are at hand, but consider two other areas of publishing. Additional background data on the economic climate of the Caribbean may be needed, so we might consult the latest volumes of two annual works, one of which was mentioned earlier in our discussion of statistical sources. These are the *Economic Survey of Latin America* and *Economic Activity in Caribbean Countries.* In addition to their statistical content, each of these reviews the economic picture for the past year on a country-by-country basis, so if we turn to the chapter in each of them on Jamaica, for example, we will see sections captioned "background and overview" and "trends in economic activity." By reading the few paragraphs that make up each of these sections, we would probably gain enough understanding of conditions in the Caribbean to see President Reagan's initiative in better perspective.

Any assessment that we wish to make about the probability of success for this initiative will have to come from our own understanding of the Caribbean and, perhaps more importantly, from the informed opinions of others. *Facts on File*, newspaper articles and editorials, and the records of congressional hearings probably represent a fair sampling of opinion, but let us now look at one final area of publishing, as outlined in our search parameters: the journal article.

The shortcomings of annual bibliographic publications such as *HAPI* and *HLAS* for researching current events topics have already been noted. Perhaps there are relevant journal indexes that appear more frequently. Turn once again to Sheehy, this time scanning the section entitled "Social Sciences–General Works–Indexes and Abstract Journals." There are several choices of indexes, but a reading of the annotations points toward two that seem especially appropriate: the Public Affairs Information Service *Bulletin* (PAIS) and the *Social Sciences Index*. The former appears weekly, with five cumulations per year plus an annual, and the latter appears quarterly, with an annual cumulation. *PAIS*, as it is generally referred to, lists books, parts of books, government publications, and the selective contents of about fourteen hundred journals, in English, that touch on various aspects of governmental affairs. The *Social Sciences Index* provides access to some three hundred English-language journals. Because of the currency of these two indexes and the types of journals that they review, most of the recently published articles on our topic can be identified by looking under a subject heading such as "Caribbean Region," with the subdivisions "Foreign Relations—United States" or "Economic Rela-

tions—United States" or under the heading "Economic Development—Caribbean Region."

Having done the background reading, and armed with a number of source citations, we can now begin reading and taking notes. In this hypothetical example we relied primarily on a single "reference guide" to open up the library's resources. Other guides, or even other approaches might have been used in our search, but the essential point is that it takes only a few well-selected tools to open up the sources of information, whether in books, journals, or newspapers.

There are more reference aids, even those devoted exclusively to Latin American studies, than most of us could ever use. It is important, therefore, to become familiar with the more basic tools, such as those described in the opening pages of this chapter, and to learn how to use them effectively.

We must be ever mindful of the scope of our tools, and we should always select a bibliography or other reference aid that best matches the search parameters of our topic. This is not to say that researching, for example, the folklore of the Puelche Indians requires reference works solely devoted to that topic. It does suggest, however, that the tools chosen should *include* the best available citations or information related to the topic.

Be systematic in the way you approach library research. Define your topic, set your parameters, and do the background reading necessary to help you understand the relevancy of what you read. Select the right tools and vary your approach or search methodology to meet the particular requirements of the topic. Try to think of several possible subject headings, or variant forms or synonyms for the same subject term when searching the card catalog or other bibliographic resource. Attempt to visualize the paper's outline during the search process itself; it should guide your quest for appropriate books, articles, or other sources of information.

Finally, remember that a library is a service

institution as well as a storehouse of information. The best resource in any library will be a good reference librarian. Do not hesitate to ask the library staff for information, for instruction in using library reference works, or for help in locating specific books, journals, or other materials. The library exists solely to put you, the user, in touch with the information you are seeking.

Notes on Contributors

■ **General Editor**

Jack W. Hopkins is Professor of Public and Environmental Affairs, faculty member, and former Director of the Center for Latin American and Caribbean Studies at Indiana University at Bloomington. He is the author of *The Government Executive of Modern Peru* and *Latin America in World Affairs: The Politics of Inequality,* and the editor of *Latin America and Caribbean Contemporary Record.* In 1982, he was a resident scholar at the Bellagio Study and Conference Center (Rockefeller Foundation), Lake Como, Italy. During the period from 1985 to 1986, he was on special assignment as Provost of the Indiana University campus at Shah Alam, Malaysia, under the ITM/MUCIA Cooperative Program.

■ **Coauthors**

Robert F. Arnove has over seven years' field experience in Latin America as a teacher, researcher, and consultant. He has written on students and politics, educational policy, and education and social change. Among his publications are *Student Alienation: A Venezuelan Study; Educational Television: A Policy Critique and Guide for Developing Countries; Comparative Education;* and *Philanthropy and Cultural Imperialism: The Foundations at Home and Abroad.* His most recent research is on education and revolution in Nicaragua. Dr. Arnove has been a professor

of comparative education at Indiana University at Bloomington since 1972.

Michael Chiappetta is Professor of International and Comparative Education at Indiana University at Bloomington. His extensive experience in Latin America and the Caribbean includes service with the U.S. Agency for International Development in Peru, technical assistance projects in Chile, and educational research and consulting in the eastern Caribbean. He has been an adviser for the Ford Foundation and has served in the Bureau of Educational and Cultural Affairs for the Department of State.

Geoffrey W. Conrad is Director of the William Hammond Mathers Museum and Associate Professor of Anthropology at Indiana University. He has conducted archaeological investigations in the United States, Canada, and (since 1970) in Peru. His most recent research is concerned with the origins and development of prehistoric New World states, and in particular with the role of religion in the cultural evolution of ancient Latin American civilizations. His major publications include *The Andean Heritage* (with Garth Bawden) and *Religion and Empire: The Dynamics of Aztec and Inca Expansionism* (with Arthur A. Demarest).

Paul L. Doughty is Professor of Anthropology and Latin American Studies at the University of

Florida. He previously worked in rural community development projects throughout Mexico and El Salvador. In subsequent years he was involved in agrarian reform projects in Peru, researched and advised on earthquake rehabilitation in Peru and Guatemala, studied Andean peasantries and the adjustment of rural migrants in Lima, and codirected a medical-anthropological study of the effects of long-term cannabis use among urban Costa Ricans. Presently he is studying the relationships between development, food dependency, and peace in Latin America. He is a former director of Latin American studies at Indiana University, chair of the Anthropology Department at the University of Florida, and past president of the Latin American Studies Association.

John P. Dyson is Associate Professor of Spanish and Portuguese at Indiana University at Bloomington. His interests include contemporary Latin American fiction and drama and literary criticism. He is author of *Le evolución de la crítica literaria en Chile* and articles on Darío, Asuela, and Borges. He served as editor (1967–1972) for the Spanish-American and Luso-Brazilian sections of the Twayne's World Authors Series. Since 1975, he has been senior editor of *The American Hispanist,* a journal of critical commentary on Iberian and Ibero-American literatures.

Lawrence S. Graham is Professor of Government and Coordinator of Corporate Relations for the Institute of Latin American Studies at the University of Texas, Austin campus. A faculty member since 1965, he has conducted fieldwork in a variety of Latin American and southern European countries, notably Brazil, Mexico, Portugal, Romania, and Yugoslavia. Among his publications are *Civil Service Reform in Brazil: Principles vs. Practice; Mexican State Government: A Prefectural System in Action; Portugal: The Decline and Collapse of an Authoritarian Order;* and *Romania: A Developing Socialist State.* He has coedited and contributed to three volumes: *Development Administration in Latin America,* with Clarence E. Thurber; *Contemporary Portugal: The*

Revolution and Its Antecedents, with Harry M. Makler; and *In Search of Modern Portugal: The Revolution and Its Consequences,* with Douglas L. Wheeler. His most recent publication is "Brazilian and Yugoslav Experience with Federalism," *Technical Papers Series,* no. 43 (1984).

Robert V. Kemper is Professor of Anthropology at Southern Methodist University in Dallas, Texas. In addition to his research on migration in Mexico, with a focus on the people of Tzintzuntzan, Michoacán, he has continuing research interests on such diverse subjects as tourism, bilingual education, and the history of anthropology. He has been a visiting professor at the Universidad Iberoamericana in Mexico City, a visiting research scholar at the Center for U.S.–Mexican Studies at the University of California, San Diego, and continues his affiliations as a research associate of the Institute for Mesoamerican Studies of the State University of New York at Albany and as an adjunct professor at the University of Texas Health Science Center at Dallas. A member of Phi Beta Kappa, Professor Kemper has been a postdoctoral Fellow of the National Endowment for the Humanities, has received a Fulbright-Hays Advanced Research Award, and has served as Co-President of the Society for Latin American Anthropology. Among his numerous publications, the best known are *Anthropologists in Cities* (with George M. Foster); *Migration and Adaptation: Tzintzuntzan Peasants in Mexico City; Metropolitan Latin America: The Challenge and The Response* (with Wayne A. Cornelius); and *Migration Across Frontiers: Mexico and the United States* (with Fernando Camara).

John V. Lombardi is Dean of The College of Arts and Sciences and Professor of History, Indiana University. He teaches international business in the Graduate School of Business as well as history and Latin American studies in the College of Arts and Sciences and Graduate School. Research interests include economic development, demography, ethnic and social relations, and the study of complex bureaucratic organizations. Publications include works on contemporary political, social, and economic history of Venezuela; ethnic studies; computer applications; economic integration; and comparative economic history. His most recent book-length publications are *Venezuela: The Search for Order, The Dream of Progress; Computer Literacy: The Basic Concepts and Language;* and *A Teaching Atlas of Latin American History* (with Cathryn L. Lombardi).

John D. Martz is Professor and Head of Political Science at the Pennsylvania State University. He is the author of some dozen books and numerous articles on Latin America, with particular emphasis on political parties, elections, campaigns, and ideological movements. His most recent work, with E. Michael Erisman, is *Colossus Challenged: The Struggle for Caribbean Influence*. His research in recent years has concentrated on the Bolivarian states. From 1975 to 1980, he was editor of the *Latin American Research Review*.

Emilio F. Moran is Professor and Chairman of the Anthropology Department at Indiana University at Bloomington. His research on ecology and agriculture has taken him to Brazil, Costa Rica, and Venezuela. Among his recent publications are: *The Dilemma of Amazonian Development; Developing the Amazon; Human Adaptability;* and *Rui e a Abolição*. His journal articles and book chapters have appeared in the United States, Brazil, and Great Britain. Among these are "Ecological, Anthropological and Agronomic Research in the Amazon Basin," *Latin American Research Review* (1982); "An Energetics View of Manioc Cultivation in the Amazon," in *Peasants, Primitives and Proletariats* (Mouton, 1979); and "Estrategias de Sobrevivencia: O Uso de Recursos ao Longo da Rodovia Transamazonica," *Acta Amazonica* (1977). His research is especially concerned with how to balance conservation and development in tropical agroecosystems.

David Scott Palmer is Chairman of Latin American Studies at the Foreign Service Institute of the Department of State. He also serves as Professorial Lecturer at the School of Advanced International Studies, The Johns Hopkins University, and Lecturer at Georgetown University. He has also taught at the University of Huamanga in Ayacucho, Peru; Cornell, the Catholic University of Peru, Bowdoin, and Princeton. His book, *Peru: The Authoritative Tradition*, was published in 1980.

Glenn F. Read, Jr. is Latin American Area Studies Specialist for the Indiana University Libraries, Bloomington. He has previously worked in similar capacities with the Cornell University Libraries and the New York Public Library. He is a life member of the American Library Association and has been an active participant in the Seminar on the Acquisition of Latin American Library Materials (SALALM), having served in various posts, including the SALALM Executive Board and its presidency. He is the author of a number of articles on collection development, bibliography, and the book trade in Latin America.

Anya Peterson Royce is a Professor of Anthropology and Dean of the Faculties at Indiana University at Bloomington. Since 1967 she has done field research in Mexico among the Isthmus Zapotec of Juchitán. Her research includes ethnographic accounts of the Zapotec as well as comparative work in the areas of ethnic identity, dance, and the performing arts. Her publications include *Prestigio y Afiliación en una Comunidad Indígena: Juchitán, Oaxaca; The Anthropology of Dance; Ethnic Identity: Strategies of Diversity;* and *Movement and Meaning: Creativity and Interpretation in Ballet and Mime*. She is currently working on a book on the Venetian contributions to the development of the *commedia dell-arte*.

Helen I. Safa is the author of *The Urban Poor of Puerto Rico* and the editor of *Migration and Development; Sex and Class in Latin America; Toward a Political Economy of Urbanization in Third World Countries;* and other books. Her articles and reviews on migration, housing, race, ethnicity, education, and women and national development have appeared in a variety of scholarly journals and periodicals. She has served as a consultant on immigration and urban planning in Colombia, Puerto Rico, and the United States.

She has taught at Syracuse University and Rutgers University. She was formerly Director of the Center for Latin American Studies, and is currently Professor of Anthropology, at the University of Florida. She is past president of the Latin American Studies Association.

Thomas G. Sanders is Senior Associate for Latin America of the Universities Field Staff International. From 1959 to 1968 he was a professor of religious studies at Brown University before joining the field staff in 1968. He is the author of *Protestant Concepts of Church and State; Catholic Innovation in a Changing Latin America; Secular Consciousness and National Conscience: The Church and Political Alternatives in Southern Europe;* and coauthor of *Military Government and the Movement Toward Democracy in South America.*

John Frederick Schwaller is Associate Professor in the Departments of History and Languages and Linguistics at Florida Atlantic University. His primary area of research interest is sixteenth-century Mexico. His initial work dealt with the church in early Mexico. Recently he began a general study of politics and society in Mexico at the end of the sixteenth century. Specifically his research will focus on the life and times of Viceroy Don Luis de Velasco, the younger. He has articles published in the leading journals. His first book, dealing with the salaries paid to parish priests in sixteenth-century Mexico, was published in Mexico. His most recent book, on the origins of church wealth in Mexico, is being published by the University of New Mexico Press.

John F. Scott is Associate Professor of Art History at the University of Florida. He has specialized in Latin American art, especially the pre-Columbian civilizations of Mexico and, more recently, of northwestern South America. He and his family have lived nearly three years in Mexico on fellowships, and he has also traveled to Spain, several Andean countries, and all the Greater Antilles. He has written on early stone sculpture of Mesoamerica; his two-volume monograph on the Danzantes of Monte Albán is the standard reference on these reliefs. He taught at Bennett College, Cornell University, and Rice University before coming to the University of Florida in 1981. He has been involved with real objects as curator and consultant in New York and Houston, most importantly for the centennial exhibition "Before Cortés: Sculpture of Middle America" at the Metropolitan Museum of Art, for which he coauthored the catalog.

Anthony Seeger is Associate Professor of Anthropology and Director of the Archives of Traditional Music at Indiana University at Bloomington. He was an assistant professor at Pomona College (1974–1975) and associate professor and later chairman of the Department of Anthropology and coordinator of the graduate program in social anthropology at the Museu Nacional in Rio de Janeiro, Brazil, from 1975 to 1982. He is the author of *Os Indios e Nos: Estudos sobre Sociedades Tribais Braileiras* and *Nature and Society in Central Brazil: The Suya Indians of Mato Grosso* as well as numerous articles on ethnomusicology, Brazilian Indians, and social organization.

Sylvia Stalker is a doctoral student in curriculum at Indiana University at Bloomington. Her minor areas are comparative education, women's studies, and bilingual education. Her Latin American experiences include a two-month stay in Nicaragua, an Oxfam comparative study/tour of the Dominican Republic and Nicaragua, and visits to Colombia, Ecuador, and Mexico. She was a member of the 1984 Indiana University School of Education Exchange Program in Hanszhou, People's Republic of China.

Howard J. Wiarda is Resident Scholar and Director of the Center for Hemispheric Studies at the American Enterprise Institute for Public Policy Research in Washington, D.C. Before joining AEI he was a visiting scholar at the Center for International Affairs at Harvard University from 1979 to 1981 and a visiting professor at MIT. He is professor of political science and adjunct professor of comparative labor relations at the University of Massachusetts in Amherst.

Professor Wiarda has been the editor of the journal *Polity* and served previously as the director of the Center for Latin American Studies at the University of Massachusetts. He has served as a consultant and adviser to a variety of private foundations, business firms, and agencies of the U.S. government. He was a consultant to the National Bipartisan (Kissinger) Commission on Central America. He is a member of several honoraries and has held grants from the Rockefeller Foundation, Fulbright Program, Mershon Center, the Social Science Research Council, American Philosophical Society, National Endowment for the Humanities, and National Institutes of Health.

Dr. Wiarda has published extensively on Latin America, Southern Europe, the Third World, and U.S. foreign policy. His most recent books include *In Search of Policy: The United States and Latin America; Rift and Revolution: The Central American Imbroglio; Politics and Social Change in Latin America; Human Rights and U.S. Human Rights Policy; The Dominican Republic: Caribbean Crucible; The State, Organized Labor, and the Changing Industrial Relations Systems of Southern Europe; Corporatism and National Development in Latin America; The Brazilian Catholic Labor Movement; Latin American Politics and Development; The Continuing Struggle for Democracy in Latin America;* and *Corporatism and Development: The Portuguese Experience.*

Darrel Young is a Latin Americanist with varied experience in the region. His initial exposure came in Colombia as a member of the first Peace Corps group, from 1961 to 1963. In the summer of 1971, he participated in colonization efforts on Bolivia's eastern frontier. A Fulbright grant enabled him to spend 1975–1976 at the Universidad del Pacífico in Lima, Peru, conducting a study on choice of technology in Andean metalworking firms. His most recent residence in Latin America was during 1981–1982 when he served as acting dean of the Business School at the Universidad de las Américas in Puebla, Mexico. At present, he teaches economic development and international trade at the University of Texas in Austin.

Index